MW00657697

"This is the book for which all wood-fired oven owners, hopeful owners, and serious bakers have been waiting. Richard Miscovich's descriptions and instructions are both practical and inspirationally poetic—dare I say, soulful. He ignites the fire within and compels us to want to know what he knows and to bake as well as he bakes. In this book, he shares it all."

—PETER REINHART, author of *The Bread Baker's Apprentice* and *Artisan Breads Everyday*

"When it comes to anything wood-fired, Richard Miscovich has set the new gold standard with his comprehensive book, *From the Wood-Fired Oven*. Both well written and inspiring, his book takes the reader on a journey that will delight and educate amateur and professional bakers alike. Richard is a master of this ancient craft, and his expert command of formula development, along with his knowledge of the classic *and* cutting-edge concepts in wood-fired oven construction, use, and maintenance, make this book unique and a must-have for any baker's library!"

—CIRIL HITZ, author of *Baking Artisan Bread* and *Baking Artisan Pastries and Breads*

"So, you want a wood-fired oven to bake bread and have pizza parties? What should you build? How does it work? What else can it cook? As an ovenbuilder I hear these questions a lot, but the books I can recommend for cooking with fire say little about ovens, and the ones about bread and ovens don't take you very far with cooking.

"So I'm glad to now be able to recommend Richard Miscovich's *From the Wood-Fired Oven*. He speaks with the authority of a professional baking instructor (and cook), an experienced mason, and a neighborhood baker; he also writes well, takes beautiful photos, and has a wealth of stories to tie it all together. He's worked with leading professionals in many fields, and teaches from extensive experience with bread, pizza, meats, vegetables, desserts, etc., as well as ovens, masonry, fire, heat, and more."

—KIKO DENZER, author of *Build Your Own Earth Oven*

From the
WOOD-FIRED
OVEN

From the
WOOD-FIRED OVEN

NEW AND TRADITIONAL TECHNIQUES FOR COOKING AND BAKING WITH FIRE

Richard Miscovich

FOREWORD BY DAN WING

Chelsea Green Publishing
White River Junction, Vermont

Project Manager: Patricia Stone
Editor: Makenna Goodman
Copy Editor: Laura Jorstad
Proofreader: Eileen M. Clawson
Indexer: Lee Lawton
Designer: Melissa Jacobson

Printed in the United States of America.
First printing September, 2013.
10 9 8 7 6 5   18 19 20

Our Commitment to Green Publishing
Chelsea Green sees publishing as a tool for cultural change and ecological stewardship. We strive to align our book
manufacturing practices with our editorial mission and to reduce the impact of our business enterprise in the environment. We print our books and catalogs on chlorine-free recycled paper, using vegetable-based inks whenever possible.
This book may cost slightly more because the text pages were printed on paper that contains recycled fiber, and we
hope you'll agree that it's worth it. Chelsea Green is a member of the Green Press Initiative (www.greenpressinitia-
tive.org), a nonprofit coalition of publishers, manufacturers, and authors working to protect the world's endangered
forests and conserve natural resources. *From the Wood-Fired Oven* was printed on FSC®-certified paper supplied by LSC
Communications.

Library of Congress Cataloging-in-Publication Data
Miscovich, Richard, 1968-
  From the wood-fired oven : new and traditional techniques for cooking and baking with fire / Richard Miscovich ;
foreword by Dan Wing.
    pages cm
  Includes bibliographical references and index.
  ISBN 978-1-60358-328-2 (hardcover)—ISBN 978-1-60358-329-9 (ebook)
  1. Cooking (Bread) 2. Cooking. 3. Baking. 4. Roasting (Cooking) 5. Stoves, Wood. 6. Fire. I. Title.

TX769.M557 2013
641.81'5—dc23
                    2013019887

Chelsea Green Publishing
85 North Main Street, Suite 120
White River Junction, VT 05001
(802) 295-6300
www.chelseagreen.com

For my parents
and my daughter, Morgan Leigh Wilson

Contents

Foreword

Are there more cookbooks than cooks? Sometimes it seems that way. How about bread books? Yes, there are plenty of great ones, by Calvel, Leader, Glezer, Hamelman, Robertson, and others. How about masonry oven books? Sorry, but there are a number of those, too—I even wrote one myself, with my late friend Alan Scott.

So where do I get off telling you that there's another cookbook, another bread book, another oven book you need to have? Well, here's the deal: Richard Miscovich's book is the only one that's really all three. The re-evolution of masonry ovens and their uses over the last 15 years thanks to bakers like Richard, cooks like Judy Rodgers, masons like those in the Masonry Heater Association, and hundreds of online oven hobbyists has created a pile of new ingredients that are now formed and baked into tasty loaves. We have needed a book that addresses everything a wood-firing baker and cook has to know, and here it is.

Over the years I had thought about writing a new edition of *The Bread Builders*. But that book was sui generis, a one-off piece of work that required two horses in harness, not one. Without Alan Scott it could not happen again. Also, "The Next Oven Book" (as I had thought of it) had to be written by a real baker and real cook, and I am not that person—Richard is. That means he brings technical proficiency, extensive experience, a great variety of wonderful bread formulas, and recipes for a wide range of baked and roasted foods to this volume. Many of these are foods I have never imagined making in my oven. (Scalloped Tomatoes! Beef jerky! Infused oils!)

You might think giving you all those formulas and recipes would be enough. No! That's not enough. Somebody needs to tell you how to manage your oven to cook all that stuff, and that person, too, is Richard

Miscovich. If you've ever baked or cooked anything, you have learned that "to all things there is a season." In this book Richard will tell you how to use the "falling heat" of a masonry oven to cook or bake just about everything from pita breads (REALLY HOT) to dried fruit (lowwww and slowww). Using this book you can learn to obtain the proper temperature, moisture level, and radiant heat intensity for any oven task.

If you haven't baked in a masonry oven, you may not know that some things are usually baked, roasted, or cooked with a wood fire burning. (Pizza comes to mind.) Or you may not know that some things can be baked after the ashes of that fire have been brushed out, using the immense store of heat that remains in the masonry mass of the oven dome and the oven floor. (Loaves of bread are the common example here.) Think about that for a moment and you will realize that from the time you scrape those ashes out, the overall store of heat in the oven mass and the temperature inside the oven will start to fall. And that is a *good* thing. This book is going to tell you how to easily and naturally use all the conditions of temperature, humidity, and radiant heat that the oven produces as it gradually cools.

Now, I have to warn you that having a masonry oven is not without its problems. The first of these is crowd control, and it doesn't matter much in this regard whether you live in town or (as I do) in downtown Nowhere. Here's how it works: You make delicious stuff to eat, people try it, people get used to eating it, people come to expect it, and pretty soon there are people checking surreptitiously to find out when you will be, or if you are now, or if you just have been cooking or baking something great in your oven. The only practical solutions to the crowd problem are: (1) Make them bring the beer or wine, and (2) see whether some of them will bring fruit pies and tarts to bake as the oven cools. After that, you're on your own.

Other problems? Well, you might think you'll gain weight, with all that baking. I doubt it. By the time you've built the oven, cut the wood, made the dough, built the fire, shaped the dough, tended the fire, baked the bread, refired the oven for a pizza party that night, and finally sat down to rest with a glass of wine, you are going to have the phenotype of a champion marathoner.

Or you might worry that all this might cut into your TV time. (Seriously, where are your priorities?) Perhaps it might cut into your time with the kids? Don't worry. Your masonry oven is going to *become* your new TV, cell phone, tablet, and what have you—and will probably have the same effect for your kids. Because there is only one thing more attractive to a junior high kid than handheld electronics, and that is . . . *fire.* This has been proven countless times in "actual clinical tests" (well, maybe not) conducted by the Edible Schoolyard

Project and at schools across America. The distraction effect is, of course, increased if the kids get to make the oven (stomping in wet clay, for example), but it's plenty strong enough if they merely become the ones to start and tend the fire. Then, just when their interest (and energy) might start to flag, we unleash the secret weapon . . . *pizza.* And we have them at our mercy.

Seriously, this book is going to change the way I use my oven—how I make and control the heat and steam, the things I bake and cook, and how much of the heat of the oven I use instead of waste. And when I build my next oven (because that is a nasty habit, and I can't stop) it will change how I build it—the type of bricks I use in the arch, how I lay them, and how I insulate the oven. If you are just starting now to plan a masonry oven—or if you have been using one for 20 years—you are still going to want to own this book. Thank you, Richard.

DAN WING
Vermont, 2013

Preface

There is nothing like hearing birds sing in the middle of the night when a masonry oven is swept of ash in preparation for baking. The smell of wood smoke is still in my shirt and the oven is equalizing, cooling to the proper baking temp. Heat completely saturates the thermal mass. The oven ticks. The dough proofs. Dawn blurs the edge of the horizon. The first sound of the morning commute comes across the fields. And then it all comes together. The proofed loaves are fluffy and asking to be baked. The oven is ready. Gentle, steady wood-fired heat seems hungry for dough. Steam is injected into the oven; I hold the scoring razor conveniently in my mouth. And then load after load, into the oven endlessly baking. The sun is full now, loaves are high-graded, somebody stops by the ovenhouse to get an early pick. Then the last load, going in with the hope of sufficient heat. It is out. The loaves are loaded for delivery and taken to town. Magdalena sits, resting, waiting for the next bake day.

In 1996 I was baking bread every couple of days at home using an old American-style baking book—one with lots of yeast and not too much water. I started thinking about bread all the time, and soon found out about a new organization called The Bread Bakers Guild of America. This was right before the American Bread Movement gave us the voluptuous handmade breads that are now part of the American food culture. My wife, Stephanie, bought me a copy of Dan Leader's book *Bread Alone*, one of the first books that explained European methods and techniques to Americans. I immediately started using a sourdough starter and the color of my loaves deepened, as did the character and complexity of the flavor. My bread took a step into a different bread-baking tradition, one that concerned itself with controlled fermentation, wet dough, and local, whole-grain flour.

But there was something else about *Bread Alone* that captivated me and ultimately changed my life—its information on wood-fired ovens. Dan told stories of huge French ovens and the special routine required for this type of baking. I was intrigued, and wanted to reproduce something as authentic. There hadn't been much of this type of baked goods around when I was growing up in mid-Michigan during the 1970s, although I feel lucky to have had Polish aunts and uncles who brought Old World, handmade baked goods like rye bread, walnut rolls, and chrusciki up from Hamtramck, Detroit's Polish suburb.

I responded to the centuries-old draw of flour, leaven, and fire described in *Bread Alone* by baking at home almost every day. Stephanie and I were living in an apartment in her hometown on the coast of North Carolina, and at that time we didn't have the space, or knowledge, to build a masonry oven. I did line the apartment oven with common red bricks in a quest to bake thoroughly fermented sourdough bread on hot masonry. These first loaves seemed authentic and made me feel like I was connecting to a past era. Plus, they tasted great.

This was a dynamic time in the American baking scene. I got in touch with The Bread Bakers Guild of America, and asked where I could learn how to bake this type of bread. I found out about the San Francisco Baking Institute and enrolled in two consecutive weeks of classes, their first ones ever. I didn't know that, as a young American baker, I was poised at the right place at the right time. Baking education was emerging everywhere; I stumbled into it because of a book purchased in a sleepy bookstore on the coast of North Carolina.

During my first week at SFBI, I learned the fundamentals of bread baking and realized this was something I wanted to do professionally. The class was taught by Lionel Vatinet, a French baker who had gone through the Compagnon du Devoir apprenticeship training and was one of the first French bakers to bring Old World techniques to the American Bread Movement. On the first day of class he found out I was staying with friends just a few blocks from where he lived. After that, he gave me a ride from Hayes Street to South San Francisco and back again in the evening—an extra hour and a half to learn about baking from a French Compagnon!

Before I traveled out to San Francisco, I found out about a man named Alan Scott who built brick ovens, taught workshops, and lived an easy drive north of the city. There wasn't a workshop on the weekend between my two SFBI classes, but when he returned my call he said I was welcome to visit and see his oven in action. When I met Alan at his beautiful Victorian home in the rolling hills of Petaluma, he gave me a somewhat stern lecture about the importance of a whole-grain diet before he took me out back and showed me his oven. This was the first time I'd seen a wood-fired oven in action; it was unforgettable! This was also the first time I'd smelled bread-infused steam rolling off bricks heated by a fire of oak and eucalyptus, and felt the oily wholesomeness of fresh flour falling from the grain mill. Alan also explained that wheat can be grown in a small golden plot by a house—it doesn't have to be monocultivated on 1,000-acre plots somewhere in the

Great Plains. This visit to Alan Scott's home sealed my conviction: This is what I wanted to do. I saw the beauty of his vision, and knew I was going to build a brick oven and bake organic hearth breads. If it hadn't been for Alan, I might not have done it—or been *able* to do it.

I bought a set of photocopied oven plans from Alan. Those plans were the basis for *The Bread Builders*, a seminal book on oven building and bread baking co-authored with Dan Wing and published in 1999. By that time the American bread-baking scene was on fire, and the book quickly became both a classic and a bible. The original oven plans included edits and omissions handwritten over the typed instructions—the mark of a man who continued to refine his system of oven building. His writing in the plans was sometimes non-linear, but his philosophical spirit shone through:

> *For the poet and mystic in us, building an oven, gathering the wood, tending the fire and baking in this way connects us experientially with one of our oldest civilized rituals. "Remembering" our past . . . helps us to momentarily touch base with our deeper selves and awaken briefly to our place in the broader web of the biosphere that supports and sustains all life.*

The cost of the plans included phone consultations with Alan, but his responses did not always entirely answer my questions. Part of the pleasure, he said, should be learning through my own discoveries, and his matter-of-fact style was positive and encouraging. Alan offered not only instruction but also inspiration and the confidence I needed to build the oven that became such an important part of my life.

Once I got back to North Carolina I immediately started to build Magdalena, the oven that ultimately gave me the opportunity to learn so much about cooking and baking with fire. I based her on Alan's plans but had the good fortune to meet Tom Trout, a masonry heater builder who lives in the mountains of North Carolina and explained the advantages of making some slight construction changes in Alan's plans. He also made me aware of other building materials like refractory mortar, silky enough to create thin mortar joints, as well as highly insulating kiln blankets.

Alan Scott in 1988 PHOTO BY ART ROGERS COPYRIGHT © 1988 BY WWW.ARTROGERS.COM

A plot of wheat growing behind Alan Scott's home circa 1996

Oven building was just as stimulating as bread baking! I wondered if maybe I should become a professional mason. I had surreal dreams where the universe was made of bricks and masonry, thrust lines extended into space, dough transubstantiated into mortar and mortar into dough. It took over a year of weekends and several periods of focused, intense work to finish Magdalena.

And then came the bread. Suddenly my life had two new-to-me (yet ancient) schools of thought to explore: making European-style hearth breads, and baking them in wood-fired ovens.

I started with Pain au Levain, a traditional French sourdough based on Lionel's formula. The crust was dark, the fins of bread created by the quick pull of a razor baked into a dark —but not quite burnt—crust. The crumb inside was fragrant, unbelievably so, a fragrance I had never smelled before, like caramel, wheat, and ancient temple walls. (The crumb is the body of the bread—everything inside the crust, not

the particles on your cutting board.) The random holes scattered throughout the loaf—called alveoli—were glossy, their iridescence a sign of starch gelating during the baking process. This open structure was something that had been lacking in my bread, and I learned that I could increase it by ensuring a vigorous, but controlled, fermentation and by increasing the hydration.

I used organic flour from a North Carolina mill, 25 percent whole wheat, the rest white flour, salt, and liquid sourdough levain elaborated from some starter brought back from SFBI and hydrated with 69 percent well water pulled from the Castle Hayne aquifer. That formula has changed over the years—the hydration has increased in particular—and is the basis for the Pain au Levain in this book.

People loved the bread but soon asked for other varieties. I was fully drawn into the world of bread—varieties, flour mixtures, and leavening systems. I realized the general method I learned from Lionel applied—more or less—to all types of bread. I could create a diverse selection of breads by changing ingredients, their ratios, and fermentation methods. This was a fun and creative period of doing research and going through the reverse-engineering process of duplicating traditional breads, formulating and tweaking other ideas and requests, and ending up with a new bread on the production schedule. I wanted to offer a roster that included white breads, whole-grain breads, rye breads, naturally leavened breads, yeasted breads, breads that used copious cuttings of fresh rosemary, spelt breads, breads suited to be baked in a hot oven, and those suited for a cool oven. This roster comprises the selection of breads—with additions and evolutions—that appears in this book.

I was lucky to be actively learning to bake during this time. The Bread Bakers Guild was fulfilling its mission of providing an education in artisan baking, and classes and conferences were becoming regular occurrences at culinary schools and bakery trade shows. The largest event during this time was the Coupe du Monde de la Boulangerie, a baking competition at Europain, a huge international baking trade show. We sat in the bleachers and watched day after day as international teams competed. It was a four-day demonstration of hand skills, fermentation techniques, and production efficiency, all punctuated by forays onto the trade show floor where we ordered display baskets handmade in a French village and bought books unavailable in the United States. Standing around watching the competition or having drinks, my new guild friends and I talked bread, bread, bread and participated in the generous exchange of ideas and knowledge, a hallmark of the American Bread Movement and an industry characteristic for which I am grateful. That knowledge, and its evolution over the past 15 years, grounds the bread-baking sections of this book.

Back home in North Carolina I baked with new inspiration buttressed by a load of information. But there was something special about our own little bakery fueled with pecan and coast oak—not better or worse, but different from the competition breads coming out of deck ovens.

It was a sense of providing food for my community. I was learning the most fundamental aspects of bread baking. Changes in the weather, customer demand, or production schedule often affected the consistency of the loaves. I baked commercially out of Magdalena for three years, until I felt the need to learn more than I could at workshops, trade shows, and through the guild's newsletter. In the fall of 2000 I left the coast of North Carolina to bake at the King Arthur Flour bakery in Vermont. It was very difficult to leave Magdalena, my all-night companion, but Vermont brought the promise of goods things to come. I learned from and baked with Jeffrey Hamelman and other talented bakers at King Arthur. A steady population of students came through the Baking Education Center for professional classes taught by Jeffrey, and I learned from their questions. Some of them became friends and colleagues, and I've watched them transition from their old life to the life of a baker or bakery owner. I was especially fortunate to work with visiting instructors like Maggie Glezer, author of *Artisan Baking Across America*, and James MacGuire, the chef/pastry chef and baker who was my direct link to the teachings of Professor Raymond Calvel, the French bread scientist who developed the autolyse and preached the value of proper dough temperature. I assisted James and then co-taught with him. My formulas for Pain Rustique, 67% Rye, and Miche came from Calvel and James.

Vermont offered a concentration of bakers and ovens, and many people I'd read or heard about seemed to live within an easy drive. Most notable was Dan Wing, coauthor of *The Bread Builders*. I met Dan when he trailered his portable brick oven to King Arthur for a weekend intensive. At the time, portable masonry ovens were a rare precursor to today's pizza catering and farmer's market scene. Dan's class quickly sold out, and I started to hear questions that are still asked today and addressed in this book: "How long do I fire the oven? Why is steam important? How do I get open holes in my bread? What is the best type of oven for me to build?" Interest in wood-fired ovens was growing.

I started teaching baguette and sourdough classes after my shift in the bakery. There I encountered the joys of helping people learn the skills to bake good bread at home with their own two hands. I realized that bread is a social leveler. There is an attraction to bread that transcends age, gender, race, socioeconomic stratum, and any other category you can think of. I was humbled to realize in class one day that I was teaching handmade bread techniques to a woman who had been baking bread longer than I had been alive.

The teaching continued to draw me in, just as bread baking had. So it was hard to turn down the opportunity to make the move to full-time teaching at Johnson & Wales in Providence, Rhode Island. Although we were sorry to leave our sweet cabin in the Vermont woods and our good King Arthur friends, it was a great chance to gain experience in another part of the baking world. Plus, it provided a summer teaching break and the chance to go back and bake in Magdalena again!

It was a perfect time to get back into small-scale brick oven baking. I had learned a lot about baking by that time, and the organic, local food scene had gone mainstream. The greater awareness of, and demand for, high-quality local food increased the acreage of organic wheat, and this greater supply allowed millers to draw and blend from more sources and create flours with more consistency. My old customer base remembered my role as village baker, and word got around that once again there was bread on Golden Farm Road. The tourist industry was perfectly in sync with my summer teaching break, and Kyle Swain's Blue Moon Bistro, my favorite restaurant, was happy to serve my bread alongside his delicious coastal cuisine.

The larger wood-fired oven world continued—and continues—to grow. King Arthur installed a wood-fired oven in the Baking Education Center, and I started regularly guest teaching classes there. I met people who installed similar oven kits, built clay ovens or masonry ovens based on Alan Scott plans. Some students wanted input on what type of oven to build. And still I heard the common questions I'd been aware of since that first class with Dan Wing about firing times, steam, and open crumb. The tips Tom Trout gave me when I was building Magdalena began to filter into the amateur wood-fired oven world.

By this time the wood-fired oven scene was populated by many different styles, shapes, and designs. Domed brick Pompeii ovens. Clay bread ovens from Quebec. Backyard bread ovens. Commercial production ovens. Scandinavian ovens, necessarily efficient in a land where wood has long been scarce and precious. Colonial beehive ovens unearthed from plaster walls during renovations in old homes across the northeastern United States. But the Alan Scott oven design became a reference point by which other wood-fired bread ovens are described. Chances are a North America stonemason and oven builder knows the Alan Scott oven. *The Bread Builders* spawned countless micro-bakeries across the country, because it showed aspiring bakers how to build an economical brick oven that could turn out artisan hearth loaves earmarked with the seal of Old World artisanship.

In addition to Alan's inspiration—and under the guidance of professional masons—the possibility of building or having a wood-fired oven has become pretty accessible to everyone. You do not have to be a mason to build an Alan Scott oven, and many people came to the endeavor through their journey as bread bakers or piazzalos, very often with no prior masonry experience at all. Like me, for example. I followed Alan's plans, built this magic thing, and became enchanted by the primal essence of the fire.

Alan's design and *The Bread Builders* still inspire and encourage many segments of society: folks living off the grid, affluent foodies, entrepreneurs, budding masons, community builders, bread heads, fifth-generation immigrants reconnecting with their Nonna's food traditions. All these folks, helped along by input from professional masons and combustion experts through online chatgroups and construction site epiphanies, have led us to this exciting time in wood-fired ovens, fueled by a sense of community focused on fire.

Not only is there excitement for baking and oven construction, but we're also seeing the resurgence in regional, small-scale grain production and milling. The rise and almost obsessive interest in handmade bread, surge of community farmer's markets, and availability of local, small-scale artisan food is helping recalibrate our culture and economy. Not to mention a food-truck phenomenon that includes mobile wood-fired pizza ovens! Alan's vision of communities gathering around wood-fired bread ovens has caught on, big time, and momentum continues to grow nearly 15 years after *The*

Bread Builders was published. Alan took action to see that this centuries-old tradition was kept alive, and he did it well. Look around. Somewhere near you, there is likely someone baking bread in a wood-fired oven and sharing it within the community. Not only is Alan's vision happening, it's thriving.

I wrote this book to share my love and interest in cooking and baking bread in the wide spectrum of wood-fired oven temperature environments; to spread the thrill (and responsibility) of efficient combustion; and to brief you on important innovations and refinements in oven design, construction, and materials.

Acknowledgments

Stephanie Miscovich has always encouraged me to know bread baking, oven building, and combustion at a deeper level. Many words and concepts in this book come directly from her and her imagination. Stephanie invented the concept of the temporary brick firewall to create a small chamber within a larger oven, a huge step forward in using a wood-fired oven to its fullest potential.

Elaine and Richard Barber, Stephanie's parents, reviewed the text and contributed extensive comments. Having the input of a keen-eyed and insightful proofreader and a world-class scientist helped this project beyond words. In addition, Elaine taught me about North Carolina coastal cuisine. I first encountered many of the recipes in this book at her generous dinner table.

Renaissance men Dan Wing and Alan Scott have had an enormous impact on my opportunity to work within the world of wood-fired ovens. Without their influences my bread-baking career and this book might not have happened.

I was fortunate to become involved in the nascent American artisan bread-baking scene and to learn the fundamentals of an emerging American food culture from Lionel Vatinet, Michel Suas, and Craig Ponsford. I use skills and techniques I learned working alongside Jeffrey Hamelman and James Macguire every time I am at the bench. Thom Leonard has been an inspiration for me since I first began to bake, and I'm honored that Thom gave his valuable comments on the manuscript during early editing. Cheryl Maffei and Jonathan Stevens of Hungry Ghost Bread have been soulful, innovative, and diligent in helping forge a place at the American table for wood-fired bread made with local flour, and I'm thankful for all the times they have welcomed me into their bakery and home.

I work with a diverse group of extremely knowledgeable educators at the Johnson & Wales College of Culinary Arts. Much of the information in part three of this book was drawn from promptly returned emails, recommended resources, hallway questions, conversations over shared meals, and opportunities to observe their areas of expertise in laboratory kitchens. Ciril Hitz and Mitch Stamm, in particular, are deep wells of baking knowledge, and they generously share that with me. I'm grateful for these two friends and the phenomenal opportunity to bake with them for the past decade.

The Bread Bakers Guild of America, The Masonry Heater Association of America, and The Kneading Conference/Maine Grain Alliance have provided overlapping networks of good-hearted individuals and copious amounts of reliable information, much of which appears within this book.

My tenure on the Board of Directors of The Bread Bakers Guild gave me the opportunity to work with a fun, creative, and hard-working group of people dedicated to shaping the knowledge and skills of the artisan baking community. It helped me see the impact of good bread and solid baking education on the American diet. This continually ongoing effort is greatly supported by staff members Laverne Dicker and Cathy Wayne.

Norbert Senf, who may know more about combustion than anybody on earth, gave valuable input on the manuscript. Norbert also maintains the MHA website, a diverse, organized, and information-dense resource. Tom Trout, William Davenport, Alex Chernov, Pat Manley, Marty Pearson, Albie Barden, and Kiko Denzer are also all highly skilled oven builders and combustion experts. The information I received from all of them greatly increased my understanding of masonry, thermodynamics, and combustion.

David S. Cargo was generous with his time spent reviewing the manuscript and offered useful comments and detailed proofreading expertise.

Dick Bessey worked closely with Alan Scott and is an important source about Alan's design. In addition, he has contributed his own creative ideas to the construction of wood-fired ovens. I appreciate learning so much about ovens and bread from all the projects and discussions Dick and I have shared over the years.

Jenn Sheridan is a recipe tester extraordinaire. Our weekly meetings to review bake tests gave me great insights on the formulas, and her friendship is another example of the strong relationships that come to be through the shared act of baking bread.

This book was researched with a massive amount of resources provided by the Fox Point Library, part of the Providence, Rhode Island, Community Library. Barbara Janson and the staff at the Johnson & Wales Harborside Library consistently helped procure materials through their own extensive collection and that of the greater HELIN network. Richard Gutman, Erin Williams, and the staff at the preeminent Culinary Arts Museum at Johnson & Wales University have been invaluable to this book and to my career as an educator at Johnson & Wales.

In addition to the named people and animals who appear in and on the pages of the book, I especially appreciate the help I received from: Melina Kelson-Podolsky, master baker, dough sister, and round-the-clock texter of manuscript comments; Stu Silverstein, baker, filmmaker, and down-to-earth role model; and Susan Miller of the King Arthur Baking Education Center, who first gave me the opportunity to teach.

I am also thankful for all who contributed photos. I learned copious amounts about photography from Jonathan Beller, who possesses the ability to light the inside of a dark oven with Heliosian virtuosity. Andrew Janjigian and Melissa Rivard lent a focused eye and an understanding of bread baking in order to capture that process.

A special "Hi-Neighbor" for Dan Schwartz. His friendship, shared meals, cold Narragansetts, and *Scarlet/Fire* recommendations gave me an enormous amount of encouragement and energy to keep writing. Rich and Cheryl Merola are beautiful people with a beautiful oven in a beautiful home, and I appreciate their space and time that we used to conduct fun and delicious baking classes.

The staff of Chelsea Green Publishing embraced this book with a meticulous fervor. Senior editors Makenna Goodman and Ben Watson steered this project from an idea expressed on a phone call to a finished book. Pati Stone's attention to detail and thoughtful design considerations created a book I never could have envisioned. The time I spent interacting with Pati and designer Melissa Jacobson taught me a great deal about grammar, editing, design, and photography. Plus, it was fun. And how are copy editor and proofreader Laura Jorstad and Eileen Clawson able to distinguish a hyphen from a dash and know how to rearrange a sentence to make it say what I actually intended? Amazing. Margo Baldwin, cofounder and president, deserves special thanks for her vision in publishing many valuable books dealing with the politics and practice of sustainable living. One of them changed my life. I am so lucky to have fallen in with this employee-owned company.

Finally, Bettie Kitty, another Golden Farm Road angel, kept me company during the last big pushes and literally watched the manuscript turn into a book.

INTRODUCTION

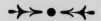

Remembering How to Cook with Fire

It is in our human spirit to build ovens, behold fire, bake bread, cook food, and provide for ourselves. Every one of us has a part in that story.

Cooking and baking with the heat of a wood fire is not an exotic foodie trend, but a skill known and practiced by everyday people since the dawn of humanity. Early American housewives built and managed fires for cooking, first on hearths, then in the firebox of cast-iron cookstoves. It was only by the mid-20th century that this basic knowledge began to be lost, so that now in the early 21st century, it is foreign to many of us. This dissipating knowledge mirrored the loss of other traditional practices like keeping small-scale chicken flocks, knitting, and plant medicine. These life skills were largely depleted (but luckily not lost) in the mid-1900s as "better living through chemistry" and the dramatic rise of a consumer culture trained us to seek products on a shelf instead of being self-reliant. Luckily, beginning with the back-to-the-land movement in the 1960s and then again in the 1990s, a whole generation began to rediscover Rhode Island Reds, their grandmother's needles, and the plants our ancestors once relied on for spiritual and physical medicine. And we were also building ovens, playing with fire, and fermenting grain to bake bread.

Living with the products of these lifestyles has a cumulative tonic-like effect on your health and quality of life. Your own eggs with yolks the color of a beautiful sunset. A favorite knitted hat. An old-growth medicinal garden. Pizza parties, the annual turkey, and countless batches of bread. How satisfying it is to see the neighbor children improve their pizza skills, make a comforting casserole, put up some venison jerky, and practice a routine that provides handmade bread to your family, friends, and community.

Resilience

In addition to the romance of masonry, fire, and food, this book is written out of the reemergence of, and need for, resilience in both our global food culture and everyday lives. I've always been interested in being self-reliant. As a child I loved reading stories of mountain men and pioneer families who blazed trails to open the West with only their wits, their courage, and the equipment they thought to take along. Mountain man Hugh Glass survived a mauling by a grizzly bear, was left for dead, and *crawled* 200 miles to safety without his firearm. And how about Laura Ingalls's family, breaking prairie sod, knowing nothing *but* a snout-to-tail approach to using livestock, and cobbling together a Christmas celebration even when the brutal winter of 1880–81 closed railroad service to the Dakota Territory? These stories inspired me to sharpen my own survival skills—keeping warm when Michigan's gales of autumn came early, making satchels out of squirrel hides, dehydrating wild apples in my parents' 1970s-era avocado-colored gas oven. For years I thought those impulses were due to Cold War anxiety, but over the course of writing this book I realized I'm simply interested in being prepared for any event so I can rebound and deal with systemic changes over which I have no control. To me, being resilient means having the foresight to have systems, skills, and infrastructure in place that provide basic physical and emotional needs when things change beyond my control. My pitcher pump, within sight of Magdalena, and a source of fresh water even when power is interrupted during a hurricane, gives me great satisfaction.

So it is not surprising that I was eventually compelled to build a wood-fired oven, my own power plant providing heat, food, and the magic of fire . . . even when modern utilities are disrupted or obsolete.

Wood-fired ovens aid resilience: the ability to return to an original form after being bent, compressed, or stretched. Resilience shouldn't be confused with robustness—although that quality is beneficial in resilient systems. And adversity isn't necessary to exhibit resilience. In fact, resilient systems can help avoid adversity. The resilience that comes from having a wood-fired oven draws its strength from flexibility (of design and materials), diversity (of how the oven can be used), and applications that enable self-sufficiency.

In the autumn of 2012, Superstorm Sandy churned up the eastern seaboard of the United States and crashed into New Jersey and New York City, leaving behind scenes from post-apocalyptic films. Dark below 39th Street. Debris scattered in the streets. Light traffic. It was hard to imagine, even with the not-so-distant memory of Hurricane Katrina. Flooded subways? Wall Street shut down? Suddenly there was a new cognizance and appreciation of previously under-considered priorities such as electricity, gasoline, hot food, and mobility.

Over on Spring Street, however, Lombardi's brick oven pizza was open. An off-the-grid oven isn't affected when the grid goes down. It just rolls along, unconcerned with the lack of electricity or breakdowns of the system delivering fuel. Storm-stressed and obsessed, hungry citizens paid candlelit cash for the good fortune of buying a hot meal. "Thank God for brick oven pizza,"

one of them expressed to graduate school reporters from the Columbia University School of Journalism.

In these times of uncertainty, it is important to avoid having all our eggs (free-range or not) in one basket. A quest for efficiency has consolidated our culture's dependence on fewer and fewer providers, most of which are dependent on the petroleum industry: food production from the Central Valley of California, trucks to transport the produce across the country, lights in the market, registers to ring up the sales, the range in your home. But what if the food you eat is grown in your backyard—or in your community, where farmers gather without the need for lights or registers? And what if you can cook that food in your own oven and with regenerative fuel that was harvested in your community? Being lucky enough to live in this way makes me feel secure *and* luxurious.

Does this mean we should put all our eggs in that "local" basket and return to medieval fiefdoms, cut off from adjacent communities? No, but shouldn't we build the strength of our local food systems and economies so we are more resilient in the event of short- or long-term disruption of our supply chain?

"Green living" is different from resilience. Most of us are now environmentally aware enough to know it is important to use high efficiency lightbulbs. But resilience is about designing buildings to take advantage of natural light so electric lights are less necessary. Resilience is also about the mind-bending task of planning for the unknown. This is important when you are planning to build your oven. What size should it be—not for what you are cooking now, but for what you may want to cook five years from now? This isn't to say sustainability isn't important—just that we may end up sustaining a system that ultimately may need to collapse, for instance if the power grid becomes permanently unavailable or economically inefficient. This may actually be okay and a positive evolution for our cultures. Consider the systems that went away after people decided to stop politically or financially sustaining them: British rule of the American colonies, slavery, Prohibition, the Vietnam War.

When the US embargo cut off Soviet supplies from reaching Cuba, it wasn't long before tractors ran out of fuel and were left to rot in the fields. What were the Cubans to do? They turned back to agriculture's roots and started growing food on a small, community-based scale. Urban gardens were started—a full decade before they became fashionable in American cities—fertilized by rooftop vermicomposting. These weren't a bunch of back-to-the-landers. These were resilient people figuring out a way to build a reliable food supply.

Wood-fired ovens provide reliability and resilience and the foundation of Maslow's primary needs: food production and also, if need be, warmth, sanitation, and community. Wood-fired ovens fulfill resiliency's requirements: flexibility, diversity, and a backup system to ensure self-reliance, instead of helplessness.

This resilience is societal mise en place, the idea that everything is in its place and organized for the task ahead, even when that task is weathering the storm for six days while power lines are repaired or when the details of the task—or the task itself—are not yet known.

Generous sharing of information among bakers, millers, and oven builders increases our community's resilience. Even wood-fired oven construction is resilient. That is why 100-year-old ovens reliably bake away, churning out bread and taking days or weeks to cool down after the last fire.

How to Use This Book

This book is separated into three broad categories: (1) How wood-fired ovens work, a brick menagerie of ovens, and techniques to catch a fire, (2) how to make bread, especially in the context of wood-fired ovens, and (3) enjoying the ride: using a live fire or retained heat to make something to eat. These ideas are explored in parts one, two, and three, respectively.

PART ONE, OVENS AND FIRE

The first chapter begins where Alan Scott and Dan Wing's book, *The Bread Builders*, left off and describes how ovens have evolved over the past 15 years.

Chapter 2 explores how wood-fired ovens work—through either retained-heat or live-fire applications—and explores thermal mass, insulation materials, and thermal breaks.

The question "What makes an oven a bread oven?" is answered in chapter 3; classifications based on firing method, shape, and building material are discussed as well. This will help you decide what type of wood-fired oven is right for you.

There are also things to know about fire. One goal of this book is to educate people about how to burn and manage wood fires as efficiently as possible to restore the reputation of wood as a viable, sustainable, and environmentally responsible source of fuel. This is addressed in chapter 4, *Fuel and Combustion*. Using these techniques will make you a more responsible oven burner and add a warm ripple to the satisfaction of a wood-fired lifestyle.

Chapter 5, *How to Operate Your Oven*, is the manual for scheduling, firing, producing, and monitoring any type of wood-fired oven. A short list of tools you should seek out to facilitate use of your oven is included.

PART TWO, BREAD BAKING: THE PROCESS

Chapter 6 explains how to make bread, the staff of life, in both wood-fired ovens and home ovens. The process described in the first chapter of part two is reinforced by a closer examination of the *Essential Ingredients for Wood-Fired Breads* in chapter 7.

Chapter 8, *Standards and Conventions for Bread Formulas*, makes note of this book's terminology, ingredient standards, and codified formula methodologies. In addition to discussing systemic fundamentals of the bread-baking process, there is a tip of the hat to some of a baker's most reliable tools: thermometer, timer, and the metric system.

PART THREE. USING THE FULL HEAT CYCLE

Chapter 9, *Cooking with Fire: Tips and Techniques to Get the Most Out of Each Burn*, sets the contemporary context of cooking with fire, and offers easy ways to adapt and/or alter the cooking environment.

Turn to chapters 10 through 14 if you want to just start cooking. Many wood-fired ovens are used for pizza and bread—and indeed, those two staples are well treated within this book—but there are rich opportunities for cooking at a wider range of temperatures. Imagine standing on the eve of a weekend set aside for wood-fired cuisine. What comes first, and how much can you send through the oven before it returns to ambient temperature? How exciting to have a blazing fire contained in a masonry box or a gentle dehydrating environment, held there solidly for 12 hours by tenaciously warm bricks! You can create inferno whiplash cooking environments for blazed tomatoes or gentle thermo-cradle oil infusion spas. And so much comfort food to be had two days after the pizza party. You have the heat; why not use it?

Look to the appendices for materials supporting the text. Appendix A provides design recommendations to construct an oven as energy- and personally efficient as possible. Modifications to the Alan Scott design anyone can make in order to get the most out of his or her oven are included. Other appendices focus on baking and include a selection of micro-bakery commercial yield formulas, a treatment of the powerful and essential baker's percentage system, templates for production schedules, oven temperature logs, and sourdough starter genesis and maintenance.

PART ONE

 ## OVENS AND FIRE

CHAPTER ONE

→• ◦ •←

Wood-Fired Masonry Ovens

At the time I'm writing this book, good handmade artisan bread is available across the United States and many other nations. Thirty years ago this was the case only in certain communities with Old World bakeries; through the rest of the nation, real bread was a scarce commodity. This change has happened, in part, because of the success of the Alan Scott oven. The oven attributes Alan Scott

promoted were high thermal mass, a low vault, and a sealed baking chamber to retain the steam—design components that aid the production of artisan bread. Alan was also interested in helping community-based micro-bakeries establish a foothold by teaching them to economically build *the* major piece of equipment necessary for a hearth bread bakery—the oven itself.

The Simpkins Improved Bakers' Oven.

or soft coal, coke, wood, oil, or gas. Has a perfect steam generator. Thirty gallons of hot water at all times. Always ready for service. Requires only one firing in 24 hours. Has a perfect and even heat. Can be fired while baking. Retains the moisture arising from the bread during the baking process.

COSTS LESS TO BUILD.
LESS FOR REPAIRS.
LESS FOR FUEL.

DOES THE BEST WORK.
THE MOST WORK.
THE CLEANEST WORK.

This we claim and this we warrant.

Patented August 3, 1886, and January 4, 1887.
THE ONLY SOFT COAL BURNER.

This externally fired commercial oven was advertised in an 1890 issue of *The Baker's Helper* and marks the beginning of widespread use of white ovens. The ad boasts the oven can do the same things we value today: "Always ready for service. Requires only one firing in 24 hours. Has a perfect and even heat. Can be fired while baking. Retains the moisture arising from the bread during the baking process." IMAGE COURTESY OF THE RETAIL BAKERS OF AMERICA

The Rise of Small-Scale Commercial Production

But scaling up to a production that provides a livable income and sustainable lifestyle has been a problem. A story I've heard over and over again is of dedicated hardworking young bakers who build an Alan Scott oven and try to make a living as bakers. The bread becomes wildly popular, everyone loves it, and the community responds to it . . . getting customers is not a problem. However, baker burnout and exhaustion make it hard for this business model to be sustained. The Alan Scott design works well, but it does not scale up in a way that produces efficient commercial production of high-quality hearth breads. The baking day is long—tending the fire extends the day even longer than the traditionally long hours of bakers who work in ovens fueled by gas or electricity. So while the bread quality has created strong demand, big bake days means retained heat may run low. The last bake drags on while the delivery route waits for today's bread. After the bread is dropped off, wood needs to be split or hauled before the whole cycle begins again tomorrow.

So can the micro-bakery idea work? Yes. Just look to Europe, where wood-fired bakeries are commonplace and sustainable in the modern era. Why is this? Around the turn of the 20th century French commercial bakeries began to switch to indirectly fired ovens, which are fundamentally different from directly fired high-mass ovens. There is less thermal mass in an indirectly fired oven, and the mass itself is permeated by masonry channels through which exhaust travels. This style of oven heats the chamber from the outside in, so baking can happen even when a fire is burning. The primary heat does not come from the fire inside the baking chamber, as it is in the Alan Scott design and most other ovens that are easy to build and keep springing up in backyards and micro-bakeries around the world. Indirectly fired models include the famous ovens of Poilâne and of Andre LeFort, who built the ovens for Dan and

Sharon Leader's Bread Alone Bakery. These wood-fired ovens with an external firebox make the baking day more sustainable, albeit the design and construction are more complicated than in an oven like Magdalena.

By the late 1890s, the commercial American baking scene also moved toward an externally fired wood-fired oven for commercial ovens. However, American affluence and industrialism allowed American commercial bakers to forgo the use of more finicky wood heat in favor of gas, oil, and eventually electricity. The American food culture—already on the way to mass production—embraced factory-made breads. Small community bakeries, whether wood-fired or not, fell by the wayside. And familiarity with using a wood-fired oven went along with them.

Enter the Oven Masons: The North American Masonry Heater Pedigree

When Alan starting spreading the word about an easy-to-build wood-fired oven, it was to a population that was unfamiliar with this type of cooking and baking, not to mention construction.

In 1987 the Masonry Heater Association was formed. This group was initially interested in building masonry heaters—a type of home heating device that has been used for centuries in cold climates where wood is scarce, and is a way to maximize the heating potential.

Masonry heaters rely on fast, hot fires to produce heat that is then stored in the copious thermal mass and radiated out into the room over a long period. The rate and ferocity of combustion is not reduced in order to prolong the delivery of heat. Fast hot burns result in complete, or very nearly complete, combustion and greatly reduced particulates. In contrast, the wood-stoves that are familiar throughout the United States were manufactured on this continent beginning in the early 18th century, at a time when the supply of wood fuel seemed limitless. These devices do not radiate heat for very long after the fire is gone, because there isn't a lot of dense thermal mass to soak up and slowly release the heat; you are only warmed while there is a fire. To keep your home warm all night long while you're asleep with a woodstove, the rate of combustion needs to be slowed so the fuel in the woodstove lasts until morning; this is done by reducing the air supply, thus choking a hot vigorous flame into smoldering embers. However, smoldering combustion results in incomplete combustion, a dirty burn, lots of air pollution, and particulates that are harmful to public health.

Thanks to the Masonry Heater Association, more and more masons in this country became trained to understand the principles of retained heat. And because constructing Alan Scott–style ovens from scratch is similar to building masonry heaters, these same masons started being contracted to build backyard wood-fired ovens.

This organized group of masonry oven builders applying combustion principles and more efficient materials to the bread oven that Alan Scott introduced had a profound and positive effect on how backyard and commercial wood-fired ovens are built and used. And while the forefront of masonry bread oven design innovation is happening in the context of commercial ovens, the technology, design principles, building materials, and combustion knowledge are quickly seeping into the world of backyard bread ovens, providing richer cooking and baking opportunities for the wood-fired oven lifestyle.

A heating system built by Tom Trout for his own home. The green tiled heater is a Finnish contraflow design. It has lighter mass so it can heat up and radiate heat more quickly than a more massive oven. There is enough mass, though, on two firings a day, the heater can warm a 24-foot by 24-foot room with 10-foot ceilings, as well as making the rest of the home comfortable, unless the temperature is less than 25°F (-4°C). If the outside temperature is that low, the house temperature is augmented with a larger oven that can be seen in this photo directly behind this heater. PHOTO COURTESY OF TOM TROUT

CHAPTER TWO

✦ ● ✦

How Wood-Fired Ovens Work

I once told somebody I had just met that I baked bread in a wood-fired brick oven. We talked about the fire—how it was built and how it burned. I briefly described the process and mentioned how different it is to bake with heat retained, and slowly released, by masonry. Not better or worse than baking in an electric or gas oven, but different. He didn't understand, though. "How can it be any different," he asked. "Heat's heat, right?"

Heat *is* heat, I suppose, but there is a different *quality* of heat when it is retained and released by hot masonry than if emitted from a flame or the red-hot electric element in your home oven. And the difference has to do with how the heat moves in and around masonry compared with how it moves in and around an oven lined with a thin sheet of metal.

The first drafts of this book's cooking sections were originally organized around "Cooking and Baking with Fire" and "Cooking and Baking Without Fire." That fundamental division is one that should be understood before a conversation about heat and heat transfer. Using a live fire to prepare food is more like using our modern home and commercial ovens: The heat can be controlled, so there is a sustained and even temperature. Yes, there are variations due to door openings and other factors, but the oven is attempting to return to a baseline temperature of, say, 450°F (232°C). The thermostat turns off once the chill that arrived with newly loaded dough has been overtaken.

Whenever you open the door and the rush of cool air drastically reduces the temperature, the oven kicks on; close the door and the temperature recovers. This can (theoretically) go on forever—an endless adjustment to create a relatively stable heating environment. Retained heat, on the other hand, continues to dissipate. There are no other increases in heat levels until another fire is started. Bakers refer to this as a "falling oven."

Radiation, Conduction, and Convection

Wood-fired ovens are supercharged by a thermal power trio composed of radiation, conduction, and convection. The combination of these three heat-transfer systems is what makes masonry ovens distinct, especially when used to bake bread.

RADIANT AND RETAINED HEAT

To bake bread in the simplest, most common type of wood-fired oven, the baker must use heat stored in the thermal mass. To get heat into the thermal mass, a fire is burned inside the oven. The fire releases heat, which is absorbed by the bricks. Ideally, the fire releases as much heat as possible and the bricks absorb as much as possible. Because bricks are dense, they can store a lot of heat—more than the thin sheet of metal in a conventional gas or electric oven can. More heat is stored in dense mass than in less dense materials, so, therefore, more dense materials = more heat storage. Eventually the fire is removed—or consumes all of its fuel and burns out—and the oven, swept clean of ash, begins to cool. Once the temperature comes into the range for what you're making (unless what you're making requires the presence of a live fire, in which case you wouldn't have let the fire expire) you load your oven and begin cooking with retained heat.

A fire gives off *radiant* heat, and so does hot masonry. This energy is emitted in *rays* that travel in a straight line and in all directions until they are absorbed or reflected by another body. (This is why I like to keep the oven free of ash, both by managing an efficient fire so there isn't as much ash—or embers and such, smothered on the hearth by excess ash—and by removing ash whenever possible.) Radiation is what you feel when the sun shines down upon your face. The intensity of heat from a radiant heat source is inversely proportional to the square of the distance between the radiant surface and the object being heated. This means that up close to a radiant surface, a small change in distance makes a big difference in heat intensity, while far away from the radiant heat source the same change in distance matters much less. Simply put by Marty Pearson, an experienced Rhode Island oven builder, "The mass is the mass as far as heat storage, but the lower the arch, the more intense is the radiant cooking heat."

THE ROLE OF CONDUCTION IN A WOOD-FIRED OVEN

The function of the junction between hot hearth and loaded dough is as a heat exchanger, delivering heat from a hotter body to a cooler one. This is conduction, the transmission of heat between different bodies of different temperatures.

Heat moves from hot areas to cold areas, and it moves more quickly when there's a large temperature difference than a smaller differential. Heat is egalitarian and wants to be equally distributed until it can't

spread anymore. If there's heat on the side of the brick closest to the fire, it will eventually migrate to the side of the brick that's farthest from the fire. The heat will continue to migrate and spread until it has distributed throughout the entire brick. This is the second law of thermodynamics.

Sometimes heat moves swiftly. Sometimes it doesn't. Some materials move heat along very quickly, like aluminum. Others move it along slowly, like bricks. The slow conductivity rate of bricks means it will take longer for one to heat up, but it will also take longer for it to cool down. This is great for wood-fired oven lovers. We want to enjoy a nice fire in the oven and we want to have a long period after the fire when heat is sequestered in the thermal mass. If our oven was made of steel it would heat up more quickly, but also cool down more quickly. It wouldn't *retain* much heat. Materials that have high diffusivity move heat through themselves more quickly than materials that can't diffuse heat as well.

Here's another example of conduction. Just now, before writing this, I went out to touch my oven. It has been more than several days since there was a fire, but the hearth bricks just inside the door were 143°F (62°C). Twelve inches above, the metal lintel was 150°F (66°C). I could place my hand on the bricks and leave it there without wanting to pull it away. I touched the lintel, however, and immediately drew away my hand. Why such a dramatic difference with only a 7°F (4°C) difference in temperature? Because metal conducts heat into my hand more quickly than bricks do. This is also why cedar benches in a 180°F (82°C) sauna are comfortable. The increased conductivity of a metal bench holds more heat and would conduct it into our skin more quickly, creating an intense heat junction that would make us spring away. Steel is three times as dense as concrete but twenty-five times as conductive.

When fully risen dough is loaded into a hot masonry oven, the retained heat in the hearth conducts itself into the bottom of the dough. Heat then spreads through the loaf, which expands. Random holes in the gluten matrix, created by the accumulation of carbon dioxide in the dough, expand in the oven's heat. Score marks rip open as the loaf swells during the first minutes of oven spring (the expansion of dough during the initial moments of the baking period). The dough is getting baked by conduction.

The flow of heat from deck to loaf is greater than the transfer of heat due to convection. To compensate for the copious amounts of hearth heat spent on baking bread, the hearth usually holds 15 percent more mass than the walls or dome of an oven. Baking bread is an energy-expensive practice. An oven will stay hot longer if it doesn't have a load (or loads) of bread being baked one right after the other.

CONVECTION: "BRINGING TOGETHER" RADIANT AND CONDUCTIVE HEAT

Hot air that rises, cools, then sinks again is convective energy serving as a bridge between the heat flowing through the hearth into the dough and the radiant rays pounding down from above. Convection circulates, and aids in the transfer of heat.

The surface temperature of heated brick inside an oven is higher than the air around it. This is because bricks are denser than air and, therefore, can store more heat. However, heat in the bricks flows into the air in its quest to equalize. As the air takes on heat, it begins to move more dramatically, as we all do when we're energetic. This motion circulates hot, moist air around the oven and over the surface of the dough. Heat is transferred from the air to the cooler dough, valiantly resisted by the evaporation of water. The steam produced by this evaporation increases the heat capacity of the air inside the firebox, which means the air becomes more dense and can therefore absorb more heat and get hotter. Currents of air in the steamy oven cool as they contribute heat to the dough on the deck. Hotter and more energetic air displaces the now cooler and more lethargic air, herding it up against the well-charged thermal mass. Once again, the mass transfers heat to the cooler air, infusing it with enough energy to displace the previous displacer. Hot air swirls around in steamy currents. Now the bread is being baked with convection.

Why is all this different from baking in an oven that isn't full of thermal mass? Because the heat transfer system is different. Yes, there can be conduction, radiation, and convection in all ovens, but the manner and speed in which heat is transferred differ between masonry and sheet metal ovens. This is not to say you can't bake good bread in an oven other than a wood-fired masonry oven. This is just saying it's *different* to bake in a wood-fired masonry oven.

The Holy Trinity: Mass, Thermal Breaks, and Insulation

The three main components of a wood-fired oven—in regard to how much and how well it stores heat—are the mass, thermal breaks, and insulation. This is true if you have a small backyard oven or a large commercial model. Their relationships are interconnected and determine how much heat you can store and how long you can keep it there.

Also, I recommend reading the discussion of mass and insulation materials in chapter 8, "Masonry Materials, Tools, and Methods," of *The Bread Builders*.

MASS: STORE AND RELEASE HEAT OVER TIME

The mass—all the masonry that is contiguous to the firebox—serves as the thermal battery of your oven, storing heat and then slowly releasing it. Dense materials have the ability to hold more heat than less dense materials. However, dense materials take longer to heat up since there is more matter to heat. There are two questions you should ask if you're trying to determine how much mass you need for your intended application: *What density of mass should I use?* And *how much mass should I use?* More mass means a longer heat-up time but more heat storage capacity. If you want a simple backyard oven that heats up easily, it doesn't need thick walls. On the other hand, be sure to have plenty of dense thermal mass if you intend to start a commercial venture where you need to store and release substantial heat over an entire long baking cycle. An oven intended for pizza parties does not need as much mass as an oven intended to produce multiple loads of hearth breads baked with retained heat.

A recurring topic among wood-fired oven users is what *shape* of oven has a faster heat-up time, better heat retention, and so on. Somebody always brings the question back to earth and reminds everybody that heat-up time is based on mass and that to have an oven perform the way you want, you need the appropriate *amount* of mass for the application. It's not the shape that affects heat-up time as much as the amount and density of thermal mass. Choosing just the right amount of thermal mass for your needs is the key to a satisfying wood-fired oven experience.

THERMAL MASS MATERIALS

All mass subjected to high temperatures will experience thermal cycling: the expansion and contraction that comes with heating and cooling. Thermal cycling is also why expansion joints are built into ovens. The extra space receives the extra volume the masonry gains when heated.

Bricks

Bricks provide the thermal mass and structure of the majority of wood-fired ovens. In fact, bread and bricks are so tightly associated that wood-fired ovens are often generically called "brick ovens." Working with bricks is a joy and easy to learn; it's a grand craft, full of hard work, forethought, a certain amount of fearlessness (after all, your creation will hopefully be around for a long time), and satisfaction.

COMMON RED BRICK

Common red bricks are designed to be used in applications without high temperatures, although some porous, low-fired red bricks can have good thermal shock resistance.

If you decide to construct a brick facade, you'll have the opportunity to work with common bricks. Brickyards have pallets and pallets of bricks with different colors and styles, so look around good and hard before you decide

on a variety. They may have more in the yard than they do in the showroom. Be sure to ask the price: It varies greatly.

FIREBRICK

Firebricks are larger than most common bricks, are fired at a high temperature, and—due to increased density—weigh more than the equivalent volume of common bricks. They also come in several grades based on the alumina content, but there is no reason to spend the extra money on high-duty. In fact, low- or medium-duty will be better because high-duty bricks are less resistant to thermal cycling, which means repeated cycling will cause the bricks to spall and degrade. (*Note:* There is also a material called "insulating firebrick" or

Firebricks also come in arch bricks. The tapered shape creates a strong arch with a desirably thin mortar joint or no mortar joint at all.

"soft firebrick." You will instantly recognize this if you pick one up, because it's similar to pumice, light and soft. It's actually used for insulation, not thermal mass.)

Firebricks also come in different shapes, which can make your construction easier because bricks won't need to be cut. Arch bricks in particular make arch construction easier and more solid. The shape of these tapered bricks allows you to construct any arch with any particular rise and run. Straight bricks (the familiar rectangular shape) can also be used to throw arches, but the mortar joints tend to get very fat on the outside of the firebox and mortar joints should be as thin as possible, especially in the case of refractory mortar. Arch bricks make a more monolithic structure, better than brickwork that relies on mortar to span the distance necessary to ensure structural integrity. (See appendix A for more information about arch bricks.)

Firebrick is also manufactured into a shape called splits that are half the thickness of full bricks. I've found them convenient to level courses and to help fill in irregular spaces when working on firebox corners or chimney transitions. Splits are also an economical option to a purchased pizza stone for your home oven. You can place them directly on the oven rack but it is faster to remove them if they are fitted onto a sheet pan. Splits break easily with a hammer and a chisel-like tool called a brick set; you can increase the surface area by fitting as many as possible on the rack or in the pan.

Soapstone

Soapstone is a very dense material with a large specific heat capacity and high conductivity, making it prized for masonry heaters. In fact, this material's high conductivity compared with firebrick is why bakers generally shy away from a soapstone hearth; it tends to scorch the bottom of a baking loaf before the interior is baked. In masonry heater applications the firebox is usually lined with firebrick to protect any soapstone layers, as soapstone tends to spall when exposed to live fire and has low resistance to thermal shock compared to firebrick. Soapstone is soft enough that it can actually be carved. This is another reason it's rarely used as a hearth for bread ovens: It would degrade and require replacement more quickly than firebrick.

Castable Refractory Concrete

This material is less romantic than the others we've discussed, but it's still a viable way to span spaces without constructing an arch from individual bricks. Forms are constructed, and oven components, such as lintels, are poured in situ or poured off-site and assembled. You may need some experience with building forms and casting in order to use castable refractories to span large expanses of your oven, but premixed high-temperature concrete (which is calcium aluminate cement plus refractory aggregate) is available for retail purchase. Castable refractory material takes less energy to produce than bricks, which may be of interest if you're tracking your total carbon footprint. Some brick, however, can be recycled, which means the cost of the embodied energy required to initially produce the brick is not incurred an additional time. Some companies cast manufactured parts that fit together into a dome; this is sold as a kit that can be assembled. Le Panyol makes oven components out of kaolin clay (literally "white earth") mined in France. For more information, see *Manufactured Oven Cores/Kits* in chapter 3.

Earth

Earth ovens are a simple and inexpensive way to bring wood-fired cooking and baking into your life. The self-reliant practice of using what's literally under your feet to cook and bake builds a connection with earth and fire, and who doesn't need that in their life? Earth ovens are often partially made of a material called cob, a mixture of clay, sand and straw. The heat storage capacity of an earth oven isn't as great as one made with firebrick, so these ovens are less able to store heat than are their brick or refractory material counterparts. See chapter 3, *Types of Wood-Fired Ovens, and What Makes an Oven a Bread Oven?* for more information about building ovens out of earth.

Poured Cladding

Cladding is not part of the firebox, per se, but additional heat storage can be provided by economical materials that are poured in direct contact with your firebox mass. It is often made with regular portland cement or high-temperature calcium aluminate cement.

Magdalena's exposed cladding. The cement pavers were mortared into place after initial construction. When my production needs increased I added this extra thermal mass to increase heat storage capacity.

MORTARS AND CEMENTS

Mortar's role is to provide bearing so compression or thrust can be distributed over a larger surface area. It sticks thermal mass together, but its performance shines when that boundary between bricks is in compression and has sufficient bearing. Mortar has little resistance to shearing forces which is why brick walls can support tremendous weight, but can easily have their structural integrity compromised if struck from the side. You may be able to build without mortar. Dan Wing and Dick Bessey built an oven at Camp Bread in 2007 and used no mortar between the walls of bricks laid in the vertical soldier orientation as described in *The Bread Builders*. Dry laying bricks means less time, cost, mess, and skin abrasion. Plus, I consider mortar joints a weak part of the oven, especially for mortars that crumble after repeated exposure to fire and flame.

Still, you will probably use mortar at some point. There are fewer mortar and cement options to choose from than you'll find of mass or insulation. The options you do have can be broken down into mortar that is mixed from fireclay, portland cement, or sand. There are also high-temperature—or refractory—mortars (two common brand names are Heat Stop and Sairset) that come dry or premixed. The high-temperature mortars are more expensive than cement mortars amended with fire clay, but splurge—you'll eliminate the need to buy portland cement, fireclay, and sand and it will simplify construction. More important, these mortars withstand high temperatures without crumbling better than do fireclay mixtures, and they're required by code in some areas.

Refractory mortar is much smoother to apply, making it easier for amateur masons to create the desirable ⅛" thick mortar joint. Or the mortar can be mixed

Repointing Mortar Joints

Years after Magdalena came into heavy use, I noticed that some of her mortar was crumbling away. By this time, I had learned about refractory mortar. I began an annual maintenance program, cleaning away any loose mortar and refilling joints as necessary. This is called repointing. It's a strange experience being inside an oven, still, dry, and alkaline. Arched ovens are more tomb-like, whereas round ovens feel more like a burrow—not as ominous as an arched vault. I always wear a dust mask, eye protection, and gloves. And of course, the oven has to be completely cool.

I begin by brushing away loose mortar and the scale that accumulates on masonry as minerals are left behind by evaporating steam. Then I fill all recesses and voids with a thin layer of refractory mortar, trying to keep it as smooth as possible.

Beads of high-temperature mortar thicker than ⅛" tend to develop cracks between the mortar and brick interface. Spiderweb cracks on the firebox are disconcerting but, luckily, don't affect the integrity of construction, as long as the bricks have proper bearing and transfer thrust. It is a concern if a heat heave widens the crack or fractures bricks. The joint needs to be repointed if it widens enough for fire and smoke to escape the firebox.

Cracks in the surface of poured cladding shouldn't worry you one bit. The cladding isn't carrying a load and will hold together as long as you include reinforcing mesh when you pour it.

to yoghurt consistency so the face of the brick can be dipped in mortar, instead of buttering the mortar on the brick. Thin mortar joints mean your oven is actually more dense, because the density of mortar is less than that of firebrick. Increased density is another reason to dry lay bricks if possible. Refractory mortars contain sodium silicate, which lends them a greasy consistency, making it easy to spread thin mortar joints. The sodium silicate also holds on to water tenaciously enough that the brick doesn't suck all the moisture out of the mortar, which would create a crunchy mortar that's too crumbly and dry for a thin mortar joint.

Refractory mortar's water-retentive properties also mean you don't need to dunk bricks briefly in water before you mortar them in place, a common practice when fireclay mortar is used. The constant wetting of your hands will soften your skin, and the abrasive nature of the work will really chew up your hands—even if you're wearing coated masonry or gardening gloves. Plus, your curing period for the oven core will be shorter if you don't have to wait for all that water to get out of the bricks before you start your first fire.

Cleaning old mortar off reclaimed bricks can be laborious, even if it is simple mortar made from cement and sand. However, it is impossible to cleanly and easily chip cured high-temperature mortar away from bricks so avoid using it for temporary ovens.

Curing a New Oven

The mortar and cement in a freshly constructed oven hold water that will eventually evaporate. A drying or curing period is important to rid the freshly constructed thermal mass of water before a fire is started. Resist the urge to build a raging fire so you can dry out the oven more quickly. Rushing the cure means you'll be heating water trapped in the mass, and the expansion of the water will exert unnecessary outward pressure on new construction. Letting your oven dry naturally will help preserve its structural integrity.

A couple of weeks is sufficient to let a firebox—whether masonry or earth—cure. More if you have a thick cladding layer. Don't apply your insulation until the oven is cured, to prevent the evaporating water from steaming or condensing inside the insulation. Small fires can be started and slowly increased in intensity over the next week or so, but there's no need to rush it. An electric heater with a fan is a good way to help facilitate evaporation from inside the firebox. You can monitor the rate of evaporation by checking how much condensation appears under a piece of plastic placed over part of the outer masonry.

NEVER THE TWAIN SHALL MEET: THERMAL BREAKS AND HEAT BRIDGES

If you lean against an oven and after a while it feels too hot on your skin, you probably have a heat bridge helping heat make the passage from deeper inside the mass to out there on the edge. The best insulated thermal mass is one that comes into contact with materials of the lowest possible density. Anywhere hotter mass comes in contact with cooler mass, the heat spreads from hot to cold. Open air space between the hearth and the hearth slab creates a thermal break between these two components. An ash slot provides a thermal break between the baking chamber and the outer hearth. If there's a thermal break between the firebox and the front of the facade—especially if the facade is brick or stone—you can lean against it all day and it won't become uncomfortably hot. Make thermal breaks clean and complete in order to keep heat energy isolated in the mass. Make the breaks and break the bridges.

SEQUESTER HEAT WITH INSULATION

If dense materials conduct heat more effectively than less dense materials, then we can halt thermal advance by introducing air gaps to help prevent heat from being transferred from solid to solid. This means the thermal mass will hold on to its heat longer. The reason double-pane windows get homeowners so giddy is that the dead air space between the panes is going to slow heat's escape more effectively than a single pane will. The single-pane window is solid, and heat more easily migrates through it from the warm, living side to the cold outdoors. Before you know it the heat is leaving your home and taking your heating dollars with it. Introduce an air gap, though, and the heat can't make the leap as easily. Remember . . . heat moves from hot to cold.

Oven insulation serves the same purpose as a double-pane window—it keeps stored heat in the thermal mass, so it's ready to do the work that ovens do. Not only does insulation help your oven hold heat longer, it also helps your oven heat up faster. And it decreases the differential in temperature between mass and ambient temperature, helping decrease the rate of heat loss.

INSULATION MATERIALS

It may be a problem to have too much thermal mass for your needs, but there is no downside to having too much insulation. Better insulation means your oven stays hot for longer, giving you more opportunities to cook and bake. And that insulation—no matter how much you have—should be of the most efficient kind you can afford. The upfront cost will be offset by years of increased fuel efficiency. Also, some more modern insulation is much easier to install and less bulky, so you save construction time as well as avoiding a monolithic oven in favor of something sleeker.

Dramatic increases in insulation efficiency and availability have occurred over the past 15 years, and we should expect that to continue. The nanotechnology industry is already busily creating aerogels and other new insulators that exceed the efficiencies we've seen even since *The Bread Builders*.

Rigid Under-Hearth Insulators

These insulators are among the new materials being used in the new generation of ovens. They are more expensive but much more efficient—and they also save considerable time because they're easy to install. Expanded cellular glass (ECG)—often referred to as foam glass—is the most popular form of rigid under-hearth insulation. ECG can be purchased in pieces, four or six of which will cover your hearth slab with less than five minutes of work. Grill bricks used in restaurants to clean flattop grills are made of ECG; these also work well as insulation even though they come in smaller pieces.

There are other types of rigid insulation, including calcium silicate board and RockBoard, all with similarly high compressive strengths. There are differences

A piece of expanded cellular glass on a length of ceramic fiber blanket. Gloves and respirators (not a simple dust mask) should be worn when handling insulating materials.

in insulating properties, but you can easily compensate for this by adding another layer. Calcium silicate board is more rigid than expanded cellular glass and has slightly greater compressive strength—4" of calcium silicate board is equal to about 6" of ECG. The compressive strength of a rigid insulator is around 100 psi, which means it won't be crushed under the weight of your oven. You can pour or place a hearth slab or hearth bricks directly on rigid insulation, or you can cap the insulation with cement backer board to prevent physical abuse and abrasion.

Flexible Ceramic Fiber Blankets

These highly efficient kiln blankets are 1" to 2" thick. Their flexibility makes it easy to mold them around corners, and they're stiff enough to hold themselves in place. They're much more effective than loose vermiculite (which is often used as the main insulation)

although much less affordable. Still, the investment will pay off in fuel savings and increased baking and cooking capacity. This is another oven material you should splurge on. I was lucky to learn about ceramic fiber blankets not long before I built Magdalena. Adding ceramic kiln blanket insulation to my oven greatly improved her heat retention (allowing me to bake two additional loads of bread) and slowed the loss of heat after the bake was over. Ceramic fiber blankets may be available locally, but they're easy to order online with economical shipping costs.

Rock and Mineral Wools

Rock and mineral wools are often used for soundproofing; they're also non-combustible and have a melting point above 2,000°F (1,093°C). They're more affordable but less efficient than ceramic fiber blankets. You can likely purchase rock and mineral wools at your

This mobile oven is so well insulated that snow does not melt from the roof, even though temperatures in the thermal mass below are around 500°F (260°C). PHOTO COURTESY OF OTTILIE SHORT

local well-stocked hardware store. Fibers from these insulating blankets are friable, so you need to take care when handling them: Keep your skin covered, wear gloves, and use high-quality dust masks.

Vermiculite and Perlite

Vermiculite is a mineral that, when puffed by heat, forms into light pieces filled with dead air cells, just as a piece of puffed cereal is lighter and more full of air than the original grain of rice or wheat. The air cells—and vermiculite's resistance to high temperature—make vermiculite a common insulator. It's often used as a loose fill over and around ovens and contained by the oven housing. It is available in 4" cubic-foot bags from masonry supply yards and shipping supply specialists; garden centers often carry it as a growing medium. A layer of vermiculite is also placed directly underneath many swimming pool liners, so check with your local swimming pool installer to see if you can get it in bulk.

Vermiculite is readily available and affordable, but it has several downsides, including much less impressive efficiency, compared to the aforementioned materials. When it's first poured into the cavity between the oven and the facade, vermiculite is fluffy. As it shifts and settles over time, it becomes more compact and dense, because air spaces decrease in size and number. Heat migrates through the vermiculite more easily once its compacted state turns it from insulator to something closer to mass.

Earth, Straw, and Dung

If you're interested in cob ovens, check out the work of Kiko Denzer and his wife, Hannah Field, authors of *Build Your Own Earth Oven*. Kiko and Hannah have been making—and teaching others how to make—beautiful and artistic earth ovens since the beginning of the American Bread Movement.

Before the American Bread Movement, before Jesus, before there was *bread*, there were camels and open fires. Fibrous desert plants don't break down in the digestive tract of camels, so the dung, especially when dried, is full of dead air cells created by plant fibers that rotted or will burn away. This makes dung a fairly useful insulative material compared with other earthen materials.

MASS CONFUSION

There's a class of materials too light for good heat storage but too dense for insulation. Material in an oven exists either to store and release heat or to prevent its loss, but never will those two goals be met most efficiently by just one material. Consider the function of the materials and choose them for their best thermal mass or insulative properties.

Sand

For years sand was used as a layer to surround an oven, but its density and lack of air spaces make it better suited for thermal mass than for insulation. It did prevent the baker from getting burned on a blazing-hot firebox, but it didn't efficiently keep the heat sequestered in the thermal mass. Instead, in a relentless pursuit of equilibrium, the sand draws heat to the outer edge of the mass. Sand doesn't have copious dead air cells so it isn't a good insulator. Don't confuse yesteryear's necessary or frugal practices with prudence. Sure, people used to bury their ovens in sand, but that doesn't mean we have to.

Vermicrete

Vermicrete, made by mixing vermiculite with wet cement, is also a material with a split personality. Many vermiculite pieces are compressed during the mixing process, reducing the material's effectiveness as dead air space. And once the vermicrete is solid, the cement structure will act as a heat bridge, conducting heat through the mass more effectively than something less dense.

Vermicrete adds about a day of work in building forms, mixing the vermicrete, placing it into the forms, and striking it off level. However, rigid insulation is easy to install: Just lay it on a well-supported hearth slab.

WHEN INSULATION DOESN'T INSULATE

Here's a dramatic story illustrating the relationship between a material's density and its insulative property. I know an oven owner who ran his chimney pipe up through the rafters of a renovated workshop. The attic floorboards were cut away a few inches to receive the flue pipe. The space between flue and floorboards was packed with high-quality insulation. The logic was that more insulation means more protection from combustion. However, the insulation was packed in so tightly it ceased to function as a thermal break, the way insulation is designed to, and became instead an effective *heat transfer* material! Thankfully, a whiff of hot wood was detected—a precursor to combustion—before the fire broke out. My friend quickly climbed up and pulled the insulation away from the rafters; tragedy narrowly averted, lesson learned.

CHAPTER THREE

➤ • ⧴

Types of Wood-Fired Ovens, and What Makes an Oven a Bread Oven

If tending a fire bounded by rocks and masonry is as elemental as we all know it to be, then it stands to reason that ovens have evolved concurrently throughout human existence. Variations are usually based on indigenous building material, fuel supply, permanence, and affluence. These filters may still greatly affect the oven you choose to build or buy. A primary distinction between ovens is how an oven is fired—or where the fire is in relation to where the bread is baked. There are three major categories: black (direct-fired) ovens, white (indirect-fired) ovens, and gray ovens (which use a hybrid firing method).

Black (Direct-Fired) Ovens

The vast majority of backyard ovens are black ovens—the type of oven that earns the French appellation *pain cuit au feu de bois*, "bread baked in a wood-fired oven." In *The Book of Bread*, Jérôme Assire further describes the requirements of this firing method: "Theoretically, it should apply only to bread baked on the sole of the oven in the baking chamber where the wood is actually burnt."

The thickness of the walls—the thermal mass—will depend on how you intend to use the oven. You want enough mass to store the amount of heat you need, but not more. Another way to think about it is being able to thoroughly heat the *entire mass* in a reasonable amount of time, with a reasonable amount of fuel. One firebrick thick (and when I say one firebrick I mean the 4.5" thickness of the brick, not the thinner 2.5" dimension) is adequate for an oven that will be used primarily for pizza—and even that can handle more than one load of lean, hearth bread, depending on when you stop firing and the size of the loaf.

The baking environment inside a retained-heat oven is most stable (the temperature falls most gradually) when the *entire* thermal mass is heated to or above the desired baking temperature. Baking in a retained-heat oven that has a significant temperature gradient between the inside (hearth/arch surface temperature) and the outside of the thermal mass will create a system that loses heat in two directions, because heat continues to cook the food and bake the bread even as it migrates away from the cooking/baking surface into the cooler parts of the mass until the whole thing equalizes.

For bread and other products that are baked with retained heat, the main downside of a black oven is that you only get one shot to heat the thermal mass per bake cycle. If you find the temperature is falling too quickly, it is not easy to jack the heat back up or to alter the rate of decline. There are effective ways to prevent or deal with this, though:

- Make sure there's enough thermal mass to store as much heat as you need for the intended use (but not more).
- Develop a firing schedule that ensures the *whole* thermal mass is brought up to or near the target baking temperature. (This slows the rate of decline by eliminating a temperature gradient within the mass, pulling heat away from the baking chamber in order to bring the whole mass to equilibrium.)
- Make sure there are thermal breaks everywhere necessary to completely isolate the thermal mass from any potential heat sinks.
- Use plenty of excellent insulation. Err on the side of too much insulation—unlike thermal mass, there is no functional downside to too much insulation.

White (Indirect-Fired) Ovens

In a white oven the baking chamber is heated by exhaust gases that travel a convoluted path on the outside of the thermal mass, conducting heat to a baking chamber that doesn't feel fire's flame. The firebox is beneath or to the side of the baking chamber.

The idea of having a convoluted exhaust path has its roots in Scandinavian masonry heaters, where a large thermal mass uses these exhaust paths to wrench as much heat energy as possible from the combusted wood. The thermal mass then slowly radiates the heat, creating a long-lasting cozy environment. A huge advantage of this design is its efficiency and lack of emissions—more of the combustible material (including gases) is burned (due to a secondary combustion chamber), and that means less smoke and particulate coming out of the chimney.

The advantage of a white oven is that it can continue to bake, because heat is replenished without having to start a fire in the bake chamber (and that requires raking out the embers, allowing the oven to cool, and so on). If the heat is dropping too low in a white oven, the firebox can simply be stoked; that heat will permeate the bake chamber from the inside out, creating the proper hearth bread-baking environment.

In general, the main downside to white ovens is not having the option of live fire and embers on the hearth. Flames and embers deliver different types of heat and unique baking environments that cannot be achieved in their absence, no matter the temperature. White ovens are great for many cooking and baking methods: baking, roasting, braising, low and slow cooking, dehydrating. But black ovens can do all that stuff just as well. The benefit of the black oven is that it expands your possibilities to include the elemental pleasure of baking and cooking with fire.

Gray Ovens (Hybrid)

Gray ovens generally have an external firebox and channels that direct the flue gases around the baking chamber just like white ovens, but they also give you the option of directing the flue gases from the external firebox through the baking chamber (as in the French gueulard oven), as well as building a fire directly in the baking chamber just like black ovens.

Imported European gray ovens continue to be a popular option for wood-fired bakeries in North America, but American high-mass oven design continues to evolve in an attempt to incorporate the convenience of the gray ovens while keeping the best qualities of the high-mass retained-heat ovens, the chief characteristic being the very constant, stable heat that a saturated, very well-insulated high-mass oven can deliver.

Note: These terms are referring to stand-alone bake ovens rather than those built within a heater. Bake ovens are often built into masonry heaters as optional features. In masonry heater lexicon, *black oven* is often used to describe any firebox that encounters flue gases, including gray ovens that are part of the flue path from the firebox. These otherwise white ovens do get black

Max and Eva Edleson and the Barrel Oven

A barrel oven is a white oven made out of brick, earth, or stone and built around a metal drum. This is a lower-cost oven that can get up to 350°F (177°C) in about 15 minutes. Barrel ovens have been commonplace for a few decades in rural parts of South America and elsewhere, but they are only now being discovered in the United States, a promising new option among the choices for backyard or community wood-fired ovens.

Max and Eva Edleson are pioneers in the next generation of earthen oven and rocket-mass heater masons, like Kiko Denzer and Ianto Evans and the work that has come out of the Aprovecho Sustainability Institute. They work primarily with mud, clay, adobe, and natural plasters, although Max and Eva are also both skilled metalsmiths, fabricating metal parts for the oven kits they sell through their business, Firespeaking (www.firespeaking.com). Eva and Max are young and strong and impassioned about their craft, constantly asking good questions, trying new ideas, moving things forward. They are creating the future they hope for, simply by gathering people together and building it, handmade brick by handmade brick.

The barrel oven operates on a fundamentally different design principle than a retained-heat black oven and serves a different, and significant, niche: maximizing fuel efficiency and heating up to temperature in as little as 15 minutes, for everyday wood-fired baking, roasting, and cooking. It does have heat retaining thermal mass, however, which provides similar descending heat temperature windows as a directly fired oven.

The barrel oven is fueled by a small hot fire in a narrow firebox beneath the barrel. Flue gases from the firebox below flow up around the barrel, quickly heating it and bringing the oven to temperature. See Max and Eva's book *Build Your Own Barrel Oven* for more information, including instructions for building your own barrel oven and a bevy of recipes designed for barrel ovens.

The flames from the firebox are washing into the bake chamber in the oven at Slow Rise Bakery on Gabriola Island, British Columbia. PHOTO COURTESY OF DIMITRI TZOTZOS

Seeing into the Future:
Noah Elbers and Orchard Hill Breadworks

I can't remember when I met Noah Elbers—it was that long ago, and our paths through the bread and wood-fired oven world have crossed that many times. I think it was when I traveled from King Arthur to Orchard Hill for an oven raising led by Alan Scott. We received a flyer at King Arthur announcing the workshop, and I immediately called and reserved a spot. It was the start of a decade-long friendship and an opportunity to watch and learn from a great baker who has tremendous insight into commercial wood-fired baking.

Noah knows so much about wood-fired ovens because over the course of his career, he has built and baked in an earth oven, an Alan Scott–style oven, and a Spanish Llopis, so he has had the opportunity to see how each of these ovens performs.

Like many micro-bakeries, Orchard Hill Breadworks evolved out of an interest in bread and traditional living. It didn't come into being via a business proposal and a decision to enter the bread business. It just happened. Noah and his wife, Dove, with their two children, Greta and Asher, live above the bakery built in a renovated barn. The beautiful farm is located in southwestern New Hampshire and was purchased by Noah's grandparents back in the 1970s. Since then, three generations have

The circular hearth inside a Llopis oven

turned Orchard Hill into a great model of the small, diverse, sustainable family farm and cooperative. Noah's grandparents and father and mother, Anton and Eleanor, tended orchards, nurtured bees, raised livestock, built and taught in a private school, and helped to create an awareness of a community-oriented food web.

Naturally, the family at Orchard Hill had close ties with the neighbors. Elliot Burch, who had a small clay oven down the road, once asked Noah to help with the bake. Noah was transfixed with the process of making bread from fire. Along with family and friends, he made his own oven using *The Bread Ovens of Quebec* as a guide, but at the time had no idea he was destined to become a baker. The oven was just one more feature of a self-reliant farm life. However, bread began to be sold at Orchard Hill in 1997 and the first community Pizza Night was held, a tradition that continues to this day.

Orchard Hill Breadworks was on the cusp of the artisan bread movement. The popularity of Noah's naturally leavened bread made with organic flour quickly made it clear that a commercial operation needed more capacity, and greater heat retention, than that provided by the small cob oven. An old barn was renovated into a commercial kitchen with space for an oven built in a 2002 workshop led by Alan Scott himself. The response to the workshop was fantastic. Orchard Hill added some spaces for observers, so that people could see the oven under construction, even though there wasn't enough hands-on room for everybody to pick up a trowel and brick. But there was plenty of mortar to mix, bricks to carry, arch forms to construct, and people to chat with about building and baking.

Alan quietly went about the business of organizing the two dozen participants and led us through the steps of constructing the firebox on the beautiful foundation (built in advance of the workshop) made from local fieldstones. The hard work of the day gave way to great food in the evening, including pizza from the cob oven and relaxed opportunities to get to know the other participants. This was an oven raising, just like communities used to raise barns. Dan Wing brought his Gypsy Wagon and gave a talk about bread and ovens in the school on the last full day of the workshop.

By 2007 the bakery had once again grown to the point that more oven capacity was necessary. Noah researched different designs and eventually decided to import a Llopis from Spain. It came in an entire shipping container (as in a tractor trailer). A few days later, two Spanish oven builders showed up and a local mason was brought in to help with construction.

A Llopis is a wood-burning oven unlike no other—it has a round hearth that rotates when the baker turns a helm-like wheel. The hearth is masonry, as is the large shallow dome under the hearth that also serves as the roof of the firebox. Both components hold and radiate heat just as in a black oven. The rest of the oven is metal and reminiscent of a horizontal Ferris wheel.

The Llopis is indirectly fired, which means the firebox is separate from the bake chamber. The heat produced in the masonry dome under the hearth also circulates through flues that run around and over the bake chamber. This heat is then transferred to the ceiling and walls of the Llopis, where it radiates back to the masonry hearth (keeping it hot) or directly to loaves when the oven is loaded with dough. This indirect heating allows Noah to continually fire the oven while baking bread, a more efficient and less nerve-racking way to bake commercial-sized batches of bread than with retained heat. In a retained-heat oven, the firing schedule must adequately soak the thermal mass with heat; once the fire is removed, no more heat can enter the thermal mass. Once heat is used to turn dough into bread, the baker needs to either refire or stop baking. Refiring is inconvenient—a fire needs to be built, burned, then raked out. And then there's the period while the oven cools to proper baking temperature. All the while the bread is fermenting. (Its rate of fermentation can be slowed by retarding—although this is only effective for a certain amount of time depending on dough temp, ambient temps, and the amount of prefermented flour and/or yeast, plus all the other variables that affect the rate of fermentation. Noah compares baking with "seeing into the future" so the dough is at its optimum when it is loaded.) And stopping is not an option if the bread has been mixed, is shaped, and is waiting for the chance to enter the oven. An indirectly fired oven eliminates this problem. The fire is separate from the bake chamber so a fire can continue to burn and heat the oven even while bread is being loaded and baked.

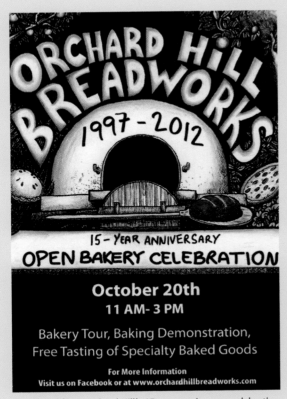

A postcard from Orchard Hill's 15-year anniversary celebration

The construction crew, with help from Noah and Anton, spent eight days building the round oven. Noah's oven is fired with wood, although a Llopis can be fitted to burn gas. The baker loads the hearth in pie-shaped wedges, slowly rotating the hearth to bring another empty wedge-shaped space in front of the loading door. There's a pan on top of the combustion chamber to provide steam, but many Llopis users start off a bake with several sheet pans loaded with wet towels. This creates steam for the first loaves. Then the steam given off by those first loaves provides steam for successive batches so no additional steaming is necessary. Even though the oven is large (a little over 11 feet in diameter), only one small, narrow door gives Noah access to it—and that small door also helps prevent the escape of steam.

Noah burns about 17 cords of wood a year to bake around 80,000 loaves of bread (about 125,000 to 140,000 pounds of dough). Twenty-five hundred loaves a week are baked during the busy summer months, a number that shrinks to 1,500 during the slow winter. Noah bakes three days a week and burns the oven for five hours, from 8 AM to 2 PM. He then closes the oven and allows the heat to equalize. Dough is mixed and fermented during the firing period. Once the dough is shaped, it's placed on speed racks and rolled into a walk-in retarder—an insulated room whose temperature is regulated by a CoolBot. The dough slowly ferments until midnight, when Noah and his small crew of dedicated bakers start pulling racks of dough from the retarder and loading the Llopis. Noah continues to fire the oven until about three-quarters of the way through the bake, when the breads at the end of the schedule don't need as much heat. Five hundred to 900 loaves later, the last loaf is pulled from the oven. This is a rate of about 100 loaves per person per hour. For years, that person was usually just Noah, but recently he brought on additional bakers to help manage the workload and provide some time so he can take care of office work. One reason Noah likes to work through the night is that everyday distractions are greatly reduced and the absence of phone calls and questions allows him to focus on the bake.

The oven temperature lives in the range from 300°F to 500°F (150–260°C). Noah's typical loading temp is around 420 °F (216°C).

Once the loaves are packed, Anton heads out on a delivery route while two other drivers take off in opposite directions. Between the three of them they will stop at about 30 different locations throughout southern Vermont and New Hampshire.

After the Llopis was up and running and a baking schedule was implemented, Noah designed a system where hot gases exiting the oven heat water in four heat exchangers made from copper coils that snake across the top of the upper flue chamber. Hot air passes through the flue and heats the bake chamber below and the water coils above. A circulator, pressure release valves, and regulation gadgets help maintain the safety and usefulness of the system, which holds 700 gallons of water and provides all the hot water for their home upstairs (including radiant floor heat) as well as hot water for the bakery. Noah saw no further fuel usage once the system was installed so he feels the heating system doesn't affect the baking efficiency of the oven. This is because the heat is captured after it exits the combustion chamber. As the flue gases flow up the thin-walled chimney, there is no mass to absorb and hold the heat. Is this wasted heat? It is if it's simply released into the atmosphere. But in Noah's case it's trapped and put to good use.

Not only does Noah bake delicious bread with high-quality ingredients for the community, he and his family have also created and augmented a farm and bakery system that offers many goods and services: education, honey, and an outlet for locally produced foods such as lacto-fermented kimchi and sauerkraut and bread. They have even converted the 1798 farmhouse into a rentable retreat with a complete kitchen, common rooms, and an ideal location next to a great bakery. Hard work, an evolving decades-old vision of sustainability, diverse revenue streams, and good bread make Orchard Hill Breadworks one of the first wood-fired micro-bakeries to pace its growth in order to avoid burnout and become profitable. Noah Elbers: leader in the American wood-fired Bread Movement.

when the flue gases initially pass through the chamber, but after a good burn the soot burns off and the oven interior becomes gray.

Mobile Ovens

Dan Wing, coauthor of *The Bread Builders*, helped start the mobile wood-fired oven concept. It has since gained substantial popularity, even helping to fuel the food-truck phenomenon.

Portable ovens have grown in popularity because micro-bakery operators can bake bread all night, then hitch up and travel to a farmer's market where they sell bread and make pizza. This business model creates greater income than a bread-only operation could. There are two big hurdles regarding trailered ovens, however. First, you need a roadworthy chassis that is street-legal, can handle the load, and protects the oven from cracking by having proper suspension. And second, if you plan to have a high-thermal-mass mobile bread oven, you may need a truck with a substantial towing capacity (around 7,000 pounds). This expense is in addition to the fixed costs of fuel, maintenance, and insurance. Mobile ovens, like backyard ovens, are generally direct-fired.

One of the benefits of a mobile oven is the opportunity to get started baking while waiting for building permits and other slowdowns that always seem to come with opening a food service establishment. In addition to gaining exposure for your market, you may even be able to sell the bread at a farmer's market, if allowed by your local health regulations.

Types of Black Ovens Based on Shape: Arched and Dome

If firing method is the overarching way to categorize ovens, then shape is the most familiar and passionately debated. It's a common misperception that dome ovens are for pizza and vaulted ovens are for bread. Nor is it true that dome ovens heat up more quickly than vaulted ones. I have baked fine bread in dome ovens and fine pizza in vaulted ovens. More important, heat-up time is more dependent on the amount of thermal mass, not the shape of the firebox.

VAULTED OR ARCHED OVEN

The arched oven Alan Scott made popular through his plans is—like the practice of baking whole-grain bread—yet another way he connected us to ancient knowledge. Arches are beautiful to behold and an amazing experience to build. When I removed the arch support after I completed my first arch and saw a span

Byron Fry

Byron Fry is a creative young baker providing the all-important field-testing of the next generation of bread ovens and reporting back to the designer regularly with feedback that helps shape the evolution of oven design. Byron lives on the filigreed coast of British Columbia, one of the world's wood-fired oven hot spots, like Vermont and the mountains of North Carolina.

Baking runs in Byron's family, although it skipped the last few generations. Byron's great-great-grandfather was a baker who built a brick oven in Victoria, British Columbia, in the 1920s. The oven was torn down in 1963, but Byron does have a *Victoria Daily Times* newspaper clipping that shows the huge oven being deconstructed. The first line of the short article says, "A memory of the days when bread smelled like bread and cost a nickel bobbed up this week out of a broken building." Byron is part of a community of bakers who know what bread should smell like and have access to local grain, an eager customer base, and copious amounts of fuel.

We met Byron when he and his girlfriend, Ottilie Short, were traveling on a cross-continent motorcycle trip from Vancouver across to Montreal; down the East Coast to Bettie, North Carolina; and then back across the Great Plains and up the West Coast to Vancouver. This wasn't just a leisure ride. It was a fact-finding mission. Both Byron and Ottilie are photographers, and they were making this trip to visit bakers and bakeries, take photos, and soak up the North American bread-baking scene. Byron was also collecting sourdough starter from each baker to create a communal starter and forming a plan to open a wood-fired enterprise once he returned to the lush BC coast.

After a continent's worth of field research, Byron was the first—with the help of his father—to build his own oven from the plans of William Davenport, of Turtlerock Masonry. As a testament to good design—not just the skill of the oven builder, because Byron was yet another amateur mason—the oven performed admirably from the start. This was a mobile oven, built on a trailer, which allowed Byron to bake on his family's property until he established a retail bakery. Byron's signature item is his organic, naturally leavened country bread—traditional and large. He sells half loaves and whole, and many of his customers have learned to time the week's meals so the last of the 4-pound loaf is eaten just in time to visit Byron at the next farmer's market. The rectangular oven is 3.5 by 4.5 feet and holds 16 of these loaves at a time. He bakes several loads, bookended at the high end with focaccia and at the bottom with sweeter breads better suited to the lower temperatures of declining

Byron Fry unloads bread from his mobile wood-fired oven. PHOTO COURTESY OF OTTILIE SHORT

heat. Loading surface temperatures for the country bread are around 500°F (260°C) on the dome and between 450°F and 480°F (232–249°C) on the hearth. Bake time is about an hour; the second bake is only slightly longer than the first. Wood-fired production baking involves progressive learning—it's good to be able to start small and let experience, skill, and practice build (with some quick and dramatic evolutions in efficiency) until you're able to bake more bread in the same amount of time—or better yet, more bread in a shorter time.

Once Byron's production schedule smoothed out, he was able to customize a firing and baking schedule that works for him. Two years after he began baking in the oven, Byron was baking about sixty 500g focaccia, thirty 350g baguettes, twenty-five 1kg spelt/kamut loaves, and twenty-five 1kg and twenty 1.8kg whole wheat boules. That's about 105kg (230 pounds) of dough. Sometimes he'll push out another 60 baguettes, making about 250 pounds of dough.

To bake this much bread he fires for eight hours for the first bake when the oven starts off at a temperature of about 260°F (127°C), and four or five hours for the second bake of the week when the oven temp at the beginning of firing is around 310°F (154°C). For the first bake he closes up the oven when the oven is around 900°F (482°C) and then lets it rest for eight hours, plenty of time to prepare for the bake and get some rest. There is enough heat to make croissants and scones, but he runs those through a convection oven in order to shorten the bake day.

In an elegant example of identifying perfect heat windows for particular items, Byron started baking some heavy rye bread during the firing schedule one day in advance of the farmer's market. The first day of his firing, the oven enjoys a four- to five-hour-long firing, but the heat hasn't yet saturated the entire oven mass so he cannot bake more than two loads before the heat runs low. The retained heat is sufficient to bake some bread but not as much as Byron needs for the busy market. He waits for the oven to drop to 500°F after he rakes out on Thursday and then loads a batch of 100 percent rye. This type of bread is best baked in a receding oven—a hot oven (around 500°F) that drops quickly to about 300°F (149°C) and hangs there while the heavy, dense rye slowly bakes through, creating a rich, dark loaf. In addition to this baking environment, these rye breads should also cure for 24 hours before they are sliced. By baking this bread a day in advance, Byron is able to use some of the heat he has created and also sell bread that is at a point when it's ready to be eaten.

In October 2012, Byron opened Fry's Red Wheat Bread in a storefront across the street from where his grandfather's bakery was. The oven is 5 by 7 feet and was built based on his previous experience, along with considerable input from local mason David Johnstone and Byron's friend Graham Mcdonald. The 8.5" hearth is insulated below with 8" of foam glass. The walls and arch are also 7.5" thick and insulated with 6" of ceramic blanket piled on with about 12" of rockwool. Byron bakes on Wednesday through Saturday. The oven is fired at noon for 6 hours on the day before production. It is left overnight to equalize and at 3:00 am when Byron comes into the bakery, it is 750°F (399°C) 2" deep into the mass. If the oven seems too hot, Byron may sweep the hearth and open the damper before bulk-fermented dough that was mixed at 5 pm the day before is divided and shaped into loaves and focaccia. Once the bread is proofing, the bakers turn to laminating pastries and getting ready to dip pretzels in lye. The focaccia and pretzels help cool the hearth before the hearth loaves go in around 7:30 am.

On one slow weekday, Byron didn't have enough focaccia and pretzels to cool the hearth so he scooped some leftover construction gravel onto sheet pans and loaded it into the oven to help absorb some of the excess heat. After the pans were unloaded and cooled a bit, Byron realized they were a useful portable thermal battery and slipped one onto the bottom of his covered speed racks to make a 'Hot Rocks Proof Box' for proofing croissants and danishes.

After the hearth breads are baked, loads of pastries, heavy rye breads, and pan breads are baked in the declining heat of the oven. Fry's Red Wheat Bread also turns out plenty of savory handpies filled with seasonal ingredients and local sausage and mutton. The oven is also used to braise ingredients for the handpies or to be used as toppings for Sunday's pizza day that begins at noon and goes until the dough runs out.

Byron also continues to use his mobile oven, which allows him the opportunity for off-site catering and baking, proving once again that mobile ovens are a great stepping-stone into a storefront or wholesale baking facility.

of masonry over Magdalena's firebox and bake chamber, I felt a huge sense of accomplishment knowing I was using a construct developed thousands of years ago. The arch seemed to soar and defined a beautiful space.

Magdalena is based on Alan Scott's 36" by 48" plans. However, because of my lack of masonry experience, the oven ended up being closer to 44" by 44", more square than the plans called for. This ended up to be a good thing. I have noticed that rectangular AS ovens, especially ones that are over 4 feet deep, require a lot of rotating of loaves, because the heat differential from the front to the back of the oven is pretty large. It is quite hot back there against the wall, but much cooler near the door. Plus, bakers usually (and logically) load from back to front. The bread that is first loaded is placed in the back so it begins baking right away. By the time the oven is fully loaded, the loaves in back have been baking away in the hottest part of the oven for longer than the ones just placed up front. When I realized my oven was going to be more square than rectangular, I worried that the shape would affect the draw. It ended up being

just fine. I do still need to rotate bread, but probably less than if the oven was substantially deeper than it is wide.

I prefer to load front-to-back in rows, alternating sides (right front corner to right back corner, then left front corner to back left corner), working toward the center until the loaves get in the way of the peel, at which time I switch to loading from back to front. The reason for loading front before back is to help balance the degree of bake: The loaves in the back will be in a slightly hotter environment due to the oven's heat differential and the loaves will be more evenly baked if they are in that hot zone for a shorter amount of time than the loaves in the cooler region closer to the mouth of the oven.

An arched oven can be constructed with a ceiling that is lower, and this allows steam to come into contact with the dough more quickly, because there isn't so much space that needs to be filled with steam, as in a dome oven.

A couple of years after I built Magdalena, I gained even more respect for the structural integrity of the arch when I had to help *dismantle* an oven that had

A top-down burn in the arched oven at the King Arthur Flour Baking Education Center, built by William Davenport of Turtlerock Masonry

been built from Alan's plans. It was a sad story where rented property was changing hands and the owner decided the oven should go. Once I peeled off the concrete cladding and was down to the arch, I pounded and pounded on the top of it with a 10-pound sledgehammer. It wouldn't budge. This is the enormous strength that allows ancient bridges to still reliably carry heavy loads. The Achilles' heel of a ring arch is that it weakens when a brick falls out, but the only way for me to achieve that was to knock one out from inside the oven. Once I removed a single brick, the monolithic structure was fatally compromised, and it was short work to clear away the rest of the arch bricks.

BRICK DOME OVEN

The brick dome oven is often referred to as the Pompeii-style or beehive oven. The shape is also used for the *horno* of the southwestern United States. This beehive shape possesses a structural elegance because a catenary dome, which is illustrated by St. Louis's monument to westward expansion, is self-supporting, while other domes and, especially, arched ovens need a buttress. Arched ovens need poured cladding or an angle iron harness or buttress to prevent arch thrust from pushing out on the walls. If the walls spread too far, there will be insufficient support for the arch and it will fall into the bake chamber.

The poured concrete cladding in an Alan Scott design contributes thermal mass as well as serving as a buttress. This additional mass is why some think that arched ovens take longer to heat up. Really it's because there's more there to heat. Shape has nothing to do with it.

I do find it challenging to bake really gorgeous hearth bread in large, high dome ovens, however, because it can be difficult to create enough steam to completely fill a cavernous baking chamber (steam accumulating as it does at the top first, and only reaching the level of the hearth if the entire air space above the hearth is full of steam) so that the loaves on the hearth are bathed in steam during the crucial initial moments of their bake.

A dome oven built by Pat Manley at Wildacres during the Masonry Heater Association's 2012 annual conference and workshop

The Wildacres 2012 dome oven during construction. The sticks help prop up the bricks until the entire dome is completed, making it a self-supporting structure.

This need for excessive steam makes it much harder to get the good caramelization and oven spring that come with a nice steamy oven. The Neapolitan designs tend to have a lower dome than the Tuscan-style Pompeii ovens, so steam accumulation may not be as much of an issue as it is in a more cavernous dome. Forno Bravo manufactures oven cores but also has free, downloadable plans for a Pompeii oven on its website. See www.fornobravo.com to download the plans; you'll also find a link to the company's useful wood-fired oven blog.

Types of Black Ovens Based on Building Material

Containing fire requires resilient materials. There are a variety to choose from with different costs and heat-retentive properties.

EARTH/MUD/CLAY/COB OVENS

This may be one of the simplest and least expensive ways to build a wood-fired oven, because materials can be locally sourced—often for free. Earth is the flour of the mason. Add some water to clay and you have a material that can be shaped and baked into an oven. In one weekend, you and a couple of friends could bring a wood-fired oven into your life, no problem.

Consult Kiko Denzer's book *Build Your Own Earth Oven* for more information on building with earth. Stu Silverstein's *Bread Earth and Fire* is another tutorial on how to build a directly fired earthen oven, as well as simply a delightful read.

Earth ovens are usually made by forming damp sand into a dome shape on top of a firebrick hearth. The outer edge of the sand form will be the inside wall of your oven, so make sure to shape the oven to the right size for your intended purpose and to fit your cooking utensils. Clay mixed with sand (two to three parts of sand to one part of clay) is then mixed with water (and by your feet) to make a firm, yet pliable mixture. Be careful not to add too much water. If the mixture is too wet it will slump when a 3" to 4" shell of this clay mixture is packed around the sand form.

"Cob" is technically this same clay-and-sand mixture with the addition of straw or other fibers to add tensile strength. (Cob is a traditional building material that can be used to build walls and comfortable structures.) This oven-building approach also includes southwestern adobe-built *hornos* and simple ovens from cultures around the world. Once the layers have dried for a day or two, a door is cut out of the clay and/or cob layers and the sand is scooped out, leaving behind a clay shell oven.

It is a wonderful experience to mix clay, sand, and water with your feet and then shape the mixture into an oven with your hands. It can be even more hands-on if you dig your own clay or collect sand. If you don't have a good source where you can dig your own, drop in on one of your local potters. Often they have unfired clay

This simple oven with a chimney is built on an urbanite foundation harvested from a Providence, Rhode Island, sidewalk, but hybridized with foam glass under a 4" hearth with a parquet pattern. The same pressurized garden sprayer used to inject steam into an oven for bread baking also works well to keep the sand form moist while shaping it.

they can't use and will be thrilled to give it away and reclaim some space in their studio. It is okay if the clay is dry; just put it in a container and cover with water. In a week or so, it will be soft enough to mix with sand in order to create the layer of the oven that acts as thermal mass. If you can't dig your own or receive potter donations, dry bagged fireclay, available at most well-stocked masonry supply companies, is a good substitute. It is more expensive, but the convenience may be worth it. Clean sand is easier to dig than clay, or bulk or bagged mason sand can be purchased.

The heat storage capacity of an earth oven isn't as great as one made of firebrick, which means it is less able to store heat than one made of dense bricks. There are, however, ways to increase the heat-retaining properties of an earth oven such as adding dense aggregate, like concrete gravel to the cob. Many earth ovens have the firebrick in the hearth oriented so the hearth is 2¼" thick, but if the bricks are turned 90 degrees, the hearth becomes 4" thick. Yes, it will take more bricks, more fuel, and a longer heat-up time, but the greater amount of stored heat will give you more opportunities to bake and cook.

I very much appreciate the low cost of building an earth oven, but for my Providence earth oven I have invested in foam glass for laying under the hearth insulation, which greatly slows heat migration into the foundation. See Kiko's book and blog for an insulated hearth made with empty wine bottles and a basket enclosure that provides space for loose fill insulation.

Clay bread ovens are also profiled in *The Bread Ovens of Quebec* by Lise Boily and Jean-François Blanchette. Instead of the dome shape that Kiko and Stu discuss, the Quebecoise oven is vaulted and elliptical. Another difference is that it's shaped by blocks of clay placed over a sapling framework or basket, as opposed to the lost-sand approach that shapes the firebox of most domed ovens. This approach makes an oven with a rough interior, which creates more radiant surface area but may also be more fragile than a dome with a smooth interior surface. *The Bread Ovens of Quebec* is out of print, but luckily the Canadian Museum of Civilization has made the book available as a free download. The website is in the resources section at the end of this book.

Earth ovens are often built without a chimney. Skipping this architectural component simplifies construction but negatively impacts combustion, because chimneys create draft, pulling more oxygen into the firebox. However, a draft door can help improve combustion on an oven without a chimney. (See *Oven Doors*, later in this chapter for information on draft doors.) Channeling the smoke into a chimney does prevent any spillage from staining the oven directly above the door. Some people make a vent hole in the top of the dome when they are constructing a cob oven, but avoid this—it will make it impossible for you to retain steam while baking bread.

HAND-BUILT MASONRY OVENS

An oven made from bricks is perhaps the iconic wood-fired oven. This castle of fire is a structure intended to outlast generations. It's a firebox, a bake chamber, an ornate room of brick and masonry, a cathedral. But thankfully, just as you don't have to be a master baker to bake good bread, you also don't need to be a master mason to build with bricks.

A brick oven is more expensive, calls for a bigger time commitment, and requires more planning than an earthen oven. The density of the firebrick will increase heat-up times, but the slow release of heat means the oven will take longer to cool down, providing a longer period to use heat windows that present themselves only after the oven temperature starts to fall. (See *Bricks* in chapter 2 for more information about this oven-building material.)

MANUFACTURED OVEN CORES/KITS

A variety of manufactured oven cores come in easy-to-assemble kits. Most kits are dome-shaped and made with a similar material that is less dense than firebrick. They heat up quickly, but often don't retain enough heat to bake more than a few loads of European hearth loaves without refiring. This can be mitigated by adding more thermal mass in the form of cladding on the outside of the firebox and plenty of high-quality insulation.

Ovens made of less dense materials have this issue because air acts as an insulator, and the air spaces distributed throughout the less dense thermal mass act as insulators, inhibiting the migration of heat into the mass. This makes the mass slower to get saturated with heat. This is great for pizza and other hot-oven applications (especially when a fire is present), but the temperature drops too quickly for large commercial baking production, in my experience.

It's certainly convenient to buy all the firebox parts, but this is offset by the cost—more than you'd pay if you were building an oven from raw materials. Some manufactured cores are certified by Underwriters Laboratories (UL), which may be a necessity for commercial applications.

TEMPORARY, STACKED BRICK OVENS

A stacked brick oven is perhaps the simplest and fastest kind to construct. Bricks or concrete blocks are dry laid—that is, without any mortar—to create a rudimentary masonry oven. David Cargo, a brick oven enthusiast and curator of the widely used Quest for Ovens website, has popularized a method for quickly constructing a small temporary brick oven. He teaches this simple, fun activity in classes around the country. The Quest for Ovens website is listed in the resource section on page 310.

Oven Doors

If eyes are the window to the soul, then a door is the window to the soul of your oven. Doors are especially necessary when baking bread, because a sealed chamber retains steam necessary for beautiful loaves. A well-designed door may also increase the efficiency of loading dough into the oven and increasing combustion efficiency by controlling airflow.

An oven core manufactured by Le Panyol and installed at the Maine home of Steve and Jennifer Dionne

Custom-made swinging doors with glass at Rupert Rising Breads in Vermont. Oven by Peter Moore, doors by George Lenhardt. PHOTO COURTESY OF JED MAYER

The classic: Alan Scott's oven door, with its vertically oriented handle, circa 1996

CLASSIC ALAN SCOTT DOOR

A simple door is more than adequate for a backyard oven. It should be light and fit snugly. Even if your wooden doors are sheathed in metal, you will likely find a pile of ash in their place some morning after an exceptionally successful pizza party. A metal door is more difficult to fabricate but is much hardier over the long run. For several years, Magdalena has enjoyed a metal oven door that fits tightly and has plenty of dead air space sandwiched within its 2" thickness. A handle oriented vertically, as in the photo of Alan Scott's door, is easier to remove than one oriented horizontally.

COUNTERWEIGHTED LOADING DOOR

In 2010 I attended the annual Masonry Heater Association spring conference and gave a talk titled "Build for Bread." I recommended wood-fired oven design elements that would be useful for home and commercial applications. One of my recommendations was counterweighted doors

for commercial-sized ovens, similar to the ones used in deck ovens that fall flat when pushed open with a peel or loader. This convenience shortens loading time, retains heat, and holds in steam. I met William Davenport of Turtlerock Masonry in the parking lot 20 minutes after the talk when he motioned me over to his truck and showed me the door I had just described.

Counterweighted doors are convenient but don't offer much insulation. William designed an insulated door plug that can be put in place while the oven is being fired or not in use to avoid heat loss.

QUEBEC-STYLE HINGED OVEN DOOR

This regional-style clay oven often has cast-iron swinging doors with twist vents. Although they are beautiful, they are uninsulated and not as steam-tight as a door that seals flat against the lintel or oven frame. Some recently built ovens do have swinging doors but are custom-made and, therefore, close tightly. (See *Earth/Mud/Clay/Cob Ovens* earlier in this chapter for more information about Quebec-style ovens.)

William Davenport's counterweighted door

Andrew Heyn starts a fire in a William Davenport oven at Elmore Mountain Bread, the central Vermont bakery he owns with his wife, Blair Marvin. The bricks serve as an oxygen diverter, guiding air to the sides and back of the firebox. The insulated plugs to the left and right are in place to keep heat inside the oven during firing.

This Quebec-style oven in a community park in Norwich, Vermont, was built by Boy Scouts more than 20 years ago. It sports a traditional set of Quebec-style doors.

A cored brick draft door on Magdalena PHOTO BY JONATHANBELLER.COM

THE DRAFT DOOR

A draft door is in place while a fire is burning and is designed to increase the velocity of oxygen intake. Oxygen flow is controlled through a sliding plate adjusted by a set screw or an access port; this "throttles" the oven, upping the velocity of the oxygen into the oven as well as the rate of combustion. Alan Scott included a drawing for a draft door in his first set of plans. A draft door is visible, in appendix A on page 289, on an oven built by Pat Manley. Draft doors are available for sale by Frankie G (www.fgpizza.com), a purveyor of wood-fired oven tools and accessories.

In a pinch, cored bricks—or any material that allows the exchange of oxygen and exhaust—helps regulate combustion. The surface facing into the oven also helps reflect heat back into the oven, increasing the firebox temperature and helping to increase combustion efficiency. Keeping the door to your oven closed as much as possible (even during firing) helps prevent heat from spilling out of the mouth of the oven and into the room and up the chimney.

Choosing an Oven That's Right for You

Only you can decide what shape and building material you want for your oven, depending on application or aesthetics. However, you do need to consider the size that is right for your needs. As we discussed earlier, think of the mass surrounding the baking chamber as a battery for storing heat; the bigger the battery, the more heat you can store. But too big a battery will sap heat energy by charging itself. Cooking and baking can be easier, more feasible, and more enjoyable with an appropriately sized oven.

One of the benefits of having a wood-fired oven is sharing all the delicious bread and food you'll make. If you build your oven so it will just meet your needs, you'll miss an opportunity to spread the goodness to your neighbors and friends.

This being said, you don't want to overbuild and have an oven so large it will take too much fuel or will be too big a deal to use very often.

Jim Frisch, part of the Frisch family masonry dynasty, says he builds lots of 3-foot by 3-foot ovens for residential use. Jim and his clients find that the 36-square-inch hearth is a really nice residential size, allowing plenty of room to cook and bake lots of items at once, but not so massive as to discourage frequent use. One residential oven I built is 26" by 30", and after having the opportunity to cook in it a number of times I find it to be the minimum size I would want for a backyard oven.

What Makes an Oven a Bread Oven?

Because I am a bread baker first and foremost, I can't help but look at oven design in the context of bread baking. Except for the additional thermal mass necessary for multiple loaves and a low, sealed baking chamber, bread and pizza ovens are pretty similar. I urge you to build for bread, as this type of oven serves very well for both products, but the higher-vaulted pizza ovens present more of a challenge for baking beautiful loaves of bread because it's more difficult to accumulate and retain the amount of steam necessary to produce beautiful loaves. It's easier to make pizza in a bread oven than bread in a pizza oven. How many different kinds of ovens can there be? We must have reached a state of advanced evolution if we have the luxury of parsing out different types of ovens. But we are there, and if an oven is intended to be used for bread, there are a few key design elements that should be included in order to make beautiful hearth loaves:

- **Low chamber.** If an oven is to work well for bread, its roof (whether domed or arched) should be relatively close to the surface of the baking loaves—no more than about 16". This is a small enough space that steam can quickly collect and completely fill the oven chamber (more quickly than in a pizza oven, which would feature an expanse of space above the

Maine Grain Alliance,
the Kneading Conference, and Albie Barden

Since 2007, the Kneading Conference has been held each summer in Skowhegan, an old mill town in central Maine. The conference draws farmers, millers, oven builders, and bakers for two days of open-air workshops and companionship.

Albie Barden attended a Brick Oven Bakers Conference in Sausalito, California, in 1999. It was organized by Alan Scott, and Alan encouraged Albie to organize a similar event on the East Coast. In 2005, Albie was a speaker at "Camp Bread," the Bread Bakers Guild educational conference, and the experience of seeing several hundred people together learning about baking inspired him to start nurturing Alan's idea. The first Kneading Conference was held on the grounds of a church in the middle of town. Tewksbury Hall was just big enough to seat 150 people family-style to talk about crossover areas of interest. Everybody was interested in earth, grain, fire, and bread.

Attendance has grown each year, because word has spread that this educational event is informative, organized, fun . . . and delicious. Eventually, the Maine Grain Alliance was formed—the non-profit that now sponsors the Kneading Conference as well as the Maine Artisan Bread Fair, held the day immediately following the conference. MGA also owns a large mobile Le Panyol oven, purchased with a grant from the Quimby Family Foundation, and uses it to sell pizza as a fund-raiser but also as an educational tool.

Albie's company, Maine Wood Heat, offers an optional copper exterior cladding on its Le Panyols, a gorgeous, durable choice that has become a signature feature. Who wouldn't be drawn to such a handsome oven? It's a

The MGA mobile oven was designed by Scott Barden, Albie and Cheryl's son. The goal was to make a mobile food-service oven as self-contained as possible while giving it a cushioned ride even over bumpy roads.

wonderful people magnet. Wendy Hebb, program director for the Maine Grain Alliance, describes this draw as "a cord inside all of us that is pulled by fire." And when people ask about how the oven works, they often find out that the flour in the crust came from the Somerset Grist Mill, a project organized by Amber Lambke and Michael Scholz. Somerset Grist Mill is "working to create a staple food, grown nearby. A grist mill renovation project in central Maine, reviving local grain production and the means to process it." Wendy says the mobile Le Panyol has been a valuable tool for fund-raising and to help achieve MGA's mission: increasing public awareness of food produced in their community.

Albie is yet another Masonry Heater Association member and longtime leading figure in bringing masonry heater and wood-fired oven information to a wider North American audience. Albie co-wrote *Finnish Fireplaces: Heart of the Home* with Heikki Hyytiäinen, a Finnish oven builder who influenced the early masonry heater builders in North America. Albie himself started Maine Wood Heat along with his wife, Cheryl, building masonry heaters. But anything with masonry and fire interested him, and he introduced Le Panyols into the lineup of wood-fired oven options. The pieces of oven core are much lighter than you would think, which makes Le Panyols excellent candidates for installing on a trailer.

In fact, this is how the Kneading Conference is able to turn a vintage fairground into a thriving weekend of wood-fired baking in just a few days—the half dozen Le Panyol ovens used in workshops and meal preparation are all mounted on trailers or portable enough to be moved around with a forklift.

Several earth ovens are also made at each Kneading Conference by Stu Silverstein and a group of students, who have the ovens ready to fire by the end of the second day. These ovens are portable, too, and will go home with a lucky oven builder.

The number of bread, grain, and oven conferences continues to increase. Maine Grain Alliance held its first West Coast Kneading Conference in 2011. The Northern Grain Growers Association gets together every spring to share information about grain cultivation. Down south, Jennifer Lapidus has started Carolina Ground, an organization dedicated to milling locally grown grain for a concentration of artisan bakers in the Asheville area of western North Carolina. Cooperation and the free exchange of ideas continue to grow through the relationships among farmer, miller, oven builder, and baker.

Perspective from Across the Pond

Ideally, wood-fired ovens bake bread that features large volume, an open crumb, and shiny crusts. These characteristics are easier to achieve in a modern steam-injected commercial deck oven, however. The American Bread Movement educated us about this style of bread and we all got on board, even those using wood-fired ovens. But bread with these characteristics isn't the only kind of good bread.

I was once baking at a national Bread Bakers Guild of America educational event in a wood-fired oven with a high dome and a door that didn't seal well. I was terribly self-conscious about the bread that came out, even if it did give me a chance to talk to the students about the benefits of steam. (It's much more fun to point out why beautiful bread is beautiful than to explain why a loaf doesn't look so hot…) Then I looked up and saw the honored guest, Christian Vabret, MOF* and organizer of the Coupe du Monde de la Boulangerie, approaching us as we gazed at loaves misshapen and uncharismatic due to the lack of steam. I immediately started apologizing to him through the interpreter about the state of the loaves. Christian listened, shook his head, and said, "You Americans are too hard on yourselves. This is the type of bread I ate my whole life growing up."

---

* MOF stands for *Meilleurs Ouvriers de France*, a prestigious French national award that recognizes impeccable craftsmanship and mastery for a variety of trades.

A Word of Caution
About Oven-Building Workshops

I have found that ovens built during workshops tend to have problems over the long run. The lack of precision and/or experience among the workshop participants can accumulate and contribute to what ends up a major, if not cataclysmic, failure. Arches sag. The hearth is uneven. Heat seeps into the foundation. I've been at workshops thinking, *I wouldn't want my oven built that way*. Still, oven workshops are great for spreading the knowledge about wood-fired ovens and building community, and I highly recommend attending as many as possible.

There is a perfectly acceptable solution to preventing structural deficiencies due to the "workshop effect": Use temporary clay mortar instead of cement mortar for the workshop. This still gives workshop participants the opportunity to cut brick, create construction components, and actually put together an oven, but it can be easily dismantled and then permanently reassembled with high-temperature mortar, avoiding any need to finish the oven with inexperienced bricklaying labor. At the Masonry Heater Association's annual conference, all the ovens—experimental designs, temporary pizza ovens, and so forth—are held together with clay. At the end of the conference they are deconstructed, and the bricks are stacked for the next year. It is a relief to know that designs can be revised after the draw and combustion are tested—and it reduces the material cost for the next year. For the micro-bakery or community oven workshop, the relief comes when you look at your workshop-built oven and realize that some bricks may be out of alignment, or the mortar joints too thick. In this case you just number all the bricks, pull the oven apart, and take your time putting it back together with an eye for accuracy and a consideration for proper building techniques.

---

bread). Steam creates shiny crusts, more volume, and cuts that open.

- **Sealed chamber.** This ensures that all the steam is trapped inside. An oven's seal is dependent on the door and whether the chimney is inside or outside. The chamber should not be perforated by an ash dump, chimney, or any other opening that will allow steam to escape.
- **Sufficient thermal mass.** A bread oven needs enough mass to store retained heat sufficient to bake bread after the fire has been removed. If the stored heat dissipates to a point too low for baking, you'll need to build another fire to recharge the thermal battery. Instead, it's better and more efficient to rely on stored energy. In addition, a "conditioned" baking environment creates more beautiful loaves.
- **Lots of best insulation.** You have the heat, why not keep it? The best use of your heat is for baking bread, so you want to minimize heat loss. The best insulation you can afford not only increases the number of things you can do during any one firing, which is the idea of this book—but also means you will spend less money on fuel.

The Benefits of Baking in a Comfortably Full Oven

A comfortably full oven bakes better than one only partially full. A hearth full of freshly loaded dough properly conditions (or mellows) the oven environment. The loaves in a comfortably full oven buffer their neighbors from the dry masonry heat, creating more volume, shinier crusts, and a more even, relaxed bake. If an oven is overfilled and the loaves touch during oven spring, the result will be a crust marked by underbaked, doughy sections, referred to

Pat Manley, Oven Builder

One reason improvements from the professional baking world have trickled down to backyard ovens is due to a non-wood-fired technology called the Internet. Pat Manley, a 30-year veteran of building masonry heaters, pizza ovens, and bread ovens, participates in a dynamic online Yahoo! forum dedicated to wood-fired ovens where he passes on information about design and efficiency. His comments are backed with experience and candor, driven by his desire to increase oven efficiency and propagate sound construction principles. How lucky the amateur oven enthusiasts are to receive his insights. And Pat is able to gently ask questions that eventually explain crucial concepts, like the difference between thermal mass and insulation.

One of the important design innovations Pat has introduced to the barrel vault oven, for example, is the reduction arch located at the front of the vault just before the chimney. The height of the arch is reduced, the skew bricks are one course lower, and the vault bricks are cut to eliminate sharp edges so there is a smooth reduction

in arch height. This helps prolong the amount of time that gases linger inside the firebox. This extra time allows more time for secondary combustion to happen and for the heat to get absorbed by the thermal mass. The reduction arch is now standard on most second-generation ovens being built today.

These gems are direct links from professional masons to backyard oven builders. Pat, like so many of the people who have contributed to the advancement of wood-fired ovens, is a member of the Masonry Heater Association, so he is knowledgeable about combustion, heat transfer, and conductivity.

Pat contributed backyard and commercial upgrades that apply to many different styles of oven. And his dissemination of oven-building information goes beyond online chat groups. For the past five years or so, Pat has taught a two-day workshop at the annual Kneading Conference in which he builds an oven with temporary mortar. So in addition to being a mason, he's also a teacher, passing along his experiences and the collective knowledge of the wood-fired community. Pat is a little like Prometheus, bringing fire from the professionals to the laypeople who want to gather with their family around a fire and share a meal.

In 2000, he started a non-profit volunteer organization called Masons on a Mission. Pat and a group of volunteers travel to Guatemala every winter to build vented cookstoves in the homes of rural Mayan families who currently do their cooking on open fires on the floor of their one-room homes. The lack of chimney or vent means smoke accumulates inside the homes, blinding women over time and causing respiratory disease in children. Pat describes the inside of these homes as blackened and covered with a thick deposit of creosote and soot.

The new cookstoves, called *estufas*, carry the smoke out of the home, creating a direct and immediate improvement in the health and safety of every family that receives one. The masons source all materials locally, and an important component of their mission is to engage aspiring local masons, who continue to build *estufas* after the masons return home. Contact Masons on a Mission for more information, to donate funds to buy materials, or to join Pat on a trip. No experience is necessary—you needn't be a mason when you go, but you will learn the basics of constructing a simple, clean, efficient cookstove from a master mason as you do this good work. Visit www.masonsonamission.org for more information.

A reduction arch. The rear of the oven is to the left. The slot on the right is the opening of the chimney.

as baisure or kissing crust. An overloaded oven also takes longer to bake due to the lack of circulation among the loaves.

How Masonry Is Similar to Baking

Tom Trout once told me, "All bakers used to be masons in order to build their own ovens—and masons had to know about baking in order to build good bread ovens." It took me about 10 years of baking and a couple of ovens before I started to see and understand the truth of this statement.

Like bread baking, masonry is a traditional and revered skill. Who built the beautiful cathedrals in Europe? Masons. And what did everybody eat when they came to the cathedral? Bread.

Dough maturation and mortar maturation are similar—both change over time and are dependent on time and temperature. Each craft depends on a few simple hand tools.

I prefer to use a margin trowel, a rectangular trowel shaped like a cake decorator's palette knife, to apply mortar. It's easier to apply a consistent bead of mortar with a margin trowel than with the traditional triangular trowel that many amateur masons instinctively reach for. Coated gloves protect your hands no matter what type of mass or insulation you use to build your oven.

CHAPTER FOUR

Fuel and Combustion

THE SPIRIT OF THE FIRE

By Lars Helbro

Imagine yourself as a fire.
What do you need to burn clean?

You need to breathe.
The harder you work
the more you need to breathe.
If you don't get enough oxygen, or
if the oxygen doesn't reach every part of your body
you'll get sick.

You need to keep warm.
Even though the purpose of your life is to make heat
* for others*
you need some of it to keep yourself alive.
Don't give everything away at once!

You need space around you to grow.
If you're fed too hard, you will grow too fast,
and there might not be space enough around you
and then you cannot breathe.
You need to get around to find the final freedom.
Every sharp edge will slow you down and weaken
* your strength.*

When you have found your way to the chimney,
you need to have just enough power left to rise up
* into the sky,*
as just the spirit of the fire that you have become,
and who successfully fulfilled the mission of your
* short life.*

Fire is the spirit of any wood-fired oven, the primal entity that attracts and holds our attention. We bring it to life and it, in turn, provides warmth, food, community, and calming entertainment.

An efficient combustion environment requires time, temperature, and turbulence. Potential energy loss occurs when gases remain uncombusted, as well as when wood is uncombusted (if the oven box is overloaded, for instance, or the oven simply needs to be raked out). I use the term *flame devils* to refer to those diaphanous scrims of fire that waver through your firebox and lick across the roof. In fact, this phenomenon is the visible combustion of gases that have been released from burning wood. The devils' swirling motion is caused by turbulence, beneficial because it causes gases to roll through the firebox, increasing their residence time and the potential for combustion.

These gases will only combust if the fire is hot enough and the gases are around long enough. The amount of time that's long enough is called residence time, and it must be sufficient enough that the gases have the opportunity to flame away and give off heat to be absorbed by the thermal mass. Masonry heaters include a secondary combustion chamber for this purpose; it's located above the firebox and provides a place for collected gases to combust. Most wood-fired ovens don't have a secondary combustion chamber, but you can increase residence time by restricting the flow of exhaust either with a reduction arch (see *Pat Manley, Oven Builder*, in chapter 3) or with the constriction of the oven door or the aid of a draft door.

Flames roll over Magdalena's arch.

transferred to both the thermal mass and the oven environment, making things hotter and more energetic. Once the masonry absorbs heat, it is reflected from the sidewalls of the oven back *toward* the fire, creating a hotter environment in which it can burn.

Is Wood Fuel a Responsible Choice?

A great deal of research has been done by both the Environmental Protection Agency and academic researchers to determine the pollution emission factors of many kinds of wood-burning appliances. The researchers have not yet measured emissions for masonry ovens per se, but they have studied the performance of masonry heaters. The result? Although masonry heaters are exempt from the EPA's New Source Performance Standards (NSPS) certification requirements, they have shown a low particulate emission factor.

The definitive EPA report cited above states:

Masonry heaters achieve their low emissions by burning wood at a high rate (i.e., high temperature complete-combustion conditions) during a short time period. A large mass of masonry material is heated rapidly by the high-temperature fast burning fuel load. The stored heat is radiated from the masonry materials into the space being heated after the fire is out.

We all need to spread the word that wood combustion is not inherently dangerous to human health; clean and safe combustion is possible, and in fact is a natural consequence of the way masonry ovens are designed to function—with high-temperature, complete-combustion conditions for a short period of time. If the fire is managed correctly in a masonry oven, it is environmentally safe. Let's do all that we can to emphasize the results of the academic and government research and teach efficient combustion practices to ensure that wood-fired baking can be considered an ethical activity in terms of its impact on human health.

The fire itself, as described in Lars's poem, needs heat itself to thrive. It should get as hot as possible as quickly as possible. This creates a combustion environment that feeds itself—higher temperatures means the fuel gasifies and ignites more easily. The release of energy gets

Table 2.1: Emission Factors, in Mass Emission per Mass of Dry Wood Burned

Appliance	Particulate Emission Factor	
	lb./ton	g/kg
Conventional woodstove	37	18.5
Non-catalytic woodstove	12	6
Catalytic woodstove	13	6.2
Masonry heater	6	3

Carbon Footprint of Wood Burning

Wood burning is carbon-neutral, but that doesn't mean it's without a carbon footprint at all. The carbon footprint of wood burning is the amount of carbon dioxide added to the atmosphere not by burning the wood itself, but by the activity of cutting the wood (with a chain saw), transporting it, and splitting it. The biggest contributor to the footprint is probably the use of a pickup truck to haul small loads of wood from the cutting site to the drying and burning site.

What Wood Works Best

You may be wondering why this book doesn't include a list of the BTUs produced by different species of wood, as is so commonly seen. In my opinion, that would be a bit misleading—it gives the impression that some types of wood are capable of producing more heat than others. In my experience, the BTUs produced by the combustion of any wood is a function of that wood's density and its moisture content. Assuming dry, seasoned wood, a given weight of wood—any type—will produce the same BTUs. It's just that some wood is much denser (oak as opposed to balsa), and since wood is commonly measured by the cord, which is a given volume of wood (a stack 4 feet wide by 8 feet long by 4 feet high), a cord of dense wood (oak) will produce more BTUs than a cord of less dense softwood. But pound for pound, dry seasoned wood of any type will produce the same.

Cutoffs are an option to split cordwood. If you live near a wood mill, ask if you can buy the bark-sided slabs left over when tree trunks are squared off. In eastern North Carolina we have a lot of cedars that come down in high winds due to their shallow root system. We also have a good supply of old pecan, which is brittle during the winter and often cut back, yielding 6" limbs that will burn down into small ash in a properly managed firebox.

Whatever species of wood you use, it should be seasoned so the moisture content is in the 20 to 25 percent range. Moisture content can be measured with a moisture meter. Split the wood to about wrist thickness. Increasing the surface area of the fuel promotes more efficient combustion. Splitting is enjoyable exercise and a good opportunity to become familiar with the fuel that you ultimately use to cook your food.

Also, a cord of greenwood should cost less than a cord of seasoned wood. If you have the space, it makes sense to buy green and season it yourself. You'll save money and guarantee yourself well-seasoned wood.

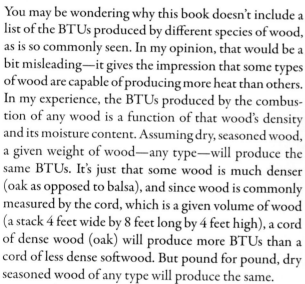

A multi-bay woodshed helps you organize your wood by age, size, or type. I try to salvage anything burnable, even sticks from the yard. These dry more quickly than split cordwood, offering a good use for good wood. PHOTO BY JONATHANBELLER.COM

Keep Your Fire Organized

A fire becomes disorganized when the rate of combustion is no longer optimal. Lack of fuel, oxygen, and temperature all lead to disorganized and smoky fires. Allow the fire to settle into a groove before adding more wood. I try to load a batch of fuel and then allow it to burn down undisturbed (resist the urge to continually poke at the fire) until another batch of fuel should be added to maintain or increase the rate of combustion. Adding unheated fuel to a fire causes the thermal momentum to falter as the temperature of the fire drops momentarily, reducing the combustion efficiency (and increasing emissions). To reduce this effect, I often preheat wood for several minutes near the mouth of the oven or along the inside walls, near but not in the fire, before adding it. Heated wood bursts quickly into flames, increasing the temperature rather than dragging it down by consuming heat energy as it heats up.

When it's time to add more wood, I also do it gradually. A big addition of wood will break the skeletonized top-down burn structure, cutting off oxygen to the source of most intense heat. The new wood will smother the fire, in other words, and it'll take time for the system to restabilize and support a clean burn. Once I've placed fuel along the sidewall of the oven, I may use a piece as a support so that—after the oven temperature has risen again—I can add another piece that spans the firebox, from the fire itself on one end to the recently added support on the other. The support piece is usually burning by then, and the newly added wood creates a bridge, joining the fire while still allowing oxygen to be pulled all the way to the back of the oven. There it's heated and washes over the masonry where it is (hopefully) absorbed.

Beginning to add wood after the top down burn has died down. The fire burned the soot off the back wall of the oven, but some still remains in the corner. The space under the wood that is resting on the supports allows oxygen to be pulled all the way to the back of the oven.

Respect the Fire

Play with fire and you're going to get burned—literally—so I like to cultivate aloe in a pot near every oven. In the heat of the moment you may bump into hot masonry or accidentally brush your forearm against a hot iron lintel. You'll know if you really get burned; it's a real physical shock as opposed to a quick contact that just singes your skin.

When you get burned, stop whatever you are doing. Immediately go treat the burn by icing it to stop cell damage caused by high heat. Then apply a generous amount of freshly squeezed aloe plant juice. Time is of the essence! The sooner you apply curatives, the less damage is incurred, and the faster a burn will heal. If you get to the icebox quickly enough, you might not yet see the boundary of the burn on your skin—but be assured it will appear later. Apply ice and aloe to an area large enough to completely cover the burn and surrounding skin. If you don't have ice, a bag of frozen vegetables or even cool running water does fine.

Ash Insulates

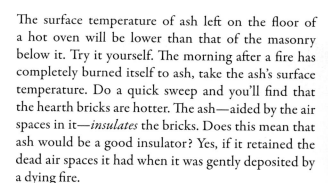

The surface temperature of ash left on the floor of a hot oven will be lower than that of the masonry below it. Try it yourself. The morning after a fire has completely burned itself to ash, take the ash's surface temperature. Do a quick sweep and you'll find that the hearth bricks are hotter. The ash—aided by the air spaces in it—*insulates* the bricks. Does this mean that ash would be a good insulator? Yes, if it retained the dead air spaces it had when it was gently deposited by a dying fire.

Dry Wood, Clean Burn

Use cured/well-seasoned/dry wood. It takes energy to evaporate water—energy that could be used to heat the oven. Uncured wood also keeps the oven temperature from increasing, leading to inefficient combustion, a long heat-up time, and creosote buildup. Cured wood is easier to start, produces more recoverable heat (as opposed to having the heat used to evaporate water), and burns cleaner. Also, as the water evaporates it dilutes the gases that may be given off, once again reducing the rate of combustion.

You can use a moisture meter to determine whether your wood is properly cured. If it's not completely cured, you'll be able to feel that moisture in the air—it adds humidity to the oven. The smell is green and

These flames illustrate wasted heat going up the chimney.

vegetal. Although energy loss happens when *wood* is uncombusted (if the oven box is overloaded or unburned wood needs to be raked out), most energy loss occurs through lost and/or uncombusted *gases*. Once the fire starts, the masonry absorbs radiant heat.

Don't build the top-down structure too high—it will suffer from lack of oxygen. And if it's too wide, it will hinder the flow of oxygen, especially to the back of the oven.

I move the top-down fire to different areas of the oven to wear the oven evenly. I know of one restaurant that had to replace some parts of a prefab dome core because they intensely fired the oven seven days a week with the fire always in the same spot. And I've seen a colonial beehive oven in Massachusetts that had a deep depression right in the middle of the hearth—obviously where the fire had always been positioned. Move your fire around, but not so close to the door that full flames escape the oven. Flames licking up the chimney are a sign of an inefficient burn.

The Top-Down Fire

The science and art of wood burning is as old as humankind. Regardless of which came first, fire and humans are intertwined, and the primal association of fire building and burning is programmed into us.

The wood-burning impetus in America in the 1970s was surely fueled by this genetic imprint, but because so many people lived in the suburbs, few had a clue about the importance of building hot fires. The wood burning we practiced was hazardous to our health and the environment, but the problem was not inherent in wood burning; it was inherent in our inexperience.

The solution is the "top-down" fire, which provides more heat from less wood, is safer, and produces fewer pollutants. The biggest logs are at the bottom. On these, lay six or seven more layers, each built of thinner logs and splits of logs. The top four or five layers are gradually smaller kindling, and the very top is a pile of shavings. The graduated construction of the upside-down fire starts rapidly with a burn that is from the beginning very hot and super clean. As the middle and bottom logs heat up and release their volatile organic carbon compounds to rise through the burning wood, enough heat and flame are present to ignite them. In the conventional bottom-up fire the first gases driven out of the wood are released unburned into the environment. The top-down burn produces much less smoke and, therefore, much less hazardous particulate pollution.

Why is the top-down burn important? For one thing, it creates a faster heat-up, less smoke, and less management, which means you add cold fuel to a fire less often. How does it work? Heat radiates equally in *all* directions, including down, so fuel below is preheated by radiant heat of the tinder fire above. The time it takes until the fuel combusts is reduced by the tinder fire above, more completely (and therefore more cleanly) using the gases given off due to that ignition. Rapid heat-up time helps to quickly warm the chimney as the hot air rises through it. This draft pulls fresh oxygen into the oven, fueling the fire and increasing the rate and efficiency of combustion. The fire on top of the unburnt fuel, rather than beneath it, also eliminates the risk of unburnt fuel falling down onto and smothering the fire.

A tall chimney increases draw more than a shorter one. If you have a short chimney, you can encourage a draft by lighting a piece of newspaper or parchment and holding it up the flue. Even a propane torch or hair dryer can heat the air in the chimney enough to rise, creating a draft and pulling fresh air into the fire. All these influences—helping to create a draft, radiant heat gain, and an organized fire—will, in concert, help increase combustion efficiency. Combustion is like fermentation—adjustments to the entire system create an optimum environment.

Oven-drying the wood brings it to a point where the gases are released, but the temperature isn't yet hot enough to combust. The scent of the hot, but not combusted, gases and organic compounds is like smelling the essence of tree, until eventually a steady heat volatilizes the sap and resin into flammable gases. On the other hand, it's important not to lay the fire if the oven is too hot. I like to build a top-down fire structure when the hearth temp is below 300°F (149°C). Oven temperatures above 450°F (232°C) would start to pyrolize the wood

A top-down burn just after ignition. You can help get a fire going easily by laying the top-down structure when the oven is still warm. At this point in the photograph, Magdalena is likely too cool for live-fire cooking.

The stratification between smoke and clear air shows that oxygen is being pulled in along the hearth and fueling the fire. A small fan blowing into the oven at this time can really help get things blazing. But otherwise, don't mess with the fire; let its vigor build.

The top-down structure will eventually fall in on itself. I let it go until it's completely skeletonized, which takes an hour or so depending on how much wood I used to start the fire and whether the oven was cool or warm when I did so. Black soot is just starting to burn off the oven bricks, indicating that the temperature is around 650°F (343°C)—plenty hot enough to be cooking.

Even after the oven is blazing hot, I still add fuel in a loose stack so the oxygen supply remains adequate. The soot is nearly completely cleaned off the bricks, and Magdalena is ready for live-fire cooking or a pizza bake.

(charring it, even without the presence of flame), driving off gases from organic material and allowing them to escape up the chimney unused. This can be dangerous: If you open the door and allow a rush of oxygen to reach the hot wood, it can initiate a flash much like the backdraft feared by firefighters. Plus, you don't want to use heat to dry fuel—you want the fuel to be dry when you place it in the oven so that the heat pulled into the masonry from the last fire can be used to bake.

It's much easier to start a new fire in a warm oven than a cold one, especially when you can use wood ovendried by the residual heat from the last firing to build it. A top-down burn will help start a fire from a completely cold oven, but can also be used in warm environments.

Don't Overload Your Firebox

Heikki Hyytiäinen, coauthor with Albie Barden of *Finnish Fireplaces: Heart of the Home*, asserts that the firebox should be about 30 percent full of wood. Too much wood, without adequate oxygen, creates a smoldering fire that may be hot, but isn't hot enough to quickly combust those gases that, due to the huge available fuel resource, are flooding the firebox but without enough heat impetus to torch to radiant life.

A pair of andirons raises wood off the hearth, allowing greater oxygen flow and combustion.

Beware of Overfiring

Overfiring is a mistake that comes from trying to push the oven beyond its ability. It's a waste of fuel and can potentially damage the firebox, but the most serious consequence is that you run the risk of creating conditions in the firebox for a backdraft to occur. A backdraft is a rapid explosive combustion that can occur when oxygen is suddenly introduced into an oxygen-starved combustion environment that has very high temperatures and abundant fuel.

I know owners of a micro-bakery who once experienced a serious—and scary—backdraft through the mouth of the original Alan Scott oven in the bakery they bought. The old oven wasn't quite able to retain enough heat to bake the amount of bread they needed to produce, so they had gotten into the habit of firing the oven more and more, trying in vain to charge the mass

with enough heat to get them through the day's production. Once, after an oxygen-starved environment had been created in the firebox by adding too much fuel all at once to a raging-hot fire, a baker pulled the draft door away to check the fire; a big tongue of flame exploded out of the mouth of the oven toward him. He ducked to the side. The flame went over his shoulder and across his back, singeing the hair on that side of his head. This was a wake-up call about pushing a wood-fired appliance beyond its limits.

A less dangerous consequence of overfiring is simply that the oven might still be too hot when your dough is ready to bake. It's a tough call, knowing how much firing is enough, and the only way to learn is through experience with your own oven.

Using Andirons

The same type of iron andirons that hold logs off the hearth of a fireplace can be used in a wood-fired oven to allow oxygen to circulate under the wood, contributing to dynamic combustion. The elevation of the fire also allows flames to roll up over the vault or dome, creating a broiler effect and helpfully giving the last bit of blaze to the top of a pizza.

I salvaged a pair from an old woodstove and place them along the side of the oven, as far back as I can reach. If the andirons are too close to the door, flames may escape the oven proper and waste their energy in the chimney. I reach for long pieces of fuel so the fire

stretches along as much of the wall as possible and stack it in an andiron crib loosely but securely. I set this up while there is fire somewhere else in the oven. Once the andiron stack is ready, I grab a burning piece of wood and place it on top of the stack. The heat of the oven, the warmth of the wood, and the oxygen flow that's being pulled into the oven will quickly combust this new fuel addition. I like to keep the hearth clear under the andirons, so I clear out embers with a poker and let them continue to combust adjacent to the andiron structure.

Be careful when setting andirons in your oven. I reach in and place them, instead of dragging or pushing them, so the legs don't damage the hearth. The efficiency of andirons is great but they do require additional firebox space—another reason to build an oven large enough to accommodate all potential cooking techniques.

CHAPTER FIVE

→➤ • ◄←

How to Operate Your Oven

This is it! Your oven has been built, you know how to lay a clean-burning, top-down burn, and you are ready to fire it up. So what's the best firing method? Keep in mind that there is no one right way to do this. Different firing methods exist based on amount of thermal mass, the design and construction of your oven, and the amount and type of bread or food you want to make. You do, however, want to burn efficiently.

All retained-heat ovens start to cool once the fire is extinguished or raked out, because no more heat is being deposited into the thermal mass. This downward trend happens faster or slower depending on the amount of heated mass and the efficiency of the insulation. Once you learn your oven's cooling curve, you can anticipate the timing so you'll know the oven will be "about this temperature at about this time." One of the biggest challenges of preparing food in a wood-fired oven is being organized and prepared so you're ready to cook when the temperature falls into the proper zone. The oven will be waiting for you as long as you are ready to use it.

Using your oven to its full potential is an overarching theme of this book. Not only is it a responsible way to use BTUs created by burning wood fuel, but it also provides a full range of bounty from your oven. One of the benefits of a retained-heat oven is that the descending temperature trend is relatively slow even in an oven without a huge amount of thermal mass. This means that if you don't get to baking some granola today, you still can start infusing rosemary olive oil two days from now. In our fast-paced world, wood-fired ovens offer a continually, but slowly, changing array of ways to slow down and enjoy life.

The Importance of Saturating the Thermal Mass

If you're planning on using the oven for cooking rather than baking bread, it isn't as crucial to thoroughly saturate the thermal mass because you'll be working with fire, not retained heat. (Live-fire cooking is more intense, though, with a saturated mass. The heated environment helps the fire get hot faster and burn more efficiently.) Bread is baked with retained heat, however, which means you have to store enough heat to bake all the dough you're planning on using. This might mean storage for multiple bakes, but even a single load of bread benefits from a strong steady heat that slowly dissipates as opposed to a lot of heat stored in the part of the masonry closest to the bake chamber.

Use the Different Temperature Zones Within the Oven

You can cook several things at once, even if they all require different temperature/heat environments, by using different areas in the oven. A dinner of braised lemon chicken, fire-roasted asparagus, and a pot of rice can be made all at once by keeping a small mature fire in a back corner (tossing in small fuel to bring forth brief heat and flames). The chicken can braise across the oven far enough away from the fire to have the right, slow temperature; the pot of rice can be pushed close to the fire at first to bring the water to a boil, and then pulled back into the doorway to cook at a very low simmer

until it's done. This is a bonus of having a hearth at least 30" by 36" or so; one smaller than that won't have such a range of temperature zones at the same time.

The Oven Log: Anticipate Your Oven's Temperature Curve

Good record keeping is another tool for oven management and an effective way to learn your own oven's thermal characteristics so you will be better able to anticipate the timing of its declining heat and plan your cooking and baking schedule accordingly. A simple homemade oven temperature log (see appendix E) helps keep track of temperatures over time, as well as

Recording temperature and conditions in an oven log will help you learn your oven's characteristics so you can anticipate when it will reach the proper temperature. This type of record keeping is especially useful when you're baking bread as opposed to live-fire cooking.

recording what you're cooking or baking. For general cooking and baking I fill out the log just out of habit and interest, but for production baking it's essential to track the timing of multiple loads. Once you gather enough data you can learn from previous bake records and fine-tune your firing schedule. Was the bottom a bit scorched the last time you baked Pain Rustique? Check the oven log from the previous bake, and consider loading at a slightly lower temperature or baking for a little less time.

Production Schedules

Bringing together bread and oven successfully will be easier if you keep an overall schedule that helps you remember important steps of oven management in relation to the forward momentum of the dough. This level of detail applies mostly to production baking, although such a schedule can be used anytime, even for a single load of bread. (See appendix D for a sample production schedule.)

Oven Tools and Accessories

Before you start in on a wood-fired weekend, you may want to invest in some simple, everyday tools and accessories that make it easier, safer, and more enjoyable to use a wood-fired oven.

FIREPLACE OR WELDING GLOVES

Oven mitts are often used for wood-fired cooking and baking, but welding gloves offer much better articulation. Kevlar-lined leather gloves protect your hands from the heat of the fire or cookware while allowing control and finesse that oven mitts cannot. Welding gloves also come in various sizes, further increasing the control—and therefore safety—of the wearer. An extra-large glove renders a small hand clumsy no matter your skill, but too often large or extra-large gloves are the

default purchase in an attempt to accommodate everyone with a single pair. Seek out properly fitting gloves; there is no need to sacrifice nimbleness for protection. Note, though, that the proper fit should be a little loose for best insulating capacity. Just as with all insulation, a little air space between hand and glove prevents conductive heat transfer much more effectively than the direct contact of a tight fit.

ASH RAKE AND POKERS

One of my favorite oven tools is a simple garden hoe that doubles as an ash rake. I look for one made entirely from wood and metal. The hoe eventually burns enough that the scraper breaks off—creating a poker that will be around for several more months. I prefer wood over metal handles, even if they do burn and have to be replaced. They don't get as hot, and the entire tool

Welding or fireplace gloves in different sizes give every cook in the house equal control and protection at the hearth. PHOTO BY JONATHAN-BELLER.COM

A hoe and poker are crucial for manipulating the fire and removing the ash once it has burned out.

is lighter and less likely to bang into the oven wall and damage it. A simple garden hoe is economical, functional, and easy to procure. Just make sure you have a safe way to extinguish the tip of the poker if it catches fire when you're fussing around in the oven.

BRUSHES

I love oven and baking brushes. A brass-bristle pizza oven brush is ideal for a first sweep of the ashes after all the wood is combusted. There should be only ash and the slightest collection of glowing embers, so a hoe is often not necessary—I love it when the brush can handle the job. I then follow up with a natural-bristle oven broom to remove the last traces of ash from the hearth. This is often done with a damp or wet mop or a "scuffle," which you can make by attaching a towel to the end of a broom handle. I prefer the dry-brushing method; it does a fine job, and there is no risk of pitting or spalling of the hearth bricks as a result of the sudden thermal shock caused by applying water to the hot hearth. Unlike wire-bristle brushes, natural-bristle brushes will burn—so make sure there are no live embers when you sweep the oven.

I like long-handled tools designed so that I draw ash toward the ash dump as opposed to sweeping from side to side. The point is to get the ash out of the oven. And I always have a hand brush at the oven so I can dust inside the corners and around the outer hearth altar.

CAST-IRON COOKWARE

What to say about cast iron? It holds up to the heat of the oven, and because of its density it retains heat, compared with other metal cookware. I consider it a wood-fired oven staple.

A collection of brushes for cleaning the oven, proofing baskets, and couches

I'm always very aware of protecting the hearth from unnecessary wear and tear. For this reason I use only Dutch ovens that have a flat bottom that won't damage the hearth when they're slid back and forth. Camp ovens with legs are best used in open-hearth cooking, over a fire or anytime you can easily lift the heavy cookware and set it down without dragging the legs across a masonry surface.

You may be tempted to use a nice piece of non-stick cookware. But in addition to the fact that food cooked in non-stick pans doesn't brown as well as it would in cast iron, the high temperatures of live-fire cooking exceed recommended temperatures for the use of Teflon and other non-stick coatings. Teflon breaks down around 500°F (260°C), releasing fluorocarbons and beginning to blister and flake. There are ceramic and silicone non-stick pans, but they also start to break down at higher temperatures, albeit without releasing fluorocarbons.

Look for cookware that has loop handles or a hole in the handle. Those holes will give you a place to grab onto with a long-handled hook—another handy tool to have around the oven.

CORNINGWARE AND PYREX

Oh, America's cookware of yesteryear! I grew up with CorningWare but didn't realize how useful it is until I started cooking with fire. Pyroceramic glass has high-deformation temperature and thermal shock resistance that enables it to withstand wide temperature swings without cracking, from freezing to inferno. It was developed during the space race by Donald Stookey, a researcher at Corning. Once it was offered to consumers as cookware, those tough casserole dishes, adorned with the now familiar blue cornflower, became a standard. CorningWare's ability to withstand high temperatures

A collection of resilient cookware: copper pans, insulated cookie sheets, cast iron with and without enamel. The wrought-iron hook in the middle is indispensable for pulling cookware pieces out of the oven by their looped handles (*above*), CorningWare (*upper right*), and covered Pyrex bakeware (*lower right*).

and direct exposure to live fire makes it perfect for use in a wood-fired oven. There is a line of CorningWare that is not safe for direct flame exposure, however. Released in the late 1990s, it was designed to meet the needs of home kitchens that relied more and more on microwave cooking. Due to popular demand, however, the original CorningWare has now been reintroduced to the market.

Pyrex can't be exposed to direct flame, but it's quite a tough material. I like the lidded baking containers. Unbaked casseroles can be frozen in them, then thawed and placed in a gentle 350°F (177°C) oven. About an hour later you have a freshly cooked meal in a stylish dish.

I scour resale shops and find some amazing pieces that are no longer available or are expensive to buy new. Plus, the quality of much retro cookware surpasses today's manufacturing standards. Of course look for cookware with heatproof handles. Plastic will obviously melt, but be aware that wood becomes brittle after exposure to the dry heat of an oven.

PEELS

I have a wide variety of peels for different uses. I prefer wooden peels for loading hearth breads—dough slides off more easily than from a metal peel. However, metal peels are good for unloading or rotating because the thin metal easily slips under a loaf. A banjo peel is one of our favorite specialty tools—the small round head makes it easy to rotate pizzas or reach over loaves to fetch something in the back. If you're loading more than a few hearth breads, collect several peels so you can turn out and score multiple loaves at once. This will

A collection of oven peels. My trusty wooden loading peel is at the bottom. The thin wooden transfer peel helps place bâtards and small loaves in tight places. It is also handy for nudging loaves into better position once the bottom crust has set. The metal peels are great for unloading hearth loaves or live-fire cooking. The banjo peel at top is especially handy at moving pizzas.

help retain heat and steam, because the door will be open fewer times.

Commercial bakers often use a loader—a canvas-covered stretcher that allows faster and gentler loading of loaves. A similar tool for home bakers, called the Super Peel, allows you to smoothly deposit your loaves on the hearth, in a home oven especially.

OTHER TOOLS AND EQUIPMENT

Tongs are essential when working in a wood-fired oven, just as they are in any kitchen. Being able to reach into the oven and quickly and securely flip a flatiron steak or remove charred onions is easier and safer to do with a good set of tongs. The strong and smooth-rolling **Zyliss pizza cutter** easily and neatly cuts pizza. **Sklips** are aluminum brackets that fit over the lip of a sheet pan and provide sturdy support to stack additional pans so you can dehydrate numerous pans of beef jerky in the same space as one. See the resource section for Sklip's contact information.

A garden mister is necessary for steaming the oven. Pressurized sprayers are better than a simple spray bottle because they create finer droplets, which evaporate more easily than larger ones; the pressurized sprayer is also capable of pumping a larger volume of water more quickly. A pump sprayer works best when the chamber is full of water, but be sure to store it empty and open to keep it clean and fresh.

I prefer commercial kitchen equipment for lots of everyday kitchen items. Commercial versions are usually more economical, space-efficient, and resilient than their residential counterparts. Today's thriving food

Sklips help create a stack of sheet pans holding beef jerky. A fan facilitates the drying process.

culture has spawned physical and online restaurant supply stores that welcome the general public to purchase items at retail. Some commercial items we particularly prefer over the common home-style version include:

- **Parchment paper.** There are a thousand sheets of parchment paper in a case. Use them to bake on, to line sheet pans, and as bread wrap.
- **Plastic wrap and aluminum foil.** These giant rolls last forever. Commercial plastic wrap is especially useful because it actually clings to what you're wrapping. Plus, the expanse means you can wrap things well enough to prevent leakage or to protect from an extended freeze.
- **Sheet pans and half sheet pans.** The regulation size of a full sheet pan is 18" by 26". They also come in half and quarter sizes if a full pan is too big. These are super tough. You may also be able to find doughnut screens or enrobing screens that fit inside sheet pans and make great cooling and drying racks.

- **Rolling speed racks.** The mule of the food service industry is a rolling rack that holds sheet pans. Proofing boards full of resting or proofing dough can also be held in a smaller footprint than if they were spread all over your horizontal area. Plastic rack covers with zipper access are convenient for keeping drafts off your dough.
- **Commercial food storage containers come in all kinds of sizes and shapes and are stackable.** Prepping 10 to 12 different pizza toppings is more convenient when you have abundant containers all with the same-size lid.
- **Dough tubs.** If you start making bread in any sizable amount, you'll need a good-sized container to hold the dough when it's fermenting. The tubs are also handy for storing weighed-out ingredients and as kneading troughs. A bus tub intended for carrying dirty dishes works well for this. I prefer dough tubs that have a flat bottom—these are easier to clean than the kind with drainage channels.

Temperature Monitoring

Pizza is made at 700°F (371°C). A 450°F (232°C) hearth temperature is needed for sourdough loaves. Granola is slow-roasted at 300°F (149°C). As in all cooking and baking, temperature is an important variable in wood-fired cuisine. But there is no knob to turn and no thermostat to indicate the temperature of the oven. There are, however, a variety of devices that can detect temperatures on the surface as well as how much heat has penetrated into the mass.

It's more crucial to have the proper temperature when baking yeasted or naturally leavened products than with other baked goods or cooking. Oven temperatures for bread must be high enough to caramelize the residual sugars of fermentation and impart good enough spring, but not so high that the loaves are scorched—or burned—during the bake cycle. Cookies, on the other hand, are more tolerant of different baking temperatures. If the temperature is a little low, bake them longer. Too hot? Use an insulated sheet and be ready to remove them right on time.

READING THE FIRE, READING THE OVEN

There are plenty of instruments to help monitor temperature, but the ones you always have with you and don't need to buy are your senses, especially sight and touch. There are clues to broad temperature ranges: Soot burns off at 600 to 700°F (316–371°C), for example, leaving the firebrick clean. You will know when you are burning cleanly, because there will be little or no smoke and the secondary combustion flames will dance along the top of the arch.

Your hand and forearm make a remarkably reliable thermometer. Stick your hand in the oven and count how long you can comfortably hold it inside. The longer you can hold it in there, the lower the temperature. Everyone's definition of *comfortable* is different, of course, so it's hard to give a specific range, but this is a simple method. You'll get the hang of it. Before thermometers, all cooks and bakers judged oven temperatures this way. This is why old recipes ask for a "hot" or "moderately hot" oven instead of a specific temperature.

Being able to sense these differences partly depends on the oven. In an oven with more thermal mass you may have a sense that the heat bears down more heavily than it would in a lighter-mass oven. The more massive oven also holds more heat, so it will cool more slowly. But again, you'll learn what the correct temperature feels like on your arm.

Another simple test is to toss a bit of flour on the hearth and see how quickly it browns and gives off a toasty smell. When Magdalena is ready to begin baking this takes about 13 seconds, but it could be different in your oven. The hearth is too hot if the flour burns or smolders, and too cool if it takes a long time for the flour to brown.

Another method is by seeing how quickly a piece of paper will burn in the oven. The auto-ignition temperature of paper is about 450°F (232°C), depending on density of the paper and the available oxygen. (I use parchment because it is always handy.) If the paper immediately burns I know the temp is well above 450°F. If it slowly blackens and falls away in brittle pieces, I know the oven is around 450°F. And if the paper stays intact and doesn't really change in color, I know the oven is down below 450°F.

STANDARD OVEN THERMOMETERS

Sometimes you want to know the air temperature in the oven more precisely than just the "thrust your hand in and gauge it by feel" method. A common oven thermometer can be purchased in most grocery stores for less than $10 and is perfect for measuring the temp inside the oven. I keep several around Magdalena so I can check temperatures in different parts of the oven. I leave them in the oven most of the time, but take them out when there's a live fire so the heat doesn't crack or smoke the lens. A camp toaster raises the thermometer up off the hearth, giving a more accurate reading of the air temperature because the thermometer isn't affected by the steady conductive heat flowing from the hearth. Look for one with a scale that goes as high as 600°F (316°C) and with

Low-tech air thermometers. There's a bent wire stand on the left, a hacked camp toaster on the right.

a font size as large as possible so it's easy to see when you peer into the oven. Read the air temperature quickly after taking off the door: You want to note the temp before outside air cools the oven environment.

HANDHELD INFRARED THERMOMETERS

The use of handheld infrared thermometers has increased dramatically since *The Bread Builders* was published. These thermometers have become more economical and their upper range has increased; you can read temperatures well over 1,000°F (538°C). I consistently check four spots—inside the left door, middle of the hearth, dead center in the back wall, and top of the arch—so I can monitor temperatures and anticipate when the oven will be ready. (See the oven log in appendix E to view the four points I monitor in Magdalena.) The infrared thermometer measures surface temperatures, which are usually higher than the temperature of the air inside the oven. Be sure to

purchase an IR thermometer that goes up to 1,000°F. Many on the market top out at 600°F (316°C) or so—temps that will be reached not long after you light a fire.

THERMOCOUPLES

The most precise—and expensive—way to monitor temperatures throughout an oven's mass is through the use of thermocouples. Thermocouples, which are placed throughout the masonry, are made of two different types of metal. The junction between the two creates voltage based on temperature. The heat generates a current that is read by an analog or digital meter. The advantage of thermocouples over the previously mentioned techniques for determining surface temperature is that they indicate how far into the masonry the heat has penetrated. Heat that is stored deep in the mass will be available for baking or cooking once the fire is removed. Knowing when the entire mass has reached a saturation point means you can gather as much stored heat energy as possible without unnecessarily burning more fuel.

K-type thermocouples have the most appropriate range, up to 1,250°F (677°C), and they resist corrosion better than the J-type. Premade leads with a braided stainless-steel sheath can be purchased, or you can make your own by buying T/C wire, twisting two pieces together, and welding the tip.

I like to get two cross-sectional profiles of the temperature: one under the hearth and one in the thermal mass above the arch. A good spot is halfway back in the oven so you can average the heat differential between the back (hottest) and front (coolest) parts.

If you want to install six thermocouples, place one a third of the way into the mass, another two-thirds of the way in, and the last one near the outside. If six thermocouples are too many, then having four is fine, with one halfway through the thermal mass and another near the outside. The one on the outside of the thermal mass is most useful, because you can monitor the heat saturation of the outer mass.

Be sure to clearly and permanently label the ends of the thermocouples so that you'll know what point you are monitoring. If the gauge ever needs to be replaced or if it is removed for maintenance, you want to be able to reconnect it properly.

One problem with thermocouples is that they tend to fail eventually. They can be replaced more easily if during construction you place a Pyrex tube to serve as a well for the thermocouple. (Metal wells are not recommended because they compromise the efficacy of the thermocouples.) Because the thermocouple placed in Pyrex won't be encased in mortar, it can be replaced as long as you have access to the tube.

I placed four thermocouples in Magdalena. Monitoring the temperatures gave me an opportunity to observe how deeply the heat penetrated and helped me adjust my firing schedule. By the time the gauge failed several years later, I had developed a firing routine and learned less technological ways to determine how hot the oven was. I never replaced the gauge, but the thermocouples are still embedded.

Wireless thermocouple monitoring is also available. An advantage with this technology is that you can record and graph temperatures directly on your computer. My friend Ron Rathburn has a monitoring device from

Omega Engineering that scans all his thermocouples. It is exported via a serial port on his laptop, where he can extract data to construct tables and graphs based on the spreadsheet data.

THE MANLEY THERMOSCOPE

A temperature reading innovation contributed by Pat Manley is leaving an opening in the facade that leads all the way to the outer edge of thermal mass. You can "shoot" the temperature of the outer edge of the thermal mass with an infrared thermometer and then close the hole with a brick plug to prevent excessive heat loss. Monitoring the surface temperatures of the inside and outside of the thermal mass will give you a good idea of how saturated the mass is.

A thermoscope well on the side of the oven at Bootleg Bâtard, a community-based oven owned by Melina Kelson and Pete Podolsky, in Chicago, Illinois. The oven was temporarily constructed in a workshop led by Pat Manley, then disassembled and rebuilt in their edible yard, in part, to help their commitment to "Build community by nourishing neighbors." PHOTO COURTESY OF BOOTLEG BÂTARD.

Firing a Backyard Black Oven

Handmade ovens are unique and have personalities and thermal characteristics all their own. So remember that in all likelihood you will need to fine-tune these instructions. Getting to know your oven is part of the fun; you will easily learn its subtleties.

One of the best parts of writing this book was visiting many different ovens and seeing how people fire and use them. It's always impressive to hear commercial wood-fired bakers tick off the parts of their process made predictable by a daily or weekly routine. It's also refreshing to use a low-mass backyard oven with the goal of baking a load or two of bread and then firing it up again for an evening meal. (If you ever want to have people over to enjoy all your oven has to offer, schedule the day so you have baked your bread before you need to fire up to live-fire cooking temperatures. The heat taken up by the thermal mass will make your cooking more predictable, and you won't risk burning the bread in an oven that, right on the heels of a pizza bake, is up in the 700°F/371°C range. This is how Dan Wing schedules a pizza party.) I do love baking hundreds of loaves of bread in one day, but I also appreciate having just six or eight coming out of a single bake day in a backyard oven. There are fewer loaves so they seem more precious, and it's an easily manageable amount of work. A backyard wood-fired oven is one of the most enjoyable ways to bake bread. Even if the loaves aren't as perfectly shaped as you wish or the bottoms are a little scorched, it will still be great. And with a little practice, you'll be turning out impressive bread.

Another benefit of baking in your backyard is the chance you'll meet people you otherwise might not have. A friend who had an oven built in her backyard tells of how her neighbor, whom she had known for 15 years only through an occasional wave hello, soon became one of her best friends. Why did they suddenly connect after all that time? Linda was curious about the oven and came over to check it out. Add to the list of things a wood-fired oven can provide—unexpected friendship.

In general, it's best to fire an oven (especially for bread production) numerous times in advance of the bake day, as opposed to just once. What I have found is that heating an oven several days in advance gives me more and more reliable heat windows for bread baking. This has played out in many different types of ovens that I've baked in at bakeries, businesses, homes, and education centers. If I'm traveling to a wood-fired oven to do some consulting or teaching, I always request that an oven be fired in advance of my arrival.

Take a little more care when you're firing up a cold oven in winter. Allow the heat to build more slowly so the bricks don't go from freezing to blazing hot too quickly. And, of course, adequate insulation is important if you are located in a cold climate and plan to use your oven during the winter months.

Firing Methods and Schedules

Here's the sequence of events that will prepare your oven for baking bread: Build a fire, let it burn (and burn cleanly!), allow sufficient time to have the heat migrate to the outer thermal mass, remove any ash, and then let the oven cool to proper baking temperature.

Proper baking temperature is hard to quantify. As we've discussed, different products want to be baked at different temperatures. Flank steak should be cooked hot and fast, while your Thanksgiving turkey will be roasted at a much lower temperature for a longer time.

But proper baking temperature is also influenced by the amount of thermal mass in the oven. If mass is low—say, one firebrick thick—you can start baking at a higher temperature than in a lower-mass oven, because you will draw down the (lower) amount of retained heat more quickly. If there's more thermal mass—say, the walls are made of a double thickness of firebrick—the heat will be more stable and cool more slowly. Therefore, you can start loading at a lower temperature than in a lower-mass oven.

A fun part of the process that can be easily managed with a variety of techniques is fine-tuning the oven environment in the period just before bread baking. I'll offer some advice on what you can do to control the heat as you prepare to put the dough on the bricks. Ideally, you won't have to artificially cool the oven, instead of letting it cool slowly; it's better to have the cooling slope be as flat as possible. Imagine heat is like a heavy rock you are rolling down a hill. If you keep the descent slow, you are more in control. If the mass suddenly starts to plunge, it's difficult to stop. Here are some ways to adjust for an oven that is too hot or too cool.

- **Keep the door (or damper) open rather than closed.** More air intake will enhance the transfer of heat to the cooler air that will soon rise out of the chimney, taking heat with it and leaving behind a cooler oven.
- **Use the high temperature for baking or cooking other things.** Many commercial bakers integrate a varied selection of breads—partly for reasons of product diversification, but also as a way to use high hearth temperatures and cool off the hearth a bit. Pita and focaccia are good examples of flat breads that can handle very high heat.
- **Jump loading.** Quickly loading another batch of dough after unloading the last one will eliminate the recharge period when heat from the outer masonry transfers back to the baking chamber. If the temperature is low, however, you want to be patient between loads to allow it to recover. (See chapter 2 for a discussion of how heat flows through masonry and other media, including air.) Jump loading is less effective when the walls and ceiling of the oven are hotter than the hearth. The loaves pull more heat out of the hearth, because the dough is in direct contact with this surface (as opposed to the walls, ceiling, or dome) and draws more heat out of the masonry. That contact permits conductive heat transfer. If the dome is too hot (in relation to the hearth), the baked loaves will have too much top color and soft or pale bottoms.
- **Stacks of empty sheet pans can act as a heat sink.** They will draw heat right out of the top layer of masonry, and the heat can then be removed from the oven. Also, you can place water in the pans; evaporation is another heat transfer process that will speed the cooling of the hearth. Be careful when removing

pans: If the water hasn't completely evaporated, it could slosh and burn you.
- **Don't mop the hearth to cool or clean the baking surface.** This damages the hearth and squanders heat. Just sweep cleanly. Use a natural-bristle brush or the terminal end of a tree branch.
- **Pray to Fornax, Roman oven goddess.** Her festival, the Fornacalia, is celebrated on February 17. I've never been able to find out too much about Fornax, and no images exist, so one night I made up my own story. I imagine Fornax monitors all the wood-fired ovens in the world, and if you pray to her she will come to your aid. If your oven is too hot she will absorb that energy and take it to underfired bakers who are wishing they had a bit more heat to finish the day's baking. And if your oven is cool, she will bring excess heat from some baker who is wishing to lose a bit.

I love the period when bread is about half an hour away from baking. Use it to prepare for loading. It's exciting. The steaming system is in place, and there's a new blade on the *lame*. The dough and the oven are literally and figuratively full of energy. It is impossible for me to bring these two independent but related energies to life without getting caught up in the nurturing that comes with creating the right moment so that luscious loaves are put to bake in a heat-conditioned masonry oven.

Loading Bread

Loading is dramatic, a performance really, and as with all performances you need to think through the process and how to move smoothly through it. This mental exercise will help you be prepared during what should be a fast-paced procedure. It's important to load the oven both with deliberate speed and with great care. The tools you need are few but important. Have them within easy reach so you can work quickly and efficiently:

- Several peels. You want to open the oven door as few times as possible. Several peels will allow you to load more than one loaf at a time.

Ron Rathburn and Jim Linakis, Community Bakers

Ron Rathburn has an oven largely based on the Alan Scott plans published in *The Bread Builders*. He did incorporate some changes after monitoring the posts on the Yahoo! brick oven chatgroup. Most notably, Ron used foam glass under the hearth and kiln blankets for insulation instead of vermiculite over the thermal mass. The hearth slab is suspended, and the vault is constructed from ring arches. The chimney transition was a difficult part of the construction for Ron, as it is for all of us. Ron's oven is pretty close to Alan's plans, with the exception of the insulation system. Ron did not use vermicrete and employed insulation with higher efficiency. The oven works great. Ron and his good friend Jim Linakis, an equally enthusiastic bread baker, have spent the past several years honing their skills baking bread from fire.

I met Ron and Jim when I taught a class in a Mugnaini prefab oven at the home of Richard and Cheryl Merola. Ron and Jim took the Sesame Semolina formula (the same one in this book) home and have been baking it ever since with great results. Ron and Jim are the type of home bakers who have taken advantage of the information about baking and ovens that's readily accessible via the Internet. Baking is a hobby for Ron and Jim, and although they take it seriously, they have a good time doing it!

Ron started building his oven in 2007 and completed it in 2009. He took a corner of the patio next to his in-ground pool in a suburban Rhode Island neighborhood to place the oven. Once the oven was complete, he built a nice compact building with plenty of windows and a sliding glass door that opens toward the pool. Fresh pizza while you relax on an air mattress, anybody? The room

Loaves of Sesame Semolina in Ron's ovenhouse

holds a wooden worktable, a wire cooling rack, and a little cupboard space for couches, baskets, and other baking tools. It's a clean, well-lighted place for baking, and the only heat is provided by the oven and from the excitement of making bread from fire. This is plenty of warmth, even in the dead of a northeastern winter on the east side of Narragansett Bay. I like Ron's bakeshop. He has paid attention to detail and constructed a building that will help him take advantage of all his oven has to offer. For instance, on either side of the oven face is a panel with holders for peels or to hang couches so they can dry well before storage. The panels are removable to allow access to both sides of the oven vault. Ron also built a 6" concrete retaining wall next to the oven foundation. Not only does the retaining wall help further insulate the oven, but it also helps to contain the kiln blankets Ron uses to insulate the top of the hearth. He installed an exterior door that provides an additional entrance to the space on the right side of the oven. It was intended for storage space for Ron's window screens during the winter. This small space is kept warm and dry; one thinks of the beds built on the top of masonry heaters in Russia and Eastern Europe, a place to spend cozy winter nights.

Ron's 32" by 36" oven is the smallest size plan available from Ovencrafters, but it's the perfect size for baking multiple loads of hearth bread on the weekend and still having plenty of heat to roast a chicken, make some taralli, cook a pot of baked beans, and put up a batch of granola over the next couple of days. Ron has experimented with firing schedules and is constantly tweaking his approach so the burn is more efficient and the retained heat lasts longer.

Like many with backyard wood-fired ovens, Ron doesn't keep his oven fired up on a regular basis. It would take too much fuel and become another chore. It usually has cooled to ambient temperature when he starts to get ready for a weekend of baking. This means he has to bring it from cold up to baking temps and maintain it there for the five to six bakes of 12 loaves each that Ron and Jim tag-team on throughout an enjoyable day of baking, eating chili, and watching Patriots football. This size of oven is great for backyard baking. It takes a little more than a wheelbarrow full of wood, which Ron starts burning the afternoon before he wants to bake. Starting from a cold oven, he can achieve solidly hot pizza temps in about two hours. (And remember—making a couple of pizzas for

yourself and family doesn't have to be a big thing. Use one of the doughs in this book and keep the toppings simple. You probably have all you need in your pantry and fridge.) Ron maintains the burn through the night. Toward 10 pm, between mixing preferments and getting ready for the next day's bake, Ron will build up a lot of hot fuel in the oven by slowly adding wood and allowing it to combust before the next addition. Once combustion equilibrium is achieved, he installs his draft door, which is concrete block, positioned to restrict—but not cut off—oxygen and exhaust flow. It is always disquieting to sleep when there is a fire in the oven (especially when you also might be fretting about your preferments), but Ron manages to get some rest while the heat of the fire slowly seeps into the masonry.

Ron also experimented with starting a small fire two days in advance of baking and maintaining the rest of the schedule. He found the heat stability and length of retention better with his current method.

In the morning there may be some coals buried in the ash. Ron decides whether to rake them into the ash dump or add some very thin kindling in order to create a quick fire. This flash fire helps stall a temperature drop, ensuring there will be enough heat once the last load of the day rolls around. Jim comes over later in the morning with the dough he has mixed at home. Following this firing schedule, Ron and Jim are able to start loading between 1 and 2 pm. The oven is small enough to be adequately steamed with a simple handheld pressurized garden sprayer. Surface temps for the first load are around 575°F (302°C). At this temp, the 570g loaves take about 30 to 35 minutes to bake.

You can see from the photo how skilled Ron and Jim have become at nurturing their dough and managing the oven. Ron doesn't sell the bread, for myriad reasons, so he and Jim act as community bakers for their families, neighbors, friends, and co-workers. Jim's wife teaches preschool, and the families of her students often get a loaf of fresh wood-fired Sesame Semolina. Ron volunteers to go into the class and help teach the kids how to bake. They donate bread to fund-raisers, make sure people learn about and get real bread, and field questions from aspiring home bakers who find out these guys are for real—they bake well-fermented loaves in a backyard wood-fired oven.

- Dusting flour. Keep a container of dusting flour within arm's reach. I always use white flour for dusting, mainly because I always have it around, it doesn't burn, and I can get an even (but thin) layer over a large expanse of peel or sticky dough. Some people like something more coarse—I recommend semolina flour over cornmeal because the abundant oils in cornmeal burn more easily.
- Woodstove or welding gloves. Keep these within easy reach. We have several pairs of different weights. I prefer the dexterity I get from gloves compared with oven mitts.
- Light source. A built-in light, flashlight, or headlamp is good to have if you're baking in the early hours of the morning or if the oven is deep enough that ambient light cannot reach its deepest recesses.

- Garden sprayer. A garden sprayer, filled with water and pressurized, is the most expedient and simple way to fill an oven with steam.
- A wet towel or two. Have a tub of water with soaked towels so you can seal the door with them when you're finished loading.
- Loaf pans. A couple of old loaf pans full of boiling hot water just inside the oven to the left and right of the door will contribute to the steam in the oven. If necessary, they can be removed at the end of loading to make room for more loaves.
- Sheet pans. Placing a half or full sheet pan half filled with water and holding an old towel (or even a metal pie tin for a smaller oven) just inside the door or way in the back of the oven will help mellow the heat of the hearth. Because the sheet pan has a low profile,

Aidan helps unload. Note the oven log and infrared thermometer in the foreground. A pressurized garden sprayer is standing by on top of the oven.

you can use it at the mouth of the oven and still load over it. It can be removed at the end of loading if you need the space to slip in a few more loaves. If there's enough room, you can also leave it inside the oven where it will help create a steam in the sealed bake chamber. Bill Freese of Bill's Bread on Vashon Island, Washington, uses a cast-iron corn bread pan filled with water . . . perfect because it holds plenty of heat and doesn't slosh water on the hearth.

Once your oven is clean and mellow and your bread is ready to bake, you can move ahead to what I think is the most dramatic part of the bread-baking process—loading the oven. The most beautiful loaves enjoy being baked in a steamy environment, so part of managing a bread bake is making sure to inject an adequate amount of steam into the oven. See *The Effects of Steam and How to Steam a Masonry Oven* in chapter 6.

PART TWO

BREAD
BAKING:
THE PROCESS

CHAPTER SIX

+>—•—<+

Baking Bread in a Wood-Fired Oven

My baking colleagues who have come before me have done a wonderful and thorough job describing the process of baking bread and the functions of ingredients, and the American Bread Movement has given rise to a canon of reliable bread-baking information not available back when I got started in 1995. What I've presented here is the information I feel is most crucial to making good bread, whether in a home, wood-fired, or commercial deck oven. Throughout, I have considered the question: If this were the only bread book readers had, could they make good bread? Keep in mind that the bread-baking knowledge this field has accumulated runs deeper than the information in these pages and beyond the scope of a book that focuses on wood-fired ovens. Explore the bibliography to deepen your own understanding of baking. Bread is communal—even in the sharing and exchange of information.

I like dining in a restaurant and anonymously watching people eat the bread I baked that morning. I like the way bread baking is a great social equalizer. I've never met anybody who didn't like bread, the smell and satisfaction of it, its ability to recall to poignant memory a childhood, an era, a romance, a simple meal shared with friends. Bread brings people together in many ways. In the bread classes I teach, a compelling interest in bread transcends age, gender, politics, and race. I feel fortunate that I get to meet so many people with whom I would not ordinarily have crossed paths.

100 Percent Touched by Human Hands

To make good bread in any oven it is important to have a basic understanding of the ingredients, the fermentation process, and how to combine knowledge and intuition in order to successfully shepherd the dough along its journey from raw ingredients to baked loaf. Baking beautiful, crusty loaves of European-style hearth bread is perhaps the most challenging use of a wood-fired oven. This primer on artisan bread baking is given in the context of bread baking in a wood-fired oven, but the techniques and formulas are also applicable to home ovens. In fact, most of the recipes are sized for—and tested in—a domestic gas or electric oven.

Baking bread in a wood-fired oven is just like being in love—simple and complex at the same time. Four fundamental ingredients—flour, water, salt, and yeast—are mixed into dough and baked in a hot brick box. Simple. It gets complex due to the myriad variables present in wood-fired oven bread baking—the absorption rate of the flour, the temperature of the dough, the health of the starter, and the temperament of the baker, for example. And then there is the oven. Is it the proper temperature? The bread is ready to be baked, but your intuition tells you the hearth is a bit hot because this is the first time you've fired the oven with some of the dense live oak that came down in the hurricane two years ago. Can you figure out a way to cater to the needs of the oven and dough and still be satisfied or, better yet, charmed by the baked loaf? These variables—time, temperature, quality of ingredients, attitude, dough health, heat retention—can be controlled, however, and the process can be learned, practiced, and refined. As your relationship with the oven and experience in baking bread evolve, so will your ability to turn out beautiful loaves with wonderfully evocative tastes of properly fermented grain. And when all these simple ingredients and dependent variables are put together and controlled with care and awareness, the results are incredibly satisfying—just like being in love.

Producing good bread requires only a few critical elements: the basic ingredients of flour, water, salt, and leaven or yeast; some way to incorporate them—a mixer can be used, although I enjoy mixing with my hands (and I once had a student with only one hand whose dough was beautiful); and time. Good bread takes time. Brinna Sands, matriarch of King Arthur Flour, likes to tell a story she heard from Lionel Poilâne, the great French baker who championed the cause of naturally leavened bread to a Paris enthralled with the baguette. He said, "You can't take nine women and make a baby in one month." But that doesn't mean you have to be a slave to the bench for 18 hours, even if it takes that amount of time—start to finish—to make the bread. You can create a production schedule that doesn't require you to be physically present with the dough for 18 hours, even though some or all of the flour is slowly fermenting in a controlled environment for that long. Time is necessary to make flavorful, Old World loaves, but luckily we know how to create handmade breads without our constant attention.

When flour and water are mixed and kneaded, they begin to form gluten strands. Salt and yeast are then added to make flavorful, leavened bread. The flour provides complex carbohydrates that are converted, through enzymatic activity, into simple sugars. Yeast consumes these sugars and gains energy for growth and reproduction, and fermentation begins. Carbon dioxide is the product of yeast respiration, just as it is

of human respiration. Alcohol and organic acids, by-products of yeast fermentation, help create complex flavors and contribute to dough maturation. The relatively small proportion of salt brightens the flavor, strengthens the dough, and gives some control over the fermentation process. Simple. And yet complex.

Any bread you bake from scratch will be satisfying, but to consistently bake bread well in any type of oven you have to balance obsession with flexibility. Call on—and amass—baking experiences and your intuition to determine the needs of the dough and oven. The dough responds to your attitude; it's difficult to achieve beautiful, charismatic loaves if you are tense, worried, or troubled. Strive from the beginning to control variables, but when things go awry, learn to recognize the signs of improper dough development and fermentation. Then you can manipulate the variables to create a more favorable environment for controlled fermentation. Is your dough cool? Get it in a warmer place to increase primary and secondary fermentation. Is the dough warm? Get it in a cooler place to decrease primary and secondary fermentation. Does the dough seem weak? Add a fold. Is it dry when you are kneading? Add more water, even if it is not called for in the recipe. Is the oven hot? Put the dough someplace cool and encourage the oven to mellow out. Is the oven too cool? Get the dough someplace warm, keep the oven door closed, and think hot thoughts. Fermentation, fire, and the oven roll on, and you have to respond to these forces in order to control and accommodate them. If all this seems overwhelming, don't worry. The way to consistently baking good bread is to sometimes bake some bread that isn't so good.

A Method-Based Approach to Bread Baking

What I learned from Lionel Vatinet when I took that first class at SFBI was that to bake well requires an understanding of method. Dough-handling and fermentation techniques are the keys to success, as opposed to a specific recipe or secret ingredient. Lionel showed me how to put together different kinds of flour, different ratios of water, salt, and some leavener in the morning and have a loaf of bread in the afternoon.

If you know the fundamental steps of baking—and the requirements to make a good loaf of bread—you can apply that knowledge to a huge variety of leavened foods. If you know how to make Pain Rustique, you know how to make naturally leavened Pain au Levain and 67% Rye. True, you need to know the special considerations of each bread and its ingredients, but the method can be customized to achieve impressive results.

Professional baking formulas often have very sparse instructions: "Autolyse. Final dough temp 75–78°F. Short mix. Ferment 3 hours, folding every half hour. Shape: boule . . ." Professional bakers fill in the extra instructions with their knowledge and experience. Information specific to a particular product—"Let rest 20 minutes before applying a second egg wash"—is offered as an aside, a tip to the baker to be aware of

requirements specific to this dough. These tips are often the difference between a good loaf and a stunning loaf.

I incorporate the method-based approach in this book's recipes and in describing the proper use of your oven. For instance, steaming techniques are described in detail in the previous chapter, while each bread recipe that requires steam—which is most of them—simply states, "load into steamed oven." I've written the recipes this way both to simplify them and to encourage you to learn the method and the reasons behind it. *What are the best ways to steam the oven? Why am I steaming anyway? What else do I need to consider besides steam if I'm looking for bread with glossy crusts?* Start asking yourself these questions and you'll better understand the simple yet complex world of baking beautiful handmade bread. When information specific to a recipe appears—for example, "Dough with any type of sugar, in this case, honey, will take color quickly; take care that your bread does not get too dark"—you will know those specifics are in part what make that bread distinctive.

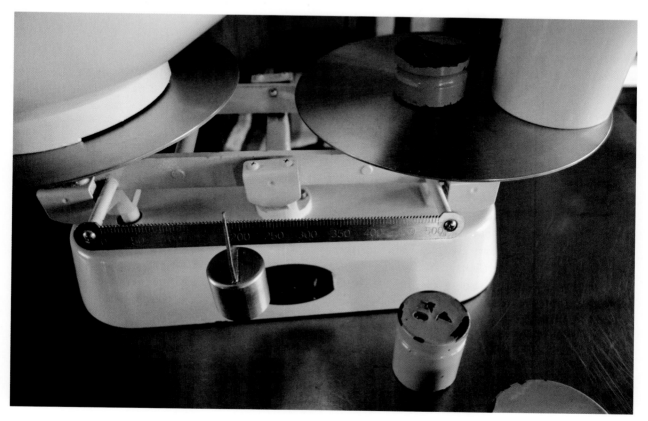

Weight Versus Volume

Get a scale! Accurately measuring ingredients is extremely important to consistently creating good bread. Because there are only four basic ingredients, the interactions among them vary widely, largely depending on the ratio of each ingredient to the others. Most scales weigh in metric and pounds and ounces so once you have a scale you can begin to weigh in the metric system if you aren't already. All the formulas in this book are expressed in metric weight and volume. I made the decision to exclude pounds and ounces because metric units offer a more convenient unit for small amounts. For instance, one ounce equals 28.35 grams. The metric system is also the artisan bread industry standard and is especially helpful when using the baker's percentage system, because both are based on 10s. (See appendix C for information about the baker's percentage system.) Volumetric measurements were included for those who prefer that approach (or don't have a scale), but again I urge you to use the metric system to weigh your ingredients. It is faster, cleaner, and more accurate.

Weight is the most accurate way to measure ingredients—454 grams of flour is 454 grams of flour, but a cup of flour will contain more or less of it depending on how you fill the cup. Fluffing the flour with a spoon and transferring it to the cup yields the proper amount of flour, while scooping it directly out of the container with the measuring cup will yield too much flour. Yes, both are "cups" of flour, but one has more flour packed into it, which can make a big difference. Variances in ingredient ratios will affect the metabolism of fermentation (dry dough ferments more slowly than wetter dough, for instance), the volume, and the crumb structure.

When shopping for a scale, look for something with enough capacity to handle the amounts of flour you need. (Having to weigh half of it, empty that into another container, and then scale the remainder is burdensome—and it leads to scaling errors as well.) Also look for a scale that weighs in 1g increments. A scale with 5g increments will likely give you inaccurately measured salt and yeast. (How can you be sure you estimated correctly and got 3g?) I also appreciate a scale platform large enough to hold the weigh-out container while the readout screen remains visible. In addition to my large digital and balance-beam scales, I rely on a small wallet-sized subgram scale. The capacity of such scales is around 100g, but they measure in 0.1g increments. Subgram scales are very handy for getting that 0.1g of yeast for a home-sized preferment. (See *Hand Mixing Technique* later in this chapter for an explanation of the term *preferment*.) They're used in the gem and jewelry industry but can also be found online. Larger scales are available online or in any store with a well-stocked kitchen department. You can go digital or analog. For years I used a balance-beam scale and it did just fine. It does take longer to measure your ingredients, however, because you need to manually tare the scale, instead of just pushing the tare button. On the other hand, there are no batteries to wear out.

Baker's Percentage Primer

Baker's percentage—sometimes called baker's math—is a system that expresses the amount of each ingredient in a bread formula relative to the amount of flour. Because the ingredients are presented in ratio form, we refer to these as "formulas," not recipes. If you understand and can leverage the power of the baker's percentage system, you'll be able to analyze, troubleshoot, develop, and resize formulas. It's easy and fun. Plus, it will allow you to more effectively communicate with other bakers, because bread bakers always speak in percentages, not fixed quantities.

If a dough is 69 percent hydrated, it means that for every 100 units of flour (whether those units are grams, ounces, pounds, kilograms, what have you), there are 69 units of water. (For the non-baking world this would be about 40 percent hydrated.) Your educated fellow baker will know what a 69 percent hydrated dough is, but won't be able to easily imagine the consistency of a dough if you tell her it contains 2,700g of water. She'll need to calculate the total flour and total water in the entire formula (preferments, final dough ingredients, and soaker if there is one) and then whip out a calculator and divide total water by total flour to know the overall hydration. Speak in the language of baker's percentage and you will be more easily understood, at least in the professional baking world.

In addition to metric and volume the formulas in this book include a column of percentages titled "Baker's %." The "Baker's %" column in the final dough table gives a "snapshot" of all the ingredients, including a preferment if there is one. In other words, the flour percentage in the final dough table includes the flour from the preferment and the water percentage in the final dough includes the water from the preferment. (There is also a percentage column in the preferment table, if a dough has a preferment. Those percentages refer to the subset of preferment ingredients. This is useful information. For instance, it gives a clue on the hydration of the preferment. However, it does not reflect the ratio of ingredients present once all the components are brought together when the dough is mixed.)

Here is a story of why percentages are more useful and accurate than quantities. A group of students in one of my Johnson & Wales classes developed a savory scone with cracked black pepper, caramelized onions, and a mix of three cheeses. Once baked, those things went fast and everybody was all atwitter about them. They could be served with a salad or soup! Add some eggs and a glass of wine for an easy brunch! We were sorry when the last one was gone.

Two days later another student wanted to make more and asked the group who'd developed the scones how much of each ingredient had been incorporated. Stephanie Agana (who helped with some of the photo shoots in this book) called out the quantities and percentages for each of the ingredients. But the other student wrote down only the quantities of ingredients, not the percentages. When she got back to her bench, the rest of her group had already scaled out a biscuit formula instead of the scone formula. Incorporating the same percentages of ingredients into the biscuit formula would have produced a flavorful savory biscuit. However, there was a crucial difference in the yields of the two products. The biscuit had less flour than the scone, and that made the presence of the inclusions

more distinct—especially the powerful pepper. The same quantity of ingredients in a recipe with less flour (and dough) created a biscuit that was too peppery. Guess who wandered in and sampled one of the biscuits fresh out of the oven? The dean. He picked up a biscuit and started eating it while talking to some students. Midway through he set it down and said, "I'm just not enjoying this anymore." After he left, we tried it and found out what he meant—it was indeed too peppery. All of which is to say that quantities mean nothing if the percentage is not respected! (Percentages and proper quantities of those savory ingredients as a ratio of flour weight are included as a variation of the Cranberry Pecan Buttermilk Scone formula in chapter 12.)

I'm confident understanding the system described in appendix C and doing simple arithmetic on a calculator will make you a more skillful and knowledgeable home bread baker. To make the leap to the professional level, you *must* understand the baker's percentage system and how it affects fermentation and the characteristics of the baked loaf. If you're already conversant with the workings of baker's percentage, move ahead to the next section. If you aren't, but just want to make some bread right away, follow the recipes and take care to scale ingredients accurately. For now, don't worry about the percentage column that appears in the bread formulas.

The Process

There's a fire burning in your oven. You want to make Pain au Levain and your starter is ripe and ready to use. Here is the basic process of turning raw ingredients into a baked loaf of handmade bread. Good bread bakers understand the following process but adjust each dough for hydration, folds, fermentation vigor, depth of score mark, and so forth, based on observation and intuition. In other words, follow the recipe but keep in mind the information in the rest of this book.

One of the most important things you can do to ensure success is to RTF—read the formula! Not only does it give you the opportunity to envision how the process unfolds, it also informs you of equipment and oven requirements. First . . . when do you need to start to have the bread ready on time? Is there a levain to mix? Do shaped loaves go into baskets or couches? And then there is the oven. Will it be at the right temperature at the right time? Do you need a high baking temperature or low, slow, steady heat? Being prepared in advance is key for having a stress-free and successful day in the kitchen, backyard, or bakery.

Mise en Place

Prescaling ingredients is one of my favorite ways to be prepared. If all your ingredients are ready to go, and the water temperature has been calculated, you can focus on the dough as it mixes. I love to walk up to my bench first thing in the morning and have everything arranged: metal dough cutter and plastic scraper, formulas stacked

Proper mixing and kneading are all about mise en place, feeling positive, and gently ensuring proper dough development.

in order of use, thermometer with probe in prescaled flour, and bucket for scaling water right next to the scale. The radio is tuned to the morning station so all I need to do when I walk in is turn it on. In addition to helping the bread-making process go more smoothly, organization like this allows you to rest easier the night before. No more anxious moments in the morning scaling ingredients when your impulse is to start mixing as soon as possible. A little bit of prep time lets you approach the day more smoothly and methodically.

The food service industry refers to this system of being prepared as mise en place or "everything in place." The *Larousse Gastronomique* definition of *mise en place* is: "All the operations carried out in a restaurant prior to serving the meal. In the dining room, this constitutes laying the tables; in the kitchen it means setting out the ingredients and utensils required for the preparation of the dishes on the menu." If that perspective seems too industrial, just remember the Girl and Boy Scout motto: "Be Prepared."

Mixing and Kneading

Professional bakers tend to use the term *mix* to refer to the entire stage when all the ingredients are brought together and then kneaded into a final dough. That term confuses some home bakers who believe mixing is simply incorporating the ingredients, while kneading is a separate step. This is true—there really are two parts to the process of turning raw ingredients into bread dough: incorporation of ingredients and gluten development. However you refer to it, this stage of bread making includes mixing the ingredients to a homogeneous stage and then adroitly kneading the dough until it is rife with strength, but not so strong it becomes overly elastic or "bucky."

The incorporation phase is complete when the mixture is homogeneous—no dry flour or extra water is pooling up around the edges of the dough. In addition to your senses, use the Force when you mix. This is a type of birth and you need to be mindful. Surround and penetrate your dough with love and nurturing instincts in an effort to bind it together. Sometimes I ask myself, HWYB? (How would Yoda bake?) Just posing that question makes me focus on the dough, and the rest of the world falls away for a few minutes. I feel the dough I mix in this state is better, is more energetic, and in the end creates a more charismatic loaf than dough mixed when I am tired, cranky, or distracted.

Pay attention. If something seems wrong, it probably is. Start figuring it out by taking a deep breath—stop mixing for a second, and go over the checklist in your head. Did you remember the salt? Does the dough seem thirsty? If you identify something wrong, fix it and then go back to mixing. This same quiet reflection is also important when firing your oven and getting ready for the bake. Follow your hunches.

Establishing a mixing routine helps you avoid mistakes and focus on the dough.

The man who taught me to bake, Lionel Vatinet, encourages his students to operate under the dictum "Work with love." In other words, treat your dough with kindness and respect. It is especially important to remember Lionel's advice when mixing. This is the birth of the dough. I believe the energy you use to "reanimate" a dough from raw ingredients will infuse the dough and affect its fermentation gestalt, flavor, volume, and charisma. I want the bread I make to contain positive energy that will be consumed by people and become part of their heart, hands, and head.

The Autolyse

In most of the formulas presented in this book, the incorporation phase is followed by an autolyse. The autolyse was developed by Professor Raymond Calvel, a French baker who studied and codified European baking techniques, and helps reduce mixing

Adding water to the preferment before the flour is incorporated makes it easier to mix the ingredients into a cohesive dough. PHOTO BY MELISSA RIVARD AND ANDREW JANJIGIAN

Combine the flour, water, and liquid preferment (if there is one) and mix until homogeneous. Yeast and salt are not added during the autolyse, to prevent the tightening of gluten.

It is not necessary to develop the gluten at this point, but all the flour should be incorporated.

Add yeast (if it's called for), mix it in, and then add the salt.

Once the salt is added, the dough begins to tighten.

time, enhances extensibility, and gives the flour an opportunity to absorb more water—an effortless way to increase hydration. All of this brings the dough more easily to proper development. The term, which roughly means "self-relaxation" or "self-dissolution," refers to breakdown of weak gluten bonds by protease enzymes naturally occurring in the flour, aiding extensibility and oven spring.

Yeast is held back (if it is being used), because the organic acids produced through yeast fermentation swell gluten proteins. This dough development will be beneficial later on, but right now we want the dough to relax and "self-destruct." Dough consistency preferments should be held back during the autolyse period for the same reason. However, liquid preferments (100 percent hydrated or so) must be added or else the autolysing dough will be too dry. It will take a long time to work in the liquid preferment after the autolyse and it is very likely that some lumps of dry dough will never be fully incorporated.

Salt also increases the strength of the gluten strands in two ways: It strengthens the ionic bonds between gluten strands, and it slows the activity of protease, the enzyme that cleaves peptide bonds in the gluten strands. Withholding yeast and salt for the autolyse period allows continued breakdown of gluten bonds, creating a soft dough that will re-form into well-organized, linear gluten strands once yeast and salt are added and the dough is kneaded.

Whether mixed by hand or in a mixer, most wheat-based, lean doughs benefit from an autolyse, while rye breads and enriched breads such as brioche do not.

Following the 20- to 30-minute autolyse period, add the yeast and mix the dough with your hand, a dough scraper, or a dough hook to get it incorporated. Once the yeast is incorporated, add the salt and mix until it nearly dissolves, at least a minute. The dough will become firmer once the salt is added (a baker might refer to this as the dough "tightening"). At this point, all the ingredients except inclusions should be in the bowl and incorporated. It is now time to develop the dough—the kneading part of the process. (Inclusions—olives, nuts, or other ingredients—will be introduced to the dough after it has been developed.)

When you see the dough development during the autolyse, and salt's subsequent strengthening effect on the dough, you may think little kneading is required, and this may be true. With naturally leavened bread the autolyse is particularly effective; after you add the salt and knead for a minute, you may have nothing more to do than cover the dough and let it ferment.

Hand Mixing Technique

The next step is to combine the water and preferment if there is one. A preferment is a mixture of flour, water, a small ratio of domestic or wild yeast, and sometimes salt. These ingredients are combined and fermented, sometimes for as little as 30 minutes—but usually for a slow, cool fermentation of up to 16 hours. (See *Yeasted Preferments* and *Naturally Leavened Breads* in chapter 7 for more discussion about domestic and wild yeast preferments.) I then add the flour and mix these ingredients until homogeneous. Hold back the yeast (if you are using it) and salt if you're incorporating an autolyse.

A trick for incorporating the flour more easily when you're mixing by hand is to add it in two stages. You don't need to wait a long period between the two additions—about 30 seconds of mixing is sufficient after the first addition—but this will help disperse the flour more quickly in the water. The dough at this point should have all the flour incorporated. It doesn't need to be super-smooth, but make sure it is homogeneous with no lumps. Cover it and allow it to rest for about 30 minutes—this is the autolyse.

The traditional kneading movements we are familiar with from before the American Bread Movement—the pushing of the dough against the work surface with the heels of your hands until it smoothens out into a firm dough—are rendered less effective by the higher hydration of artisan-style bread. Wet dough—typical of European-style hearth bread—will smear against the work surface if you try to give it this same move. Lionel Vatinet taught me a process he learned as a Compagnon, or apprentice, of the ancient guild of French bread bakers. Even large batches of wet dough can be

Your thumbs should be away from you and try not to get your palms stuck in the dough. A quick release of your hands helps do this.

Orient your hands as in the photo and cut the dough with the webbing of your hands. A quick opening flick of your fingers and thumbs helps prevent dough from sticking. If dough get stuck to your palms, remove it with a scraper.

Cutting off small pieces of dough and bringing them back together is also an easy and reliable way to develop gluten. I go back and forth between squeezing the dough between my hands and cutting it with a scraper. Dough seems to develop more quickly by using both of these techniques instead of just one or the other.

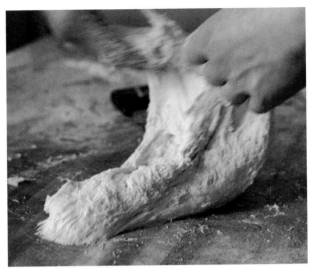

The "flippy move" helps organize gluten and creates a smooth skin with good surface tension. PHOTO BY KATE KELLEY

effectively mixed with this technique. The rhythm of mixing dough while watching and feeling it develop is one of my favorite parts of making bread; it's fascinating to watch a shaggy mass develop into a luscious and dynamic piece of dough.

Here's how to do it. Turn the dough out onto the bench, making sure to scrape all the dough bits into the mass. Starting with the side of the dough closest to you, cut the dough in sections with the webbing between your thumb and forefinger. Once you complete one pass, fold the dough over on itself, turn it 90 degrees, and cut through it again with the same action. Perform this several times. It seems counterintuitive to develop gluten by cutting it, but this action organizes the gluten strands into an extensible matrix. Remove the dough from your hands with a dough scraper and repeat.

A second way to knead is to cut the dough mass into small pieces—about 90g each—and pile them up together. Again, it seems counterintuitive that cutting the dough will help it develop, but the process helps organize the gluten strands. I go back and forth between these two steps, cutting the dough with the webbing of my hand for a minute or so and then cutting it into pieces with my dough scraper for a minute or so. You will see and feel the dough begin to strengthen. I also employ the "flippy move"—picking the dough up from the bench, *lightly* slapping it back down, and then drawing it over itself. This motion develops surface tension that helps keep the dough from sticking. It also gives a visual cue about how developed the dough has become. When I demonstrate this technique to students, they often say, "A good way to take out your frustrations." But guard against this inclination! There is never a good time to take out frustrations on the dough.

Gluten development during the kneading process does not need to be taken to the level necessary when the dough ultimately hits the hearth. Yes, dough development is created during mixing and kneading, but fermentation and its sidekick "the fold" also contribute a great deal to gluten development. The amount of gluten development that comes from fermentation is evident in the overnight metamorphosis of a preferment like a liquid sourdough starter or poolish. On the day it is mixed, the consistency is like pancake batter. By the next morning the organic acids swell flour proteins, which strengthens the gluten into a more cohesive network.

Folding the final dough greatly increases its development and adds to its maturation. The often sought-after gluten window test of a thin extensible dough membrane is not necessary at the end of mixing. Be patient. Let your dough ferment and fold it. It will become strong, fluffy, and extensible by the time you divide and shape it into individual loaves.

Experienced bread bakers are wary of overmixing, which can easily happen in a mixer. Overmixing oxidizes carotenoid pigments—important flavor and color carriers—and strengthens the gluten excessively. The result is a cottony and white crumb with little flavor. Allowing the dough to develop or mature throughout the bread-baking process yields a creamy and open crumb.

Even if you want to use a mixer—or start baking in quantities where a mixer makes a larger production more feasible—mixing some dough by hand lets you train yourself to feel how the dough changes and develops through the mixing or kneading process. And if you don't have a mixer, just pick up your hands and go to work. It's called handmade bread for a reason—you can create wonderful bread from fire by mixing by hand, just as people have been doing for thousands of years.

It's All in the Wrist

After 44 years of constant use, my wrists developed a severe case of carpal tunnel syndrome. I had fooled myself into thinking that baking offered a full range of motion for my body that would avoid the repetitive-motion injury I'd expect if I spent 40 hours a week assembling widgets. When people found out about my wrists, they often said, "And with your line of work! That must be so difficult!" Fact is, we all use our wrists all day and every day. The thrill of the bake was usually enough to make me forget about the numbness and tingling, but the next morning my hands, wrists, and forearms reminded me of the work I'd performed.

The carpal tunnel is a tunnel of connective tissue that acts as a sheath for two nerve bundles that run down the arm and into the hand. When the tunnel becomes inflamed from constant, repetitive, or non-ergonomic work, it presses on the nerve bundles, delaying impulses to the hands, causing numbness and tingling. To remedy the situation a ligament band that runs around the inside of your wrist is severed, releasing the pressure on the nerves. The symptoms go away immediately, well before the small incision and low-level surgery trauma have healed. I was grateful to have such a simple procedure make such a huge improvement to my quality of life.

I developed modifications to help me in all my work, from typing to baking, especially after a nonplussed physician said about human wrists, "Well, it's a weak part of our bodies." A special problem for tall people is the angle your wrist has to make when you are working on a bench that is too low for you. Modify your work space if possible to avoid having a sharp angle in your wrists for a good part of your bake day.

Using a Mixer

You can use a home mixer to make any of the breads in this book. Timing varies with bowl size, hook revolutions per minute (rpm), and size and shape of the hook. Remember what you have learned about dough development from hand mixing and try to achieve those same characteristics. I always add liquids to a bowl first—this helps prevent flour from sticking to the bottom of the mixing bowl. Incorporation of the ingredients will take about 2 to 3 minutes on low speed, depending on the capacity of the mixer. A bowl with plenty of room incorporates the ingredients more easily and quickly than a mixer that is full to the brim. Stop the mixer several times and scrape the bowl to make sure no dry flour is stuck to the bottom or sides.

Increase the speed to medium. Unfortunately, there is no standard medium speed, but it's a little less than halfway on most types of home-sized stand mixers, about 4 or 5 on a KitchenAid. (If your wood-fired oven is large enough to make more than 12 loaves of bread, you may want to shop around for a 20-quart Hobart mixer. It won't be inexpensive, but it will be reliable—even an old one—and you will find it very useful if you make bread for friends and family, or make enough pizza dough for the parties your neighbors will start asking you to host!) Be sure to use a spiral-shaped hook attachment as opposed to the C-shaped—the spiral version makes a nicer dough.

You will likely have to stop the mixer occasionally and scrape the dough that the hook pulls up. It's important to do this, because dough spinning around on the socket end of the hook isn't being worked; it's just going for a merry-go-round ride. Get it back into the mix so the dough is evenly developed. Remember, the amount of mixing is tied to proper dough development, not a certain length of time. In a stand mixer, it will likely be 2 to 3 minutes, perhaps a little less if the autolyse was particularly effective. The surface of the dough will be slightly smooth and shiny. It may still be sticky but should offer some resistance if you give the dough a light tug.

One of the important things to remember with using a mixer is that the shape and rpms of the dough hook will greatly affect the amount of time the dough has to be mixed. *Mixing times are guidelines, not cardinal rules.* Getting a feel for properly mixed dough is important, and it's something that comes with practice. Use the instructions as a framework, but use your own experience and intuition to determine whether a dough is sufficiently mixed. Use all your senses when you mix. *Look* to see if all the ingredients have been incorporated. *Taste* for salt. *Smell* the aromas of fermentation—are they more distinct because of the salt? *Listen* to the way the dough slaps against the bench or side of the bowl once it gains some strength—is it the crisp sound of something smooth hitting a flat surface? *Feel* the dough and tug on it gently. If it rips easily, it needs more development, but if there is some resistance—if the dough tugs back—then you have built in enough strength. Passing these sensory tests indicates that the dough is sufficiently mixed.

This diving arm mixer, at Elmore Mountain Bread, is an efficient and gentle way to mix hearth bread dough.

Stand or Planetary Mixers

Stand or planetary mixers are not ideal for mixing bread dough, but they can be used, especially if you allow your dough to mature with fermentation and folding. The most efficient and gentle way to mix a nice dough is with a commercial spiral mixer or a diving arm mixer, but both are expensive. A home-sized spiral mixer is available through TMB Baking, but I'm not aware of any home-sized diving arm mixer. Planetary mixers such as commercial Hobarts are larger versions of the home-sized versions made by KitchenAid, Bosch, or Viking.

What I've described so far is the mixing technique for wheat-based hearth breads that are lean (they contain little or no fat or sugar). Rye breads and dough with enrichments like butter will require a longer mix time because rye flour has less gluten, and because fat molecules lubricate gluten strands, making it more difficult to organize them into a strong, three-dimensional matrix. In the recipe section (part three), special mixing considerations are addressed in the appropriate formulas.

Primary Fermentation, the First Rise

Once the dough is mixed you can transfer it to a container to ferment; it's also fine to leave it in the bowl in which you mixed it. Before you cover it and allow it to ferment, be sure to take the temperature of the dough and adjust its environment accordingly.

The skin on the breast of your newly born dough will dry out very quickly. I like to ferment dough in containers or tubs that have tight-fitting seals and that are large enough to accommodate the increase in volume that occurs as dough swells with carbon dioxide. Placing an upside-down bowl on top of the bowl in which you mixed is a good way to prevent a skin from forming on the dough, and it eliminates the need for a piece of plastic. If you do use plastic wrap, make sure it clings securely to the rim of the bowl. Plastic wrap can stick badly if you let it come in contact with the surface of your dough.

Containers with lids or bus tubs available at restaurant supply stores are convenient for holding dough. When you shop for tubs, look for those that are completely smooth on the bottom. Many bus tubs have channels that make it hard to scrape the tubs dry at the end of the day. I don't oil or spray the inside of the bus tubs for two reasons: First, oil gums up the inside of the tub, which will then require several good washings before it's clean. Second, pan spray is an energy-intensive product I would rather not use. When the tubs are not oiled, dough remnants and dusting flour are easy to remove by a dry scraping followed by a quick wash in hot soapy water.

Now your bread is fermenting. Bid it farewell until you return for the next step. As you go about other business, the yeast comes to life and fermentation commences in earnest. Flavor evolves; dough strength increases. We'll talk about what is happening during this step in chapter 7, but for now be aware that the dynamic change in the strength and fluffiness of dough at the proper temperature during primary fermentation is an amazing process to observe. The accumulation of organic acids strengthens the dough by swelling proteins in the gluten strands, and the carbon dioxide released during this process forms bubble-like spaces (alveoli) within the extensible, yet firm, gluten matrix. As long as the food supply and temperature support fermentation, the dough will continue to develop, transforming itself from a mass of freshly mixed dough to a supple cloud, full of complex aroma and flavor. The dough feels alive (and it is, at least in the sense that it's an ecosystem with both living and non-living components) and it responds to environmental changes (like temperature) and to stimuli (like folding).

The majority of flavor and dough strength happens during primary fermentation (as opposed to the secondary fermentation or final rise). This is partly because bulk dough ferments more effectively than smaller pieces of dough. The larger mass of dough, having more thermal inertia, responds more slowly to changes in ambient temperature. It also benefits from enhanced fermentation activity initiated by the folding process.

Folding

Folding is a simple series of movements that help your dough have active fermentation, by redistributing oxygen and stimulating the enzymes and yeast to continue their work. The process also helps the dough develop by de-gassing accumulated carbon dioxide and elongating and organizing the gluten strands. Some people fold the dough right in the tub, but I prefer to do it on a lightly floured surface.

Lionel Vatinet taught me to "Work *with* the flour, not *in* the flour." You will become a better bread baker when you learn how to spray a thin layer of flour onto your work surface. The ideal flour cover will be even and of sufficient surface area. Wet dough, especially, will flow when it's turned out of the tub. If it runs into an unfloured stretch of bench, it's likely to stick. Once the dough sticks, things go rapidly downhill. On the other hand, excessive flour on the bench will become incorporated into the dough, leaving visible ribbons of raw flour in baked loaves. More important, too much flour makes it difficult, if not impossible, to seal the seam on the final loaf, resulting in loose shapes and insufficient volume in the final loaf. Work with the flour, not in the flour!

Getting a perfectly even layer of flour, that in some cases might need to be only one flour particle thick, is easy to learn. Keep in mind that this is a spraying action, not a sprinkling (which would result in uneven distribution). Grab a light handful of flour and hold it in your fingers, not the palm of your hand. Contain the flour with your thumb and hand but leave some space between your fingers. Move that arm through space horizontally over the work surface and then stop

A light dusting of flour keeps dough from sticking to the work surface.
PHOTO BY KATE KELLEY

it suddenly. (Think about zipping a fast Frisbee or snapping a wet towel; that's the wrist action you want to use.) The forward momentum of the flour causes it to fly through the space between your fingers, disperse through the air, and settle onto the work surface. Suspending a cloud of flour in the air is beautiful, especially when each flour mote is illuminated by beautiful morning light. However, I hold my breath while I do this to avoid inhaling flour particles into my lungs.

I prefer to use a plastic dough scraper when releasing dough from a container in order to execute the folding sequence. A metal cutter may scrape curls of plastic off dough tubs and simply won't follow the contours of a round proofing container. The folding sequence is illustrated on the following page and described in the photo captions.

This dough is ready to be folded. Before it is turned out of the bowl, apply a light covering of flour to the work surface and to the top surface of the dough.

Release the dough by sliding the plastic dough scraper around the inside of the bowl. Flip the container over and allow the dough to drop to the lightly floured surface. A bit of coaxing may be necessary.

Stretch the dough into a larger rectangle. The actual folding is usually four moves. Fold the left side toward the right, covering about one-third of the dough, and then make the same move from right to left.

Now fold the bottom toward the top, covering about one-third of the dough.

Finally, fold the bottom toward yourself. These four moves constitute one fold.

Return the dough back to the container with the fold seams underneath. Cover and continue ferment.

This is dough handling. Use gentle but firm motion and only the force necessary to accomplish the fold. Think of the way a mother deftly picks up her child and swings him onto her hip, or the way a hockey player slick in the crease flips the puck past the goalie's shoulder into the net. All it takes is practice and confidence. Confidence comes through practice, so the more you bake the better you get.

Handling wet dough can be challenging, but the development of the dough over the course of three or more folds will make it stronger and easier to handle. The first fold will need a heavier dusting of flour, but use less and less for subsequent folds. As the dough develops, even a thin wisp of added flour completely covering the bench can be enough to ensure the dough won't stick.

A fold is a great way to increase the strength of your dough. Some dough receives only one fold, while extremely wet dough might need a fold every half hour or so. Each formula in this book calls for a specific number of folds, but you can increase or decrease the recommended number if your dough seems to need a different treatment. You will know that the primary fermentation period is over when the dough is fluffy yet strong, with a nice balance of extensibility and elasticity.

Dividing

Once the primary fermentation is over, it's time to divide the dough into individual loaves. It's important that all pieces are the same size so that they will bake at the same rate and conform to labeling requirements should you be selling your bread. Get the dough out of the container and onto the bench in the manner

Divide dough into individual pieces . . . PHOTO BY MELISSA RIVARD AND ANDREW JANJIGIAN

described under *Folding*. Remember, work with the flour, not in the flour.

The large surface area of the dough facing up (toward you, that is) will be sticky, but you can easily remedy that by giving it another light puff of flour. Remember, you want just enough flour coverage to create a surface that isn't sticky, not a thick layer. Too much flour will prevent you from gaining the required friction on the bench for preshaping and shaping the divided pieces. Focus on cutting pieces of dough that have a regular shape, have a nice skin, and aren't torn or frayed. One way to help achieve this is by patting out the dough to about 2″ thick. Reach your hand completely under the dough and gently pull it out. De-gas and flatten the dough while holding your hand as if you were making a handprint in wet cement. Avoid poking dimples into the dough. If the dough is too thick when you cut it into pieces, you will expose a large amount of sticky

dough as you cut into the interior. That sticky surface area, which will likely stick to *something* (bench, hand, scraper, your other hand), is not the smooth, non-stick skin you want during the dividing process.

Cut decisively with your metal scraper. This is a guillotine-like move—a swift cut with each fall of the blade. It is not a horizontal sawing motion, which tears the dough. Pull the pieces away from the rest of the dough so that they don't fuse back together. Weigh each piece. Ideally, you'll be within 10g of the target weight. You can cut off some dough if it's too heavy, or add a little nugget to bring the piece up to the proper scale weight. To reduce wear on the scale, move the dough to the bench before you cut off more. Cutting on the scale platform wears heavily on the scale's mechanism and accuracy—especially in the case of an electronic scale. Treat your scale as if it were a delicate instrument, because it is!

. . . with decisive cuts of your metal scraper. PHOTO BY MELISSA RIVARD AND ANDREW JANJIGIAN

Scaling Is Big Fun

For 680g (1.5-pound) loaves, accept anything between 670g and 690g. Scaling is really fun, trying to get each piece of dough right on the mark each time. What a thrill when that happens. Five hundred grams. Not 499. Not 501. Five hundred. On rare occasions you score a hat trick, three perfect weights in a row.

At this point you should follow a FIFO (First In, First Out) approach to usher the dough through the rest of the process. The first piece of dough that is divided should be the first piece of dough that is preshaped, the first that is shaped, and the first into the oven. This way, each piece of dough experiences the same amount of rest or proof time between steps. It minimizes variations between dough pieces and makes a more consistent product. Moreover, it's a systematic way to approach the process of handling high volumes of handmade bread.

Preshaping

After all the pieces have been divided, whether two or 200, you need to start leading the dough toward the final shape. First comes an intermediate step called preshaping. Again use your hands assertively but gently. I use the same preshape for both boules and bâtards, working around the edge of each piece, pulling the perimeter to the center, and pressing it there with the flat of my hand. Preshaping also helps establish a taut skin

Preshaping pieces of dough. The piece of dough at upper left is unshaped; the piece at lower left is already shaped. PHOTO BY MELISSA RIVARD AND ANDREW JANJIGIAN

to the dough, an attribute that will help greatly once you execute the final shape.

Not all breads require a preshape. With heavy rye breads, for example, the preshape is sometimes skipped because the consistency of the dough is firm. Rustic shaped breads like Pain Rustique do not require a preshape because they are distinguished by their rough shape—the divided piece is simply placed on a well-floured couche (a piece of baker's linen).

After preshaping, pull an air-impermeable cover over the dough. I often use a couche that's also covered by a large piece of plastic to keep out drafts. A bakery speed rack with an airtight cover is very useful for holding a lot of dough without using all your bench space. Keep the boards as high up on the rack as possible. Dough near the bottom tends to dry out more because of drafts coming up under the rack cover. You need to bench-rest the dough for about 20 minutes between preshaping and shaping because each time the dough is worked, the gluten firms up. Time is all it takes to get back to a relaxed dough.

Relax

Dough tightens anytime it's handled—especially when it's folded, preshaped, or shaped. The dough feels more firm and bouncy. Less slack and more elastic. Once the dough sits undisturbed for about 20 minutes, it slackens and becomes more extensible as the tension dissipates. The dough may spread somewhat and become *relaxed*. What's happening here?

I asked Andrew Ross this. He shared the podium with Lee Glass at WheatStalk: Three Days of Baking and Learning, the Bread Bakers Guild of America conference held at Kendall College in Chicago in July 2012. Andrew is an associate professor of crop and food science at Oregon State University. Here's what he said about dough relaxation:

Dough relaxes because of structural changes in the gluten at the molecular level. Glutenin strings are entangled and stressed and gradually disentangle. As this is happening disulfide bonds break and re-form

in less stressed configurations, and the gliadins, which are globular (roughly spherical) in structure, add some slip to the overall gluten structure, allowing things to slide past each other. All these pieces added together allow greater mobility in the dough structure, and we perceive this in part as increased extensibility.

Later over lunch, Thom Leonard, one of the great-uncles of the American Bread Movement, and I discussed the same concept. Here is the way Thom explained it to me and how he describes it in *The Bread Book: A Natural, Whole-Grain Seed-to-Loaf Approach to Real Bread,* his early and important contribution to the wood-fired baking canon:

Gluten, the primary protein in wheat, responds to certain elements in much the same way as do our muscles, the primary proteins in the body. Take a plunge in an icy mountain stream and your body tightens. Soak in a hot spring and it unwinds. Work your muscles hard, without stopping to relax, and you'll increase your chances of pulling one. Cold water tightens gluten and slows fermentation. Overworked dough will tighten and not be able to relax and rise fully. And unless it is allowed to rest between each working or kneading, dough will tear instead of stretch.

Shaping

Properly shaped loaves are uniform, perky, and smooth. Repetition and practice are the keys to shaping pieces of dough into symmetrical loaves with skins taut enough to contain accumulated carbon dioxide, but extensible enough to stretch during the final rise or "proof," imparting good volume to the baked loaf. Experienced bakers make shaping look easier than it is; inexperienced bakers make it look harder. One way to approach shaping is what James MacGuire calls "an iron hand in a velvet glove." You have to make it do what you want it to do, but in a gentle way, like raising a child or training a puppy. The best way to improve your shaping skills is through practice and repetition.

Start to shape a boule in the same way you preshaped the dough right after it was divided.

Roll the dough over so the seam is on the bottom and drag it across the work surface at about 15-degree angle so the surface of the dough tightens against the friction.

Encourage the dough into the seam of the loaf with the tips of your fingers. PHOTO BY KATE KELLEY

Turn the loaf so the seam is toward the side.

Push the dough away . . .

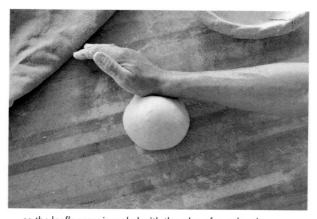

. . . so the loaf's seam is sealed with the edge of your hand.

To begin to shape a bâtard, fold in the sides of a preshaped round into the center, creating a shape like a bike seat.

Bring the point of the seat into the center of the round, turn the whole loaf 180 degrees and repeat.

Lightly press the entire loaf together into a packet.

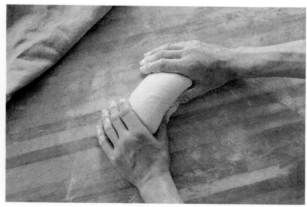

Roll the loaf over. Place thumbs and base of the hand along the seam and push away, using the friction of the board to tighten the loaf.

Push on the seam with the thumb of one hand while sealing the final seam of the loaf with the heel of the other hand.

The seam sealing movement helps to tighten the loaf, creating more surface tension.

Once the loaf is shaped it needs to be held for the final proof in a well-floured proofing basket, on a couche, or even on an appropriately floured board. I use a sifter so I can get an even and light layer of white flour in the basket. Too much flour will be dry in the mouth. I prefer to place the shaped loaf upside down so the flour is pressed into the top surface of the loaf. I use white flour to give maximum contrast between the grigne (the cut part of the loaf that is exposed when the dough's surface is scored just before loading) and the white floured surface.

Couche is coarse linen material made from flax stems—it's the same textile as what you'll find in linen clothes, just with a lower thread count, and it comes in running lengths that exactly fit a proofing board. It allows you to proof more bread on a board, due to the folds that separate loaves from each other. The material also wicks water away from the surface of the dough, making it a bit more leathery and easier to score. The basket can be a German coiled wicker brotform or the French-style banneton, a wicker basket with a couche liner sewed into it. Couches and bannetons both prevent loaves from spreading during the final proof.

Professional couches and baskets are the best; if you want to augment your bread-baking tools with something pleasurable to use, work some of these into your collection. You can also fashion materials in a pinch. A tea towel is a good stand-in for a couche, or you can use it to line a bowl and use that as a proofing basket.

As always, cover the dough so it doesn't develop a skin during proofing.

Use only as much flour as is necessary to prevent shaped loaves from sticking to the basket or couche during the final proof.

Proofing, the Final Rise

Fermentation continues after the dough is shaped. Carbon dioxide is generated by the yeast and trapped by the gluten matrix, swelling the loaf. Once again the dough becomes fluffy and increases in volume as it rises in the last stage before it gets baked.

Here's what I look for in a properly proofed loaf. The volume should be about two-thirds larger than when the loaf was shaped. Then there is the classic push test: If an impression of your finger springs back quickly, the dough needs to proof more. If the impression stays and the dough seems to deflate, the dough is over-proofed and should be hustled into the oven as soon as possible. A properly proofed loaf will spring back slowly—after about 5 to 15 seconds, depending on the dough. The best section of the loaf to test for proofiness is dough that has been protected from drafts and the resulting dry skin. The side of the loaf protected by the couche or basket, for example, is a good place to feel the dough. The presence of subsurface carbon dioxide bubbles is evidence of a properly proofed loaf, but be aware that this evidence is more visible in doughs made with white flour than in those made with whole-grain flour.

Be patient. There's a tendency among new bakers to underproof loaves that come from the European tradition of long, cool fermentation. If you're proofing naturally leavened dough and are unsure whether it's ready for baking, you probably need to wait longer. I learned this patience from Dave Krishock, now a grain

Bread beginning to proof in a linen-lined banneton

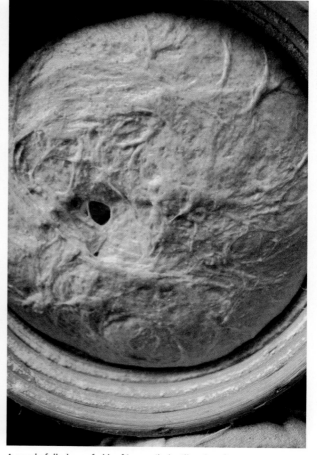

A nearly fulled proofed loaf in a coiled-willow brotform

science instructor at Kansas State University, who was already working at the King Arthur Bakery when I arrived there. There were some other pastry bakers there, along with Jeffrey Hamelman who went back and forth between the two ends of the bakery, but most of the time down in Breadtown it was just Dave and me. We'd confer about whether we should load. "Give it another 10 minutes" was his usual response, and I learned how taking the proof to the max—but not beyond—was the way to achieve the most volume and an open crumb. Proof times in this book's recipes describe proofing under ideal conditions. Environmental conditions—is it especially humid or dry in the room?—and dough temperatures, *especially* dough temperatures, will greatly affect the proof time.

The Baker's Strength

The baker's strength flows from the Force. Here, when you are determining if the loaf is properly proofed, is another time to use the Force, much like when you were determining whether the dough was properly mixed. There is a quivering energy you need to sense and recognize in order to nail the moment when the loaves are ready to be scored and baked. Be mindful and follow your gut.

If your baked loaves bulge through the score mark and seem heavy for their size, they were probably underproofed. In successive baking sessions, keep extending the proof time to determine the maximum proof boundary. Your loaves are overproofed if they collapse when you score them, have insipid oven spring, and bake out with a pale, thick crust. These undesirable characteristics of overproofing can be eliminated by reducing any or all of the following: the yeast ratio, the water temperature, or the primary or secondary fermentation time. Simple and complex.

When to Load the Oven

Once the fire has been removed from the oven, the temperature starts to fall. You want hot masonry that

holds enough heat to provide good oven spring so the loaves will get a good rise, but not so hot that the bottom of a loaf scorches during the bake cycle. In addition to an infrared surface temperature reading (see *Temperature Monitoring* in chapter 5 for a discussion of reading and monitoring oven temperatures), a reliable test for when the oven is ready to load is tossing some flour on the hearth. If the flour browns nicely after about 13 seconds and gives off a lovely toasty smell, the oven is ready. The oven is too hot if the flour bursts into flames or instantly starts smoldering. To cool the oven more quickly leave the door off; if you think the bread may still need some time to proof, however, keep the oven closed. *Having the dough ready to bake at the same time the oven is at the right temperature for baking is one of the challenges of baking bread in a wood-fired oven.*

What's the best temperature to load bread in a wood-fired oven? That question gets asked all the time. There is a range of temperatures that are appropriate, but other aspects of the oven (including mass, insulation, and thoroughness of heat saturation) will help determine the best temperature for the dough when it hits the deck. The temperatures I refer to in the formulas and recipes are surface temperatures. Thermocouple temperatures can also be compared from oven to oven, but their depth in the masonry would have to be the same to ensure the accuracy of the comparison.

Here are some more factors that influence loading temperatures.

THE PRODUCT

Some things just want to get baked at a higher temperature. To expand into a pocket, pita bread needs a heat high enough to scorch even a baguette. But a baguette can go in at a higher temperature than a 680g boule. And so it continues down the line from bread type to bread type. One of the goals of this book is to teach you how you can use all of your wood-fired oven's heat, from firing to the long, slow tail-off of a falling oven. The recipes in part three are arranged in this order, and the methodologies note different loading temperatures.

THE AMOUNT OF THERMAL MASS

An oven with more mass will maintain its loading temperature for longer than one with less mass. The temperature of the lighter oven will drop more quickly than that of a heavier oven, and it won't have as much stored energy to rebound. So a loaf loaded in a lighter oven (or one with less insulation) bakes at a temperature that descends more quickly compared with the heavier (or more insulated) oven, which bakes at a more sustained temperature. And it's not just how massive the oven is that affects loading time; it's also how thoroughly the mass is heated. A massive oven that is still conducting heat to the outer masonry couldn't support as sustained a heat as a massive oven that's thoroughly heated.

COLOR

Your personal aesthetic in how much color you like to bake into your loaves will help you decide the best loading temperature in your wood-fired oven. If you like a lighter color and a softer crumb, you can load at a higher temperature and bake for a shorter time than if you bake at a lower temperature for a longer time.

Stencils should be applied immediately before baking. CHELSEA GREEN LOGO STENCIL BY KAYLA KOEHN AND ASHLEY REY

For years I have loaded 680g Pain au Levain between 450°F and 475°F (232–246°C) and baked it for about 50 minutes, and I would consider it underbaked if the crust softened *at all* after it cooled. Often I would finish baking the loaves by taking off the door and letting the loaves dry out a bit more but not give any more color to the well-caramelized crusts. This is a great way to make tasty bread, but the downside of this long bake is that more water is evaporated from the dough, creating a loaf that's more dried out than one baked at a higher temperature for a shorter time. I'm not encouraging you to underbake your loaves. A doughy crumb is just not pleasant to eat, and a caramelized crust is crucial for a well-flavored crumb. See *Cooling* later in this chapter for more information about how flavor is related to a well-baked crust.

Transferring the Loaves

Using a peel is one of the best parts of baking in a wood-fired oven. This tool is an extension of your arms and hands. It will quickly become familiar, and you'll confidently and deftly load and unload loaves in and out of the oven.

Load the loaves in when the dough is at its most delicate state . . . full of, but not yet ruptured from, accumulated carbon dioxide. The gluten strands are extended to their maximum and still maintain structural integrity. This is proofiness. Use a gentle and soft hand when you transfer the loaves to the peel.

Apply a light layer of flour to cover the peel. I use white flour to prevent loaves from sticking. However, semolina and rice flours work well—their coarse grain size makes them act like ball bearings, and loaves properly transferred to the peel will easily slip from peel to hearth. Cornmeal is also "slippery," but its oils make it burn more acridly than semolina or rice flours. You may also need to apply a light layer of flour to the bottoms of the loaves themselves. If they're shiny, they're sticky. If the risen loaves are in baskets, check to make sure the dough isn't sticking to the baskets. Use the side of your hand to pull the dough back from the side to see.

Invert the baskets and lightly tap them onto the floured peel. They may need a little coaxing. If so . . . next time just use a bit more flour in the basket and/or strive for a tighter final shape. If you're transferring a loaf from a couche, use the material as a kind of handle that flips the dough onto a transfer peel or just your hand spread wide.

Be mindful of the loaf's seam. It should be down on the peel so that it will be down on the hearth once it's slid into the oven.

If it seems the dough has absorbed much of the flour, it's okay to apply a bit more with the palm of your hand. If there's too much, palm that off, too, so you don't have a thick layer of dry flour on the crust of the baked loaf. If you are transferring several loaves, give the first ones down a jiggle every now and again to make sure they don't adhere to the peel. Once all the loaves are sitting on the peel, it's time to score.

Scoring the Loaves

Scoring is generally done just before loaves are loaded into the oven. The score marks allow the loaf to open at a predictable place when expansion starts due to oven spring. If a loaf isn't scored, it might open randomly at the weakest spot or not at all, yielding a dense crumb and a twisted appearance in either case. I prefer to use a traditional French *lame* (rhymes with "mom") with a changeable blade for scoring loaves. (Avoid *lames* that have a blade fixed to the handle; these are single-use tools. Once the blade is dull—and it won't take long—all you can do is throw the *lame* away. A changeable-blade *lame* is a tool you can have the rest of your life.) It's a simple tool that allows more dexterity and agility when making cuts. Some *lame* handles are bent, which curves the razor, allowing the baker to easily make an undercut when scoring the loaf. This flap of dough will lift up and create a deeply caramelized ridge of crust. A straight *lame* is good for making cuts that are perpendicular to the surface of the dough. Use only the tip of the blade to prevent the back edge of the blade (which doesn't have a sharp cutting edge) from bulldozing and snagging the surface of the dough.

Determine your score mark in advance and make quick, confident moves. Even a brand-new blade will drag and snag the dough's surface if you use it in a slow and hesitant manner. Ideally, the motion is continuous, with the moving blade cutting neatly through the dough and continuing on its trajectory—follow-through is important for making confident cuts. If multiple loaves

A *lame* handle with a removable blade is the best tool for scoring bread. PHOTO BY JONATHANBELLER.COM

are being scored and loaded, make all the parallel cuts on all the loaves and then go back to finish the pattern. This will save time because you won't have to reposition your arm for each segment of the score mark.

An important adjustment to consider in scoring is the angle of the blade in relation to the surface of the dough. Undercutting the surface of the dough will allow the flap of skin to rise up during the oven spring period, creating an "ear" or ridge of dough. Making a cut with the blade perpendicular to the surface forces the parts of the dough on either side of the cut to migrate away during oven spring.

Finally, the depth of the cut depends on the hydration of the dough and how proofed the loaf is. Very wet dough, like Ciabatta, is not scored because this bread has little surface tension; cutting it would reduce surface tension even more, leading to a loaf that would spread too much. A drier dough needs a deep and decisive cut. If you realize while loading that the dough is still a bit young (slightly underproofed), make the score marks a bit deeper to give some release to the excess force that will be released during oven spring. If the dough seems slightly overproofed or delicate, make the cut a bit shallower.

Simple score marks that cover the entire surface of the bread are easiest to execute and allow the loaf to expand in all directions. Complex cuts with lots of curves are difficult to execute; often the detail is lost in the oven spring.

The Effects of Steam and How to Steam a Masonry Oven

Steaming the oven is the other part of the loading process that makes the difference between good bread and really beautiful loaves. Steam in the oven chamber during the loading process and in the first 10 to 15 minutes after loading creates loaves with more volume, allows the cuts to open, and creates well-caramelized crusts. Heat transfer is greater in a humid environment. Therefore,

a steamed oven will more quickly bring up the surface temperature of just-loaded dough, gelatinizing starches as fuel for the important—but fleeting—Maillard and caramelization processes.

Here is a rundown of the baking phases that take place when loaves are placed in a properly heated and steamed oven. These phases are not strictly successive; they may overlap one another.

- The loaf swells rapidly during oven spring.
- Steam condenses on the surface of the loaf, delaying the formation of the crust. This supple outer layer allows for greater oven spring.
- Proteins coagulate at 140°F to 160°F (60–71°C), giving a more rigid structure to the loaf. By this time oven spring has ended.
- Starches also contribute to structure when starch granules absorb water and swell. This process, gelatinization, begins at about 105°F (41°C) and is mostly complete at 200°F (93°C).
- Alcohol and water evaporate. Dough can lose approximately 20 percent of its scaled weight during the baking process due to evaporation. Water loss depends on dough hydration as well as exposed surface area.
- When surface temperature exceeds 212°F (100°C), the boiling point of water, the crust begins to develop and gain color. At this temperature, residual sugars (those that remain in the crust after fermentation) begin to caramelize and the Maillard reaction takes place. Caramelization and Maillard browning are separate processes: Caramelization occurs when sugars break down, producing flavor molecules and the caramel color; Maillard browning occurs when sugars react with amino acids and form bonds with the proteins, producing complex flavor as well as darker crust color. Caramelization and the Maillard reaction contribute significantly to the pleasant taste of well-baked bread. If residual sugar, adequate steam, or sufficient heat is absent, these processes will not occur and the baked loaf will be dull, pale, and lacking in flavor.

To summarize, steam affects yeast-raised doughs by:

- Providing a humid environment that allows the crust to stay supple so it can expand to its greatest volume during oven spring. Dough placed in a dry oven quickly develops a skin that keeps the loaf from full expansion.
- Promoting a shiny crust by enhancing caramelization and the Maillard reaction.
- Allowing cuts to open dramatically and form distinct "ears."

To create and maintain a full head of steam in a wood-fired oven, several methods can be used. As described previously, I use all of the following tools and methods:

- Pans of water heated and steaming before loading begins, which may be removed at the last minute if hearth space is needed.
- A pressurized garden sprayer that injects mist into the oven before and between unloading each peel.
- Working quickly and closing the door between loads when scoring raw loaves.
- Several peels so that each time I open the door I can place more than one loaf on the hearth.
- A wet towel for sealing the door. I hang it on the inside of the door to introduce more water and hence more steam. Perhaps more important, however, once the loading is finished, fold the wet towel over the door back to the outside in order to create a seal that prevents the steam from escaping. Be careful when you open the door: Steam may come rushing out.

Once some color appears on the loaf, no more steam is necessary. In fact, baking with too much steam for too long into the process will create a crust that is too thick.

Completely Baked

Knowing when to take bread out of the oven is easier to learn than determining when to put it in. Before the American Bread Movement, most bread we ate was underbaked. This is why those of us who were alive in the 1970s remember rolling dough up into a slightly gray ball, doughy enough to take the impression of a fingerprint. The North American interest in European-style hearth loaves provided unbridled liberation to bake things to an über-caramelized point and beyond. A bold bake. I've been to the dark side, and believe me, I like the primal candy crust made when fermented grain is subjected to the pyro-epic experience of retained masonry heat baking. The bread is evocative. The flavor is complex. The crust is thick. Teething toddlers are drawn to this bread. The memory of a loaf like this is the Platonic perfect loaf.

However, I do appreciate the extended shelf life afforded a loaf pulled from the oven before it is baked to within an inch of its life. Don't get me wrong. I like it dark, but sometimes a bit of a lighter bake means some water is retained in the loaf, providing softness two or three days after the bake. You'll develop your own aesthetic to determine when bread is done.

Here are cues I look for when determining if the time has come to peel the loaves out of the oven and into the world. First, has the loaf been baking for the length of time noted in the formula? Even the lightest 680g (1.5-pound) boule will be underbaked if it is baked for only 18 minutes and the formula calls for 40 to 45. (If there is too much crust color at 18 minutes, it's because the oven was too hot when the bread was loaded. If you're breaking open papier-mâché-like burnt crusts to find a semi-molten core of dough, you are loading at too high a temperature and baking for too short a time.)

In addition to a realistic amount of baking time, I consider color, weight, and sound when I'm deciding whether the bread is ready to take out of the oven. Color—especially deep inside the grigne—is your portal into the loaf's subcutaneous layers. I want the dough at the bottom of that crevasse to have taken on some color—no lighter than the color of cornflakes; it shouldn't be completely pale or still look damp. Loaves sometimes achieve enough crust color even though the center of the bread is still underbaked. Such a loaf softens as it cools, because water remaining in the center migrates throughout the bread (much the way heat migrates through thermal mass) until it's evenly distributed.

Simulating a Wood-Fired Oven at Home with a Combo Cooker

The best way to get good results baking in a home oven is by using a cast-iron combo cooker. A combo cooker provides thermal mass, and its tight-fitting lid retains steam. There are other ways to bake in a home oven, but they are either dangerous (pouring boiling water in a heated container); ineffective (throwing ice into the oven); or in vain (a gas oven is vented by design; any steam in the oven environment escapes). To use a combo cooker, heat it as you preheat your oven. When the dough is ready to bake, turn it out carefully into the shallower part of the cooker, trying to keep it centered. Score and quickly replace the top. Place the combo cooker in the heated oven and close the door. In approximately 15 minutes, *carefully* remove the cover, opening it away from you so the accumulated steam does not burn your hand. Leave off the lid in order to give some color to the crust, and return the cooker to the oven. Once the loaf acquires enough structural integrity, you may want to remove it from the cast iron and finish baking on the wire rack or inverted sheet pan—the conductive properties of the cast iron may scorch the bottom of the loaf.

You can use a combo cooker in a wood-fired oven, especially if your oven is larger than the amount of bread you're making, because you won't need to steam the oven.

Any cover over your bread that traps steam will work. I've used a paper-lined sheet pan with an inverted stainless-steel bowl. Rectangular containers, such as a simple aluminum roasting pan on a sheet pan, will give you the spatial freedom to bake bâtards. The parchment paper helps makes a tighter seal and, because it can be easily slid around, allows the loaf to be repositioned on the pan if it doesn't land right where you want it to. A cloche or a flower pot with the drainage hole blocked also works well.

A combo cooker provides thermal mass and retains heat. It is the best way to bake bread in a home oven. It is also handy in a wood-fired oven if you aren't baking enough bread to fill the entire bake chamber.

Curing Rye Breads

Some rye breads need 24 hours or so until they're ready to eat, as opposed to just a few hours. Increased hydration and the higher pentosan ratio in rye breads (pentosan is a particularly water-absorbent carbohydrate) demands this additional period.

A well-baked loaf will feel lighter than it looks like it should, and this especially applies to dough made from highly hydrated, low-extraction flour.

And there is always the thump hollow test. A well-baked loaf will sound hollow when it is thumped on the bottom.

I rarely take the internal temperature of a baked loaf; it seems unnecessarily invasive to push a thermometer into the fragile, freshly baked crumb. Okay, okay, okay, I've done it more than a few times to confirm for this book that a well-baked loaf is about 200°F (93°C), more or less, depending on size and shape.

Cooling

It's hard to get people to not eat bread still warm from the oven. A natural instinct draws us to eat warm bread—it makes us feel good. I can't bring myself to insist that people not do things that make them feel good. However, there are benefits to thoroughly cooling bread before breaking into it, beyond the fact that "carry-over" cooking caused by the heat held within the body of the loaf means it still continues to cook after it is removed from the oven.

The gelatinized structure of the crumb continues to set as the loaf cools. The crumb will be gummy if it's opened before completely cool. The crumb smears

across the knife, and the alveoli are torn. It is also physiologically more difficult for the human tongue to taste flavors when they're still hot as opposed to at room temperature. This is why cheese should be served at room temperature. Some would also make the assertion that bread is more digestible when cool. But to me, one of the most interesting effects of proper cooling on flavor is what I call flavor osmosis. As a loaf cools, the crumb contracts, creating a pressure differential that pulls outside air through the crust, infusing the crumb with flavor from the crust. In other words, as a well-colored loaf pulled from the oven cools, pressure decreases inside the crumb. The pressure differential is equalized by air outside the loaf being pulled in, and as the air is sucked into the crumb it is filtered through a (hopefully) well-caramelized crust. As it passes through the crust, the air is infused with the complexity of caramel and Maillard, depositing in the absorbent crumb. I have to say, though, that I follow an all-things-in-moderation diet, and if I break (warm) wheaten bread at the end of an all-day class, then I gain the opportunity to participate in an important social custom. *Compagnon* means roughly "with bread," and I'd rather not miss the opportunity to share bread with a group of people I have been baking with all weekend simply because the bread isn't yet at its peak flavor and texture. If you do indulge in warm bread, tear it instead of slicing it.

Freezing Bread

Bread freezes well, especially if you follow this protocol: Freeze a loaf as soon as possible after it's thoroughly cool. Wrap it well or place it in a double freezer bag. Freeze. Let it thaw still wrapped so any water that escapes the loaf and forms ice crystals inside the plastic will melt and get resorbed by the loaf. It will be fine to use as soon as it's thawed, but you can freshen the taste and texture if you pop the whole loaf in a 350°F (177°C) oven for 5 minutes or toast individual slices.

CHAPTER SEVEN

→→•←←

Essential Ingredients for Wood-Fired Breads

Yeast is the ingredient that exemplifies bread baking. Flour, water (or another ingredient that contains water), and salt are present in almost every baked good. But yeast provides fermentation, the process that has made bread a food standard for eons. Fermentation is the process you need to control in order to make good bread. All other ingredients, as well as variables such as time and temperature, affect fermentation. That's why this discussion of the ingredients of bread baking begins with a consideration of the alchemy created by this single-celled fungus, yeast.

I have never met anybody who didn't like bread—the satisfaction of making it, its comforting smell as it bakes, the sense of community while breaking it. These are the gifts of yeast. It's easy to be romantic about human history, tactile pleasure, and all the sensuality bread provides, but yeast is simply a living single-celled fungus doing its work. It is our charge to understand its biological requirements and create the best environment for it to flourish.

Upon Which Life Depends

Enzyme (énzaim) n. one of a large class of complex proteinaceous substances of a high molecular weight formed in and produced by living matter which are responsible for promoting the chemical reactions upon which life depends (e.g. digestion, respiration, reproduction.) . . . [fr G. enzym fr. Mod. Gk enzumos, leavened]

The New Lexicon Webster's Dictionary of the English Language, 1987

Yeast-raised and naturally leavened doughs need the same things we need to be healthy: water, high-quality food, oxygen, proper temperature, appropriate salinity, loving attention, and enzymatic activity.

In bread baking, the food comes in the form of grain and flour. Yeast cannot metabolize these starches until a biological posse of enzymes present within it, including alpha-amylase, beta-amylase, and maltase, convert starch into complex sugars, including sucrose and maltose. Another group of enzymes, collectively known as zymases, ferment maltose, producing alcohol and carbon dioxide. Enzymatic activity is directly proportional to temperature; it's reduced by half for every 18°F (10°C) decrease in temperature and doubles for every 18°F increase until it reaches a lethal temperature (for yeast, about 140°F/60°C). Understanding enzymatic activity will lead to better bread.

Our salivary glands produce amylase to help break down carbohydrates in preparation for complete digestion. Consuming enzymatically active foods (like sprouted grains) gives our digestive tract a boost in helping break down our food so it's easier for our bodies to assimilate. Oral enzymes are also a way to stimulate fermentation. In *The Art of Fermentation*, Sandor Katz describes a process that involves chewing boiled potatoes as a way to inoculate potato starches with salivary amylase, converting them to fermentable sugars that, when introduced to yeast, create alcohol.

Once these simple sugars have been created, yeast can get right to work—or right to its daily life—because what yeast is programmed to do is use the energy derived from the consumption of simple sugars to digest, respire, ferment, and reproduce asexually. It's fortuitous for bakers that in the course of this cycle, yeast produces carbon dioxide gas, alcohol, and organic acids.

Carbon Dioxide Gas

Carbon dioxide gas, a product of the respiration of yeast, leavens the dough and helps create baked loaves that are light and have volume. As it accumulates during primary and secondary fermentation, carbon dioxide is trapped in, and constrained by, strong sheets of viscoelastic gluten that stretch under the internal pressure and the yeast's last exhalations of the expanding gas. The same gas further expands (as does the water in the dough) when it encounters the heat of the oven. This process is called physical leavening. All baked goods—whether they have yeast, a chemical leavener such as baking powder, or no leavener (as in unyeasted flat breads)—undergo physical leavening caused by the increase in volume of the water and gases trapped within the gluten matrix of the dough or batter. The well-heated thermal mass of a wood-fired oven provides plenty of stored heat energy for properly proofed loaves to gain maximum volume. When dough is baked, starches gelatinize and proteins coagulate, giving structure to the open spaces (alveoli) created by the expanding carbon dioxide and air as well as the evaporating water and alcohol. The spaces remain, forming the open crumb so sought after in artisan bread baking.

An open crumb is largely dependent on the vigor of controlled fermentation, proper gluten development, and optimum carbon dioxide production.

Alcohol

Alcohol, a by-product of fermentation, is a flavoring and aromatic agent. Much of it evaporates during the baking cycle. I've heard bread referred to as solid beer and beer called liquid bread, and that's because both use fermentation and most of the same ingredients: grain, water, and yeast. To control fermentation, the brewer needs to monitor time and temperature as diligently as the baker. From the time of ancient Egypt up through the medieval era, bakeries and breweries were efficiently located side by side so that they could take advantage of the same ingredients, especially yeast, the "great animator." (As a nod to the power of enzymes, note that non-alcoholic beers are made from modified malts with lots of malt flavor but little enzymatic activity. Without the enzymes to convert grain into sugar, there can be no alcohol production.)

Organic Acids

Organic acids, mainly lactic acid and acetic acid, create more complex flavor, increase dough strength, and lengthen shelf life. Lactic and acetic acid impart different flavor profiles to bread and are created under different conditions. Lactic acid imparts the natural flavor of grain and a buttery essence, subtle and wholesome. Acetic acid is sharper and more sour. (Table vinegar is usually 4 to 8 percent acetic acid.) The production of these acids in bread making varies with time, temperature, and hydration.

Different environments favor the production of different acids. For example, lactic acid is produced in doughs and preferments that have a higher hydration and are fermented at ambient temperatures; it is also created earlier in the fermentation cycle than acetic acid. Acetic acid is produced in drier doughs and preferments, at cooler temperatures, and later in the fermentation cycle. The inclusion of whole-grain flour also promotes the production of acetic acid due to the higher enzyme concentration in wheat and rye bran.

The flavor profiles of lactic and acetic acids can be combined to create more complexity. A drier preferment can be incorporated into a wet dough that is fermented at ambient temperatures. Or two preferments can be used in conjunction with the same dough. In addition to flavor, acids increase dough strength greatly by swelling flour proteins. Acidification also inhibits microbial growth, so properly fermented bread lasts longer, just as lacto-fermented or vinegar-processed pickles last much longer than fresh cucumbers. However, if too many acids build up in the dough, the gluten strands begin to deteriorate, and the bread has off flavors and a tighter crumb.

There is a point of diminishing returns in the world of fermentation and we, here in the United States especially, tend to run with the "more is better" philosophy. Once, when I was first learning how to bake, I had some extra Pain au Levain dough. I stashed it in the fridge and added it to the next day's mix. I thought, *This batch will be really good—think of all the extra flavor!* What came out of the oven were the dreaded acidic hockey pucks. I introduced too much fully fermented flour in which all the sugars had been consumed, and too many organic acids had accumulated.

In addition to residual sugars, two other elements are required to achieve beautiful crusts: plenty of heat and steam in the baking chamber. If you fail to provide any of these elements, you will have uncharismatic crust with an insipid color and cuts that don't open to create the ridges of dough that caramelize into incredibly tasty pieces of grain candy.

Life Continues

Yeast continues to ferment until it either runs out of simple sugars or is killed when its temperature reaches about 140°F (60°C). Residual sugars, unconsumed by the time the dough goes into the oven, contribute to shiny crusts and rich color because they caramelize and contribute to the Maillard reaction. If there are too few residual sugars remaining when the bread enters the oven, no caramelization can occur and the resulting loaves will be dull, with muted colors, cuts that don't open, and a thick, dry, overbaked crust.

Yeast's metabolic rate is directly proportional to temperature and hydration, so wetter and warmer dough will ferment more quickly than drier and cooler dough. The ideal fermentation temperature for most bread dough is 75°F to 78°F (24–26°C). Controlling fermentation means preventing the dough temperature from exceeding roughly 78°F for wheat-based breads and around 80°F (27°C) for rye breads. Cool fermentation temperatures are acceptable, however; this technique, called retarding, is described under *Extended Fermentation* later in this chapter.

Wild Yeast and Domestic Yeast

Wild yeast (*Saccharomyces exiguus*) is all around us—it settles on grain growing in the field and is visible as the white film on grapes and other fruits and vegetables. A mixture of flour and water regularly "fed" with more flour and water will support an active colony of healthy yeast that can be used to make naturally leavened breads. This colony is what creates a sourdough starter. "Domestic yeast," the type available in fresh and dry forms, was discovered and cultured by Louis Pasteur in the 1850s. (This is the clay-like blocks of yeast that were once widely available in the refrigerated section of local supermarkets, but have been largely replaced by dry yeast for most home bakers. Professional bakers still have access to fresh yeast.) Pasteur's yeast quickly moved into the baking world, replacing, in part, naturally leavened breads. Two reasons were convenience and economy—no need to maintain a healthy starter and no reason to use precious flour for starter feedings. Also, domestic yeast worked more quickly, and that meant brutally long commercial baking shifts could be shortened.

During World War II dehydrating techniques were developed so bread could be baked in the field without the need to refrigerate stored fresh yeast. This first dry yeast was oven-dried active dry yeast. It requires a 15-minute hydration period that allows water to seep through the outer layer of dead yeast cells damaged during the dehydrating process. Eventually, a more sophisticated air-drying method was developed that didn't damage the yeast. This product is instant active yeast, and it doesn't need to be hydrated before being added to dough; it's simply mixed in with the water or flour. I prefer to mix it with the water, as long as the water's temperature is between 65°F and 85°F (18–29°C). If the water temp is outside this range, the yeast can be shocked and may not ferment as reliably. I judge whether the water is too hot or cold by sticking my hand in it, reasoning that if my hand is comfortable (not too cold or too hot) it will be okay for the yeast. If the water temperature is so uncomfortable I want to pull my hand out of the water, I mix the yeast in with the flour to buffer the temperature.

It's much more economical to purchase yeast in 1-pound vacuum packages from a supplier like King Arthur Flour than in the little strips of envelopes found in the supermarket. If you do buy yeast at the grocery store, look for names that suggest the process will be fast: Quik-Rise, Fast-o-matic, Nevr-doze 4 Yr Doughs. Such products are most likely instant active yeast. Confused because you know the handmade bread process revolves around cool, *slow* fermentation? Don't worry. It's the ratio of yeast that is important. The proper ratio of instant active yeast to flour is 0.3 to 0.4 percent. At that amount you will have no problem controlling fermentation as long as the dough temperature is correct. Instant active yeast is shelf-stable at room temperature until the package is opened. After that, keep it in an airtight container in the fridge.

Fermentation Techniques

There are numerous ways to manage fermentation, from simple straight doughs made with off the shelf yeast to naturally leavened sourdough that requires an active levain and extended fermentation.

STRAIGHT DOUGHS (MÉTHODE DIRECTE)

Straight doughs are those in which all the ingredients are mixed *at once* at the beginning of mixing the final dough. In other words, they don't have any preferments. That's not to say straight doughs don't have a lengthy fermentation period. The pizza dough in the straight dough section needs 4 to 5 hours to slowly ferment, becoming very extensible in the process.

YEASTED PREFERMENTS

Most handmade, crusty hearth breads use preferments to create flavorful bread with more dough strength and a longer shelf life than a straight dough. A preferment is a mixture of flour, water, a small ratio of domestic or wild yeast, and sometimes salt. The ingredients are mixed together and fermented for as little as 30 minutes—but they usually have a slow, cool fermentation of up to 16 hours. The majority of breads baked over the past

The yeast on the left is labeled active dry. Instant active is on the right, but not clearly identified.

6,000 years have used a preferment because wild yeast sourdough starters were the only way to leaven bread.

Organic acids produced through fermentation enable preferments to confer on the bread strong dough, complex taste, and long shelf life. A short fermentation time doesn't allow enough time for the acids to accumulate as they do in a preferment—slowly and exponentially.

All the recipes in this book indicate how much of the flour is prefermented. This is important, because a higher proportion of prefermented flour will increase the rate of fermentation. However, a higher rate of fermentation means that more sugars are being consumed, so it's especially important to regulate time and temperature to control a vigorous fermentation. A prefermented flour of 20 to 30 percent is common, but occasionally an outlier, such as Calvel's Pain Rustique, can have as high as 50 percent prefermented flour.

Whole-grain flours can be used in preferments. In fact, they benefit from the overnight "soak," because the bran has a long time to absorb the increased hydration required with whole-grain flours. The overnight period also means that large pieces of bran will soften, limiting the damage that harder, unsoaked pieces might wreak on the developing gluten. Weaker flours benefit from being prefermented, too. Those reliable aids to gluten development, the organic acids, help tighten the gluten matrix by swelling the proteins.

However, you should not assume that preferments are necessary to make good bread. Dough without a preferment can still make good bread. Some breads, like Pain de Mie, that do not call for a preferment are far from dull or insipid; the texture of the crumb is simply different. (Remember: One of the attributes of a preferment is greater dough strength, which affects the texture of the baked loaf. Breads thoroughly fermented during their dough phase will be chewier than a straight dough that did not mature, because the resulting organic acids created more dough strength.) Preferments are not magic bullets that turn a poorly fermented loaf into an Old World masterpiece. And straight dough can receive a lengthy primary fermentation period, in which case all the flour in the recipe is slowly fermenting.

The section *Naturally Leavened Breads* on page 108 includes an explanation of sourdough starters, because naturally leavened bread must have a preferment (or sourdough starter). It's the starter that contributes the yeast necessary to initiate fermentation and leaven the dough. Preferments can also be made with domestic yeast. And there are some traditional options like poolish, Italian biga, or simply dough from a previous batch, called *pâte fermentée* by the French.

Poolish

The poolish is one of my favorite preferments, and not just because it's of Polish origin. It has a standard hydration of 100 percent (for every unit of flour there is one unit of water) and is the consistency of pancake batter when first mixed. Because it's wet and has a lengthy fermentation period (about 15 hours), a poolish creates an environment that favors the production of lactic acid; the result is a nutty, wheaty, and buttery flavor. Poolishes also create protease, an enzyme involved in the process that makes dough extensible. This extensibility is why poolish is the standard preferment for baguettes—it aids the multi-step process of shaping a nice baguette. The extensibility also aids oven spring because it allows the crumb to expand more than a less extensible dough.

A poolish is mixed about 15 hours in advance of final dough mixing. Of course, that time can be increased or decreased by manipulating temperature and ratio of yeast to flour. A poolish with 0.1 percent yeast held at 75°F (24°C) will be ripe in about 14 to 16 hours. The ripe poolish will have nearly doubled in size, be extremely active (with bubbles occasionally and lazily breaking the surface), and have a crevasse in the surface where it fell after reaching maximum volume. The ideal time to use a poolish is right *before* it falls, but of course, we don't know when that will be until we receive that visual cue of the crevasse. The accumulation of organic acids changes the consistency of the poolish. What was pancake batter on the day it was mixed transforms, by the following day, into a glutenous mass. The easiest way to get it out of a container is to loosen it with the water that has been brought to the proper temperature and weighed for use in the final dough. Poolishes were developed by Polish bakers (thus the name) and were quickly adopted and made popular by French bakers.

You Can't Go Back and You Can't Stand Still

You may be asking yourself, *If my poolish is ripe but suddenly my schedule changes and I can't bake right now, how long will it keep? Will it last in my fridge until next weekend like a starter would?* No. You have one good shot at using a poolish at its peak of ripeness. Even a couple of extra hours is detrimental to the quality of the final dough, although it can still be quite good. Instead of improving the poolish over the extended time, the yeast consumes all of the residual sugars and overferments; the dough strength suffers due to overacidification. This is true of other preferments, too.

NATURALLY LEAVENED BREADS

For about 97 percent of the 6,000 years humans have been baking leavened bread, wild yeast levains or sourdough starters provided the leavening power. The roles and rules of fermentation are pretty much the same as with yeasted preferments—with a few microbiological variations—but naturally leavened breads represent the side of the fermentation family tree that requires a sourdough starter to be nurtured and cultivated in order to make bread. In the case of a yeasted preferment the ingredients are mixed and used in their entirety, but some portion of a naturally leavened starter always needs to be held back to propagate more—one of the more romantic parts of a romantic practice. (All the naturally leavened preferments in this book are "spun off" from a 100 percent hydrated liquid sourdough starter. If the final preferment [or levain] maintains this hydration, the formula methodology instructions point out that the original starter should be removed. However, if other flours or hydrations are used to elaborate the starter into a preferment, the methodology does not include notes to remove the original liquid sourdough starter.)

Wild yeast fermentation involves another enzymatic step. Wild yeast cannot metabolize maltose, one of the simple sugars created through the enzymatic conversion of starch. Luckily, *Saccharomyces exiguus* has a symbiotic relationship with beneficial bacteria. These bacteria are either homofermentative, which create only lactic bacteria, or heterofermentative, which create both lactic and acetic acid. These bacteria and the acid they create as by-products are major contributors to dough strength and to the flavor, aroma, and keeping qualities of the baked loaf.

In addition to this major difference, naturally leavened bread, in its finished form, has different characteristics from those of bread leavened with commercial yeast. The following table indicates how they differ.

A ripe 100 percent hydrated levain should be bubbly, increased in volume by about two-thirds from when it was mixed. The crevasse visible in this photograph is a sign that the levain is ready to be incorporated into the final dough. A poolish is also 100 percent hydrated and made with white flour; it looks the same as this levain when it's ready to use.

Table 7.1: Comparison of Bread Characteristics in Naturally Leavened Breads and Yeasted Breads

Characteristic	Naturally Leavened Breads	Yeasted Breads
Crust	Thicker	Thinner, crisper
Shelf life	Longer	Shorter
Crumb	Chewier	More tender
Total time to make	Longer	Shorter
Flavor profile	Varies regionally depending on local strains of yeast and bacteria	Consistent, regardless of where a particular yeasted bread is made
Nutrition	Deactivates phytic acid allowing minerals in our food to be available to our bodies	Does not deactivate phytic acid

Part of the appeal of naturally leavened bread is the routine of holding back some of the starter to feed, ripen, and use for another batch of bread. This same starter can be lent to friends and passed down through families, creating an actively bubbling family heirloom. Sourdough starter can be maintained into perpetuity—this is some of the intrigue of naturally leavened baking. Wild yeast populations are different around the world. A given locale supports wild yeast and lactobacillus cultures that create particular characteristics in the bread baked there. This wild yeast starter is just that, a *culture*.

Culture [kuhl-cher] n. b. The cultivation of . . . micro-organisms in prepared media, or a product of this.

—*The New Lexicon Webster's Dictionary of the English Language*

You can, however, change your bread's flavor profile by making adjustments in the fermentation schedule, the hydration, or the proportion of prefermented flour in the dough. The *Extended Fermentation* section later in this chapter explains how you can make your bread dramatically more sour by cooling the fermenting dough, which allows for more acetic acid production. Whole-grain flours also ferment differently, so, in addition to the flavor that comes from the bran and germ, you get different flavors from fermentation. Professional bakers always consider how much flour is prefermented (whether it's a natural leaven or a yeasted preferment). Using more

prefermented flour means you're adding aromas and flavors that were created in the preferment along with extra dough strength that comes from acidification. However, as the amount of prefermented flour increases, so does the risk of overfermenting your dough—too many of the residual sugars may get consumed.

Caring for a sourdough starter is a little like caring for a pet: You need to feed and water it on a regular schedule. See the sidebar for care and maintenance information, but remember that flexibility can be built into a feeding schedule by balancing time and temperature.

RYE-BASED BREADS AND RYE SOURS

A major consideration when making rye breads is the high amylase activity level of rye flour. Because amylase converts starch to sugar, which does not absorb water at the same rate as starch, there may be free water in the rye bread dough. Acidifying some of the rye flour will reduce amylase activity. Also, overmixing a rye dough can "squeeze" more free water out of the weaker gluten matrix.

Overhydrated, overfermented, and weak dough may lead to flying crust—a thin layer of the top crust that covers a large cavernous hole often running the entire length of the loaf. This can happen in wheat-based doughs, too, although it's less common.

The gelatinization of rye starches begins to happen around 122°F (50°C) and ends around 176°F (80°C).

My Bettie Starter

A microbiologist friend once isolated and grew out 12 or so of the wild yeast isolates that collectively formed my Bettie starter. He brought them to me in petri dishes; each gave off its own smells of fruit, old wine, wet pine bark, and green banana, among others. People change when they move to another culture—how they speak, what they do, the pace of their daily schedule—and so does wild yeast. My starter moves back and forth with me between Providence, Rhode Island, and Bettie, North Carolina, and as I take it from one place to the other it becomes populated with the local culture of its current home. This is not something to lament—it is a change, not a passing. When I return to school in the fall, my starter and I adapt to our new environment. Sourdough starters, then, are local food. And if ever you are traveling and have the chance to pick up some of, say, Elvis's sourdough starter at the Memphis airport, be aware that it will soon become just like the one you have waiting for you at home.

Wheat starches begin to gelatinize at 140°(60°C) and cease around 194°F (90°C). The lower gelatinization temperature in the rye dough means amylase has a lengthier opportunity to convert it to sugar, especially when it's at its peak activity—around 145°F (63°C). Eventually, amylase is deactivated at around 176°F (80°C). The extra time for amylase to convert rye starches to sugar—and at the peak of their activity—is called starch attack.

Acidifying the flour with a rye sour restrains amylase activity and reins in starch conversion during fermentation. Failure to acidify rye flour when the total rye is greater than 30 percent of total flour means the baked loaf will remain gummy—even if you let it cool for 24 to 48 hours.

Here are some other ways rye-based breads differ from wheat-based:

- Rye breads don't usually employ an autolyse.
- As the rye flour percentage in the dough increases (in relation to wheat), the final loaf becomes more dense.
- Final rye dough temperatures are higher than final wheat dough temperatures. Rye bread can finish mixing at 78°F to 82°F (26–28°C), a step higher than the 75°F to 78°F (24–26°C) final dough temperatures for wheat-based breads. Breads made with 100 percent rye—of which there are none in this book—may have final dough temperatures of 84°F (29°C).

- Bulk fermentation and proof times are shorter for rye breads than for wheat breads.
- Rye breads with more than 30 percent whole rye are usually not retarded.

Rye sours are often of a stiff consistency.

Care and Maintenance of the Starter

Here is a basic outline of how a naturally leavened starter is maintained. Either a starter is given to you by a friend, or you start one from scratch. (See appendix F for instructions on how to make a starter from scratch.) A stable culture requires regular feedings of flour and water. Timing of these feedings and amounts of ingredients vary depending on when you plan to bake. The last feeding before you bake will create enough healthy levain to leaven your bread and a bit extra to withhold and feed in order to keep the process going.

Starters are resilient and can be stored in the fridge for months without perishing. They will, however, break down and go dormant. A gray layer of alcohol—called hooch—will accumulate on top. The wild yeast physiologically transitions to spore phase and rides out the period until it receives another feeding of flour and water.

A starter can be easily revived from dormancy. I took a mason jar full of starter with me when I moved from North Carolina to Vermont to work at King Arthur Flour. Because I was working in the bakery, I didn't need to refresh my starter at home. I put the jar of 100 percent hydrated starter in the fridge, pulled it out nine months later, and opened the jar. Even though the smell was sharply acidic, I was instantly homesick because the smell was distinctly from back home. I put it on a feeding schedule of 100g starter to 100g flour to 100g water. Within a week, it became vigorous and bubbly, although the essence of my North Carolina starter had disappeared—replaced by a smell similar to the starter we were using at work.

Starters can also be frozen or dried as an emergency backup. Frozen starters need to be thawed and then put back on a regular feeding schedule. Active starter can be dried by spreading a thin layer on a piece of parchment paper and allowing it to dry. Once the starter is completely dry, crumble it into an airtight jar. When you need to revive it, just mix the starter flakes with water and some fresh flour and continue feeding until it's active again.

- Heavy rye sourdoughs often call for the addition of commercial yeast, while naturally leavened wheat breads commonly do not. Yeast helps make heavy rye breads lighter and gives them greater volume.
- Hydration is usually higher in rye breads than wheat. Rye flour contains high levels of the carbohydrate pentosan, which is particularly water-absorbent. (Another reason to avoid overmixing when putting together the dough for rye breads is to avoid having the pentosan-absorbed water break loose in the dough.)

I use whole rye flour, sometimes called pumpernickel flour, in all my rye breads. There are medium rye and light rye flours with more or less of the bran and germ removed, but I prefer to go for the most rye flavor and texture and use as high an extraction as possible. I have used Joe Lindley's 100% Organic Whole Rye Flour for years, but all of the recipes in this book were tested with off-the-shelf rye flour available at mainstream supermarkets.

Rye is a resilient grain, able to grow in poor soil and harsh climates. Its hardiness makes it ideal for small-scale grain farmers. The American Bread Movement is already bringing delicious and unique rye bread to the market.

EXTENDED FERMENTATION: THE RETARDING PROCESS

Retarding dough is a method of extending its fermentation period by cooling it. Dough can be retarded in bulk (that is, after it has been mixed but not yet divided into loaf-sized pieces) or after it has been divided and shaped into individual loaves. Retarding often happens overnight while the baker is resting but the yeast is busily—albeit slowly—fermenting the dough.

Ideal retarding temperatures are around 50°F to 55°F (10–13°C). In commercial bakeries, appliances similar to refrigerators called "retarders" are often used to provide this temperature. (Retarders can also control the humidity, and they can get warm to create a warmer environment for the final proof. A baker would call this a proofer/retarder. They can be programmed to change from cool to warm.) You may have a wine cabinet, root cellar, or other spot in your house or property, like a porch or shed, that can provide the ideal temperature—at least during part of the year. Refrigerators can also be used as retarders, but their 39°F (4°C) or lower temperature will greatly slow fermentation. That slower fermentation rate can be compensated for by giving the dough an hour or so (depending on dough temperature) at room temperature before you put it into the fridge overnight. You may need to give it some time to finish proofing the next day once you take it out of the fridge.

Commercial bakers retard shaped dough so they can immediately start baking in the morning, producing fresh bread for sale or delivery early in the morning. While the day's first mixes are happening, retarded dough can be loaded into the oven. Retarding dough is also efficient from a production perspective, and it can provide opportunities to diversify the products you make. When I worked at King Arthur, most of the naturally leavened dough was mixed one day, shaped into loaves and retarded overnight, and baked the next day. However, some of the dough was mixed, molded into the beautiful fougasse shape, and baked the same day. This gave us a distinctive item baked on a separate day from the loaves.

Home bakers can retard dough as a way to have bread early in the morning without having to get out of bed at 2 am. (Still, I recommend baking bread through the night as a way to experience the graceful interactions between dough preparation and oven management without the interruptions that come during the daytime. Tending a fire beneath the stars and loading bread as the sun rises make my heart swell. We are fortunate to participate in this process that celebrates fire and grain.) For instance, if you want to have some rosemary sourdough for a Sunday brunch, all the mixing and shaping can be done on Saturday. The next morning, the loaves can be baked in an oven still hot from last night's pizza party.

Naturally leavened sourdoughs retard better than yeasted breads, because yeasted breads *may* overferment during the retarding period if the ratio of yeast is too high. (Again, adjust the ratios to create a bread that fits into the system that works for you. You are in charge as long as you create a formula and a system that control fermentation. If you have a favorite yeasted bread and a retarded schedule works well for you, simply reduce the yeast in the final dough until you find a ratio that will adequately ferment the bread without having so much fermentation that all those wonderful residual sugars are consumed.) Of the recipes in this book, the Pain au Levain and its variations are the best candidates for retarding. The Miche and Sprouted Wheat Flour Sourdough are a bit too active, as are most of the yeasted breads. Pain Rustique with 50 percent preferment flour and an additional 0.3 percent instant active yeast is too active to retard with good results. The vigorous enzymatic activity of heavy rye breads at the proper temperature means they don't retard well. Again, the bread-baking process can be adjusted (to a point) to fit your schedule. Final dough temperatures should be a bit lower (about 73°F/23°C) if you want to retard yeasted bread, but a more reliable adjustment would be to reduce the ratio of yeast indicated in the formula. On the other hand, if you are retarding two loaves of Pain au Levain in your (relatively cold) home refrigerator, you may want a slightly warmer final dough temperature—or to let it achieve some fermentation activity before it's chilled.

Typically, dough is retarded after it's shaped. The final rise is extended, and if the bread is fully risen the next morning, it can be immediately baked—there is no need to allow it to come up to ambient temperature. However, it may still need more time to proof. (See *Proofing, the Final Rise*, in chapter 6 for more information about determining if your dough is ready to bake.) I prefer to use baskets for retarding instead of a couche, because a dough cradled in a couche overnight tends to spread during the extended proofing period and the baked loaf is flat.

Proofing baskets that hold dough overnight will need more flour than baskets that will be held only for a room-temperature proofing period. I always use

Factors That Affect Fermentation

- Temperature
- Time
- Extraction rate of the flour
- Hydration of the dough
- Presence of sugar (Various forms of sugar, e.g., sucrose, honey, and molasses, increase the rate of fermentation.)
- Presence of spices (Spices, such as cinnamon, can inhibit enzyme and yeast activity.)
- Mass of dough (A smaller mass will cool and heat more quickly than a larger one. This applies to preferments and final dough.)
- Attitude of the baker

linen-lined banneton for retarded bread instead of the coiled willow brotform. The convoluted interior of the brotform, and/or insufficient flour, will make for a more difficult release of dough from the basket when the loaves are turned out to be baked the next morning.

Try this experiment, which illustrates the flavor and volume effects of retarding a loaf of naturally leavened dough. Mix a batch of Pain au Levain and give it the prescribed amount of primary fermentation. Divide it into three loaves of equal weight, and shape them into boules. Place them in well-floured proofing baskets. Take two of the loaves and retard them after about an hour or so of proof time. Allow the third one to proof and bake it according to the unretarded schedule described in the formula methodology. Bake one of the retarded loaves 12 to 15 hours later. And bake the third loaf 24 hours later. The unretarded loaf should have more of a lactic acid flavor profile and the largest volume of the three loaves. The loaf baked second should be tangier and a little smaller than the first loaf. In addition, there will probably be blisters on the crust from carbon dioxide that has accumulated and migrated to the skin, where it could not escape because of the strength of the gluten. The third loaf should be the sourest and the smallest in size. Its decreased volume is caused by the dough-tightening effect of the acetic acid created during the retarding period. (You may want to mix a double batch for this experiment so that you will have some bread to eat as the experiment unfolds.) The idea here is to eliminate baking variables—a bit of a trick in a wood-fired oven. You may want to try

this in your home oven. (Check the sidebar *Simulating a Wood-Fired Oven at Home with a Combo Cooker* in chapter 6 for instructions on how to replicate the characteristics of a wood-fired oven in your home oven.)

You can also retard in bulk by mixing the final dough, giving it some primary fermentation and several folds to build strength, and then stashing it in a covered dough tub in the fridge. The next day, divide and shape the dough and allow it to proof. Proof time for a dough fermented with this retarding method will likely be longer than you'd need if the same dough wasn't retarded.

Remember that dough should be covered during retarding to avoid drying out the skin. Commercial retarders provide humidity to accomplish this, but home bakers can cover each loaf with plastic. If you're using proofing baskets, simply tie each one up in a plastic grocery bag and place it in your fridge. Baking retarded dough in a wood-fired oven allows you to load into an oven that is slightly too hot for room-temperature dough. The higher-than-usual oven temperature is offset by the cool dough placed on the deck. The firing schedule will have to be fine-tuned, and it will take some observation to learn the characteristics of an oven that's ready. On the other hand, retarded dough may squander some of your precious stored heat. Whether to bake retarded dough in your wood-fired oven depends on the type of flavor profile you want to create in your bread, what you want your baking schedule to be, and how many loads of hearth breads you want to bake on a single firing.

Water Temperature Formula to Achieve Desired Final Dough Temperature

I run the water temperature formula every time I mix. Dough temperature is affected by the temperature of each ingredient (water, flour, and preferment), the room temperature, and the friction factor (the amount of heat added to the dough through friction during the mixing process). In general, aim for a dough temperature between 75°F and 78°F (24–26°C). Breads with commercial yeast are usually about 75°F, while naturally leavened breads like to be a bit warmer, around 78°F. Rye breads are aided by a final dough temperature of 78°F to 84°F (26–29°C) depending on the percentage of rye. The desired final dough temperature for each bread in this book is given in the formula.

Is it really a big deal to have dough temperature that is drastically out of the optimum range? It's not uncommon to be several degrees out, but a 5°F (3°C) difference will bring about very slow or very fast fermentation activity. Imagine if our body temperature was raised 10°F (6°C), from 98.7°F to 108.7°F. You'd be approaching death. Luckily, having doughs with high temperatures is not as dire a situation as having a feverish family member, but this is an important factor in the health of your dough.

Here's how to calculate the water temperature to use in order to finish the kneading step with the desired final dough temperature.

For a bread that uses a preferment: Multiply the desired dough temperature by 4, then subtract the flour temperature, preferment temperature, room temperature, and friction factor. The result is the water temperature you should use. Or:

$$\text{water temp} = (4 \times \text{desired dough temp}) -$$
$$(\text{flour temp} + \text{room temp}$$
$$+ \text{preferment temp} + \text{friction factor})$$

The friction factor will vary depending on hydration of the dough and whether you mix by hand. Most mixers add approximately 30°F (17°C) to a properly mixed hearth bread, while hand mixing might add about 10°F.

A very wet dough (above 80 percent hydration) might not generate any friction heat, while a drier dough in a mixer will create more friction. Also, a fast mixer will add more heat to the dough than a slower mixer, given the same mixing time.

Don't know the friction factor for your mixing method? Take the temperature of the dough when it first becomes homogeneous during the final dough mixing process and again when kneading is complete. Subtract the first value from the second; the difference in those quantities is the friction factor.

Here is an example, calculated in Fahrenheit. You are mixing Pain au Levain. It's a cool day, and you want the temperature to be on the warmer side of the 75°F to 78°F desired dough temperature. The room temperature is 69°F, the flour is 68°F, and the levain preferment is 75°F. You are mixing by hand, which you have determined adds 10°F to the dough.

$$\text{water temp} = (4 \times 78) - (68 + 69 + 75 + 10)$$
$$\text{water temp} = 312 - 222$$
$$\text{water temp} = 90°F$$

If the environment is warmer than in this example, the calculated water temperature will be cooler; if it's cooler, the water temp will be warmer.

For a bread without a preferment: Multiply the desired dough temperature by 3 instead of 4, because there is no preferment temperature to take into account when determining the desired water temperature.

Calculating the proper water temperature to start your bread's fermentation cycle at the optimal point is necessary to creating a beautiful and delicious loaf of bread that follows a specific production schedule. Controlling water temperature is a way to control an important variable and is required to get properly proofed dough into a wood-fired oven that is at the proper baking temperature.

The desired final dough temperature for each bread is included in the formula.

Water

It is crucial for bread dough to be properly hydrated, just as it is for the human body. Water is necessary to develop gluten—and there are other, more subtle effects of proper hydration. Hearth bread bakers strive to get as much water as possible into the dough and still have it manageable. As you become more proficient with mixing and handling wet dough, you'll be able to increase hydration. The benefits of increased hydration are a vigorous fermentation and more open crumb. Another advantage to using more water in the dough—especially for commercial bakers—is lower ingredient cost per loaf of bread.

I've used all types of water—well water, bottled water, city water—and they all seem just fine as long as they're the proper temperature. Highly chlorinated water can reduce fermentation activity, but you can still easily achieve a healthy dough with proper dough temperature and handling. Chlorine will dissipate if the water sits uncovered overnight—an option if you live somewhere with highly chlorinated water.

Water is the ingredient that can most easily adjust the final temperature of dough, and dough temperature has a huge impact on the timing and final results of bread baking. When the dough temperature is too low, fermentation is inhibited, the process slows down, and the baked loaf is dense, with low volume and flavor that lacks the desired complexity that comes with thorough—but controlled—fermentation. When the dough temperature is too high, fermentation is too vigorous, the process speeds up, too many residual sugars are consumed, and the dough can become gassy and hard to handle. Neither situation is desirable. Manage proper dough temperature by determining the temperature of the water used in the dough.

The information in the preceding sidebar will help you accommodate the temperature of your environment and ingredients by adjusting the temperature of your water. This is one of the fundamental techniques that help ensure consistently good bread.

Flour: The Body of Bread

We are fortunate at this point of human evolution to have a diverse selection of high-quality flours within easy reach—unlike the not-so-distant past, when flour was low-quality, bleached, adulterated, or simply unavailable.

The largest percentage of breads baked today are made with wheat flour because wheat has the best quality and highest concentration of gluten compared with other grains. Gluten traps carbon dioxide gas, allowing us to have lighter loaves with a crumb full of alveoli. Gluten is made of two proteins—gliadin and glutenin. Gliadin creates extensibility in dough, a desirable quality that allows dough to stretch or expand without pulling back when being shaped or during oven spring. Extensible dough is easier to shape and creates baked loaves with more volume than loaves that have an overly elastic gluten structure. Glutenin creates elasticity, also desirable because it gives dough the strength to retain carbon dioxide and stand up on the hearth without spreading into a flat loaf. A dough with both extensibility and elasticity can be created by selecting flour with the proper protein levels, using the appropriate mixing method, controlling fermentation, and incorporating techniques such as folds during the bread-making process.

Protein content in flour is an indication of how much gluten the flour can develop. The level of gluten in different wheat flours depends on several variables. Soft wheat has less than hard wheat, and within the same type of wheat, gluten levels vary from year to year, from field to field, and even from plant to plant. For this reason, larger flour companies blend flours to create consistent protein content.

Most of the white flour in this book's recipes is identified as "bread" flour, but a more meaningful description is that it should have a protein percentage of about 11.5 to 11.7 percent. (For instance, King Arthur's Sir Galahad is 11.7 percent protein—and it's nearly the same flour, with some ash variations, as that sold as the familiar King Arthur All-Purpose Flour. A flour with this protein percentage also performs

A Flour by Any Other Name

The milling industry does not have standardized names for bread flours, which makes it difficult to go to a supermarket and buy a flour with the protein content recommended for the breads in this book. You might see a bread flour and think it's what you want because you're making bread, but the protein content is likely 12 percent or higher. All-purpose flour also seems an incorrect choice. Isn't that what you use for biscuits and pound cake? For years I have asked bakers, millers, farmers, and sales reps if they had any accurate and catchy names for white flour with about 11.5 percent protein to be used for artisan hearth breads. The best default options are the ones I used in this book: "bread flour" and "high-gluten flour." I urge the flour industry to establish standard names for flours based on protein content and include that information on each bag, much the way high-end chocolate bars notify the consumer how much cacao bean solid is found in different varieties of chocolate. Bittersweet is not interchangeable with unsweetened chocolate, just as cake flour is not a substitute for high-gluten flour. C'mon, flour companies, can't we all speak the same language? It will help us make your products perform better . . .

well for this book's Pie Dough, Apple Galette pastry, Baking Powder Biscuits, Cranberry Pecan Buttermilk Scones, Rustic Potato Pie, Pound Cake, and Taralli.) However, some flours labeled "bread flour" have a much higher protein percentage of around 12.7 to 14. This is the flour used in America's pan bread tradition. White flours with protein above 12 percent contribute useful gluten to heavier, whole-grain breads where the larger pieces of the whole-grain flour may cut and abrade the gluten strands, preventing them from developing into the long, extensible strands that form the gluten matrix. In this book, I call this type of white flour "high-gluten" flour and use it as the white flour component in breads with high percentages of gluten deficient rye flour. (By the way, whole wheat flour has a higher protein content than white flour.) Traditionally, farmers have been paid more for higher-gluten flours, and millers still tend to tout their higher gluten content. However, the movement toward local, small-scale grain growing and milling (without the ability or inclination to blend wheats from around the continent) means the baker has to learn how to manage the lower or higher protein levels that might come from any given growing season.

It's also important to consider that protein *quality* is more important than protein *quantity*. A grain that has been properly grown, harvested, and milled may yield a 10.5 percent protein flour that's better for bread baking than one with 11.5 percent protein that came from grain harvested too late in the season or improperly milled. Late harvesting could result in flour with unusually high levels of enzyme activity caused by preharvest sprouting.

There are many wonderful flours on the market—some locally grown and milled, others that are available nationally—that will perform well in this book's recipes. I appreciate the consistency and quality of King Arthur's All-Purpose. I've used it for years, and it was the standard flour for testing these recipes. King Arthur sells the exact same flour in a 50-pound (22.7kg) bag called Sir Galahad. The organic version of Sir Galahad is called Select Artisan.

Living with a wood-fired oven—and loving to bake bread—inspired me to explore and investigate other types of bread, many of which were made with subspecies of wheat, or grains other than wheat. The availability of heirloom and ancient grains has increased along with the popularity of handmade bread and wood-fired ovens. This book's recipes use a variety of flours, such as rye, spelt, durum, and sprouted wheat flour. Notes on their origins, performance, and intricacies are noted in the formulas. What they all have in common is some amount of gluten. Rye, for instance, has less gluten than wheat, while durum wheat flour has more protein than hard red winter wheat. The baking characteristics of these and other flours are discussed in the context of the recipes.

THE WHEAT BERRY

Many, many pages have been written on the three parts of the wheat berry. Refer to the bibliography for some excellent sources. However, I would be remiss if a brief description of the wheat berry wasn't included.

The bran is the fiber layer on the outside of the grain. (It is not the inedible husk that protects the grain while it grows and is separated as chaff.) Bran is absorbent and requires more water (compared with a dough made from white flour) in order to achieve an extensible dough.

The germ is the small part of the grain kernel that gives birth to a new stalk given the proper environment in which to germinate. It contains vitamin E, an oil that can become rancid unless the whole-grain flour is kept in a cool, dark place.

The endosperm is the large starchy interior of the grain kernel, which stores the energy that will fuel the seed's growth into a young sprout. It's also the part of the grain that makes "white" flour.

In addition to the protein content, there are several other key flour attributes that will help you create great bread if you understand them: extraction rate, ash content, and falling number.

EXTRACTION RATE

The extraction rate corresponds to the amount of flour that was produced from a given amount of grain. If the miller starts with 100 tons of grain and ends up with 55 tons of flour, then the extraction rate is 55 percent; 45 percent of the wheat kernel—the bran, germ, and part of the endosperm—was removed during the milling process. Most white flours have an extraction rate of 75 percent, whereas whole milled flour has an extraction rate of 100 percent—everything in the wheat berry is in the flour. As extraction rate increases, so does the rate of fermentation, because there is more food available for the yeast. Likewise, for us, there is more

nutrition in whole-grain products. Treat yeast as you treat yourself. A whole-grain diet is more healthful for yeast and baker alike.

ASH CONTENT

Ash content is an indication of the amount of minerals in the flour. The minerals reside in the bran, so ash content is also an indication of how much bran is left in the flour. Concentrations are quite small, around 0.48 to 0.54 percent. High-extraction flours, of course, will have a higher ash content because more of the wheat berry is included in the flour. As ash content increases, so does the rate of fermentation.

FALLING NUMBER

The falling number is a measure of the enzymatic activity of alpha-amylase in the flour. The alpha-amylase that converts starch into simple sugars occurs naturally in grains. However, its activity varies depending on the health of the grain and whether the growing season was conducive to wheat berry germination before harvest and milling. An ideal falling number is 250 to 300 seconds for white flour, and the higher the falling number, the lower the rate of fermentation. If the flour you're using has a falling number greater than 300, it can be made more enzymatically active by adding malted barley flour. Most large-scale mills test and adjust the falling number by adding ground-up malted barley to the flour as it is milled. If you're using flour from a small-scale miller who doesn't malt the flour, you may need to add 0.1 percent of total flour weight of malt powder to your formula.

USING MALT

Dough that has a high percentage (30 percent and above) of prefermented flour (especially white flours) or a lengthy bulk fermentation time often requires the use of additional malt powder. In my first years baking in Magdalena, I was lucky to have Jeffrey Hamelman and his wife, Chiho, stop to visit us on their way down the southeastern coast. I was making a white flour,

Some Ways Humans Are Similar to Bread Dough

Bread dough and humans have the following things in common:

- We both need food, water, oxygen, proper temperature, appropriate salinity, care, and maintenance.
- Alpha-amylase naturally occurs in wheat and is also produced by human salivary glands.
- Lactic acid is produced both in bread dough and in the human body.
- Yeast and humans both exhale carbon dioxide.

Ciabatta-type bread with about 30 percent prefermented flour. It was coming out of the oven with a fully baked crust that lacked good, rich color. Jeffrey looked at it and advised me to add about 0.1 percent diastatic malt powder. I immediately ordered some, and the increase in fermentation vigor, crust color, and flavor after the next bake proved to me the power of that little 0.1 percent of enzymes.

The malt powder I added to my Ciabatta is enzymatically active diastatic malt powder. The enzyme alpha-amylase is necessary to convert complex carbohydrates into simple sugars that can be consumed by yeast. The addition of diastatic malt to a hearth bread ensures good crust color because it "unlocks" sugars, which are then available for caramelization and the Maillard reaction. Be sure not to purchase sweet malt, which is non-diastatic and not enzymatically active. Malt powder appears in the formulas of this book that require the additional enzymatic activity. Increased enzyme activity *usually* makes the use of malt powder unnecessary in dough made with whole-grain flours. (See the Sprouted Wheat Power Bars formula for more information about the sprouting process and how it relates to the production of malt.)

Breads made with whole-grain flour *tend* to have less volume because the chunks of bran cut and shorten the gluten strands. However, increasingly sophisticated milling (coupled with greater interest in whole foods) has led to the creation of flours with extraction rates higher than those of white flour. Although these new

flours contain all or some of the bran and germ, the particle size is reduced, so the decrease in the volume of the baked loaf is less severe. The high-extraction flour used in the Miche recipe makes beautiful dough with the color of a well-brewed cappuccino. The taste of the baked loaf is evocative and mysterious. This is the type of bread the great baker Lionel Poilâne insisted on selling in his boulangeries and which today gets shipped around the world on a daily basis.

The infusion of local wheats into the marketplace has taught bakers to anticipate and interpret the vagaries of local flour while continuing to produce a consistent product. Here are some ways to do this:

- Use preferments or more prefermented flour. The buildup of acids will help increase dough strength.
- Lower hydration (in the case of low-protein flours).
- Shorten fermentation times when possible.
- Add diastatic malt powder.

Salt

The proper ratio of salt to flour in handmade hearth bread is only 1.8 to 2.0 percent (for every 100 units of flour, there are 1.8 to 2 units of salt), but this small amount plays a crucial role in making high-quality bread. In addition to making bread flavorful—as salt does in all food—it helps control fermentation by giving the baker some control over the enzyme and yeast activity. Salt slows the rate of enzymatic conversion and fermentation. Bread dough without salt will quickly overferment. Salt also increases the strength of the ionic bonds among the gluten strands. Without this added strength your dough will be loose and rip very easily; this is especially evident during shaping. Properly salted bread will also have a longer shelf life than bread with less than 1.8 percent salt; salt's hygroscopic nature helps it retard microbial growth.

Of the various bread dough ingredients, salt fulfills the functions that are the easiest to explain—albeit complex and intertwined. Without salt, bread dough would be weak, the baked loaves would taste insipid, and the crust would be uninspiring.

An important thing to remember when using salt in bread dough is to weigh it, rather than measuring it volumetrically. Large crystals will yield less salt in any volume than smaller crystals, while 15g of salt is 15g, no matter how big or small the crystal size. The amount of sodium chloride within that 15g of salt, however, may vary. Sea salts have other mineral chlorides that affect the saltiness of your bread. Also, some sea salts are very hygroscopic and contain more water than the salt you buy in the supermarket. When you weigh a "wet" salt, part of what you are weighing is just water, in which case your ratio of sodium chloride to flour could decrease to a level below 1.8 to 2 percent.

Questions about salt always come up. What type of salt should I use? The formulas in this book all use Morton kosher salt. I chose this brand because it is what I can get in rural North Carolina and I feel that is a good test of national availability. Other salts will work—just be sure to weigh them and adjust the ratio if they are noticeably more or less salty than usual. (See also *Salt Standard* in chapter 8.)

Is regular table salt okay? Yes. How about sea salt? Also fine to use, although you might want to reduce the ratio if there are other mineral chlorides that make the final loaf taste too salty. Iodized? I try to avoid it, but it will do if it's all you have. Will it make my bread better if I use salt from the Wieliczka Salt Mine in southern Poland? Not necessarily. As long as salt is weighed, rather than measured volumetrically, the differences in the final loaves of bread made from different kinds of salt, if detectable, are subtle. Making good bread is a matter of controlling variables; there is no one magic ingredient that, on its own, will elevate your bread to sublime status.

CHAPTER EIGHT

➤➤ • ◄◄

Standards and Conventions for Bread Formulas

The roster of bread formulas presented in this book includes white breads, whole-grain breads, rye breads, naturally leavened breads, yeasted breads, spelt breads, breads to be baked in a hot oven, breads for a cool oven, and others outside these categories. This is a well-rounded selection of breads that forms the basis of a good baker's repertoire. This chapter gives some insight into what these formulas are based on and how to re-create them in your own oven.

The Importance of the Thermometer and Timer

By now it is clear how important temperature is to bread baking. There's no need to buy a fancy digital thermometer, although it's faster and sometimes easier to see a digital readout than one on a standard, analog instant-read thermometer. The problem with digital thermometers is that they're often inaccurate and have batteries that eventually will need to be changed. An analog instant-read thermometer can be calibrated by putting it into a bath of half ice and half water and waiting a minute or so. If the dial does not read 32°F (0°C), hold on to the nut on the back of the dial with a wrench and turn the dial until it reads 32°F. No batteries required.

The pace of production baking—and for a home baker, simply the interruptions of everyday life—make a timer a valuable tool for keeping things on schedule. Anything will work—an analog windup, a digital kitchen timer with multiple functions, your cell phone. Once the bread-baking process seeps into your soul, don't be surprised if at some point you think, *It must be about time to fold that dough*, only to check the timer and see that the alarm is due to sound in just a few seconds.

Why Metric?

The straightforward answer is that the metric system of weights, volumes, and measures is simply superior in terms of accuracy, precision, resolution, and efficiency of the user's time. Other benefits are that the metric system is understood by a worldwide community of users, it's easier to learn than non-metric systems, and its use greatly reduces errors. Nevertheless, non-metric systems of measure hang on very tenaciously; Americans think of water temperature in degrees Fahrenheit, the height of a mountain in feet, weight loss in pounds, gallons of gas for our cars, and quarts of ice cream. These entrenched patterns of thought won't be changed easily. When we take on a task like bread baking that requires both precision and frequent measurements, however, adjusting to

Useful Conversions

1 ounce = 28.35 grams	1,000 grams = 1 kilogram
1 pound = 454 grams	1 kilogram = 2.2 pounds

the metric system quickly pays off. Simply by dividing by a factor of 10, the baker using metric measurements can shift easily to a larger or smaller unit as needed, whereas converting non-metric units (ounces to pounds, for example) is a very common source of error.

So the metric system is clearly much easier to work with once you begin to use it, but another point of view is that non-metric systems are inherently flawed. For example, the US tablespoon is 14.8 milliliters; the Canadian is 15.0, the British 17.8, and the Australian 20.0. Americans unwittingly using an Australian recipe will have 29 percent less than the tablespoon(s) called for in the recipe, and Australians using an American recipe will have 41 percent more. In either case, the errors are large enough to make a difference. To become adept at making handmade bread, a baker only needs a very few tools. One of them is the metric system.

By the way, I use the metric system for mass but maintain the use of Fahrenheit temperatures, although all Celsius temperature equivalents are included in the text and formulas.

If you still haven't bought a scale, I hope you will put down this book right now and do it. It will make all of your bread-making processes easier and your finished loaves more admirable.

Salt Standard

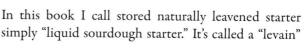

All the recipes in this book were tested using Morton's kosher salt, which is the only kosher salt available on grocery store shelves in our rural North Carolina county. Many people prefer another popular brand, Diamond Crystal, because it does not contain the 1 percent calcium silicate anti-caking agent found in Morton's. Diamond Crystal has much lighter, crystalline granules, so a given volume of Diamond Crystal will contain less than half the weight of salt as the same volume of Morton's. (Another reason to measure by weight, not volume!) If you do use Diamond Crystal and measure by volume, however, just be aware that you will need to adjust the salt accordingly. (See also the section on *Salt* in chapter 7.)

Starter Versus Levain

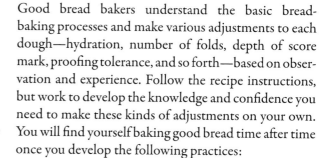

In this book I call stored naturally leavened starter simply "liquid sourdough starter." It's called a "levain" once it's elaborated into a preferment for use in a batch of baked bread.

Knead to Know

Good bread bakers understand the basic bread-baking processes and make various adjustments to each dough—hydration, number of folds, depth of score mark, proofing tolerance, and so forth—based on observation and experience. Follow the recipe instructions, but work to develop the knowledge and confidence you need to make these kinds of adjustments on your own. You will find yourself baking good bread time after time once you develop the following practices:

- Think of ingredient quantities in relation to the amount of flour (use baker's ratios).

- Weigh your ingredients as opposed to measuring volumetrically.
- Handle wet dough without getting sticky. This includes dusting the bench with a very thin layer of flour with a flick of your wrist and overcoming the urge to add flour to dough.
- Control fermentation by adjusting water temperature to provide the appropriate final dough temperature, as well as adjusting environmental temperatures for optimal fermentation vigor.
- Understand how the ingredients—and the ratios among them—interact and affect fermentation.
- Learn the idiosyncrasies of your oven so you can use it properly.
- Build your skills at nurturing clean combustion.
- Employ an autolyse period.
- Practice the doctrine of mise en place.

Practice is crucial to master the craft of bread making; the best teacher—after a good introduction to the basics—is hands-on experience.

What You Can Change and What You Might Wish You Hadn't

Wondering which parts of a recipe you really should stick to and when it's okay to go rogue? The following points will help you decide where to let your creativity run loose, and still get stellar results.

Changes that are easily accommodated:

- **White flour to whole-grain (or other grain) flours.** You may need to increase or decrease hydration, yeast, or prefermented flour when you change to a different type of flour. For instance, if you would like to replace the white flour in a formula with whole wheat flour, you will need to increase the hydration. Whole-grain flour absorbs more water, so increased hydration is required in order to achieve the same dough consistency. As long as the quantity of flour

is constant, regardless of what kind of flour it is, salt quantity remains the same.

- **Amount of yeast or starter in the preferment.** Adding a lower ratio of ripe, naturally leavened starter (or yeast, in the case of a yeasted preferment) will slow down the rate of fermentation compared to a higher ratio. This can help you fit your fermentation periods into your schedule or overcome a problematic warm, summer environment. Conversely, a higher ratio of ripe sourdough starter or yeast will make a preferment ripen more quickly, or in the proper amount of time if the environment is cool or cold.
- **Hydration.** Hydrate as needed to achieve proper consistency in the dough. Whole-grain flours, smaller grain sizes, and dry flour absorb more water than white flour, larger grain sizes, and flour that contains a higher moisture level.
- **Loaf size and shape.** A single batch of 69 percent hydrated Pain au Levain will make two large loaves of bread. You could also make three or more smaller loaves. However, the larger loaf will need to be baked at a lower temperature for a longer time, while the smaller loaves and rolls can be baked at a higher temperature for a shorter time. Changing the size of the loaf can help you dovetail your baking with the changing temperature of the oven. Like Bettie Three Seed Bread, but want something shaped better for sandwiches? Form it into bâtards. If you are baking in a combo cooker, be aware that round boules will accommodate more dough in that enclosed space than bâtards.
- **Exchange poolish for 100 percent hydrated sourdough levain.** The hydrations of these two preferments are the same, so the overall hydration of the dough will remain the same. You will likely want to add additional yeast (about 0.3 percent of total flour weight) to dough that contains a poolish, as the leavening power of a poolish needs a little extra oomph to fully ferment and proof the dough. If two breads were made side by side and the only difference was a poolish instead of a levain, the poolish dough would be slightly lighter with a more tender crumb than the one leavened with a naturally leavened levain.

Once in a While You Get Shown the Light In the Strangest of Places If You Look at It Right*

One of the most important lessons I learned about baking bread was from our dog Georgie, a wise, long-haired dachshund-esque beauty who loved good bread. Georgie was a scrappy neglected resident of our neighborhood when we moved in. She spent her days lying beside the gravel road, chasing cars, and barking at whoever would listen. Everyone on the road knew her and fed her scraps when they had some, but we fell desperately in love with her, and it didn't take long before she moved out of her makeshift home beneath a broken lawn mower and into our home. She became a princess, quite content to stay right by our side, but she never quite lost her independent streak. Over the years she would occasionally stroll down to visit the neighbors along the road, despite our disapproval.

Our neighbor Heber Golden, the old farmer for whom Golden Farm Road was named, kept treats for Georgie. We became friends and did neighborly things—he gave us fresh goose eggs, we boarded up his house before the hurricanes when he got too old to do it, he shared white iris bulbs when his patch needed thinning—but his bond with Georgie was special. They went way back.

One Saturday we were planning to have friends over for pizza after the day's baking. This was during the era when I operated the wood-fired bakery year-round, working long days and nights, the cumulative effect of overwork wearing me down. That day I was fatigued and wishing for rest more than anything, but nonetheless mixing the pizza dough, prepping ingredients, feeding the fire, getting things in order for the party. Time was getting short and I was feeling rushed. I looked around the yard for Georgie, trying to keep track of things. She was nowhere to be found. Eventually I spotted her way across the field, behind Heber's house. Off for a treat, I assumed. I called and called, but she ignored me. I had to walk halfway across the field before my commands

overpowered her defiance and she reluctantly slunk back to me. I told her what a bad girl she was and ordered her to stay in the yard before I turned my attention back to fretting about the party.

Party time was almost upon me and I still had things to do before our friends arrived when I noticed she was missing again. Sure enough, I saw her right back where she had been, out back behind Heber's house. I marched across the field again, grabbed her, and marched back

PHOTO BY STEPHANIE MISCOVICH

---

* from "Scarlet Begonias" by the Grateful Dead. Lyrics by Robert Hunter.

home, telling her what a bad girl she was. I shut her inside the house and turned back to my chores.

The next day we learned that Heber had died that evening while we were having our pizza. We attended his fire-and-brimstone funeral at the Otway Free Will Baptist Church, and were greeted by Heber's girlfriend after the service. She said, "Georgie came to see Heber just before he died. She barked at the back door, and I let her in and put her on the bed next to Heber. He opened his eyes and said, 'Oh, Georgie,' and petted her before he closed his eyes and then I put her back outside. That was the last he was awake before he was gone."

I suddenly realized how oblivious I had been that evening. Georgie was so much more aware; she sensed his waning energy and was determined to go to him. Thoughts raced through my mind. *I was right outside his back door, twice. Why didn't I ask myself why Georgie was acting that way? I should have recognized there was something wrong by the look in her eyes. What else have I been missing?* After Heber's funeral I rushed home to apologize to Georgie for my failure to pay attention and for telling her she was a bad dog, when in fact she was being an angel.

Georgie taught me to pay attention to subtle messages, a good practice always, and well suited for baking good bread in a wood-fired oven. Does the dough seem a little more dry than usual? Add more water. Is it weak today for some reason? Give it another fold. Is the heat penetrating too aggressively to the bone when you thrust your arm into the oven? Put the dough someplace cool and give the oven a little extra time to mellow. Use recommended methods and firing schedules as guidelines, but go with your gut—and the deepest part of your awareness—when it comes to making a decision about the health of your dough or the baking environment of your oven.

I regret not catching on to Georgie's odd behavior that evening so that I, too, could have said good-bye to sweet old Heber, but I am grateful for the indelible lesson about being aware of subtle things.

These differences are more pronounced in a dough made with white flour, compared with one that has a high ratio (50 percent or more) of whole-grain flour.

Changes that create a domino effect of other needed changes:

- **Quantity of flour.** All of the ingredients are in ratio with flour. If you increase the amount of flour (to make up for overhydration or simply by inadvertently using too much flour on the board when you're kneading, folding, or shaping), the amount of salt and yeast can slip below acceptable levels. Learn to handle wet dough and avoid overdusting your work surface.

- **Salt ratio.** Stick very close to a salt-to-flour ratio of 1.8 to 2.0 percent. A higher ratio will make a bread that tastes too salty. An undersalted bread easily overferments, is hard to handle, tastes bland, and has a shorter shelf life once it's baked. Yes, saltless bread is made in some parts of the world, but the flavor is bland.

- **Proper proof.** The rate of fermentation depends mainly on dough temperature, hydration, ratio and health of prefermented flour, and yeast ratio. The time it takes to achieve a full proof may vary from bake to bake. You need to be able to recognize the signs of a proper proof to achieve the voluptuous characteristics the loaves should have when you load them into the oven. You can change the amount of time needed by changing the fermentation environment—by retarding a dough, for instance. Underproofed dough will bake into dense loaves with a closed crumb. If it seems like the score marks blew out or there is an aneurysm on the side of the loaf, it was likely underproofed (or not sufficiently steamed). Overproofed bread will be flat, lack color, taste too strong, or have off flavors and a crumbly crumb. Be patient. Move the dough from warm to cool, depending on its needs. But don't expect to have control over the quality of your bread if you fail to achieve a proper secondary fermentation.

PART THREE

Using the Full Heat Cycle

CHAPTER NINE

✦➤ • ◆ ✦

Cooking with Fire:
TIPS AND TECHNIQUES
TO GET THE MOST OUT OF EACH BURN

As a bread baker I am steeped in what feels like—and is—ancient tradition: Bread has been part of the human experience since the Neolithic period, when the development of agriculture gave rise to the first urban centers and what we know as modern civilization. The human practice of baking bread has been a fundamental part of society through the ages, and this long tradition somehow infuses the physical process with a headiness that is palpable to bread bakers. During unhurried, re-flective moments during the act of baking bread, many bakers describe a feeling of direct connection with the ages, of tapping into or being part of an unbroken con-tinuum. This feeling affects us, enchants us, and imparts a subtle but deep sense of fulfillment and purpose to a physically demanding livelihood with long hours.

The 6,000-year history of bread has always seemed like forever to me, so trying to fathom our 1.5-million year history of cooking with fire—that's 250 times farther back in time—has been mind expanding. We don't even have that much time in all of human history; to fathom this we have to reach back into deep, pre-human history, even beyond the limits of the human time scale: Our history with fire is measured on the geologic time scale. If a 6,000-year history strikes a

chord as profound as the history of bread does in our lives, little wonder, then, that humans everywhere seem hardwired to respond in an elemental way to the 1,500,000-year-old practice of simply gathering around a fire to cook and share a meal.

Cooking and baking elemental dishes in a stone oven fueled by wood fire is satisfying in a way that is hard to define: fascinating, but also familiar, mysterious, and deeply fulfilling. Our ancestors learned to control fire and cook with it, and this remained the way humans fed one another, until only the last 100 years or so. It is perhaps the most basic domestic skill, yet people today who have grown up cooking with gas or electric ovens sometimes feel intimidated by the challenge. Cooking with fire has become so foreign to so many of us that it has acquired an aura of mystery, of being somehow complex or difficult to master. It should not be so.

All traditional cooking and baking methods were originally wood-fired, so rather than feature a selection of recipes for "wood-fired cuisine" in this book, I chose to concentrate on how to adapt modern cooking meth-ods—return them, really—to cooking with fire and retained heat, hopefully giving you a feel for adapting *any* recipe for the wood-fired oven.

Getting the Most Out of Each Burn

The beauty of cooking in the retained heat of a wood-fired oven is not only that it provides an appealing atmosphere and enjoyable, communal activity, but also that an organized cook can use the heat from a single firing to do everything from baking pizza and bread to roasting vegetables, grilling shrimp and steak, roasting a chicken, baking casseroles and pies, rendering fat, simmering chicken broth, drying wood for the next fire, and more.

For many years when I baked commercially in Magdalena, I did not use the residual heat for all the various uses described in this book. Then the breaks provided by my full-time teaching job gave me the opportunity to experiment, and I quickly realized one of the most satisfying aspects about having a wood-fired oven is using all the heat windows. There is some use for your oven almost from the moment the fire is lit and continuing on to the low, slow 100°F (38°C) temperature range. (Commercial wood-fired ovens tend not to get down to very low temperatures, which makes it easier to bake consistent loaves, but does not allow some of the low-temperature cooking described at the end of this chapter.) Creating and nurturing those diverse oven environments—or being able to identify and use them—is hugely satisfying. Not only do you make delicious food with wood, but you also use more of the BTUs that were harvested through careful combustion and then the retention of heat in the thermal mass. You'll learn to anticipate the varying stages of diminishing heat in your oven and choose the appropriate cooking method throughout the falling temperature gradient.

Adapting the Cooking Environment

Even after you've learned the thermal habits of your oven and planned ahead, you may occasionally find that it's too hot or cool to provide an ideal baking or cooking environment. Most of the ways to deal with this involve increasing or decreasing the distance from the heat source to the food. The methods for doing this are presented here in ascending order of complication.

CONSIDER ALL THE DIFFERENT HEAT ZONES IN THE OVEN

Does the ghee look like it will burn in a few seconds? Pull the pan closer to the mouth of the oven. Worried the oven might be a little cool for biscuits? Push them clear to the back of the oven and keep the door closed as long as possible (without peeking) in order to contain heat. You can't just reach over and adjust the temperature of your wood-fired oven with a knob, but the oven has natural temperature zones. A larger oven provides a wider spectrum of thermal environments than a smaller oven with less hearth space. For instance, pie dough needs to start off at a high temp—but you then want to finish the pie at a cooler temperature. Simply push the pie all the way to the back wall when you first load it and then pull it forward once it needs a cooler oven. After all, the only guidelines cooks and bakers had for years were instructions like "slow" or "moderately hot" oven. You can make anything in a wood-fired oven that you can make in a home oven. Make sure you install an oven large enough to create these zones.

CONSIDER A THREE-BRICK FIRE

People throughout history and all over the world have used a "three stone" approach to cooking with fire. Three stones of roughly the same size are used to elevate a cooking vessel above a fire. It is simple, but there are serious drawbacks, especially particulate emissions that people inhale when the fire is inside living quarters, as it is for about three *billion* of us each day on earth.

A three-brick fire can be easily constructed in your wood-fired oven, and the chimney draft will take the harmful smoke (although if you are burning efficiently, hopefully there won't be any) out of your immediate area and inhalation zone. Place three firebricks in a circle, pull some burning wood into the middle, and you have a cooking surface with fire directly below for sautéing, frying, or searing.

USE A FIREWALL OF BRICKS

It's nice to have as large an oven as possible. It provides enough space for the entire Thanksgiving wood-fired feast and the long, slow periods of dehydrating figs. A drawback of a larger oven, however, is the increased time and fuel required to heat her up. One solution (in addition to burning efficiently and having a well-insulated oven) is a firewall. This is a wall of bricks protecting part of the oven from the fire's radiant heat, as well as creating a smaller space—one small enough to heat up more quickly than the larger space of the entire oven. Firewalls can be placed in any configuration and built as high as necessary to offer proper protection.

A firewall allows you to quickly transition from a cooler environment to one that requires a quick, hot fire for last-minute cooking and vice versa. For instance, standing rib roast is an impressive cut of meat to cook in a wood-fired oven, but the ending temperature of the oven is significantly lower than the high heat necessary to make the classic Yorkshire pudding accompaniment. These different cooking temperatures can be accommodated by constructing a firewall in the front corner of the oven while maintaining a small fire or keeping a pile of coals dormant by covering them with ash in the opposite back corner. A standing rib roast requires a 20- to 30-minute rest time between cooking and serving. During the rest, remove part or some of the firewall if necessary, pull some coals forward, and rekindle a hot fire. Once that part of the oven is blazing hot, I can easily make the Yorkshire pudding and any side dishes, like Brussels sprouts seared for a few minutes in some bacon fat and then finished with a bit of reduced stock and some capers. I can also sear some chicken thighs and sauté onions on the fire side and then braise the

A firewall offers this standing rib roast some protection from the higher heat in the back of the oven.

The effectiveness of the firewall is illustrated by the clear demarcation line between soot deposition and firebricks that were cleaned by the heat of the fire's radiant heat.

dish at the lower temperature on the protected side of the firewall. Long-roasted food and a quick sauté out of the same oven. A searing environment immediately followed by a 350°F (177°C) braising oven. That's getting the most out of each burn.

The firewall can alter airflow patterns, so you'll want to construct it such that intake and exhaust happen naturally. A firewall may make a start-up from a cold oven a bit tricky. Wood dried during the receding heat from the previous fire helps, as do copious amounts of kindling. Avoid poking at the young fire, but do encourage it by giving it some extra puffs of air.

A similar device for holding back coals and ash in a live-fire cooking environment to dampen the effect of radiant heat is a piece of angle iron or heavy-duty metal called a fire fence. Protection is bounded by the height of the fence and size and intensity of the fire. It does help to keep your hearth organized. For instance, coals and ash are retained, which helps maintain clean hearth space for baking multiple pizzas. Andirons are especially handy behind a fire fence, because they lift a majority of burning wood above the collection of embers and ash, allowing more oxygen to the fire, aiding efficient combustion.

CONSTRUCT FLAMELESS BROILERS

Flameless broilers are even easier to construct than a firewall and are effective because they bring food closer to the radiant heat emitted by the hot mass. Simply stand up enough bricks to create a surface that holds food close to the dome or arch.

Finishing off the toppings on a pizza in this manner by holding the pizza up close to the ceiling of the oven is called doming. The intense heat radiated off the masonry arch gives more color and "cook" to the toppings

A few bricks will raise something up closer to the radiant heat of the arch. Note the inverted sheet pan in the back of the oven.

of a wood-fired pie. Raise the pizza up after you scoop it off the hearth with the peel, and hold it close to the top bricks for several seconds—and you'll have a good example of how the intensity of heat increases the closer the item is to the radiant surface.

USE INVERTED SHEET PANS

Inverted sheet pans provide air space that slows the transfer of heat cached in the hearth to whatever you're cooking or baking. This is another example of dead air space serving as insulation, just like the air gaps in the insulation around the oven. For example, if you're baking scones and you realize that the oven hearth is a bit hot, place the pan of scones directly on the hearth for the first 5 to 10 minutes in order to provide oven spring and flakiness, then move it to the inverted sheet pan so that the scones can bake through without developing

a thick bottom crust. Inverted sheet pans are great for raising any item up off the hearth—even a hearth bread—if the bottom seems to be getting too dark but the interior needs more baking time.

ADJUST COOKING TIME BASED ON OVEN TEMPERATURE

Many items can simply be cooked for longer if the oven is a bit cool, or shorter if the oven is hotter. This technique requires no special equipment. Just monitor the food and make changes as necessary. Of course, there are limits that can be exceeded, but there is a lot of temperature flexibility in many of this chapter's recipes and formulas. Granola, for example, can be made in the range of 275°F to 325°F (135–163°C), while the quality of your Pain au Levain is greatly impacted if you aren't loading at around 425°F to 475°F (218–246°C).

CREATE A WOOD-FIRED CONVECTION OVEN

Positioning a small fan by the door helps circulate the air in the baking chamber, increasing convective heat transfer. This is especially useful for dehydrated and dried items like jerky, dried fruits, and herbs. A small solar panel on the roof of my ovenhouse provides more than enough electricity to power the fan. It can't be used inside the oven at high temperatures, of course, but it's effective for removing moist air from the chamber, resulting in quicker and more effective drying and dehydrating.

Cooking and Baking Methods Adapted for the Wood-Fired Oven

There are many ways to use a wood-fired oven. Some users lean toward baking bread with retained heat; others require live-fire cooking. Once in a while, at pizza parties especially, the two come together. Part three of this book is organized according to descending temperature environments. The narrative is structured around general cooking methods, usually dictated by the presence of live fire, oven temperature, and, sometimes, humidity. This is the way professional bakers and chefs approach food. You prepare according to a general method, not a specific recipe. Most of the recipes specify quantities of ingredients, but some are akin to how your grandmother used to cook: by feel and method.

Here are the temperature ranges used in this book to group cooking methods:

- Pizza and Other Live-Fire Flat Breads: 600°F (316°C) and Above, with Fire
- Live-Fire Roasting: 600°F to 500°F (316–260°C), with Fire
- Hot Oven: 500°F to 350°F (260–177°C)
- Moderate Oven, aka the Comfort Zone: 350°F to 212°F (177–100°C)
- The Long Tail of the Temperature Curve: Under 212°F (100°C)

➤➤ ● ◄◄

CHAPTER TEN

Pizza and Other Live-Fire Flat Breads:

600°F (316°C) AND ABOVE, WITH FIRE

This very hot part of the oven temperature cycle is necessary to make Old World flat breads and pizza.

Isn't the primary role of flat breads the world over to serve as vehicles for holding or transporting other foods? Injera, the Ethiopian flat bread, is the plate and utensil used to serve and eat delicious Ethiopian wat. Baingan bharta is handled with a piece of naan. Focaccia, loaded down with savory seasonal toppings, is now mainstream American food.

The short bake time of most flat breads means you get to eat sooner rather than later, and the brevity of a fast, hot fire means you don't need a lot of wood to keep it going for the extended period needed to infuse the thermal mass with enough heat to bake hearth breads. Perhaps this is why flat breads dominate those cultures where there is little fuelwood.

Pizza: The Gateway Food to Wood-Fired Cooking

Pizza needs fiery-hot oven temperatures and cooks in a flash. Thin-crust pizza flavored by smoke and fire is incredibly satisfying, and the fun of a wood-fired pizza party with your family and friends is gratifying. So it's not surprising that pizza is often the introduction that many people have to cooking with fire, just as it serves as the introduction to this book's recipes.

However, pizza need not be a big production—in fact, if it's easy it will happen more often. If you make pizza dough (or have some in your fridge) and wrangle together some ingredients—even a selection as simple as sauce and high-quality fresh mozzarella—you can have a delicious meal without a lot of fuss. Being able to incorporate wood-fired cuisine into your meals is not only delicious, but also adds to a luxurious lifestyle. A couple of wood-fired pizzas on Tuesday night, or for lunch on a day at home? What a great way to feed yourself! In other words, there is no need to have a party to have pizza.

The best way to learn how to operate your oven for pizza is to mix some dough, prep a *small* variety of toppings, and . . . don't invite anybody over for pizza, *yet*. Oh, you will, eventually, especially when people find out you're making wood-fired pies. But it's harder to focus on your pizza skills when there's a lot going on and you're receiving people at your oven. Once all the pieces come together—you know how to fire your oven, the fermentation schedule is under control, and

you have some favorite flavor combinations—then you can bring over the crowd and expand their view of good pizza.

THE DOUGH

There is a massive rift in the pizza world about which type of flour to use for dough. According to the Associazione Verace Pizza Napoletana, "the only non-profit association that safeguards and promotes the culture of the real Neapolitan pizza worldwide," Type 00 flour must be used in an authentic Neapolitan pizza (as well as San Marzano tomatoes, fior di latte or fresh bufala mozzarella, fresh basil, extra-virgin olive oil, sea salt, and yeast—and as much of it as possible should be imported from Italy). Type 00 refers to a flour with a small grain size and a flour protein content of about 11.5 percent. I've used Type 00 and it is, indeed, a beautiful flour that makes an extensible dough and is chewy once the pie comes out of the oven. If I see bags of Caputo—a popular brand of Type 00—in the back of a pizzeria, I know it's an establishment that takes quality and authenticity seriously. Still, I balk at purchasing imported flour. And you know what? Domestic flour with a protein level of 11.5 to 11.7 percent protein makes delicious pies, and nobody has ever asked me, "Is this dough made with Type 00?" (*Note:* Imported flours are often not malted, so they may not brown if you are making pizza in your home oven—the temperatures can't get hot enough.)

A fire for pizza should blaze long enough to completely remove the soot from the firebox to leave it clean and reflective. The size and amount of thermal mass will affect the amount of time this takes. A minimum of 1 to 2 hours should be allocated for bringing your oven up to temp if you have a manufactured core or the firebox is only one brick thick with no additional thermal mass. The amount of time required to heat up the oven partly depends on how adept you are at making fires. A top-down fire structure that was laid while the oven was still warm will substantially decrease the amount of time it takes to start a strong fire and heat up the firebox. You may need to move the fire around to heat the hearth and, eventually, make room to bake the pies. Position the fire along either side (or both) of the oven, and/or against the back wall, depending on how big your oven is. The discussion of andirons in chapter 4 describes how elevating the wood off the hearth creates flames that roll over the vault or dome, providing plenty of flame to cook the toppings of the pizza, just as the hot hearth bakes the bottom crust.

Once the fire is established, sweep the hearth with a wire brush. The first couple of pizzas may be sacrificial; if the hearth is still blazing hot, it'll quickly char the bottom of the pizza. The hearth needs to be conditioned and mellowed—think of the way the first couple of pancakes help bring a freshly used griddle into adjustment.

Sweep the hearth between pies, especially when the oven is very hot. Otherwise, dusting flour will carbonize on the hearth and get baked into the bottom of the next pie.

Eventually, the oven will begin to cool and you'll need to add fresh fuel to stoke the fire and increase the temperature of the oven environment. You may also want to pull some coals or embers over the part of the hearth where you've been baking pizza as a way to recharge it. You can continue to make pizza in another part of the hearth meantime, or wait to let the area covered in coals come back up to pizza temperature. A hoe and wire brush are invaluable tools for moving around a fire and cleaning the hearth in its wake.

I prefer a slightly less intense pizza environment than that espoused by much of the live-fire pizza crowd. I know, I know, I know, pizzas are supposed to be baked for just 90 seconds at whatever mega-temp you can possibly stand working in. But sometimes that seems a little extreme, and to me the pizza ends up burned. I liked it well baked, but that's no excuse for burned, dry carbon crust. It doesn't taste good to me. Once I went to a live-fire pizzeria and the wait staff told us that we should expect 30 percent of the pizza to be burned, because "that's the way it's supposed to be." Even if that is how it's "supposed" to be, that isn't the way it *has to* be. I feel a 900°F (482°C) oven environment burns the pizza more often than imparting some special quality I can't achieve in a 650°F to 700°F (343–371°C) oven with stable heat.

THE TOPPINGS

The ingredients I like the most on my pizza are simple, and that means I can often harvest them from my yard or prepare them in the lead-up to the actual baking of the pies: simple uncooked sauce, roasted peppers and onions, fire-roasted bacon, sautéed asparagus. Your guests will come up with some extravagant pie topping combinations. Remind them to keep them simple and light! In my classes I sometimes impose a three-ingredient-only mandate in order to make sure the pies stay light and simple.

I've heard people tell of sweet pizza that has such things as chocolate and fruit on it, but I tend to steer clear of that. A big reason is that the dough recipes in this book are intended to make savory pizza. The dough isn't tough, but it also isn't the proper tenderness for a dessert application. Plus, I'm usually too full from pizza to find room for a dessert that has a large percentage of dough.

A. First, pat out the dough with the flat of your hand to form a disc.

B. Define an edge by creating a perimeter with your fingers. This edge will be the sauceless piece of crust that some people leave behind. The Italian term for this part of the pie is *cornicione*, which has the same root as *cornice* and refers to the horizontal ledge that appears on both pizza crusts and buildings. Andrew Janjigian, food journalist, associate editor at America's Test Kitchen, and ninja pizza archivist, calls it the "bones" of the pizza.

C. Next, drape the dough over the back of your hands and wrists and allow gravity to stretch it.

D. Place the dough back on the work surface and use the cornicione as a handle to gently stretch out the dough, thinning the membrane but taking care not to get it too thin. Any rips will cause you considerable grief when you attempt to slide the topped pizza from the peel to the hearth.

E. A light touch during stretching will keep the dough bubbly and light.

Easy, Uncooked Pizza Sauce

Open a 794-gram (28-ounce) can of crushed tomatoes. If you get whole tomatoes, and squeeze them, the sauce ends up a bit wet. No worries, though, if that's all you have. Just drain before you squeeze, even though that reduces the yield of your sauce. You do get more sauce with less work if you buy crushed tomatoes. And of course, you can also use fresh tomatoes. (I like the way Alton Brown prepares tomatoes for paella: Place a mesh strainer over a bowl. Halve tomatoes and squeeze them into the strainer, collecting the juice in the bowl. Grate the tomato on the large holes of a box grater and add to the tomato water. Now you have your own crushed tomatoes.) Also, I know pizza purists call for San Marzanos, but I feel other full-flavored tomatoes do just as well. And if you're keeping it local and canning tomatoes from your own yard or community, know that 3 cups of tomatoes is about 794 grams (28 ounces).

To the tomato, add a heaping tablespoon each of sugar and balsamic vinegar, 2 to 3 tablespoons of olive oil, and a couple of robust splashes of hot sauce. Add salt as necessary, and several good grinds of pepper. Then I go out and harvest a collection of fresh herbs—rosemary, thyme, oregano, and heavy on the marjoram—that will end up as about ½ cup stripped leaves. Chop the herbs finely and mix into the sauce. An immersion mixer helps make the sauce more uniform and smooth, but you can just mix it by hand, too. And no need to cook! The sauce will nearly boil when the pizza is in the oven, and applying it raw helps bring out the flavor of the tomatoes and herbs. Make a bunch of it, freeze for later use, and you are one step closer to making impromptu pizza in your wood-fired oven.

I prefer to use a restaurant squeeze bottle to apply the sauce, instead of ladling it on the dough. You may need to snip the end off the tip so the sauce can flow through, but you will have more control and less waste than if you and your guests use a ladle for sauce application.

STRETCHING PIZZA DOUGH

Once the oven is heated and your ingredients are prepped, it's time to start making pies with dough that you prepared as little as 4 hours—or as long as several days—ago. Spray a little flour on the bench and try to de-gas the dough as little as possible when you remove it from the tub. I strive to maintain as round a shape as possible, although I don't worry if the pizza isn't perfectly round and neither should you. Lightly dust the surface of the dough facing up at you.

I prefer a pizza with a cornicione (edge) full of large bubbles—the inside of each alveoli shiny, iridescent, or darkened by fire. Flat, dense corniciones are due to under- or overfermented dough, or to dough rolled out with a rolling pin—instead of stretched by hand. The rolling pin method de-gases the dough and fails to demarcate the rim of crust.

Fear not if the dough isn't perfectly round; it will still taste great. And consider making some oblong pizzas as a signature shape for specific toppings.

An oblong grana padano pizza made by Martin Phillip during a class at the King Arthur Flour Baking Education Center

Lightly flour a peel and place the stretched dough right at the end. The closer the pizza is to the edge of the peel, the less distance it has to travel before it's deposited intact on the hearth. Put on the toppings and decide what part of the hearth you want to use. Place the peel in that spot and swiftly pull it out from under the pizza so the dough drops down onto the hearth. There is a tendency for people to want to "push" the pie onto the hearth. However, the pizza will likely stop as soon as the leading edge hits the hot deck, forming an accordion shaped pizza, folded over on itself. Sometimes people try to pass these off as calzones. In addition to aesthetics, proper placement on the hearth maximizes space. Work on learning how to work the peel so you deposit your pizza (or bread) in exactly the right place.

The cornicione will begin to expand within 30 seconds, and soon after the sauce will start to bubble. Let the pizza stay in one place until you see the edge of the crust lift up off the hearth enough that you can slide the thin edge of a metal peel under the pie. Rotate it 90 degrees to expose a new section of the pie to the direct radiation of the fire, which should be strong, bold, and giving off yellow or white hot flames Anywhere from 90 seconds to a few minutes later, the pizza will be peeled out of the blazing oven before you devour it. This is what all the fuss is about.

Four-Hour Pizza Dough

I first learned about this pizza dough fermentation technique in Maggie Glezer's early contribution to the bread-baking canon, *Artisan Baking Across America*. There is no bulk fermentation; rather, the dough is divided immediately after mixing, shaped into rounds, and then allowed to slowly ferment and relax. It becomes extensible enough to easily stretch into a thin-crust pizza that, with minimal ingredients (which is how it should be), can be slid onto your 650°F (343°C) hearth and pulled out perfectly blazed in about 2 to 3 minutes. This type of pizza is what makes people dig up their yards and build wood-fired ovens. Pizza is a perfect healthy food group aggregator: It has grain, vegetable, dairy, meat, and a dab of oil on the cornicione.

The production schedule of this dough is flexible—there are several different ways to have dough ready for a pizza party. Need it this evening? Fine. Would you like to mix the dough today and chill it until tomorrow? Also no problem. The stability of the straight dough means you can use it for several pizza sessions over the course of two to three days. Here's how that can work. Mix a batch of dough around lunchtime. Take half of

the dough and place it in a container that has a light coat of pan spray and is big enough to accommodate a volume increase in the dough of about two-thirds. Give that an hour or so at room temperature and then place it in the fridge. This will be the last piece you use. The remaining dough can be divided, shaped, and placed in shallow, covered containers that have a light coating of pan spray. After another hour, place one of the tubs with divided dough in the fridge. This will be your pizza dough for tomorrow's lunch. The remaining first half of the dough will stay at room temperature until it's time to have a couple of pizzas for dinner that night.

Staggering the retarding periods helps control fermentation and, with a little monitoring, allows you to have properly proofed and extensible dough without having to mix more. There is no reason you can't have fresh pizza as an *easy* lunch if you have a hot oven, and some dough and simple toppings in the fridge.

This is a basic dough, but it nonetheless produces a delicious thin-crust pizza. If you don't need the 10 pieces of dough this formula yields, you can use one of the retarding options described above or freeze parbaked shells. You can also cut the formula in half.

Yield: 10 pieces, each 283g
Prefermented flour: 0%
Wood-fired oven temperature window: 650°F (343°C) and up
Home oven: Preheat the oven to 500°F (260°C).

Final Dough

Ingredient	Weight (g)	Volume	Baker's %
Bread flour	1,700	15 C	100
Water	1,105	4⅔ C	65
Instant active yeast	4	1 tsp	0.2
Salt	30	2 Tbsp	1.8
Total	2,839	—	—

Desired dough temperature: Adjust the water temperature so the dough is 75°F (24°C) at the end of mixing.

Autolyse: Combine the flour and water in a mixing bowl. Hold back the yeast and salt. Mix until thoroughly incorporated and homogeneous—but there's no need to develop the dough at this point. It's okay if the dough is still shaggy. Cover to prevent a skin from forming and autolyse for 20 to 30 minutes.

Mixing:

BY HAND: After the autolyse, add the yeast and salt to the autolyse mixture. Mix the dough with your hand and a plastic dough scraper for a minute to incorporate the ingredients.

Turn the dough out of the bowl and knead by hand using the traditional kneading technique we're all familiar with: Push the dough down with the heels of your hands, pull the opposite side of the dough up with your fingers, rotate the dough about 90 degrees, and repeat. This is the feel of kneading a lower-hydration dough. Mixing by hand will take 5 to 8 minutes.

BY MIXER: After the autolyse, add the yeast and salt to the autolyse mixture. Mix on slow speed for 3 minutes. Increase the speed to medium and mix for 2 minutes. Stop occasionally while mixing to scrape the dough off the hook.

When complete, the dough will be smooth and slightly tacky; it'll pull back when tugged.

Dividing/shaping: There is no bulk fermentation for this dough. Instead, immediately divide it into 283g pieces, shape into tight balls, and place in a dough box that has been sprayed with pan release.

Proofing: Allow to ferment at room temperature for 4 to 5 hours before using, or retard the dough overnight in the refrigerator. The extended rest time will make an extensible dough that's very easy to stretch.

Stretch, dress, and bake: Gently stretch dough into a thin disc, but retain a rim around the edge. Dress with simple toppings and bake at 600°F to 700°F (316–371°C) for approximately 3 minutes—less at higher temperatures.

Pizza Dough with Poolish

I've tried many delicious pizza doughs, but this formula, compliments of Brian Spangler and Kim Nyland of Apizza Scholls in Portland, Oregon, is the best ever. It's an incredibly light, fluffy dough that performs consistently and produces some of the most flavorful, tender but chewy, thin-crust pizza you'll ever find.

Yield: 8 pieces, each 283g
Prefermented flour: 20%
Minimum wood-fired oven temperature: 650°F (343°C)
Home oven: Preheat the oven to 500°F (260°C).

Poolish

Ingredient	Weight (g)	Volume	Baker's %
Bread flour	270	2⅓ C	100
Water	270	1 C + 3 Tbsp	100
Instant active yeast	0.08	pinch	0.03
Total	540.08	—	—

Ideal fermentation temperature for the poolish is 75°F (24°C). Combine and mix all poolish ingredients and ferment for 14 to 16 hours.

Final Dough

Ingredient	Weight (g)	Volume	Baker's %
Bread flour	1,085	9 C + 1 Tbsp	100
Water	715	3 C	73
Poolish	540.08	*	—
Instant active yeast	4	1 tsp	0.3
Salt	28	2 Tbsp	2
Total	2,372.08	—	—

* Best measured by weight; volume varies with ripeness.

Desired dough temperature: Adjust the water temperature so the dough is 75°F (24°C) at the end of mixing.

Autolyse: Combine the flour, water, and ripe poolish in a mixing bowl. Hold back the yeast and salt. Mix until thoroughly incorporated and homogeneous, but there's no need to develop the dough at this point. It's okay if the dough is still shaggy. Cover to prevent a skin from forming and autolyse for 20 to 30 minutes.

Mixing:
BY HAND: After the autolyse, add the yeast and salt to the autolyse mixture. Mix the dough with your hand and a plastic dough scraper for a minute to incorporate the ingredients. Turn the dough out of the bowl and knead for 3 to 5 minutes.
BY MIXER: After the autolyse, add the yeast and salt to the autolyse mixture. Mix on slow speed for 2 minutes, or until the ingredients are incorporated. Increase the speed to medium and mix for 2 minutes. Stop occasionally while mixing to scrape the dough off the hook.

Primary fermentation (first rise): 3½ hours, folding every 45 minutes

Divide, shape, and proof: Divide the dough into 283g pieces, shape into tight balls, and place in a dough box that has been sprayed with pan release. Allow to relax for 1½ to 2 hours.

Stretch, dress, and bake: Gently stretch the dough into a thin disc, but retain a rim around the edge. Dress lightly with toppings. Bake at 650°F to 750°F (343–399°C) for approximately 3 minutes—less at high temperature.

NEAPOLITAN

This is the classic style of pizza I always order. Use the best fresh mozzarella you can find, drain it well, and slice it as thinly as possible so it melts evenly. You can help make this pizza look more authentic if you put the cheese on first and then apply the sauce with a squirt bottle. This is the basic pizza. You can add other toppings, but it will no longer "officially" be a Neapolitan pizza.

PIZZA MARGHERITA

The same as Neapolitan except with the addition of basil and a drizzle of olive oil. The basil is usually added to the top of this pizza either before or after it goes into the oven, but if you tuck torn pieces of basil *under* the cheese they will be protected from the heat and retain more of their fresh flavor and bright color.

OTHER TOPPINGS

Even though we all love the traditional pizzas, we still like to add some of our favorite toppings. I like to select my toppings based on what's fresh and in season. I also prefer to roast them in the hot oven first so they become caramelized and sweet, then add them to the pizza. Not only do they become more flavorful, but they also lose

moisture in the first roasting, which helps prevent soggy pizza. My favorites include fresh corn, asparagus, red peppers, and onions. Any of the staples that I have created using the oven's diverse temperature windows, like crumbled bacon, Ember-Roasted Onions, or roasted asparagus, are perfect premade wood-fired ingredients. I always sweat mushrooms first because I find that raw ones get too dried out in the hot pizza oven. You can use fresh tomatoes, but slice them thinly so they cook thoroughly without losing a lot of water. And there's nothing like bright jewels from fire-roasted corn-on-the cob to give color and sweetness to a midsummer pizza party.

GRANA PADANO POTATO PIZZA

I learned this pizza from Paul Krcmar, wood-fired pizzaiolo at American Flatbread in Waitsfield, Vermont. Slice Yukon Gold potatoes very thinly on a mandoline. This can be done in advance; you can prevent them from getting brown by covering them with a damp towel. Stretch a piece of dough and brush the surface

A grana padano pie made by Paul Krcmar at the King Arthur Baking Education Center

Dough at the Ready

Sometimes you might want to bake some pizza, but it's late in the day and you don't have enough time to mix dough, then let it ferment and relax enough to stretch into a thin-crust pizza. There are a few things you can do in advance to make sure you always have the means to crank out a few pies without mixing a new batch of dough.

First . . . support your local baker. Many artisan bakers and pizza shops produce dough available at the bakery or in the refrigerated section of your local market.

But it's also easy to have dough stashed in your freezer. I prefer to freeze baked shells rather than raw dough, as they thaw more evenly (a defrosting piece of dough might be thawed on the outside but still frozen solid in the middle). So instead of freezing unused dough at the end of a pizza party, stretch out the pieces—but don't top them with ingredients—and bake until the structure firms but doesn't take on much color. This is called parbaking. You may want to dock the dough in the center of the pie

so it doesn't puff up like a pita. Slide it onto the hearth and bake until the dough is firm enough to slide a metal peel underneath. Spin the shell as necessary so that the entire crust has adequate heat exposure to assure structural integrity after it cools. I resist the urge to flip the dough—this flattens the cornicione's characteristics next to one baked "for real." The bubbles will have a flat side to them, and the shoulders will be weak. Once it's baked, place the firmed-up crust onto a cooling rack with good circulation. When the crusts have completely cooled (but haven't sat out long enough to dry out), slide them into a jumbo freezer bag, or double-wrap them with plastic.

Keeping a supply of stretched, parbaked, and frozen pizza shells around means you can easily have pizza anytime your oven is hot. I top them while they're flexible but still partially frozen. Place one on a well-floured peel (be careful that melting ice crystals on the dough's surface don't make the topped pizza stick), and pop it into the oven.

---

with olive oil (you can also infuse the olive oil with rosemary). Place the potatoes in a single layer, overlapping slightly. Cover the potatoes with a light grating of grana padano cheese and a sprinkling of chopped rosemary before sliding the pie into the oven. When it emerges, you can gloss the cornicione with a brushing of rosemary-infused oil.

PISSALADIERE

This is a classic Old World pizza, a bit like flat bread made with an onion filling, anchovies, and black olives. It's an attractive pie, with ingredients that will appeal to an excited minority of people. I adopted the filling described in the *Larousse Gastronomique* and made some slight changes.

Drain 1 tablespoon of capers. Peel and chop 700g onions (about two large onions). Heat a pan and melt a couple of tablespoons of clarified butter or schmaltz. Add the onions, a bit of salt and pepper, three minced cloves of garlic, several sprigs of thyme, and a fresh bay

leaf or two. Cook until soft. If the oven is hot, move the pan toward the mouth and into a cooler zone so the onions can gently break down to a jammy consistency.

I like to puree the onions at this point so they are more a filling than a topping. The capers can be thoroughly pureed with the onions or finely minced by hand and folded into the onions until evenly incorporated.

Quickly rinse six to eight anchovy fillets and halve them lengthwise. Spread the onion caper puree on a stretched dough and make a crosshatch pattern with the anchovies, placing half of a black Niçoise olive in the middle of each diamond. Pissaladiere can be baked in a slightly cooler oven. Too hot a bake makes the anchovies and olives dry out, concentrating their already intense saltiness.

The correct ratio of onions, anchovies, and olives to dough brings together sweetness, saltiness, and the flavor of fermented grain to make a delicious tart-like pizza that can be eaten hot or cold. The anchovies can be omitted, in which case you should salt the onions when you cook them.

Pissaladiere

Pita with olive oil and Za'atar

Pita and Za'atar Bread

Pita, either plain or brushed with olive oil and the Middle Eastern seasoning called Za'atar, is one of the easiest and tastiest foods to cook when the fire is too hot for most other breads. While you're waiting for the oven to cool, pop these lovelies into the oven and, in just a couple of minutes, enjoy them, or save them to use with the curry or stew you're preparing or as a pocket for other foods. A fire isn't necessary to make pita—only high temperatures. If you do make pita when a fire is burning away, keep a close eye on them so they don't get too crispy.

The pocket in a pita depends on high heat for enough oven spring so one side of a thin round of dough rips away from the other. Whole wheat flour with soft and fluffy particles is best; coarse and gritty whole wheat flour cuts gluten strands, creating weakness that may prevent the pita from ballooning.

After your first encounter with a scratch pita, you'll want to make pita yourself—easy, tasty, fun to watch. The pita baking method can also be used with other types of dough. If you have some extra pizza dough, simply roll it out in the same manner described for pita here and place it in a hot oven without any toppings. It will likely puff into a pita.

Za'atar is a Middle Eastern spice blend that varies as much as curry or garam masala, but is generally made with thyme, sesame seeds, and lemony sumac. Brush "just-more-than-a-little" olive oil on a piece of pita dough, then sprinkle on a healthy addition of Za'atar, about 2 to 3 tablespoons per flat bread. Rub the spice

Pita puffing in the oven

The pita should be rolled out to about ⅛" thick.

blend into the oil with your fingers to make a paste. Too much oil will make Za'atar flat bread soggy, but too little is just as serious. If it goes into the oven looking dry, it will come out dry. Not only is it unpleasant to eat, but the Za'atar simply falls off.

Yield: 12 pitas big enough for a sandwich
Prefermented flour: 0% (this is a "straight" dough—one that does not contain a preferment)
Wood-fired oven temperature window: 500°F (260°C) and up. Pita can be baked with or without a fire in the oven. If a fire is present, you need to tend the pitas a little more closely: They can turn from soft and pliable to brittle if left a moment too long.
Home oven: Preheat the oven to 500°F (260°C).

Pita

Ingredient	Weight (g)	Volume	Baker's %
Bread flour	350	scant 3 C	50
Whole wheat flour	350	3 C + 2 Tbsp	50
Water	476	2 C	68
Instant active yeast	2.1	½ tsp	0.3
Salt	14	1 Tbsp	2
Total	1,192.1	—	—

Desired dough temperature: Adjust the water temperature so the dough is 75°F to 78°F (24–26°C) at the end of mixing.

Autolyse: Combine the flours and water in a mixing bowl. Hold back the yeast and salt. Mix until thoroughly incorporated and homogeneous, but you needn't develop the dough at this point. It's okay if the dough is still shaggy. Cover to prevent a skin from forming and autolyse for 20 to 30 minutes.

Mixing:

BY HAND: After the autolyse, add the yeast and salt to the autolyse mixture. Mix the dough with your hand and a plastic dough scraper for a minute to incorporate the ingredients.

Turn the dough out of the bowl and knead by hand using the traditional kneading technique we're all familiar with. Push the dough down with the heels of your hands, pull the opposite side of the dough up with your fingers, rotate the dough about 90 degrees, and repeat. This is the feel of kneading a lower-hydration dough. Mixing by hand will take about 5 minutes.

BY MIXER: After the autolyse, add the yeast and salt to the autolyse mixture. Mix on slow speed for 3 minutes. Increase the speed to medium and mix for 2 minutes. Stop occasionally while mixing to scrape the dough off the hook.

The dough comes together into a firm dough with a smooth skin once it's fully kneaded.

Primary fermentation: Place the dough in a covered container and let it ferment for 1½ hours, folding once after 45 minutes.

Dividing/preshaping: Turn the dough onto a lightly floured surface and divide into 12 pieces. Pre-shape each piece into a tight round ball and place it, seam side down, on a lightly floured surface. Cover the dough, and allow to rest for 20 to 30 minutes.

Shaping: After the pitas have rested, flatten each ball of dough with a rolling pin into a disc about ⅛" thick. It's okay to use some flour when you roll them so they don't stick to the bench or pin, but use just enough to prevent sticking.

Place the rolled pitas on lightly floured couches. It's fine to stack them, but separate the layers with couche material.

Allow the pitas to relax for approximately 20 minutes. If your oven is nice and hot (about 550°F/288°C), you can rush this rest time. The push of the extra heat helps overcome the tension left over from shaping.

Baking: Transfer the pitas to a lightly floured peel and slide them directly onto the 500°F (260°C) hearth.

The pitas should begin to puff up within 2 to 3 minutes. After each one does, flip it over to lightly brown the top side—if desired—then remove it from the oven and loosely stack on a cooling rack. If the oven is very hot—or if a fire is present—you may want to remove the pitas as soon as they puff.

Wrap the stack of warm pitas in a tea towel to keep them soft as they cool. Once cool, store pitas in plastic. (This is one of the very few hearth breads that should be stored in plastic. Left in the open air, they dry out and become brittle rather quickly.)

PHOTO BY KATE KELLEY

VARIATION: SPELT PITA

This 100 percent spelt pita was the first pita formula I developed back in the late 1990s. I was looking for a product to bake in a high-temperature range, and was lucky enough to get whole spelt flour from Lindley Mills. We quickly grew to appreciate the distinctive, wholesome flavor of spelt, and a simple flat bread seemed a good fit for this ancient grain.

Hildegard von Bingen, the great Benedictine abbess, visionary, musician, poet, and healer who lived 900 years ago, gave spelt a ringing endorsement in her medical treatise, declaring, "The best grain is spelt. It is hot, rich, and powerful. It is milder than other grains. Eating it rectifies the flesh and provides proper blood. It also creates a happy mind and puts joy in the human disposition. In whatever way it is eaten, whether in bread or in other foods, it is good and easy to digest" (from *Hildegard von Bingen's Physica: The Complete English Translation of Her Classic Work on Health and Healing*, translated from the Latin by Priscilla Throop). Our respect for this extraordinary woman is immense. Much of her approach to health and wellness bears remarkable resemblance to modern understanding, particularly the principles of Eastern medicine. For balance, though, it should be mentioned she also had this to say: "From unicorn skin, make a belt. Gird yourself with it against your skin, and no strong disease or fever will harm your insides."

Follow the same mixing and baking instructions as for the pita in the previous recipe.

Yield: 12 pitas big enough for a sandwich
Prefermented flour: 0% (this is a "straight" dough—one that does not contain a preferment)
Wood-fired oven temperature window: 500°F (260°C) and up. Pitas can be baked with or without a fire in the oven. If a fire is present, you need to tend the pitas a little more closely: They can turn from soft and pliable to brittle if left a moment too long.
Home oven: Preheat the oven to 500°F (260°C).

Pita

Ingredient	Weight (g)	Volume	Baker's %
Whole spelt flour	680	4½ C	100
Water	503	2¼ C	74
Instant active yeast	2.1	¾ tsp	0.3
Salt	14	2½ tsp	2
Total	1,199.1	—	—

Desired dough temperature: Adjust the water temperature so the dough is 75°F to 78°F (24–26°C) at the end of mixing.

CHAPTER ELEVEN

✦

Live-Fire Roasting:
600°F TO 500°F (316–260°C), WITH FIRE

Live-fire roasting can happen at the same time as—or even before—pizzas are baked. The requirement for both is a very hot oven with some crackling flame to give color and flavor to whatever you're preparing. The length of firing from cold oven to roasting temperatures depends on how much thermal mass and insulation the oven has and how quickly an efficient fire can be established.

The only requirement is that the oven is hot and—ideally—has a dynamic fire. It might seem crazy to push a pan of cauliflower into a 700°F (371°C) oven. Isn't that too hot? It seems like it would burn. It does a bit, but just on the ends if you make sure to (carefully) reach in and shake the pan around a bit to expose some more edges to brazen heat. Many of the vegetables roasted at high temperature found in this next section can be made in advance of a pizza bake, and in fact will become toppings.

Roasting can also be done when there is no fire, but the oven is still hot. The density of an item affects the cooking time more than whether a fire is live or not. Potatoes will take longer to cook than asparagus and, therefore, may be a better candidate for roasting in a hot oven without a live fire.

Of course, a pizza bake isn't necessary to use live-fire roasting methods and techniques. Here are some easy ways to stock your larder with staples cooked in a live fire oven.

Radicchio and endive roast in a bed of embers.

Ember-Roasted Onions

My favorite way to have a supply of cooked onions at the ready is to roast them in their own skins. Medium-sized onions work best—small ones can become über-charred in a very hot oven, and it may be difficult to roast large ones all the way through without carbonizing the outer layers before the heart of the onion is tender. Rake some coals into an even layer just inside the door and toss a few onions onto the layer. You can also reach in with gloved hands or tongs to place them on the coals. The skins will immediately start to burn into a shell, protecting the onion as it starts to roast in its own juices. Turn the onions over a few times. You may need to pull them forward to a hot part of the oven that's free of coals so they continue to cook to the center without increasing the amount of charred exterior. They are done when a skewer penetrates to the center with no resistance. Take them out a little earlier if you want some onions that are slightly crisp in the middle and still have a hint of fresh onion flavor.

Remove the onions from the oven, place in a covered container, and let them cool in their skins so the smoky, charred flavor seeps into the flesh of the onions. Once they're cool, peel off the skin and you'll have an orb of cooked onion. Don't rinse off the small, flavorful bits of charred skin that stay on the onion. Rinsing the onion will wash away some of the juice released during roasting.

Onions can also be roasted at a lower temperature and without the fire, although the smoky flavor won't be imparted.

You can simply stash roasted onions in your fridge. Make a simple side dish by quartering them or slicing them into rings and dressing with olive oil, red wine vinegar, and salt and pepper.

This roasting method works with other vegetables, too; radicchio, endive, and eggplant are favorites.

Michael and Sandy Jubinsky's roasted pepper technique

Roasted Sweet and Pimiento Peppers

Place whole peppers close to (or on) the flame and embers. Char them, being careful not to carbonize all the pepper flesh. Turn two or three times to expose as much skin as possible to the fire. Remove with tongs and place in a sealed container. When the peppers are cool enough to handle, remove the skin and seeds under running water.

My friends Michael and Sandy Jubinsky of Stone Turtle Baking and Cooking School showed me an alternative method of roasting peppers. In their beautiful school in the woods of Maine, Michael cuts the walls off the sides of the pepper and sets them aside, just as you might do if you were adding them fresh to a salad. The seeds stay attached to the ribs. You now have a slab of pepper that you can roast and enjoy without the mess of removing the skins and seeds after the peppers have been cooked. You also conserve water because you won't have to rinse away all the seeds and bits of burned skin. Michael roasts them on a rack and places them in a covered container once they're removed from the oven. It's great to have a *slab* of roasted pepper, which stays on a sandwich more easily than julienne strips do.

For an easy appetizer, cut each slab of roasted pepper into bite-sized pieces and smear the tops with a combination of tomato paste, anchovy paste, and a bit of oil. Place them in a cast-iron pan (or other heavy-bottomed, ovenproof pan), sprinkle with salt and a few grinds of pepper, and slide the pan up to the flames until things start to sizzle.

I always glance at the marked-down produce racks in a grocery store or buy the slightly beaten-up peppers at the farmer's market. Peppers too wrinkled to sell as fresh are perfect for roasting, and come into your life at a fraction of the price. Roast and freeze them when they are available.

Pimiento Cheese Spread

Most people start with a jar of diced roasted pimientos when making pimiento cheese, but why not grow and roast your own? Pimientos are every bit as easy to grow as the more commonly grown bell, jalapeño, and cayenne peppers. A pimiento resembles a small, thick-walled red bell pepper that tapers at the bottom to a stubby point. Pick ripe pimientos and roast in the oven with a live fire just as you would bell peppers. Then dice the roasted pimientos and use them in the recipe below.

Here is Steph's recipe, adapted from Kyle Swain, chef-owner of Blue Moon Bistro in Beaufort, North Carolina. Kyle adds a healthy splash of good bourbon to give depth and complexity to the flavor, although I tend to use rye whiskey. Irish blended whiskey and even a smoky single-malt scotch can be substituted when that's all there is in the cupboard.

Spread pimiento cheese between slices of untoasted Pain de Mie for a retro lunch or serve as a dip paired with Pain de Mie Melba Toast for the best homemade, homegrown, fire-roasted pimiento cheese around.

INGREDIENTS

- 1 cup mayonnaise
- 2 teaspoons Worcestershire sauce
- 2 teaspoons rye whiskey
- 3 ounces diced pimientos, freshly roasted or from a jar (drain off the liquid from the jar)
- Salt and pepper to taste
- 1 teaspoon lemon juice
- A few dashes of Tabasco, Texas Pete, or other hot sauce if you want it spicier
- 1 pound very sharp white cheddar cheese, grated

Combine the wet ingredients, salt, and pepper in a large bowl. Add the grated cheese, folding gently if you like a chunkier pimiento cheese, or mixing with more vigor if you prefer a smoother, more whipped consistency. The mixture should seem a little too wet at first; it will thicken as the cheese absorbs some of the moisture. Sometimes I hold back a bit of the grated cheese just to make sure it doesn't turn out too dry; I can always add the extra cheddar later if it still seems too wet after a few hours in the fridge. Store the pimiento cheese in the fridge, but warm to room temperature before serving so it spreads easily.

Fire-Roasted Asparagus

For an extremely fast, easy, and delicious preparation of asparagus, begin by removing the tough lower one-third or so of each stalk. (Snap it easily; it'll break where the tender part ends and the tough part begins.) Place the asparagus stalks in a heated sauté or cast-iron pan and toss with a just a bit of clarified butter or olive oil and salt and pepper. Set the pan in a hot oven for a few minutes. Shake the pan occasionally and roast until the veggies are tender but still crisp at the heart and brightly green. Sometimes I cut the asparagus into shorter lengths, to be used later as a pizza topping.

Many vegetables—like the lightly oiled and seasoned asparagus and Brussels sprouts here—can be roasted with or without a fire.

Fire-roasted tomatoes

Tomatoes and cipollini onions are live-fire roasting.

Fire-Roasted Tomatoes

This approach to live-fire-roasted tomatoes makes a staple that can be used as a rich pasta sauce or as a thin spread on a piece of toasted bread. In a pinch it can be used for pizza sauce, although its flavor profile is more suggestive of pasta sauce.

Use the juiciest tomatoes you can find, either full-sized or cherry. Late-summer seconds and bumper-crop bonanzas are good times to make a bunch of sauce and freeze or can it. Ask yourself whether or not you want seeds in your sauce. I tend to skip removing the seeds because I don't want to reduce the yield, and out of my feeling that the whole tomato is more nutritious than a seeded one. Plus, removing the seeds is more work. The sauce will eventually be pureed, and that also breaks down many of the seeds. However, feel free to remove them if you avoid seeds in your food or prefer a smoother sauce.

Cut the tomatoes into 1" to 2" chunks and place in a roasting pan. The tomatoes will give off a lot of water, so choose a pan deep enough to contain the sauce without any liquid sloshing over the sides when it's moved around and stirred. Season with salt, pepper, and olive oil. You can add some garlic at this point, and any fresh herbs. Slide the pan into a blazing-hot oven. The tomatoes will immediately begin to cook and give off water. In about 10 minutes, give them a stir, then slide them back in the oven until the tops of the tomatoes are blackened.

You can stop at this point and serve this as a side dish or as a pizza topping. Or see the Scalloped Tomatoes recipe later in chapter 12, which uses these tomatoes.

If you are going for sauce, adjust the flavor by adding more fresh herbs (adding them after the sauce is cooked lets them retain their color and vibrant flavor) and puree the entire mixture with a food mill, food processor, or immersion blender.

Roasted Bone Marrow

Roasted bone marrow is both primal and sophisticated. Bones can be roasted anytime there's a fire in the oven; they make a low-cost, flavorful pâté-like spread to be served warm on good bread. Ask your meat farmer if you can buy thick beef bones, full of marrow. Then have a butcher cut them into lengths of about 3". Spread the top of the bone with a sauce of parsley, salt, coarse pepper, and some smashed juniper berries. Place the bones in a dish deep enough to catch fat that drains out as the marrow heats up and begins to bubble; this takes about 15 minutes in a hot oven. Avoid burning the bone itself—the aroma overpowers the nuanced taste and flavors of the marrow. Remove from the oven, cool slightly, and then scrape or scoop out the marrow with a knife or long, narrow marrow spoon. Or you can go caveman and suck out the marrow while sitting around a roaring fire.

Cedar-Planked Fish

By this time your fire might have died down a bit; if so, you can occasionally toss on a few sticks to create a flare-up of heat or light. The masonry should be hot, even if a fire isn't raging. The heat radiating off the surface of the firebox contributes significant brute thermal force to your food, cooking it quickly. And that fire or pile of embers is still going to infuse a piece of fish with the flavors of wood smoke, especially if you use a piece of cedar as a cooking surface. When Stephanie cleaves cedar into smaller and smaller pieces for use as kindling, she occasionally shears off a flat plank perfect for holding (and flavoring) a piece of fire-roasted fish. Alder planks are also commonly used in this way. Soak the planks for about 30 minutes before you use them so they don't burst into flames in the hot oven.

Bone marrow roasting in a hot fire

A relatively flat piece of cedar makes a nice surface for fire-roasting fish. After soaking the plank about 30 minutes, pat it dry and rub the surface of the plank with a light coating of oil and warm it in the oven before you place the fish on it. You'll need more time with this technique than if you were cooking in a pan, because the wood doesn't conduct heat as readily as metal or masonry does.

I use this method when preparing any type of fish cut into fillets, like mahi-mahi, or fish cut into steak like wahoo or tuna. Adjust cooking time by keeping in mind a rough timing guide of 10 minutes per 1" thickness of the fish. This timing works well in a hot oven, with or without the presence of flame.

Roast Chicken

Is there anything easier, more satisfying, and more useful than a roast chicken? The oven environment is similar to that for cedar-planked fish—a mild fire is nice, but the absolute requirement is a hot oven with the capacity to thoroughly roast the chicken to the core and give it crisp, flavorful skin. You can roast a chicken once a fire has mellowed, but make sure to have a hot oven.

Here's a simple way to yield that succulent meal. I like to use the method of salting and roasting poultry from Judy Rodgers's *Zuni Cafe Cookbook*. There chicken is salted at least 24 hours in advance and then dry-aged until being roasted at high temperatures. Salt draws and holds water, temporarily pulling juices to the surface of the bird. Eventually, this seasoned juice is resorbed into the chicken, permeating the meat with juice flavored by salt, pepper, and any other seasoning you may have used in the rub. Salting poultry in advance also helps soften otherwise tough muscle fibers.

Remove the large lumps of fat in—or covering the opening to—the body cavity. These large fat deposits might make the bottom of the chicken greasy. I add the trimmed pieces to a collection I keep in the freezer. Once I have half a pound or more, it will get rendered into schmaltz. (You'll find information about rendering schmaltz in chapter 13.)

Unwrap and pat the chicken dry. To prepare your seasoning, a ratio of ¾ teaspoon salt and ¼ teaspoon cracked pepper per pound of chicken is a good starting amount. Other aromatics can also be included in the mix. A tablespoon of pink peppercorns and a teaspoon of fennel or cumin seeds ground with a mortar and pestle is a good addition. Apply most of the salt and seasonings to the outside of the bird, but I sprinkle a bit

into the cavity. The seasonings easily stick to the slightly damp and flexible skin. However, once the chicken sits in the refrigerator for a day or two, the skin will dry out and the seasonings won't stick as well.

After the chicken is salted, place it on a cooling rack so air can circulate around the entire bird. Then set the rack on a pan on the bottom shelf of the fridge (to make sure that no chicken juice spills onto ready-to-eat food).

Over the next day or two, the skin will start to dry. This will help create a crisp skin on the roasted chicken. The body of the chicken also sags after a day or so. Once the chicken has aged for a minimum of 24 hours, loosely fill the cavity with quartered shallots or onions, a quartered lemon, and some sprigs of thyme or rosemary. (If you didn't salt the chicken in advance, you can also salt the bird now. If you have salted in advance, there's no need to add more.) Take care to not pack the chicken too tightly—this slows the internal cooking in relation to the external parts of the chicken exposed to direct radiant heat. Another way to help the bird cook evenly is to keep the legs untrussed to allow heat to more easily penetrate the cavity.

A word about roasting pans. You may be inclined to reach for your traditional speckled blue enamel roasting pan, but there is a better choice . . . unless your oven is blazing hot. A low-sided pan is best for roasting chicken because it doesn't obstruct radiant heat, which will brown more of the skin's surface. And a roasting chicken doesn't give off many juices that need to be contained. The lip of a regular commercial quarter-sized sheet pan is plenty deep enough. (You can also use a roasting rack to elevate the chicken and expose it to more heat—including circulating under the bottom.) On the other hand, if you are in a live-fire or high-heat environment, you may need the extra protection so the outside of the chicken doesn't dry out before the inside is adequately cooked.

Place the chicken in the hot pan breast side down. It will be flipped halfway through baking, and it makes for a nicer presentation to have the good side undisturbed during the last half of the cooking period.

High heat is crucial to create crackly, full-flavored skin, 400°F to 450°F (204–232°C), depending on how well your oven holds heat. Chickens can be roasted with or without a fire in the oven, although live fire browns skin much more quickly and you risk getting the bird too dark. If the skin does take too much color, move the pan to a cooler part of the oven and/or tent it with foil. Allow about 10 minutes for each pound. Flip the chicken over about halfway through to even the cooking and give nice color to the breast.

Once the internal temperature in the deepest recesses of the chicken reaches 165°F (74°C)—after about 50 minutes of roasting—remove it from the oven, cover it with foil, and let it rest for about 10 minutes. If you were to cut it immediately, the juices would run out, making the meat dry.

Searing and Using the Oven as a Griddle

Even the word *sear* sounds hot. You can sear in your wood-fired oven with or without a fire, but it's imperative that you have high heat and a heated surface on which to cook. We are still at the juncture of live-fire and retained-heat cookery. I like the wood-fire aspects imparted to a steak cooked rare on the hearth, but also appreciate masonry's heavy radiant heat, softer than the direct radiation emitted from the fire's flames.

The kind of heat transfer that takes place during searing or cooking on a griddle is conduction, and cast-iron pans and griddles are ideal heat conductors. When a mature fire has created a bed of embers, place the cast-iron pan or griddle on the embers (or directly on the hearth if it's hot enough) and allow it to get hot. Remove the hot pan and use one of two approaches for oiling it: Either

place a very small amount of fat or oil on the surface of the pan—not so much that it puddles, but enough to grease the pan well—or apply the fat or oil to the food before placing it on the dry pan or griddle. The food will immediately begin to cook when it hits the heat. Searing is what many recipes mean when they tell you to "brown" the meat. This technique can be used to quickly cook a steak—or to "brown" ground beef for a casserole that is baked at a relatively low temperature and won't reach a temperature necessary to brown the meat.

Steak on the Hearth

You don't even need a pan for this—just sear your favorite steak directly on the hot masonry hearth. Rub the steak with a mixture of salt, freshly ground pepper, and a little ground cumin if you care to add it, let it come up to room temperature, and then place it directly on

A flatiron steak cooking directly on the hearth

the very hot, dry hearth. Don't try to move it until the bottom is well seared. The high heat of the oven quickly cooks the steak, so check for doneness after just a few minutes. (You want an internal temperature of about 130°F/54°C for medium rare.) Muscle fibers contract under high heat, so let cooked meat rest for 10 to 15 minutes. That way proteins can relax and have a chance to resorb juices before the meat is cut, preventing them from gushing out of the meat and onto the platter.

Cleaning the hearth after a piece of meat sizzles its way to succulence is easy. Rake embers over the spot on the hearth where the meat cooked. Let things be for a few minutes. The hearth will be clean (and recharged with heat) once the fire is moved to another part of the oven. Sweep the ash and continue to enjoy the excitement of live-fire cookery on a stretch of clean hearth.

Seared, Oven-Roasted Triggerfish

Triggerfish is a white-fleshed fish with a distinctive nutty flavor. It began to make its appearance here in the waters off Cape Lookout, North Carolina, a couple of decades ago. Before that, triggerfish weren't found so far north. It took a little time for locals here to get to know this new fish, but it's now a highly sought-after item on menus all over the county.

To cook triggerfish fillets (or any similar flaky white-fleshed fish such as grouper, cod, or halibut) in the wood-fired oven, sprinkle them with salt and pepper and dust very lightly with flour. Be sure to brush off any flour that is more than a transparent veil on the fillet. Heat a pan until it's very hot, then add enough clarified butter or other high-temperature-tolerant cooking oil to barely cover the bottom. Place the fillets in the pan and do not move them until the proteins are seared. Flip and sear the second side, then move the pan to a slightly cooler part of the oven until the fillet has cooked through. Even in the absence of fire, this high-temperature technique gives plenty of flavor to high-quality fish. Other than a wood-fired roast-o-thon, all this fish needs is a squeeze of lemon.

Searing Meats and Vegetables for Later Braising (at Lower Oven Temperatures)

Foods gain flavor when Maillard browning and caramelization occur during the searing process. This flavor is a large part of the appeal of a thoroughly braised dish or a casserole where the meat has been browned before being cooked slowly and for a long time. But this type of comfort food requires a low and slow cooking environment after the high-temperature searing.

How do you quickly dial down your oven from searing to braising temperatures without wasting a lot of heat by leaving the door open? Use a firewall (as described in chapter 9) to create high- and low-temperature zones in an oven at the same time. You can also sear food at high temperature and then keep it in the fridge until the oven falls back down to the braising temperature range. To do this, sear or brown the meat or vegetable when the oven is in the higher temperature range—about 400°F (204°C). Turn it so it's grilled on all sides, but it's okay if it doesn't cook all the way through. Once it's browned, the food can be cooled, covered, and refrigerated for later in the day (or the next day) when you can use the oven's lower temperature to finish the cooking using the braising method described later in this chapter.

Simple Roasted Vegetables

The operative word in this method is *simple*. So simple, in fact, there's no need to include a recipe, just a few guidelines to ensure success. You needn't even have a fire. You might be at the point in your oven's cycle when the oven is swept of coals and is cooling a bit to receive a load of hearth bread. Or maybe this is the morning after a pizza party, with the fireproof oven door closed overnight to prevent heat from spilling out. Roasting vegetables, in other words, can happen at various times in the oven's heat cycle.

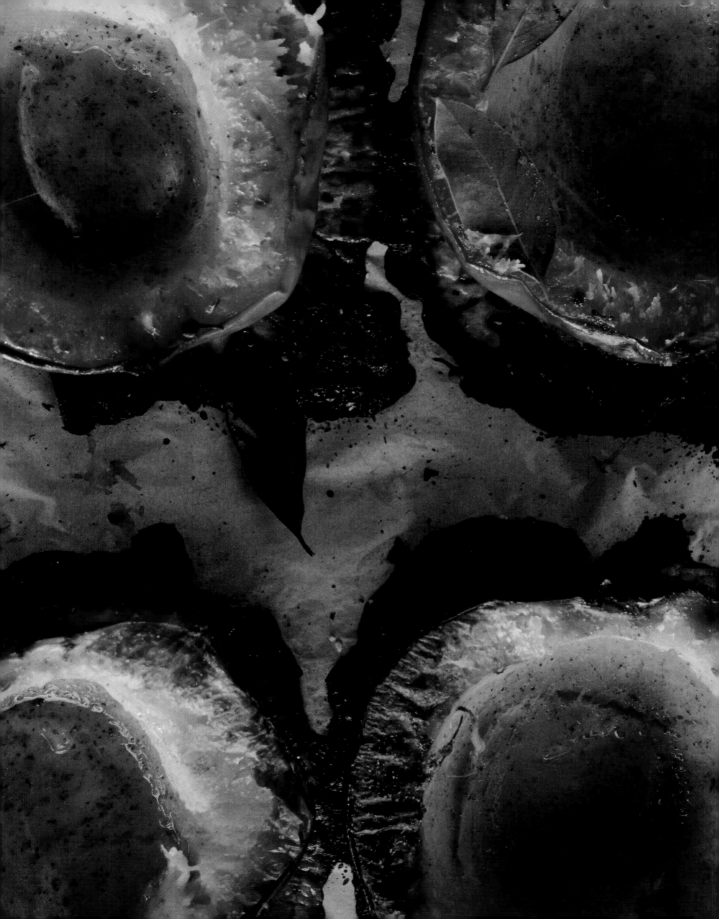

In addition to a high, flameless heat around 350°F to 400°F (177–204°C), consider these general tips:

- Wash the vegetables and cut them into pieces of a fairly uniform size. Drizzle with oil and sprinkle with salt, pepper, and whatever herbs complement the main vegetable.
- Spread the pieces on a low-sided roasting or sheet pan in a single layer.
- Roast the vegetables until tender, turning them occasionally, but not before a crust has formed.

Baked Balsamic Onions

Peel and slice or chop some onions. Toss with oil and balsamic vinegar. Throw in a bay leaf and a cayenne pepper. Place in a heavy roasting pan or something with sides tall enough to prevent the onions from spilling over when you stir them. Stir every 20 minutes or so to prevent them from sticking. A cover of foil near the end of 60 minutes of roasting will prevent the onions from over-roasting into bitterness; this also helps retain some of the syrupy glaze in the bottom of the pan.

Grilled Cheese on Pain de Mie

This grilled cheese compares favorably with the greatest sandwiches in the world. The combination of a good cheese between two slices of the delicious sandwich bread called Pain de Mie makes for a satisfying lunch every time. The closed crumb, soft texture, and rich taste make Pain de Mie a perfect bread for any grilled sandwich. Simply load a couple of these sandwiches, buttered on the outsides, on a griddle pan in a flameless oven that is around 350°F (177°C). Cook them long enough so they toast a bit on the outside while allowing the cheese enough time to melt.

One-Eyed Jacks

This delicious egg dish goes by many other names: eggs in a basket, bull's-eye eggs, gashouse eggs, eggs in a cage. I use Pain de Mie to make this breakfast, lunch, or dinner serving of eggs. The photo shows you what you're trying for here. Cut holes in the center of Pain de Mie slices by tearing out a piece of dough or using a cutter to create a neater frame. Heat enough of your favorite cooking fat (see *Rendering Animal Fat* in chapter 13 for some examples) to lightly cover the bottom of an ovenproof pan. Toast the rims and the rounds of bread; turn them over, crack an egg into each hole, and return the pan to the oven until the eggs are just set. Use the rounds to dip up the luscious egg yolks.

The oven's radiant top heat cooks the top of the egg while conductive heat cooks from the bottom. This crunch of heat means you don't have to flip the One-Eyed Jack, retaining a bright, well-cooked yolk that is a more attractive eye than either side of a cooked egg. Melt a piece of cheese on top for a heartier meal.

One-Eyed Jacks PHOTO BY KATE KELLEY

Crab Cakes

One of the quickest and lightest food preparations is the quick sauté. It's the obvious choice for many tender fresh vegetables, and it also works well with smaller pieces of seafood—very small fish fillets, soft-shell crabs, and shrimp sautéed in clarified butter, with crushed garlic and a good squirt of lime juice.

For many years we've made our crab cakes using picked local blue crab meat and a recipe adapted from A. J. McClane's wonderful seafood cookbook *Mc-Clane's North American Fish Cookery*. To a pound of fresh backfin or lump crabmeat, add ½ cup Pain de Mie crumbs, a beaten egg, about ⅓ cup mayonnaise, some chopped fresh parsley, 2 teaspoons Worcestershire sauce, 1 teaspoon prepared mustard, ½ teaspoon salt, and some freshly ground pepper. Combined lightly,

the mixture makes six medium-sized cakes that can be sautéed in a little clarified butter in a hot oven.

Steamed Littleneck Clams in Garlic Wine Broth

Littleneck clams are one of the earliest successful aquaculture products to become established here in Carteret County, North Carolina. These small clams are started from spat, grown out in tanks of circulating water from the estuary, and then placed in plots on the bottom of the estuary. Cherrystones (slightly larger clams) can also be prepared by the method given here.

Figure on a dozen or so clams per person. Use only clams that are tightly closed; discard them if they're open. Brush under running water to remove any sand clinging to the shells. Put 2 dozen clams in their shells

Matunuck Littlenecks at the Providence Farmer's Market bound for garlic wine broth

in a wide, shallow pan that has a tight-fitting lid along with ¼ cup each of white wine and water and a couple of glugs of olive oil. Add 1 minced clove of garlic (shallots are a good substitute), 3 bruised bay leaves or a couple of sprigs of thyme, and some grinds of black pepper. There should be ¼" to ½" of liquid in the pan. Don't add any salt! The clam juice will likely be plenty salty. More can be added at the table, although that is rarely necessary. Put the lid on the pan and push it close to embers or a live fire for a few minutes until the liquids start to boil, then pull the pan away from the intense heat and let it steam for 8 to 10 minutes or until the clams open. Place the clams with some of the liquid into individual serving bowls. The juice from the clams—released into the pan when the clams open—along with the wine, olive oil, and aromatics, is the perfect dipping broth for a crusty piece of hearth-baked bread. You can also pair these clams with pizza or flat bread, because the timing will be right.

Pan-Fried Flounder or Little Blues

Pan-frying differs from sautéing in that the former requires more fat. The fat should cover the bottom of the pan completely and reach a third to halfway up the sides of the food. Also, the food is often well covered in some kind of batter, be it a dusting of equal parts cornmeal and flour, or a covering of bread crumbs applied after a dip in a simple egg-and-water mixture. Make sure the fat is hot—you should see ripples on its surface—before you put food in the pan; this keeps the food from absorbing the fat.

Salt and pepper small (pan-sized) pieces of flounder fillets or little, fresh-caught bluefish. (*Note:* Bluefish, being oilier, are best eaten the day they are caught.) Lightly dust or encrust the small fillets, then fry them, turning once. Thin fillets will cook in a few minutes.

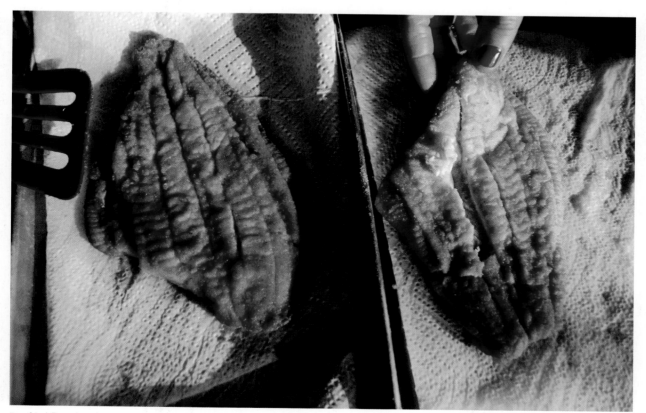

Pan-fried flounder

Dry-fried okra just beginning to brown

A tasty variation is to coat the seasoned (salted and peppered) fillets in a mixture of equal parts flour and cornmeal before pan-frying. This method requires just a bit more fat in the pan.

Dry-Fried Okra

Although a little clarified butter or oil is used to wet the pan, this method is called "dry-fried okra" to emphasize that the dish differs dramatically from stewed and deep-fried versions. If you've always disliked okra in its gooey state (in stews and gumbos), you might like this crispy presentation. Okra is an easy vegetable to grow in the South and has lovely flowers. Our local farmer George Simpson usually has a plentiful supply, so we often get our okra from him and save potager space for growing other herbs and vegetables. Cut up fresh and tender okra into ½"-thick cross sections. Then very lightly dust them with equal parts cornmeal and flour to which salt and pepper have been added. (Dust the okra in a colander, sprinkling the breading mixture over the pieces and allowing the excess to sift through. This ensures a light application.) Heat a small amount of clarified butter in a cast-iron pan. Place the okra in the pan and sauté, tossing gently from time to time, until tender, crispy, and lightly browned. These tasty, bite-sized bits of okra seem to shrink when you cook them, and I always wish we had cooked more.

CHAPTER TWELVE

✦ • ✦

Hot Oven:
500°F TO 350°F (260–177°C)

This is the heat zone where most bread baking happens. The high temperature is necessary for good oven spring, caramelization, and the Maillard reaction. However, as you know, this high temperature continues to decrease if a fire isn't present. The length of time the oven remains in this temperature zone depends on the amount of thermal mass and insulation. It's a dynamic environment to cook and bake in, because this temperature window gives a steady, penetrating heat.

Getting Ready to Bake Hearth Bread

I bake most of my hearth bread in an oven with a hearth temperature of about 450°F (232°C). The fire has long burned itself to ash, and I've swept the hearth clean of ash. The rake-out occurred while the oven was maybe still 700°F (371°C); since then it has been slowly equalizing and descending into the zone for baking hearth breads. This is the oven environment you need to make beautiful loaves of wood-fired bread. The masonry is hot, and once this heat starts to conduct into the loaves, they will swell with oven spring, aerating themselves on the inside. Water from the dough evaporates, contributing humidity to the bake chamber. This is where you want your oven to be as you move into these next formulas.

Pain Rustique

One of the many benefits of working at King Arthur was the opportunity to meet James MacGuire, the charming, longtime restaurateur of Montreal. James possesses incredible skills as a chef, pastry chef, and baker, holistic culinary competency rarely found in just one individual. His talents coalesced at his acclaimed restaurant Le Passe-Partout, where he served fine European cuisine in the evening (menus handwritten each day) accompanied by the hearth bread he made that morning. He also served the community as boulanger in the European tradition of selling bread by weight, gladly cutting just a slice or two off a loaf for elderly neighbor patrons who came by for something for their morning toast.

As a young man James was working in a French restaurant where Professor Raymond Calvel was doing what we now call consulting. James was able to observe Calvel and was intrigued by how much the restaurant's bread improved in the wake of Calvel's simple but fundamental suggestions. In 2001, James's English version of Calvel's *Le Goût du Pain* (*The Taste of Bread*) was published, a treasure for non-French-reading American bakers. This was the primary source that explained crucial bread-baking fundamentals such as the autolyse,

the importance of enzymatic activity in fermentation, and the need to control dough temperature.

James was a guest instructor at the King Arthur Baking Education Center in Norwich, Vermont, and I was lucky to assist him in classes as he spread the word of Calvel along with his own knowledge and skills. I even had the opportunity to bake with him in Montreal, where he served a delicious lunch halfway through a baking day in the white-tablecloth dining room, vacant until the evening. I learned three breads from James that are in my standard repertoire and in this book: Pain Rustique, Miche, and 67% Rye. Here is an excerpt from James's Pain Rustique notes, written down for me during those fun days:

> *. . . invented by Raymond Calvel in the mid 1980's, inspired by the ciabatta (among other influences). His idea was that a minimally kneaded, well-fermented white bread dough (i.e. baguette 90% of the time) which doesn't go through the stress of being shaped into something long + skinny will have better flavor, texture, and keeping qualities . . . it also fits today's purposes because it is* very, very fast.

On more than one occasion I've heard James compare Rustique's speed of fermentation to "a barn on fire." So keep on your toes lest the dough overferment.

Rustique is a beautiful, tasty, and elemental loaf that can be made from mixing to baking in about 4½ hours thanks to the fact that half of the flour is prefermented in a poolish. I use it in place of the baguette in a wood-fired oven, as was Calvel's intent. I used to make baguettes in Magdalena, but I transitioned to rustic shaped breads as a substitute for the flavor profile and open crumb of baguettes. Transferring baguettes off a peel into a wood-fired oven without distorting the shape can be tricky; contemporary wood-fired ovens that employ a loader are better suited to the careful placement a baguette requires. It's much easier to systematically fill the oven with Pain Rustique, with less wasted hearth space, a full oven, and greater profit for each load. If you're a home baker or micro-baker, I encourage you to fill the white bread niche with this good friend of mine, Pain Rustique.

The high percentage of prefermented flour in Pain Rustique makes it important to include diastatic malt powder. As the poolish ferments, much of the flour's starch is converted to sugar and consumed by yeast. Diastatic malt, which is enzymatically active, helps unlock more of the sugars contained in the flour. See *Falling Number* and *Using Malt* in chapter 7 for more information about malt and enzyme activity in flour.

Yield: 3 loaves, 3 focaccia, or numerous petits pains
Prefermented flour: 50%
Wood-fired oven temperature window: 425°F to 475°F (218–246°C)
Home oven: Preheat the oven to 450°F (232°C).

Poolish

Ingredient	Weight (g)	Volume	Baker's %
Bread flour	390	3¼ C	100
Water (75°F)	390	1⅔ C	100
Instant active yeast	0.4	pinch	0.1
Total	780.4	—	—

Ideal fermentation temperature for the poolish is 75°F (24°C). Combine and mix all poolish ingredients and ferment for 14 to 16 hours.

Final Dough

Ingredient	Weight (g)	Volume	Baker's %
Water	148	¼ C + ⅓ C	69
Poolish	780.4	*	—
Bread flour	390	3¼ C	100
Diastatic malt powder	1.5	½ tsp	0.2
Instant active yeast	2	½ tsp	0.3
Salt	14	1 Tbsp	1.8
Total	1,335.9	—	—

* Best measured by weight; volume varies with ripeness.

Desired dough temperature: Adjust the water temperature so the dough is 77°F (25°C) at the end of mixing.

James MacGuire: famous enough to be caricatured with his bread in a Montreal alley, circa 2000

You'll notice that most of the water in this formula is added into the preferment, with only a small amount in the final dough. For this reason, the standard method of achieving the desired final dough temperature (by adjusting the temperature of the water according to a formula that averages the temperatures of the various components) doesn't work as well as it does when a larger amount of water is added to the final dough. Although less precise than the standard calculation method, the following guide should help you arrive at the desired final dough temperature:

If the flour, room, and preferment are:
- Less than 70°F (21°C), use water that is 90°F (32°C)
- 71°F to 80°F (22–27°C), use water that is 75°F (24°C)
- Greater than 80°F (27°C), use water that is 60°F (16°C)

Autolyse: Pour the water around the edge of the poolish to help release all of the preferment. Add the water and poolish to the mixing bowl. Add flour and malt. Hold back the yeast and salt. Mix by hand or mixer until thoroughly incorporated and homogeneous, but you needn't develop the dough at this point. It's okay if the dough is still shaggy. Cover to prevent a skin from forming and autolyse for 20 to 30 minutes.

Mixing:

BY HAND: After the autolyse, add the yeast and salt and mix the dough with your hand and a plastic dough scraper for a minute to incorporate the ingredients. Turn the dough out of the bowl and knead by hand using the techniques described in chapter 6. Hand mixing will take about 8 minutes.

BY MIXER: After the autolyse, add the yeast and salt, then mix on slow speed for 3 minutes. Increase the speed to medium and mix for 3 minutes. Stop occasionally as you mix to scrape the dough off the hook.

When complete, the dough will be smooth and slightly tacky, and will pull back when tugged. Remember, the dough will develop considerably when fermenting and folding.

Primary fermentation: Place the dough in a covered container and let it ferment for 1½ hours, folding every 30 minutes. There will be a total of two folds—but if the dough doesn't seem fluffy and active, give it an additional fold and divide after another 30 minutes.

Dividing: Turn the dough onto a lightly floured surface and divide into three pieces, about 454g each, and place upside down on a floured couche. This is the final rustic shape—no preshape or further shaping is required. One of the benefits of the rustic shape is the opportunity to go from bulk dough to final shape with no preshape, bench rest, or final shaping. Proof for approximately 45 minutes.

Scoring and Baking: Just before baking, invert the loaves onto a lightly floured peel. Score with one angled cut down the length of the loaf and bake in a steamed 450°F (232°C) oven. Or place in a heated combo cooker, score, cover, and place in the oven. Bake for approximately 40 minutes.

Dividing Rustique into loaves . . .   . . . and placing them on floured couche. PHOTOS BY KATE KELLEY

VARIATION: PETITS PAINS

Pain Rustique is also ideal for rolls. You can divide the dough into whatever sizes you desire; I find pieces of 85g to 113g perfect for modestly portioned individual sandwiches. Like baguettes and other open-crumb breads, slice petits pains horizontally if you're using them for sandwiches. The top and bottom crusts do a great job of containing sandwich dressings, whereas the abundant holes in vertical slices would allow dressings to drip through.

Proof time is the same as for the larger Pain Rustique but the bake time is shorter, about 20 minutes, depending on size. Because petits pains take less time to bake, they can tolerate a bit hotter hearth than can breads that must remain on the hearth longer. For this reason, a load of petits pains can go into a hot oven ahead of a load of larger loaves, allowing you to begin production when the oven would otherwise be too hot. Be sure to inject plenty of steam when baking in an extra-hot oven—steam is driven out of a higher-temperature bake chamber more quickly than one with a lower temperature.

Petits pains PHOTO BY KATE KELLEY

VARIATION: FOCACCIA

Focaccia can be made out of any dough that gives a nice open crumb, but I make it out of Pain Rustique dough more than anything else. The whole batch in this home-sized recipe will nicely fill a half sheet pan. When the dough is turned out of the tub onto a floured surface, gently pat it into a rectangle slightly smaller than the size of the pan, and then place it into a lightly greased half sheet pan. Take care not to fold it over on itself. Pat the dough into an even layer, avoiding thin spots or a built-up rim.

The choice of toppings is wide open, but I prefer a simple combination: finely chopped fresh thyme or rosemary, thin rings of sweet onions, olive oil, and salt and pepper, layered in that order. The rings of onions and the top coat of olive oil protect the fresh herbs from dehydrating or burning.

Finish with olive oil applied with a squirt bottle, and then use a pastry brush to spread the oil evenly. Get it into all the nooks and crannies, and make sure to brush it out to all the edges so that the entire surface has a nice sheen.

Like petits pains, focaccia can tolerate a hotter oven and serve the same purpose of mellowing the hearth temperature in advance of a load of loaves so that their bottoms won't scorch. The oil provides a shine to the rim of the focaccia, so steaming isn't nearly as crucial as it is with freestanding hearth loaves, which depend on steam for rich caramelization and shine.

Raymond Calvel, Coupe du Monde 1999

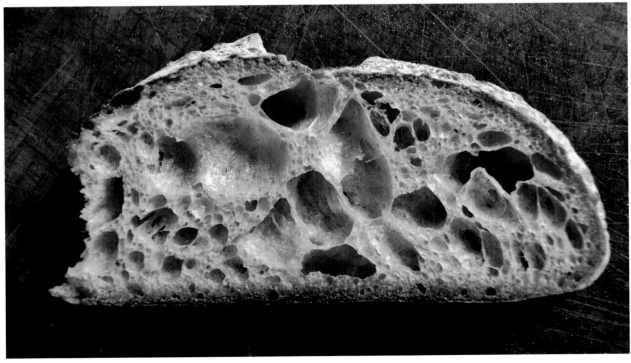

Pain au Levain, 69% Hydrated

This is the bread I made in order to learn how to make bread. Lionel Vatinet taught me this bread when I was at the San Francisco Baking Institute, and it was in heavy rotation when I got back to Bettie. I was baking in our home oven as much as I could, but I had also started baking hearth breads at Windansea, the newest fine-dining restaurant on the Crystal Coast. They opened a few months after I returned from San Francisco and had a wood-fired oven built by a local mason from Alan Scott's plans. At home I was able to control the major variable—oven temperature—allowing me to more easily observe the characteristics of the final loaf based on dough variables such as dough temperature and hydration. But at the restaurant I needed to consider the needs of the dough in the context of a brand-new wood-fired oven—the first one I'd ever baked in. I learned how to bake and how to bake in a masonry oven at the same time.

Pain au Levain means (roughly) "bread with leaven." But it's not just any leaven. Pain au Levain is a naturally leavened bread. It is a typical French sourdough that is long on earthiness and short on sourness. Although it's a dough that creates a milder lactic acid flavor profile, a retarding period will produce a more sour, acetic flavor.

Pain au Levain is probably the bread I have made more than any other. It's simple, but you could bake it every day for years and still learn something new about the bread-baking process. If I were allowed to make only one bread, this would be the one; but that doesn't mean I would be limited as to production schedule or variety. One of the beauties of naturally leavened breads is the flexibility of the production schedule. These breads can be slowed down by retarding. Pain au Levain is finicky, but it's not fickle. Pay close attention to your starter health and dough temperature. A weak (or underripe) starter or a low dough temperature will create a sluggish dough and a dense, contorted loaf. Take action to ensure fluffy and active dough! This recipe is a base formula, great by itself—quietly unassuming and sustaining—but flexible enough to take on the personalities of the following variations: rosemary, olive, and roasted onion. If dog is man's best friend, then Pain au Levain is humankind's best bread friend.

Yield: 2 large loaves
Prefermented flour: 25%
Wood-fired oven temperature window: 425°F to 475°F (218–246°C)
Home oven: Preheat the oven to 450°F (232°C).

Levain

Ingredient	Weight (g)	Volume	Baker's %
Bread flour	227	1½ C + ⅓ C	100
Water	227	scant 1 C + 2 Tbsp	100
Liquid sourdough starter	45	3 Tbsp*	20
Total	499	—	—

* Best measured by weight; volume varies with ripeness.

Combine the flour, water, and starter. Mix until smooth. Cover and allow to ferment at 75°F (24°C) for 8 hours.

You can also mix the starter and allow it to ferment for 5 to 6 hours, then retard it in the fridge for an additional 12 hours. It's important to achieve some visible activity before retarding the starter. If the starter isn't moving before it goes into the fridge, it's unlikely to become active during its tenure under cold storage: 40°F (4°C) is too cold to initiate fermentation. Activation before refrigeration!

Final Dough

Ingredient	Weight (g)	Volume	Baker's%
Water	400	1¾ C	69
Levain	454	2½ C*	—
Bread Flour	457	3¾ C	75
Whole wheat flour	228	2 C	25
Salt	17	1 Tbsp + 1 tsp	1.8
Total	1,556	—	—

* Best measured by weight; volume varies with ripeness.

Desired dough temperature: Adjust the water temperature so the dough is 78°F (26°C) at the end of mixing.

Autolyse: Remove 45g of liquid sourdough starter from the levain. Pour the water around the edge of the ripe levain to help release all of the preferment. Add the water, levain, and flours to a mixing bowl, but hold back the salt. Mix by hand or mixer until thoroughly incorporated and homogeneous, but you needn't develop the dough at this point. It's okay if the dough is still shaggy. Cover to prevent a skin from forming and autolyse for 20 to 30 minutes.

Mixing:

BY HAND: After the autolyse, add the salt and mix the dough with your hand and a plastic dough scraper for a minute to incorporate the ingredients. Turn the dough out of the bowl and knead by hand using the techniques described in chapter 6. Hand mixing will take about 8 minutes.

BY MIXER: After the autolyse, add the salt and mix on slow speed for 3 minutes. Increase the speed to medium and mix for 3 minutes. Stop occasionally while mixing to scrape the dough off the hook.

The dough will be sticky whether you're mixing by hand or a mixer, but as always, don't add any flour! The extended primary fermentation and numerous folds will eventually create a bouncy dough. Be patient and focus on creating a dough with a nice skin. When you handle it, strive to keep the skin intact and taut. Avoid poking or tearing the dough.

Primary fermentation: Place the dough in a covered container and let it ferment for 2¼ hours, folding twice approximately every 45 minutes.

Dividing/preshaping: Forty-five minutes after the last fold, turn the dough onto a lightly floured surface and divide into two pieces. Preshape each piece into a loose round ball, and place bottom up on a lightly floured surface. Cover the loaves and allow them to rest for about 20 minutes.

Shaping: Shape the loaves into boules or bâtards, place them seam side up in a well-floured proofing basket, and let them proof for approximately 2 hours. This is a pretty long proof time—you need to make sure the basket is well floured so the dough doesn't stick when it's turned out to score and bake, especially if the dough will be retarded in the baskets overnight. I prefer linen-lined bannetons instead of unlined brotforms for dough with a long proof time—the dough tends to stick more to the convolutions of the willow basket, while the linen-lined wicker gives a nice release.

Be patient! Cool dough or environment temperatures—or lack of an active dough at the shaping stage—will lengthen the proof time.

Scoring and baking: Just before baking, invert the baskets and turn the loaves onto a lightly floured peel. Score and bake in a steamed 450°F (232°C) oven for about 40 minutes.

VARIATION: OLIVE SOURDOUGH

For this variation, exchange the whole wheat flour for whole rye flour, which holds up well to the strong flavor of the olives. However, you can also make the bread with whole wheat flour with excellent results. Once the dough is developed after kneading, add 400g olives and continue mixing until evenly incorporated. (The baker's ratio of olives is 44 percent.) I like whole kalamatas but have also made olive bread with other types, including a mix of black and green olives. I roughly chop about 75 percent of the olives but leave the others whole. Some of those whole olives will get broken up during the rest of the bread-making process (and when the baked loaf is sliced or ripped apart), but it's satisfying to find some whole pieces of olive in the middle of the loaf. The smooth and oily olives tend to slip out of the dough; just keep tucking them back in as you fold, divide, and shape—they'll eventually become incorporated. The addition of the olives will increase the yield of the dough, so you may want to divide this variation into three loaves—or make one into a fougasse.

Top to bottom: Pain au Levain, Panmarino, and Pain Rustique

VARIATION: ROSEMARY SOURDOUGH

This is one of my favorite breads. I replace the whole wheat flour with white flour and add 28g fresh rosemary. The baker's percentage of rosemary is 3 percent. However, you may need to adjust this percentage depending on the pungency of your rosemary. Our grandmother rosemary was the first plant we put in the ground when we bought our property, and over the years we have planted many more; we now have a plentiful supply for bread without scalping any one plant. Rosemary thrives in coastal North Carolina and stays in the ground through the winter. The stems grow into long spears that can be used for skewers. The leaves have a strong flavor—more so than purchased rosemary. I chop the rosemary during the autolyse period, as oxidation will cause the herb to turn black if it's chopped too far in advance. Add the rosemary right at the beginning of kneading. That way, the bits of herb are evenly incorporated throughout the dough. I place a tip of a rosemary stem under the loaf just before loading.

VARIATION: ROASTED ONION SOURDOUGH

This is a hearty loaf with nice flavor—a simple and inexpensive Pain au Levain variation. Keep the whole wheat flour (from the basic formula) but hold back a bit of the water—about 28g (1 ounce)—because the onions will add to the hydration. Add 226g caramelized onions. Remember that the post-cooking weight will be less, so start with about 283g raw onion—about 2 medium onions. Chop the onions coarsely, and toss them with olive oil, salt, and pepper. Caramelize until translucent. They should still be pretty wet, not crispy and dark. Add the onions once the dough is near the end of kneading, and make sure they're evenly distributed. This bread is great for savory applications, especially when beef is involved.

A sprig of fresh rosemary placed under the loaf . . . PHOTO BY KATE KELLEY

. . . is baked into the bottom of the loaf by a hot hearth.

Sand dollar fougasse can be made out of any type of dough.

VARIATION: FOUGASSE

Fougasse is a beautifully shaped flat bread, decoratively pierced during shaping, brushed with olive oil, and seasoned with coarse salt and pepper just before baking. Fougasse does not need to be made out of Pain au Levain or one of its variations—it can be made out of any dough—but I like the texture of the crumb when it's made from Pain au Levain dough, and it's especially tasty made with olive or rosemary dough. To make fougasse, roll out a piece of dough to an even 0.5" thickness after it has been divided, preshaped, and rested for about 20 to 30 minutes. Pierce it with a dough cutter, transfer it to parchment paper, and let it proof for 1½ to 2 hours. There are traditional fougasse shapes, but you can also be creative and pierce it in a pattern of your own design. I make the olive dough into the traditional "leaf"" pattern, but coastal North Carolina inspired me also to make the rosemary dough into a sand dollar fougasse. Once the dough has proofed, brush it with olive oil, season it with salt and pepper, and slide it directly onto the hearth. Bake for about 25 minutes. I keep the bake on this shape a bit lighter than for loaves, as the thin fougasse can dry out too much if baked too long.

Naturally leavened fougasse is also efficient from a production perspective. When I worked at King Arthur, all of the naturally leavened bread was mixed and retarded, then baked the next day. However, we also made fougasse out of olive and rosemary dough, and shaped and baked it in the late morning without going through the retarding process. One mix provided an additional sales opportunity on a separate day from the loaves.

Pain au Levain, 75% Hydrated

This formula is the same as the original except the overall hydration is 75 percent, a significant increase from 69 percent. What does this mean? From a ratio perspective, it means there are 75 units of water instead of 69 for every 100 units of flour. But it also means more active fermentation, stickier dough, more folds, more open crumb, and a longer shelf life. In addition, this dough is more challenging to shape. It's prudent for businesses to increase hydration as a way to lower ingredient cost per loaf.

The mixing process for the 75 percent hydrated version is the same as for the 69 percent, although it might take a bit longer (2 to 3 minutes longer if you're working by hand, 30 seconds to a minute longer on second speed if you're using a mixer). Like the 69 percent hydrated dough, the 75 percent will be sticky, but not as bouncy as the 69 percent version. Still, don't be surprised if something seems wrong and the dough seems impossibly wet. Avoid adding flour to the mix—this will decrease the ratios of other ingredients to flour. For instance, your salt ratio could drop below the minimum 1.8 percent. Don't worry! This will develop into a gorgeous dough as long as you punctuate the primary fermentation period with twice as many folds as you use for 69 percent hydrated Pain au Levain.

Go with your intuition, and incorporate an additional fold if the dough needs more strength or vitality. Still, the dough will be sticky when you divide. At that time, maintain a lightly floured surface to prevent the dough from sticking to the bench, and make clean cuts with your cutter to avoid torn and frayed dough. Use the tips of your fingers and touch the dough as little as possible.

If you're less experienced, it may seem like something is wrong, and you might be tempted to add flour. Remember: Use enough flour to prevent the dough from sticking, but copious use will make it more difficult to get a tightly shaped final loaf with a well-sealed seam.

Finally, there is a point of diminishing returns as far as hydration is concerned. Score marks may not open on a highly hydrated dough, and the grigne can be less dramatic. Also, wet loaves spread more than dry dough, so the cross section is more flat and less round than the 69 percent hydrated loaf. I prefer shaping boules out of the 75 percent hydrated Pain au Levain. Bâtards, especially if they are raised on couche (and not in a proofing basket), tend to spread more than boules during proofing.

Yield: 2 large loaves
Prefermented flour: 25%
Wood-fired oven temperature window:
425°F to 475°F (218–246°C)
Home oven: Preheat the oven to 450°F (232°C).

Levain

Ingredient	Weight (g)	Volume	Baker's %
Bread flour	227	1½ C + ⅓ C + 2 Tbsp	100
Water	227	scant 1 C	100
Liquid sourdough starter	45	3 Tbsp*	20
Total	499	—	—

* Best measured by weight; volume varies with ripeness.

Combine flour, water, and starter. Mix until smooth. Cover and allow to ferment at 75°F (24°C) for 8 hours.

You can also mix the starter and let it ferment for 5 hours and then retard it in the fridge for an additional 12 hours. It's important to achieve some visible activity before retarding the starter. If the starter isn't moving before it goes into the fridge, it's unlikely to become active during its tenure under cold storage: 40°F (4°C) is too cold to initiate fermentation. Activation before refrigeration!

Final Dough

Ingredient	Weight (g)	Volume	Baker's %
Water	454	2 C	75
Liquid sourdough starter	454	2½ C*	—
Bread flour	457	3¾ C	75
Whole wheat flour	228	2 C	25
Salt	17	1 Tbsp + 1 tsp	1.9
Total	1,610	—	—

* Best measured by weight; volume varies with ripeness.

Desired dough temperature: Adjust the water temperature so the dough is 78°F (26°C) at the end of mixing.

Autolyse: Remove 45g of liquid sourdough starter from the levain. Pour the water around the edge of the ripe levain to help release all of the preferment. Add the water, levain, and flours to a mixing bowl, but hold back the salt. Mix by hand or a mixer until thoroughly incorporated and homogeneous, but you needn't develop the dough at this point. It's okay if the dough is still shaggy. Cover to prevent a skin from forming and autolyse for 20 to 30 minutes.

Mixing:
BY HAND: After the autolyse, add the salt and mix the dough with your hand and a plastic dough scraper for a minute to incorporate the ingredients. Turn the dough out of the bowl and knead by hand using the techniques described in chapter 6. Hand mixing will take about 8 minutes.
BY MIXER: After the autolyse, add the salt and mix on slow speed for 3 minutes. Increase the speed to medium and mix for 3 minutes. Stop occasionally while mixing to scrape the dough off the hook.

The dough will be sticky whether you're mixing by hand or a mixer, but as always, don't add any flour! The extended primary fermentation and numerous folds will eventually create a bouncy dough. Be patient and focus on creating a dough with a nice skin. When you handle it, strive to keep the skin intact and taut. Avoid poking or tearing the dough.

Primary fermentation: Place the dough in a covered container and let it ferment for 2½ hours, folding every 30 minutes. There will be a total of four folds.

Dividing/preshaping: Half an hour after the last fold, turn the dough onto a lightly floured surface and divide into two pieces. Preshape each piece into a loose round ball, and place it bottom up on a lightly floured surface. Cover the loaves, and let them rest for about 20 minutes.

Shaping: Shape the loaves into boules or bâtards, place them seam side up in a well-floured proofing basket, and let them proof for approximately 2 hours. This is a pretty long proof time—you need to make sure the basket is well floured so the dough doesn't stick when it's turned out to score and bake, especially if the dough will be retarded in the baskets overnight. I prefer linen-lined bannetons instead of unlined brotforms for dough with a long proof time; the dough tends to stick more to the convolutions of the willow basket, while the linen-lined wicker gives a nice release.

Be patient! Cool dough or environment temperatures—or lack of an active dough at the shaping stage—will lengthen the proof time.

Scoring and baking: Just before baking, invert the baskets and turn the loaves onto a lightly floured peel. Score and bake in a steamed 450°F (232°C) oven for about 40 minutes.

Sprouted Wheat Flour Sourdough

I first heard about sprouted wheat flour from Monica Spiller, a longtime proponent of whole and sprouted grains and founder of the Whole Grain Connection, a non-profit organization that brings together farmers and bakers. Recently, the North Carolina miller Joe Lindley started producing his own line of this unique and tasty flour. Sprouted wheat flour is just that—wheat kernels are sprouted (see the sidebar on page 261 for a description of the sprouting process), dried, and then ground into flour. The result is a "fatty" flour, 100 percent extracted and thirsty—it takes a high hydration but ends up as a bouncy dough once it has been fermented and folded.

The combination of whole grains, natural leavening, and sprouting makes this bread very nutritious. In addition to the entire array of fiber, vitamins, and minerals imparted by the whole grain, the natural leavening and sprouting processes create phytase, an enzyme that deactivates phytic acid. Phytic acid prevents our bodies

from absorbing zinc, calcium, and iron. Joe Lindley says, "In my opinion, one of the next branches in the evolution of wheat as a food source is to utilize the more complete nutritional potential of wheat by letting it fulfill its true destiny and sprout."

Note the small amount of sourdough starter (16 percent) used to leaven this bread. This is because fermentation is enhanced by the high extraction rate of the flour. It should be noted that the falling number for sprouted wheat flour is similar to those for unsprouted flours. Still—even without the extra vigor provided by more enzyme activity associated with a low falling number—this dough moves pretty quickly if the dough temperature is correct. The transformation from pudding-like dough at the end of mixing to the extensible and fluffy dough that goes into the oven is amazing.

Yield: 2 loaves, 680g each
Prefermented flour: 25%
Wood-fired oven temperature window: 450°F to 475°F (232–246°C)
Home oven: Preheat the oven to 450°F (232°C).

Levain

Ingredient	Weight (g)	Volume	Baker's %
Sprouted wheat flour	177	1½ C + ⅓ C	100
Water (75°F/24°C)	115	½ C	65
Liquid sourdough starter	28	2 Tbsp*	16
Total	320	—	—

* Best measured by weight; volume varies with ripeness.

Combine the flour, water, and starter. Mix by hand or a mixer until all the flour is incorporated and the dough is cohesive. Be patient and keep mixing until there is no more dry flour. Cover and let the mixture ferment at 75°F (24°C) for 8 hours. The starter is ready when the volume has increased by about two-thirds and the consistency is fluffy.

Sprouted wheat flour sourdough
with variations on the Carpal Sutra score mark

Final Dough

Ingredient	Weight (g)	Volume	Baker's %
Sprouted wheat flour	531	5½ C	100
Water	522	2 C + 1 Tbsp	90
Salt	14	1 Tbsp	2
Levain	320	*	—
Total	1,387	—	—

* Best measured by weight; volume varies with ripeness.

Desired dough temperature: Adjust the water temperature so the dough is 76°F (24°C) at the end of mixing.

Autolyse: Combine the flour and water in a mixing bowl. Hold back the salt and levain. (Note: I don't remove the original starter from this levain before incorporating it into the final dough.) Mix until thoroughly incorporated and homogeneous, but you needn't develop the dough at this point. It's okay if the dough is still shaggy. Cover to prevent a skin from forming and autolyse for 20 to 30 minutes.

Mixing:

BY HAND: After the autolyse, add the salt and levain (cut into chunks) to the autolyse mixture. Mix the dough with your hand and a plastic dough scraper for a minute to incorporate the ingredients.

Turn the dough out of the bowl and knead by hand using the techniques described in chapter 6. Hand mixing will take about 10 minutes.

BY MIXER: After the autolyse, add the salt and the levain (cut into chunks) to the autolyse mixture and mix on slow speed for 3 to 4 minutes. Increase the speed to medium and mix for 2 to 3 minutes. Stop occasionally while mixing to scrape the dough off the hook.

This dough will be very sticky, but you will see gluten strands beginning to form and the surface will become slightly shiny. It will, however, tear more easily than a dough made with unsprouted

flour. It will transform considerably between mixing and shaping, especially after the second fold.

Primary fermentation: Place the dough in a covered container and let it ferment for 2 hours, folding every 30 minutes. There will be a total of three folds.

Dividing/preshaping: Half an hour after the last fold, turn the dough onto a lightly floured surface and divide into two pieces. Preshape each piece into a loose round ball and place bottom up on a lightly floured surface. Cover the loaves, and let them rest for about 20 minutes.

Shaping: Shape the loaves into boules or bâtards and place them seam side up in a well-floured proofing basket or couche. Let them proof for approximately 1½ to 2 hours.

Scoring and baking: Just before baking, invert the loaves onto a lightly floured peel. Score with the Carpal Sutra score mark shown in the photo on page 186 and bake in a steamed 450°F (232°C) oven for about 40 minutes.

Miche

Miche is another bread in my repertoire that I learned from James MacGuire. When I tasted it for the first time, I recognized it as the flavor and style of bread I was looking for when I began thinking of making naturally leavened breads in a wood-fired oven. High-extraction flour retains much but not all of the bran and germ that remains in whole wheat flour; however, the particles are the same small size as in white flour. The baked loaf is chewy with a mysterious flavor that people have been savoring for ages. Having Miche around is like having some lean, high-quality protein. Our dog Georgie really took to Miche—as if it were meat. You can make a close approximation of high-extraction flour by sifting whole wheat flour.

To be considered Miche, a loaf needs to be large, around 2kg). This is the type of bread made famous by the Poilâne Parisian bakery where workers each bake this Old World classic in their own wood-fired ovens.

Yield: 1 large (2,000g) Miche
Prefermented flour: 20%
Wood-fired oven temperature window:
425°F to 450°F (218–232°C) and falling
Home oven: Preheat the oven to 500°F (260°C).
Once the oven is loaded, reduce the heat to 450°F
(232°C) and bake for approximately 45 minutes.

Levain

Ingredient	Weight (g)	Volume	Baker's %
High-extraction flour	216	1½ C + 1 Tbsp	100
Water	147	⅔ C	68
Liquid sour-dough starter	32	2 Tbsp + ¼ tsp	15
Total	395	—	—

Combine the flour, water, and starter. Mix by hand
or a mixer until all of the flour is incorporated and the
dough is cohesive. Cover and let the mixture ferment at
77°F (25°C) for 8 hours.

Final Dough

Ingredient	Weight (g)	Volume	Baker's %
High-extraction flour	864	8 C	100
Water	749	3 C	83
Salt	20	1 Tbsp + 1 tsp	1.9
Levain	395	all from above	—
Total	2,028	—	—

Desired dough temperature: Adjust the water
temperature so the dough is 75°F (24°C) at the end
of mixing.

Autolyse: Combine the flour and water in a mixing
bowl. Hold back the salt and levain. (Note: I don't
remove the original starter from this levain before
incorporating it into the final dough.) Mix until
thoroughly incorporated and homogeneous, but you
needn't develop the dough at this point. It's okay if

Transferring Miche from couche to peel

the dough is still shaggy. Cover to prevent a skin from forming and autolyse for 20 to 30 minutes.

Mixing:

BY HAND: After the autolyse, add the salt and levain (cut into chunks) to the autolyse mixture. Mix the dough with your hand and a plastic dough scraper for a minute to incorporate the ingredients.

Turn the dough out of the bowl and knead by hand using the techniques described in chapter 6. Hand mixing will take 8 to 10 minutes. When complete, the dough will be smooth and slightly tacky; it'll pull back when tugged. Remember, the dough will develop considerably when fermenting and folding.

BY MIXER: After the autolyse, add the salt and the preferment to the autolyse mixture and mix on slow speed for 3 minutes. Increase the speed to medium and mix for 2 to 3 minutes. Stop occasionally while mixing to scrape the dough off the hook. The overall consistency of this dough is pretty wet.

At the end of mixing, the dough will be smooth and slightly tacky; it'll pull back when tugged. Remember, the dough will develop considerably when fermenting and folding.

Primary fermentation: Place the dough in a covered container and ferment for 2 hours, folding every 30 minutes. There will be a total of three folds.

Preshaping: Half an hour after the last fold, turn the dough onto a lightly floured surface and preshape into a loose, round ball. Place bottom up on a lightly floured surface. Cover the loaf, and rest it for about 15 minutes.

Shaping: Shape the dough into a large, flat boule. A Miche has a large surface area and is quite flat, as opposed to a round boule. Once it's placed seam side up on a well-floured couche, encourage a low loaf profile by pushing down on the loaf to flatten. Two loaves will fit on a standard sheet pan, but it's nice to have one per board, especially after the proofing period when the loaves are flipped from the couche to the loading peel. You can place shaped Miche into large baskets—they won't spread as much, but you'll be able to fit more loaves into the oven (each loaf will have a smaller footprint), and the baskets can be stacked. Loaves on boards need to be kept on a rack so they don't smash one another. The dough should be bouncy by the time you're shaping, but be aware that the dough inside the skin is still wet. Make sure to flour the couche or basket well so the dough doesn't stick during the 1½- to 2-hour proof time. The impregnated flour also provides dramatic contrast when marks are scored onto a Miche's expansive canvas.

Scoring and baking: Just before baking, grab an edge of the couche and flip the fragile Miche onto a floured peel. Score in a lozenge pattern, and bake in a steamed 450°F (232°C) oven for about 1 hour.

Seven Grain boules
with a Diamant Grain Mill

Seven Grain Bread

This is one of the first formulas I created at One Acre Garden and Bakery using the baker's percentage system. It appealed to people who were looking for a bread made with whole grain flour, but 50 percent of the flour is white flour so it also served as a gateway whole-grain bread for white bread lovers. This bread was one of my early contributions to the production schedule once I started baking at King Arthur Flour. The first time I mixed it in Vermont, it was like greeting an old friend that I hadn't seen since I lived down south.

This dough can be leavened solely with your naturally leavened starter, or you can include the optional baker's yeast to speed up the process and create a slightly lighter loaf. If your sole leavening is wild yeast, be sure to give the dough more time for primary and secondary fermentation. (The French term for breads that combine wild and commercial yeast is *levain de pâte*.)

Yield: 3 loaves, 725g each
Prefermented flour: 25%
Wood-fired oven temperature window:
425°F to 450°F (218–232°C)
Home oven: Preheat the oven to 450°F (232°C).

Levain

Ingredient	Weight (g)	Volume	Baker's %
Bread flour	250	2 C + 3 Tbsp	100
Water	250	1 C + 1 Tbsp + 1 tsp	100
Liquid sourdough starter	30	3 Tbsp*	12
Total	530	—	—

* *Best measured by weight; volume varies with ripeness.*

Combine the flour, water, and starter, and mix until smooth. Cover and allow to ferment at 77°F (25°C)

for 8 hours. You can also mix the levain and allow it to ferment for 4 to 6 hours at 77°F, then retard it in the fridge for an additional 12 hours.

Soaker

Ingredient	Weight (g)	Volume	Baker's %
Grains	180	1¼ C	100
Water	206	⅞ C	114
Honey	60	3 Tbsp	33
Total	446	—	—

Combine all ingredients and soak overnight at approximately 77°F (25°C).

Final Dough

Ingredient	Weight (g)	Volume	Baker's %
Water	424	1¾ C + 2 Tbsp	88
Levain	500	all from above	—
Bread flour	250	2 C + 3 Tbsp	50
Whole wheat flour	500	5 C	50
Soaker	446	all from above	—
Salt	22	1 Tbsp + 1½ tsp	2.2
Instant active yeast (optional)	4	1 tsp	0.4
Honey	—	—	6
Grains	—	—	18
Total	2,146	—	—

Desired dough temperature: Adjust the water temperature so the dough is 75°F to 77°F (24–25°C) at the end of mixing.

Autolyse: Remove 30g of starter from the levain. Pour the water around the edge of the levain to help release all of the preferment. Add the water and levain to the mixing bowl. Add the flours and soaker; hold back the salt *and yeast*. Mix by hand or a mixer until thoroughly incorporated and homogeneous, but you needn't develop the dough at this point. It's okay if the dough is still shaggy. Cover to prevent a skin from forming and autolyse for 20 to 30 minutes.

Mixing:

BY HAND: After the autolyse, add the salt and dry yeast, if you're using it. Mix the dough with your hand and a plastic dough scraper for a minute to incorporate the ingredients.

Turn the dough out of the bowl and knead by hand using the techniques described in chapter 6. Hand mixing will take about 8 minutes.

BY MIXER: After the autolyse, add the salt and yeast and mix on slow speed for 3 minutes. Increase the speed to medium and mix for 3 minutes. Stop occasionally while mixing to scrape the dough off the hook.

When complete, the dough will be slightly tacky and will pull back when tugged. The soaker will create a dough that is more rough than doughs made just from flour. Remember that the dough will develop considerably when fermenting and folding.

Primary fermentation:
Place the dough in a covered container and let it ferment for 2 hours, folding once after 60 minutes. If you are making this bread without any commercial yeast, you may want to give it another fold at the end of the 2 hours plus another 45 minutes of fermentation time before you divide. This may be necessary to help the dough become active and fluffy.

Dividing/preshaping:
Turn the dough onto a lightly floured surface and divide into three pieces. Preshape each piece into a loose round ball, and place bottom up on a lightly floured surface. Cover the loaves, and allow them to rest for about 20 minutes.

Shaping:
Shape the loaves into boules or bâtards and place them seam side up in well-floured proofing baskets or couches. Let them proof for approximately

Getting ready to score Seven Grain PHOTO BY KATE KELLEY

1 hour if you're using yeast. If the dough is 100 percent naturally leavened, let rise for about 2 hours.

Scoring and baking:
Just before baking, invert the loaves onto a lightly floured peel. Score bâtards with five to seven diagonal lines, making sure the score mark extends down the shoulders of the loaf in order for it to open fully. Score boules with a simple square. Bake in a steamed 450°F (232°C) oven.

Or place in a heated combo cooker, score, cover, and place in the oven. Bake for 40 to 45 minutes.

Doughs with any type of sugar—in this case, honey—will take color quickly, so be careful that your bread does not get too dark. Placing the loaves on sheet pans about halfway through the bake will prevent the bottoms from scorching or darkening.

Rub the surface of the loaf before you score to help spread an even layer of flour over its skin. Add more flour if necessary, but keep it a thin layer. A light layer of flour will create more contrast between the grigne and the surface of the baked loaf. The flour is also helpful in reflecting heat so the crust doesn't get too dark during the bake cycle. The darker color of the whole-grain dough, the honey, and the (sometimes) unpredictable heat of a wood-fired oven may cause excessive crust color before the loaf is baked all the way through. The flour acts like the zinc oxide people used to wear on their noses at the beach to avoid sunburn.

Muesli

The grain mix used in the Seven Grain formula (for years I have used a Lindley Mills product, 7 Grain Cereal, that is made with cracked wheat, oat flakes, rye chops, hulled millet, corn grits, spelt, and flaxseed—which is not actually a grain) can also be used as muesli. To make muesli, simply soak any amount of cracked grain in about twice as much water overnight in the fridge. You can also add nuts or dried fruit. In the morning, the grains will have soaked up much of the water—just as they do in the Seven Grain soaker—but they will also have created a milky liquid. The muesli can be eaten as is, or with grated seasonal produce.

You can use any combination of grains, although I like them to be small enough that the particles that migrate to the outside of the crust don't get too hard when the loaf is baked. Grains are ingredients for which measuring by weight is especially important: Differences in grain size can yield an inaccurate amount if measured volumetrically.

Lindley Mills' 7 Grain Blend

Golden Sesame bâtards

Golden Sesame Bread

This bread is beautifully golden from the durum flour. Durum is a type of wheat with a high protein percentage (about 16 percent) and a correspondingly high level of absorption. The flour comes in two grain sizes: semolina and durum. Semolina looks like coarse cornmeal, while durum is as fine as white flour. I prefer durum over semolina because the smaller grain size reduces damage to the gluten network caused by the larger pieces of semolina, although even the small durum particles feel like grains of sand. *Triticum durum* is harder than the common bread wheat, *T. aestivum*. The words *durum* and *durable* have the same root, which means "hard" or "to harden."

Even though the grain is hard, this bread will easily become a staple in your repertoire. It's not only beautiful, but also versatile—good for breakfast, lunch, or dinner. This is an ideal introductory bread for those new to bread baking: It's easy to make, the baked loaves are beautiful, and even those not inclined toward crusty hearth breads will be drawn to the delicious taste. This dough is a bit drier during mixing than many of the hearth breads in this book. You can add a little water—but be patient and you'll see that the dough comes together beautifully.

I like to encrust the outside of the shaped loaves in sesame seeds. An easy way to get the seeds to stick (on any type of dough) is to roll the freshly shaped loaves onto a damp cloth and then in a shallow tray full of the seeds. (Don't get the towel sopping wet—if you hold up the towel and it dripdripdrips, it's just right. A steady stream of water is too much.) You can coat just the top of the loaf, or roll the loaf to coat it completely. Just keep in mind where the seam is so that when you place the loaf on an unfloured couche, the seam will be up. Using the couche unfloured works well: The seeds prevent the loaf from sticking to the couche, and you'll avoid the unattractive appearance of flour among the seeds. You can make the seed coating more visually interesting by adding black sesame seeds to the white ones in a ratio of about 1:10.

This bread can be made without the seeds, too, and it's just as beautiful. In that case, place seam side up on a floured couche and simply call it semolina bread.

Fermentation and proofing tolerance are lower for breads with high levels of durum than those made with common bread wheat. In other words, a lengthy primary fermentation or proof time may cause the loaf to collapse. It's time to bake when you see the seam in the tightly shaped loaves start to rip apart.

Yield: 2 medium loaves
Prefermented flour: 16%
Wood-fired oven temperature window: 450°F to 475°F (232–246°C)
Home oven: Preheat the oven to 450°F (232°C).

Poolish

Ingredient	Weight (g)	Volume	Baker's %
Bread flour	113	1 C	100
Water	113	½ C	100
Instant active yeast	0.1	pinch	0.1
Total	226.1	—	—

Ideal fermentation temperature for the poolish is 75°F (24°C). Combine and mix all poolish ingredients and ferment for 14 to 16 hours.

Final Dough

Ingredient	Weight (g)	Volume	Baker's %
Water	340	1½ C + 1 Tbsp	66
Poolish	226.1	all from above	—
Durum or semolina flour	454	3½ C	66
Bread flour	120	1 C	34
Instant active yeast	2.7	¾ tsp	0.4
Salt	14	1 Tbsp	2
Sesame seeds (optional)	142	1 C	—
Total	1,298.8	—	—

Desired dough temperature: Adjust the water temperature so the dough is 76°F (24°C) at the end of mixing.

Autolyse: Pour the water around the edge of the poolish to help release all of the preferment. Add the water and poolish to the mixing bowl. Add the flours but hold back the yeast and salt. Mix by hand or a mixer until thoroughly incorporated and homogeneous, but you needn't develop the dough at this point. It's okay if the dough is still shaggy. Cover to prevent a skin from forming and autolyse for 20 to 30 minutes.

Mixing:

BY HAND: After the autolyse, add the yeast and salt and mix the dough with your hands and a plastic dough scraper for a minute to incorporate the ingredients.

  Turn the dough out of the bowl and knead by hand using the techniques described in chapter 6. Mixing by hand will take about 5 minutes.

BY MIXER: After the autolyse, add the yeast and salt and mix on slow speed for 3 minutes. Increase the speed to medium and mix for 2 minutes. Stop occasionally while mixing to scrape the dough off the hook.

  When complete, the dough will be smooth and slightly tacky; it'll pull back when tugged. Remember, the dough will develop considerably when fermenting and folded.

Primary fermentation: Place the dough in a covered container and let it ferment for 2 hours, folding once after 60 minutes.

Dividing/preshaping: Place the dough onto a lightly floured surface and divide into two pieces. Preshape each piece into a loose round ball and place bottom up on a lightly floured surface. Cover the loaves and let them rest for about 20 minutes.

Shaping: Shape the loaves into bâtards, seed them if desired, and place them seam side up on a couche. Let them proof for 1 to 1½ hours.

Scoring and baking: Just before baking, turn the loaves onto a lightly floured peel. Score with one angled cut down the length of the loaf. The seed coating makes scoring a bit difficult. Be sure to use a new blade and score assertively. Bake in a steamed 450°F (232°C) oven.

  Or place in a heated combo cooker, score, cover, and place in the oven. Bake for approximately 40 minutes.

VARIATION: FENNEL GOLDEN RAISIN BREAD

Amy's Bread in New York City was one of the first bakeries in the American Bread Movement to scale up artisan techniques in order to meet demand for high-quality hearth breads. Amy Scherber developed this interesting bread, now a signature product for the multi-unit bakery that strives "To create a bakery and café that nourishes . . . bodies, minds and spirits of . . . communities." Amy's Bread serves that mission by "respecting the craft of traditional baking," "staying local," and "using ingredients and procedures that sustain the health of the planet." After two decades of helping shape the new American food culture, Amy's Bread still relies on small-scale ideology to create high-quality bread in a high-volume bakery. When I heard about Amy's fennel raisin variation for a semolina bread, I was intrigued and incorporated the idea into my Golden Sesame dough. I loved the flavor, and so have many of my students over the years.

  Add 4g fennel seed (1 tablespoon or 0.6 percent—coarsely chopped after weighing) and 116g golden raisins (¾ cup or 17 percent) to the dough after kneading is complete. Make sure to get the fennel and raisins evenly distributed. Follow the rest of the methodology as directed. However, I omit the sesame seed coating and proof the bâtards seam side up on lightly floured couches.

Bettie Three Seed Bread

Bettie Three Seed was developed in response to a customer request for a seeded bread at a time when I was experimenting with growing an array of culinary seeds. After numerous trials of different combinations of flours and seeds, I came up with this interesting variety, named for the North Carolina farming community, Bettie, where we live. The bread is a blend of 20 percent rye, 20 percent durum, and 60 percent white flour with three nutritious seeds: flax (*Linum usitatissimum*), sesame (*Sesamum indicum*), and charnushka (*Nigella sativa*).

Flax is such a useful plant! Couches are made of linen refined from flax stems. Old-fashioned linoleum—the genuine article, precursor to today's vinyl flooring—was made by heat treating flaxseeds, colorizing them, and pressing them into a couche-like material, scrim-thin. Ground flaxseeds oxidize quickly at room temperature and may become carcinogenic at high cooking temperatures. For those reasons, I grind flaxseeds immediately before incorporating them into the dough, and I leave flaxseeds out of the exterior seed mix to keep them from direct exposure to the high temperatures of the baking chamber. The interior temperature of a baked loaf cannot increase above 212°F (100°C) until all water is completely evaporated, a point you won't reach during the baking process unless you're aiming for croutons.

Charnushka is a seed often used in Eastern European rye breads, but it also lends an exotic flavor to Mediterranean foods. It's often referred to as kalonji or black cumin. An Armenian student I had at Johnson & Wales told me his family simply called it black seed. Gardeners will know *Nigella sativa* as a close relative of *N. damascena*, commonly known as the delicate flower love-in-a-mist, which creates swollen capsules full of the flavorful seeds. Charnushka can be easily purchased online, or you may find it in an international foods market. It's only used in the exterior seed mix that coats the outside of this bread; it isn't included in the soaker or final dough.

On a whim we broadcast a handful of sesame seeds in our garden one year. They thrived, quickly becoming

Love-in-a-mist PHOTO COURTESY OF DAN SCHWARTZ

Flax

A strong sesame plant backed by a stand of golden amaranth

a stand of lush, 6-foot-tall plants with fleshy leaves and pretty pink flowers at the top. The flowers mature into elongated seed capsules, each holding four perfect Pringle-like stacks of sesame seeds, and the whole plant gives off the subtle but persistent aroma of toasted sesame oil. For best flavor, toast the sesame seeds that will be ground and mixed into this dough, but use raw sesame seeds in the exterior seed mix—the seeds on the outside will become toasted during the baking process.

A note about propagation: All three of these plants grow easily from seeds sown directly in a home garden. Each has a pretty flower and other interesting characteristics that make us want to grow them even if we don't plan to harvest the seeds. In coastal North Carolina's Zone 8, flax is sown in February, sesame after the last frost—sesame likes it hot—and charnushka in the fall. However, charnushka has never really thrived for us in hot, humid coastal North Carolina the way it does in the cooler Zone 6 climate of Providence, Rhode Island, where it has been reseeding itself abundantly in our community garden plot ever since we sowed a single pack of love-in-a-mist seeds in 2007.

Yield: 2 large loaves or 3 medium loaves
Prefermented flour: 19%
Wood-fired oven temperature window:
425°F to 475°F (218–246°C)
Home oven: Preheat the oven to 450°F (232°C).

Levain

Ingredient	Weight (g)	Volume	Baker's %
Bread flour	142	1¼ C	100
Water	142	½ C + 2 Tbsp + 2 tsp	100
Liquid sourdough starter	17	1½ Tbsp	12
Total	301	—	—

Combine the flour, water, and starter. Mix until smooth. Cover and allow to ferment at 77°F (25°C) for 8 to 10 hours.

Soaker

Ingredient	Weight (g)	Volume	Baker's %
Flaxseeds, whole	36	¼ C	56
Sesame seeds, whole	28	3 Tbsp + 1 tsp	44
Water	64	¼ C + 1 tsp	100
Total	128	—	—

Combine all ingredients, cover, and soak overnight at approximately 77°(25°C).

Final Dough

Ingredient	Weight (g)	Volume	Baker's %
Water	400	1¾ C	82
Levain	284	all from above	—
Bread flour	300	2½ C	60
Durum flour	147	1¼ C	20
Rye flour	147	1½ C + 1 Tbsp + 1 tsp	20
Salt	15	1 Tbsp	2
Instant active yeast	2	½ tsp	0.27
Soaker	128	all from above	—
Flaxseeds, raw, ground	28	3 Tbsp	8.7
Sesame seeds, toasted, ground	21	2 Tbsp + 2 tsp	6.7
Total	1,472	—	—

Exterior Seed Coating

Ingredient	Weight (g)	Volume	Baker's %
Charnushka	24	3 Tbsp + 1 tsp	12
Sesame Seeds	200	1¼ C	100

Desired dough temperature: Adjust the water temperature so the dough is 77°F (25°C) at the end of mixing.

Autolyse: Remove 17g of starter from the levain. Pour the water around the edge of the levain to help release all of the preferment. Combine the water and preferment in a mixing bowl and add the flours. Hold back the salt, yeast, and soaker. Mix by hand or a mixer until thoroughly incorporated and homogeneous, but you needn't develop the dough at this point. It's okay if the dough is still shaggy. Cover to prevent a skin from forming and autolyse for 20 to 30 minutes.

Mixing:

BY HAND: After the autolyse, add the salt and yeast and mix the dough with your hand and a plastic dough scraper for a minute to incorporate the ingredients. Turn the dough out of the bowl and knead by hand using the techniques described in chapter 6. Mix for 4 minutes. Add the soaker, flaxseeds and sesame seeds and continue to mix for another 4 minutes.

When complete, the dough will be smooth and slightly tacky; it'll pull back when tugged. The surface of the dough should have a slight sheen. Remember, the dough will develop considerably when fermenting and folding.

BY MIXER: After the autolyse, add the salt and yeast and mix on slow speed for 3 minutes. Increase the speed to medium and mix for 3 minutes. Stop occasionally while mixing to scrape the dough off the hook. Reduce the mixer to slow and add the soaker; mix until completely incorporated. When complete, the dough will be smooth and slightly tacky; it'll pull back when tugged. The surface of the dough should have a slight sheen. Remember, the dough will develop considerably when fermenting and folding.

Primary fermentation: Place the dough in a covered container and allow to ferment for 2 hours, folding every 30 minutes. There will be a total of 3 folds.

Divide, preshape, rest: Divide the dough into two or three pieces. Preshape each piece into a loose round ball, and place bottom up on a lightly floured surface. Cover the loaves, and let them rest for about 20 minutes.

Shape and proof: With Bettie Three Seed, I like to encrust the outside of the shaped loaves in a mix of charnushka and sesame seeds in a ratio of about 1:12 using the method described in the Golden Sesame Bread formula.

Shape the loaves into boules or bâtards. Roll all sides of the loaf onto a damp cloth and then dredge into the charnushka-sesame mixture. Place the seeded loaf seam side up on a flour-free couche and let it proof for approximately 1½ hours.

Score, steam, bake: Just before baking, turn the loaves onto a lightly floured peel. Score with a large cross, making sure the score marks extend down onto the sides of the loaf. The seed coating makes scoring a bit difficult. Be sure to use a new blade and score assertively. Bake in a steamed 450°F (232°C) oven. The oven is hot enough if the seeds that fall off onto the hearth immediately start popping.

67% Rye

Rye breads can be tricky to make, especially when the rye flour percentage rises above 30 percent of the total flour weight. Part of the trickiness is a physical difference—rye has less protein (and thus develops less gluten) than wheat. Of the two gluten-forming proteins in rye, there is more glutenin (the protein that provides strength) and less gliadin (the protein that provides extensibility). A high-gluten (wheat) flour is often called for as the remaining white flour in breads with more than 50 to 60 percent rye flour to compensate for the lower gluten quantity in the rye flour. Often a product labeled "bread flour" in the supermarket will have a higher protein percentage than the ideal 11.7 percent called for in wheat-based breads. Look for something with about 12.5 percent protein or higher to use in the 67% Rye and Rugbrød formulas.

Yield: 2 loaves, 750g each
Prefermented flour: 27%

67% Rye bread by Lauren V. Hass

Wood-fired oven temperature window:
450°F to 475°F (232–246°C)
Home oven: Preheat the oven to 450°F (232°C).

Rye Sour

Ingredient	Weight (g)	Volume	Baker's %
Whole rye flour	225	2⅓ C	100
Water	182	¾ C + 2 Tbsp	81
Liquid sour-dough starter	14	1½ Tbsp	6
Total	421	—	—

Combine the flour, water, and starter. Mix by hand or a mixer until all of the flour is incorporated. Be patient and mix until the starter is the consistency of wet cement. Cover and allow to ferment at 75°F (24°C) for 12 to 15 hours.

Final Dough

Ingredient	Weight (g)	Volume	Baker's %
Whole rye flour	340	3½ C + ⅓ C	67
High-gluten flour	280	2⅓ C	33
Instant active yeast	3	¾ tsp	0.35
Salt	17	1 Tbsp	2
Water	468	2 C	77
Rye sour	421	all from above	—
Total	1,529	—	—

Desired dough temperature: Adjust the water temperature so the dough is 82°F (28°C) at the end of mixing.

Mixing:

BY MIXER: This is a dough where I don't remove the original 14g of liquid sourdough starter from the rye sour. Combine all ingredients in the bowl of a mixer. Mix on slow speed for 3 minutes. Increase the speed to medium and mix for 2 to 3 minutes. The dough will probably stick against the sides of the bowl in a thick layer. You will need to scrape down the bowl more often than with wheat-based breads.

The dough will be sticky, but gluten strands should be visible. The surface of the dough will have a slight sheen and will tug back when gently pulled.

Primary fermentation: Place the dough in a covered container and let it ferment for 45 minutes. There are no folds for this dough.

Dividing/preshaping: Turn the dough onto a lightly floured surface and divide into two or three pieces. Preshape each piece into a loose round ball, and place bottom up on a lightly floured surface. Cover the loaves, and let them rest for about 10 minutes.

Shaping: Shape into slender bâtards and place them seam side up in well-floured round proofing basket. Proof for approximately 45 minutes to 1 hour. The seam will begin to rip open when the loaf is ready to bake.

Scoring and baking: Just before baking, invert the baskets, turn the loaves onto a lightly floured peel, and score across the bâtard, about 25 percent in from each end. Bake in a steamed 450°F (232°C) oven.

Or place in a heated combo cooker, score, cover, and place in the oven. Bake for approximately 45 minutes.

Rugbrød

This bread contains two naturally leavened preferments, a rye sour and a 100% hydrated white levain. The levain will contribute a mellow lactic acid taste, while the sour will give the tang that identifies this as a heavy rye bread with a complex flavor and long shelf life. The hydrations and starter percentages have been modified so that they can both be mixed at the same time and will be ready to

Rugbørd is not scored but the oven spring of this active
dough creates a variegated surface on a well-floured loaf.

use at the same time—convenient when you are baking a bread with two preferments.

Rye chops, called for in the soaker formula, are coarsely broken rye berries, similar in size to cracked rye or steel-cut oats. I recommend mixing Rugbrød with a mixer.

Yield: 1 Pullman loaf, 13"
Prefermented flour: 55%
Wood-fired oven temperature window: 475°F (246°C) and falling
Home oven: Preheat the oven to 500°F (260°C).

Rye Sour

Ingredient	Weight (g)	Volume	Baker's %
Whole rye flour	300	3⅓ C	100
Water	245	1 C + 1 Tbsp + 1 tsp	82
Liquid sour-dough starter	55	¼ C	18
Total	600	—	—

Combine the flour, water, and starter. Mix by hand or a mixer until all of the flour is incorporated. Be patient and mix until the sour is the consistency of wet cement. Cover and allow to ferment at 75°F (24°C) for 12 to 15 hours.

Levain

Ingredient	Weight (g)	Volume	Baker's %
High-gluten flour	103	1 C	100
Water	103	scant ½ C	100
Liquid sour-dough starter	14	1½ Tbsp	14
Total	220	—	—

Combine the flour, water, and starter, and mix until smooth. Cover and allow to ferment at 77°F (25°C) for 8 to 10 hours. You can also mix the levain and allow it

to ferment for 4 to 6 hours at 77°F, then retard it in the fridge for an additional 12 hours.

Soaker

Ingredient	Weight (g)	Volume	Baker's %
Rye chops*	75	⅓ C + 3 Tbsp	100
Water	150	⅔ C	200
Total	225	—	—

* You can substitute an equal amount of multigrain mix (used in the Seven Grain formula) for the rye chops.

Combine all ingredients and soak overnight at approximately 77°F (25°C).

Final Dough

Ingredient	Weight (g)	Volume	Baker's %
High-gluten flour	130	1 C + 1 Tbsp	32
Whole rye flour	200	2⅓ C	68
Water	180	¾ C	92
Instant active yeast	2.5	½ tsp	0.3
Salt	16	1 Tbsp	2.2
Soaker	225	all from above	—
Rye sour	600	all from above	—
Rye chops	—	—	10
Levain	220	all from above	—
Blackstrap molasses	15	1 Tbsp	2
Whole fennel seeds, coarsely ground	4.5	1 Tbsp + ½ tsp	0.6
Total	1,593	—	—

Desired dough temperature: Adjust the water temperature so the dough is 80°F (27°C) at the end of mixing.

Spray a 13" lidded Pullman pan and coat the inside with the same whole rye flour you used in the rye sour. Tilt the pan all around so the flour sticks to the sprayed interior, just as you do when you prep a cake pan.

Mixing:

BY MIXER: This is a dough where I don't remove the original sourdough starter from the levain or sourdough starter. Combine all ingredients in the bowl of a mixer. Mix on slow speed for 4 minutes. Increase the speed to medium and mix for 3 to 4 minutes. The dough will probably stick against the sides of the bowl in a thick layer. You will need to scrape down the bowl more often than with wheat-based breads.

The dough will be sticky, but gluten strands should be visible.

Dividing/preshaping: There is no primary fermentation and no preshape for this dough. After mixing is complete, immediately transfer the dough into the greased and floured Pullman pan. Distribute the dough down the length of the pan, and roughly smooth the top. Dust the surface of the loaf with a generous coating of rye flour, slide the lid onto the Pullman pan, and let it proof for about 45 to 60 minutes. The loaf will be puffy and will have risen to within an inch of the top of the pan.

Baking: This bread is not scored. Put the covered pan into the oven and bake for 15 minutes at 500°F (260°C). Reduce the temperature to 400°F (204°C) and bake for an additional 15 minutes. Remove the cover, lower the temperature to 325°F (163°C) and bake for an additional 45 minutes, until the bread is done. If the bread isn't done at this point, remove it from the pan and continue baking it on a sheet pan until the sides of the loaf are firm and the loaf has good color development.

Once you've removed the bread from the oven and cooled it, let it sit at room temperature covered with a cloth for least 24 to 48 hours before cutting the loaf. This will prevent the dough from having a gummy interior.

Coming Down the Mountain

There's a change in the oven now: It's getting cooler. The fire has been removed for several hours, heat has equalized throughout the mass, and—perhaps more important—you've been using some of the heat to cook and bake. The heat is softer than the blistering temperatures needed to puff pita or sear meat. Breads with dried fruit, for instance, need to be in a more mellow environment like this so they don't get too dark. At about this point in the temperature curve, it can be beneficial to give the oven a rest period between loads. This allows heat stored in the outer masonry to migrate back toward the firebox. I like the way the heat feels when I put my arm in the oven during this zone. I don't have the urge to jerk my arm back out; it's more like a sauna. It's intense, but not overwhelmingly penetrating.

Fig Pecan Bread

One of my favorite baking books—and one that gives me a lot of inspiration to develop new breads—is *The Book of Bread* by Jérôme Assire. It's a beautiful book with great photos of breads from around the world. I was ready to put a dried fruit and nut bread into production when I saw a collection of Swiss breads that included Sauserbrot made with wheat and spelt flours and including chestnut and grape must—unfermented freshly squeezed juice. I dropped the juice and whole wheat flour but added a higher ratio of spelt flour and included walnuts, dried figs, and oats. I immediately recognized it as a slightly sweet bread that was also delicious, nutritious, and soothing. Have it at breakfast, at teatime, or as a bedtime snack.

Be sure to use old-fashioned oats or the thicker, chewy kind you might be able to get through your local miller. "Quick" oats don't give the bread the same texture and don't look as pretty on the outside of the loaf. Whole wheat flour can be substituted for the spelt flour, but the taste won't be quite so distinctive. Whole-grain spelt flour and the addition of a high percentage of pecans and figs will make a denser dough. Be aware that the dough will be delicate and that spelt has a shorter proofing tolerance than hard red winter wheat.

It took me several years to realize I should replace the walnuts in this formula with pecans, partly because a pecan tree grows right next to my ovenhouse. In the fall, local pecans are available at roadside stands and people stock their freezers with bags of the rich nut meats, more milky, tender, and fresh than those available in most stores. Enjoy fresh, local nuts if you are lucky enough to have access to them.

We're also grateful when somebody drops off a load of pecan wood. The logs split nicely, and the branches can be cut into manageable lengths with a pair of heavy-duty loppers and a reciprocating saw. Pecan wood provides fewer BTUs than oak, which means it is less dense. This is an advantage when a fire is just starting and needs heat to accumulate so that the hot firebox will support a more complete combustion. Oak requires a hot environment to get started, so it's best to add pecan early on and save the oak for later. The pecan also combusts efficiently—little ash is left over after a load of pecan is burned.

We inherited three fig trees when we bought this property. Mid- to late July is when the figs start to ripen. I like to harvest twice a day, once in the morning and again in the late afternoon when the sun warms the sweet and sensual fruit. I so appreciate these two local trees, pecan and fig, that give us beauty, shade, oxygen, fresh nuts, bountiful bowls of figs, and fuel.

Yield: 3 medium loaves
Prefermented flour: 20%
Wood-fired oven temperature window: 425°F to 450°F (218–232°C)
Home oven: Preheat the oven to 450°F (232°C).

Levain

Ingredient	Weight (g)	Volume	Baker's %
Bread flour	120	1 C	100
Water	120	½ C	100
Liquid sourdough starter	14	1½ Tbsp	12
Total	254	—	—

Combine the flour, water, and starter. Mix until smooth. Cover and allow to ferment at 77°F (25°C) for 8 to 10 hours.

Backyard figs

Final Dough

Ingredient	Weight (g)	Volume	Baker's %
Pecans, halves	150	1¾ C	26
Figs, dried, chopped	230	1½ C	40
Water	345	1½ C	80
Levain	240	*	—
Bread flour	335	2¾ C	79
Whole spelt flour	123	1¼ C	21
Oats	57	⅔ C	10
Instant active yeast	2.3	½ tsp	0.4
Salt	12	1 Tbsp	2.1
Total	1,494.3	—	—
Additional oats in which to roll the shaped loaf	as needed	as needed	—

* Best measured by weight; volume varies with ripeness.

Desired dough temperature: Adjust the water temperature so the dough is 77°F (25°C) at the end of mixing.

Lightly toast the pecans, chop them, and let them cool. (Be sure they are completely cool before adding them to the dough so they don't affect the dough temperature.)

Before measuring the figs, remove any tough stems, chop the figs, and set them aside.

Autolyse: Remove 14g of starter from the levain. Pour the water around the edge of the levain to help release all of the preferment. Add the water and levain to the mixing bowl. Add the flours and oats, but hold back all the other ingredients. Mix by hand or a mixer until thoroughly incorporated and homogeneous, but you needn't develop the dough at this point. It's okay if the dough is still shaggy. Cover to prevent a skin from forming and autolyse for 20 to 30 minutes.

Mixing:

BY HAND: After the autolyse, add the yeast and salt. Mix the dough with your hand and a plastic dough scraper for a minute to incorporate the ingredients.

Turn the dough out of the bowl and knead by hand using the techniques described in chapter 6. Hand mixing will take about 8 to 10 minutes. The dough is going to seem wet, but you'll see the pecans and figs transform the consistency when you add them at this time.

BY MIXER: After the autolyse, add the yeast and salt and mix on slow speed for 3 minutes. Increase the speed to medium and mix for 3 minutes. Stop occasionally while mixing to scrape the dough off the hook. Reduce the mixer speed to slow, add the pecans and figs, and mix until incorporated.

When complete, the dough will be smooth and slightly tacky; it'll pull back when tugged. Remember, the dough will develop considerably during fermenting and folding.

Primary fermentation: Place the dough in a covered container and let it ferment for 2 hours, folding once after 60 minutes.

Dividing/preshaping: Turn the dough onto a lightly floured surface and divide it into three pieces. Preshape each piece into a loose round ball, and place bottom up on a lightly floured surface. Cover the loaves and let them rest for about 20 minutes.

Shaping: Shape the loaves into bâtards. Roll each onto a damp cloth and then into a tray of oats. Place the loaves seam side up on a *non-floured* couche. (See the Golden Sesame Bread formula for more information about encrusting the outside of loaves with seeds and oats.) Allow to proof for 1 to 1½ hours.

Scoring and baking: Just before baking, turn the loaves onto a lightly floured peel. Score with three angled cuts across the loaf. The oat coating makes scoring a bit difficult. Be sure to use a new blade and score assertively. Bake in a steamed 450°F (232°C) oven.

Or place in a heated combo cooker, score, cover, and place in the oven. Bake for approximately 40 minutes.

Two generations of Miscovich pecan trees

Pain de Mie

Pain de Mie

Pain de Mie is an enriched sandwich bread baked in a lidded Pullman pan, so the final loaf is square. This isn't just any sandwich bread—the crumb is firm and reminiscent of pound cake, while the crust is intended to be soft. It's great for cold sandwiches but extra luscious when toasted or used for any type of grilled or pressed sandwich. Or you can cut out pieces with decorative cutters and create elegant canapés for your guests while they watch you make the first pizzas of the evening. Two favorite uses of Pain de Mie are melba toast and bread crumbs. (You'll find more information on both in chapter 13.)

You can also bake 680g pieces of this dough in a regular loaf pan, although the crumb will be a little more open because the lid won't compress the dough as it springs during the first minutes of baking. If you do bake this dough in an unlidded pan, egg-wash and score the top of the loaf right before you bake. If you fail to score the loaves, they will likely rip and shred along the edge of the pan. The smaller loaves will bake more quickly than the Pullmans. Bake for about 35 minutes at 350°F (177°C). The rich egg-washed dough will take color quickly. You may need to tent the loaf with foil or bring it into a cooler zone by the oven door to prevent overbrowning. You can also make nice 85g rolls with this dough, although these will still be heavier than southern light rolls.

In the South—where people often gravitate toward biscuits and light rolls—Pain de Mie gave me the opportunity to meet local people in our community who might not have stopped by the ovenhouse for a loaf of crusty Pain au Levain, but who loved Pain de Mie.

Yield: 1 Pullman loaf
Prefermented flour: 0% (this is a "straight" dough—one that doesn't contain a preferment)
Wood-fired oven temperature: 375°F to 450°F (191–232°C). The temperature of your wood-fired oven is a little less crucial for Pain de Mie and its sister, Cinnamon Spiral Pain de Mie, than for hearth breads.

The pan protects the loaves, so it can go into an oven as hot as 450°F. If you bake that hot, however, you may want to place the Pullman pan on an inverted sheet pan after 15 to 20 minutes to prevent the bottom crust from getting too thick and hard. You shouldn't load this big loaf below 350°F (177°C), though—lower temperatures won't give the oven spring necessary for the dough to fill out the pan completely. If you do bake at the lower end of this range, you likely won't need the inverted sheet pan. After 20 to 30 minutes, remove the lid from the pan and bake for another 10 to 15 minutes. Check the sidewalls of the loaf. They should be solid and golden brown. If they aren't, invert the pan and let the Pain de Mie slide out onto a sheet pan. Bake for an extra 5 minutes or until the sidewalls have enough structure to hold up the weight of the loaf.

Home oven: Bake at 450°F (232°C) for 10 minutes. Lower the temperature to 350°F (177°C) and bake for 25 minutes. Remove the lid from the pan and bake for another 10 minutes. Check the sidewalls of the loaf. They should be solid and golden brown. If they aren't, invert the pan and let the Pain de Mie slide out onto a sheet pan. Bake for an extra 5 minutes or until the sidewalls have enough structure to hold up the weight of the loaf.

Pain de Mie

Ingredient	Weight (g)	Volume	Baker's %
Unsalted butter	113	½ C	18
Bread flour	630	5¼ C	100
Salt	16	1 Tbsp	2.5
Granulated sugar*	25	2 Tbsp + 1 tsp	4
Dry milk solids	31	¼ C + 2 tsp	5
Instant active yeast	6	1½ tsp	1
Water	378	1⅓ C + ¼ C	60
Total	1,199	—	—

* Pureed golden raisins can be used in place of the refined white sugar, with no perceptible difference in the baked loaf.

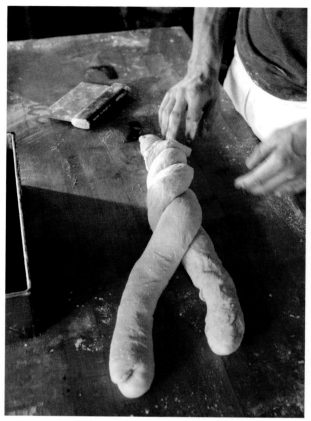

It's easier to get tightly shaped loaves if you twist together two "baguettes" of Pain de Mie dough.

Desired dough temperature: Adjust the water temperature so the dough is 76°F (24°C) at the end of mixing.

Mixing: Pain de Mie is best made with a mixer.

Remove the butter from the fridge and pound it soft with a rolling pin. The butter will be worked into the dough through the action of the mixer on medium speed. Adding melted or very soft butter will make your dough greasy. You won't need to strike it more than 10 or 12 times. Makes sure it can take the impression of your finger.

Combine all of the ingredients except the butter in the bowl of a mixer. Mix on slow speed for 4 minutes. Increase the mixer speed to medium, add half the softened butter, and mix for 1 minute. Add the remaining softened butter and mix for an additional 5 minutes. All the butter should have disappeared into the dough,

creating suppleness. Cover and let the dough ferment for 1½ hours, folding once after 45 minutes.

Spray a 13" Pullman pan with non-stick spray.

Carefully turn the dough onto a lightly floured surface. Gently de-gas the dough as you pat it into a rectangular shape. Divide the rectangle roughly in half. (It's okay if the two pieces aren't exactly the same weight—they will be twisted together and placed into the same pan.) Shape each piece into a baguette-like rope about 20" long. Lightly twist the ropes together and place in the Pullman pan.

Put the lid on the pan, but leave it open an inch or two so you can check the progress of the dough as it proofs. The dough will require 1 to 1½ hours to achieve full volume. It's ready to bake when the top surface of the dough is about ½" below the lid of the pan. Close the lid completely before baking.

Cinnamon Spiral Pain de Mie

VARIATION:
CINNAMON SPIRAL PAIN DE MIE

Cinnamon Spiral Pain de Mie is comfort food with style. Toasted pieces of this bread are great for breakfast, teatime, or a midnight snack.

A perennial problem with cinnamon swirl breads is the creation of cavities between the bands of dough. This happens as the sugar liquefies, gives off steam, and forms a "slip joint," forcing layers of dough away from each other. Baking a spiraled loaf in a lidded Pullman pan is the best way I've found to prevent cavities—the pan confines the loaf to the square shape of the pan. The dough, swelling inside the pan, pushes the layers together, creating a baked loaf compressed enough that slices don't fall apart in a curlicue.

Other dried fruits can be substituted, but Cinnamon Spiral Pain de Mie seems most elegant with golden raisins.

Yield: 1 Pullman loaf
Prefermented flour: 0% (this is a "straight" dough—one that doesn't contain a preferment)
Wood-fired and home oven temperature:
See the descriptions in the Pain de Mie recipe.

Dough

Ingredient	Weight (g)	Volume	Baker's %
Unsalted butter	95	7 Tbsp	18
Bread flour	525	4⅓ C	100
Salt	13	2 tsp	2.5
Granulated sugar*	21	2 Tbsp	4
Dry milk solids	26	¼ C	5
Instant active yeast	5	1¼ tsp	1
Water	315	1⅓ C	60
Golden raisins, room temperature	240	2 C	46
Total	1,240	—	—

* Pureed golden raisins can be used in place of the refined white sugar, with no perceptible difference in the baked loaf.

Cinnamon Spice Mix

Ingredient	Weight (g)	Volume	Baker's %
Granulated sugar	100	½ C	100
Cinnamon	30	¼ C + 1 tsp	30
Cardamom, ground	2.6	1½ tsp	2.6
Cloves, ground	1	¾ tsp	1
Total	133.6	—	—

Desired dough temperature: Adjust the water temperature so the dough is 76°F (24°C) at the end of mixing.

Remove the butter from the fridge and pound it soft with a rolling pin. The butter will be worked into the dough through the action of the mixer on medium speed. Adding melted or very soft butter will make your dough greasy. You won't need to strike it more than 10 or 12 times. Make sure it can take the impression of your finger.

Combine all of the ingredients except the butter and raisins in the bowl of a mixer. Mix on slow speed for 4 minutes. Increase the mixer speed to medium, add half the softened butter, and mix for 1 minute. Add the remaining softened butter and mix for an additional 5 minutes. All the butter should have disappeared into the dough, creating strength and suppleness. Reduce the mixer to slow and add the raisins in two parts. Mix until evenly dispersed, 2 to 3 minutes. Check the dough on the bottom of the bowl to make sure the raisins are completely incorporated. You may want to knead the dough on your work surface for a few strokes by hand to get them evenly mixed in. It won't be much work and the dough will feel good under your hands. It may seem like too many raisins at the moment, but they will get spread out during the shaping process. Cover the dough and let it ferment for 1½ hours, folding once after 45 minutes.

Spray a 13" Pullman pan with non-stick spray.

Carefully turn out the dough onto a lightly floured surface. Gently de-gas the dough as you pat it into a rectangular shape. Roll it into a 13" × 24" rectangle. Egg-wash a 2" strip along one 13" edge. Spread the spice mix over the entire piece of dough except for the egg-washed edge. Make sure to get the spice mix as close as possible to the other three borders. Roll the dough toward the egg wash, and place the rolled cylinder into the Pullman pan seam side down. Put the lid on the pan, but leave it open an inch or two so you can check the dough's progress as it proofs. It'll require approximately 2 hours to achieve full volume. (Spices like cinnamon and clove slow down yeast activity. Because of that, and also due to the raisins, this dough will take longer to proof than the plain Pain de Mie. Be patient and give it a little more time.)

The dough is ready to bake when its top surface is about ½" below the lid of the pan. Close the lid completely before baking. Use the baking instructions for the basic Pain de Mie.

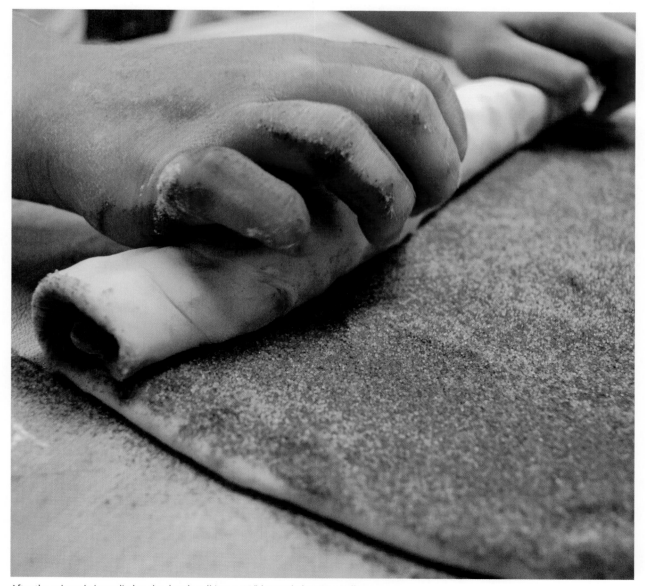

After the spice mix is applied to the dough, roll into a 13" log and place in a Pullman pan.

Chocolate Pumpernickel

Chocolate Pumpernickel Bread

One of the first loaves of crusty handmade bread I tasted was something similar to this rich chocolate bread. Stephanie brought it to me from a small bakery that was between the beach and the railroad tracks in Santa Barbara, California. The flavor was fantastic, as was the chew of the loaf, a texture I now know comes from a long, controlled fermentation. When I developed this recipe, I tried to think of anything with a dark color that might help create a multi-layered complexity in the flavor. There are a lot of ingredients, but they harmonize together very well in the baked loaf.

Once the American Bread Movement was well under way, this type of bread was lightly ridiculed, especially by the purists, who were focused on more versatile breads like Levain and Rustique. I have to admit I was a little self-conscious about this bread and shelved it for nearly 10 years until some Johnson & Wales students asked if I had a recipe for chocolate bread. I found the old 3" × 5" card and enjoyed watching my students bring this one back to life. Once I tasted it again, I realized it's a keeper. Although it is on the sweet side of things, it's also hardy and makes a nice afternoon snack or something to have with coffee when you take a break from splitting wood.

Pumpernickel (defined broadly, as is typical of bread-baking terminology) is a dense rye bread slightly sweetened by a long fermentation and baking cycle. I've had misgivings about calling this enriched bread a pumpernickel, since it swerves into the pastry side of the baking world. The students who first asked about a chocolate bread called it "Pumperdevil." However, with no other category making itself evident, pumpernickel it seems to be. You can make it less sweet by omitting the chocolate, which creates a leaner dough more akin to traditional pumpernickels.

I advise mixing this dough in a mixer.

Yield: 3 medium loaves
Prefermented flour: 34%

Wood-fired oven temperature window: 400°F (204°C) and falling. It's good to get some oven spring from a relatively hot loading temperature, but you want the temperature to then drop so that there won't be excessive browning or too thick a crust. About midway through the bake, you may need to sheet-pan the baking loaves to prevent scorched bottoms.
Home oven: Preheat the oven to 400°F (204°C). Bake in the combo cooker for 10 minutes, then lower the temperature to 350°F (177°C) and bake for another 25 minutes. Remove the lid about 15 minutes into the bake to vent the steam. Check the bottom of the loaves. If they seem to be getting too dark, remove them from the combo cooker and continue to bake directly on the oven rack.

Levain

Ingredient	Weight (g)	Volume	Baker's %
Bread flour	157	1⅓ C	64
Whole rye flour	89	1 C	36
Stout beer	312	1¼ C	127
Liquid sourdough starter	30	2 Tbsp	12
Total	588	—	—

Combine the flours, beer, and starter; mix until smooth. Cover and allow to ferment at 75°F (24°C) for approximately 10 hours.

Desired dough temperature: Adjust the water temperature so the dough is 78°F (26°C) at the end of mixing.

Mixing: This is a dough where I don't remove the original starter from the levain. Combine all of the ingredients except the bittersweet chocolate in the bowl of a mixer. Mix on slow speed for 3 minutes. Increase the mixer to medium, and mix for 3 minutes. The dough will be quite stiff, but the lower gluten content of the rye flour will create a dough that's more clay-like than one made entirely from wheat flour. Reduce the

Final Dough

Ingredient	Weight (g)	Volume	Baker's %
Bread flour	268	2¼ C	60
Whole rye flour	202	2¼ C	40
Stout beer	155	¾ C	65
Brewed coffee	34	3 Tbsp + 1 tsp	4.7
Instant active yeast	4	1 tsp	0.6
Salt	15	1 Tbsp	2
Unsweetened cocoa	7	1 Tbsp + ½ tsp	1
Ground coffee	11	3 Tbsp	1.5
Dark brown sugar	20	2 Tbsp	2.8
Blackstrap molasses	15	1 Tbsp	2
Levain	588	all from above	—
Bittersweet chocolate, chopped	179	1⅓ C	25
Total	1,498	—	—

mixer speed to slow and add the bittersweet chocolate in two parts. Mix until evenly dispersed, 2 to 3 minutes. Check the dough on the bottom of the bowl to make sure the chocolate is completely incorporated. You may want to knead it for few strokes by hand on your work surface to get it evenly incorporated.

Primary fermentation: Place dough in a covered container and let it ferment for 2 hours, folding once after 60 minutes.

Dividing/shaping: Carefully turn the dough onto a lightly floured surface and divide it into three pieces. You can skip a preshape for this dough and immediately form each piece into a bâtard. This dough is easy to shape—breads with a significant ratio of rye flour (say, above 30 percent) become as moldable as clay, an effect of the reduced amount of gluten in the rye. Place the bâtards seam side up on a well-floured couche to proof.

Allow to proof for 1½ to 2 hours. The dough will be fluffy, but be aware that its density may make the bread seem less proofed than it actually is. A loaf is ready to bake when it becomes swollen and the bottom seam starts to pull apart.

Scoring and baking: Just before baking, invert the loaves onto a lightly floured peel. Before scoring, reflour the surface of the bâtards, spreading the flour with the palm of your hand. I like to score this loaf with five parallel lines down its length. The contrast between the dark score marks and the light, floured surface is dramatic and beautiful.

Load the bread into the oven, steam well, and bake for approximately 35 minutes. Vent the steam about 15 minutes after loading.

Baking Beyond Bread

When I think of fresh baked goods, bread is at the top of my list. But a wood-fired oven is just as convenient (and perhaps less finicky) for other baked goods. In fact, it's more convenient because many products baked under 350°F (177°C) are forgiving and will bake with good results in a flexible temperature window.

Once again, there is beauty and satisfaction in being prepared in advance. Have some of your favorite cookie dough proportioned in the freezer to bake whenever your oven is at the right temperature. A wood-fired oven is a resource and therapeutic—the oven warms your hands but also your heart, by reminding you of this luxurious simplicity.

Some items are more persnickety—like cakes—but with a little monitoring you can adjust the bake environment by putting the item on an inverted pan or moving it closer to the door. You can make anything in a wood-fired oven that you can make in a home oven.

Pie Dough

At Johnson & Wales, we use the 3:2:1 ratio for piecrust: three parts flour, two parts fat, one part liquid. But which fat to use? My wife grew up making pie crust with Crisco and for years held on to this habit even after we had otherwise purged Crisco from our diets. She wasn't happy with her all-butter piecrusts: Wonderful flavor, but not quite flaky or light enough, and too prone to sagging, she thought. As an instructor at Johnson & Wales, though, I felt my own recipes should adhere to the university's policy of eliminating trans fats from the recipes in the culinary school curriculum. Pure lard was the obvious alternative, but the hydrogenated lard found in the grocery stores in rural North Carolina is no more healthful than Crisco. In Rhode Island, we found fresh leaf lard (the highest-quality lard) at the weekly farmer's market. We brought it to North Carolina, rendered it—effortlessly in the falling residual heat of a wood-fired oven—and made some of the flakiest crust we'd ever had. Properly rendered leaf lard can be nearly tasteless, but the lard from our first attempt tasted ever so slightly of pork, probably because it was rendered at too high a temperature. The taste was a little odd in blueberry pie, but tremendous for quiche and other savory pastry. Quiche Lorraine, the classic bacon-and-Gruyère quiche, seems to achieve its full potential in a leaf lard crust. Subsequent renderings at cooler temperatures had more neutral flavor and color, but at the time we ruled out lard as a good option for sweet pies and pastry. More experimentation was in order, and our next happy discovery was clarified butter.

Solid vegetable shortening and lard produce flakier crust than butter because in addition to fat, butter contains around 20 percent water and milk solids, while vegetable shortening and lard are 100 percent fat. The process of clarifying butter, however, removes the water and milk solids, leaving only the butterfat. The result performs like shortening and lard, producing gorgeous flaky crust with the wonderful flavor of butter. What a revelation.

Clarified butter is also stable at room temperature because the moisture and milk solids that could go

rancid have been removed. In their book *Home Baking*, Naomi Duguid and Jeffrey Alford note the convenience of clarified butter when you're traveling and constant refrigeration is not accessible. We had a jar of clarified butter on the counter when Hurricane Irene knocked out power for several days. Knowing the butter was fine sitting out was one small comfort, and, we added "clarify butter to have on hand when power goes out" to our Hurricane Preparedness List. (See the Clarified Butter section in chapter 14 for more.)

Clarified butter has a much higher smoke point than regular butter, so in addition to pastry crusts we also use clarified butter to sauté or brown foods with all the flavor of regular butter but with less risk of burning or smoking.

Yield: 9" double-crust pie

Pie Dough

Ingredient	Weight (g)	Volume	Baker's %
Bread flour	250	2 C + 2 Tbsp	100
Salt	5	scant 1 tsp	2
Fat	167	½ C + 3 Tbsp	67
Water, icy cold	83	⅓ C + 1 Tbsp	33
Total	505	—	—

Sift together the flour and salt. Cut the fat into the flour with a pastry blender, two knives, or your fingers until the pieces are pea-sized and evenly distributed. Work quickly to avoid melting the fat. Add half the water and mix gently with a spoon or plastic dough scraper. Add the remaining water in 1-tablespoon increments and mix until all of the ingredients are incorporated. Turn the dough onto a lightly floured surface and gather it together, gently pressing and just barely kneading until all the flour is part of the dough. The dough will be underdeveloped, and chunks of fat should be visible. Divide the dough in half, gently form into two balls, cover each in plastic or parchment, and press into a disc. Chill thoroughly—at least 2 hours but preferably overnight.

Apple Galette

Galettes—free-form tarts baked without a tin—are well suited for wood-fired oven baking. These rustic tarts are visually stunning and are a great way to feature fresh, seasonal fruit. The sweetness of the fruit may require an adjustment to the quantity of sugar.

Yield: 2 galettes
Wood-fired or home oven temperature: 375°F (191°C)

Pastry

Ingredient	Weight (g)	Volume	Baker's %
Bread flour	284	2⅓ C	100
Salt	10	2 tsp	3
Cinnamon	2	1 tsp	0.7
Unsalted butter, cold, cut into bits	255	1 C + 2 Tbsp	90
Water, icy cold	113	½ C	40
Total	664	—	—

Sift the flour, salt, and cinnamon into a bowl. Cut the butter into the flour with a pastry blender, or rub between your fingers, until the pieces are flat shards and evenly distributed. Work quickly to avoid melting the butter. Add the water and mix gently with a spoon or plastic dough scraper. If the dough seems dry or doesn't come together, add more water in 1-tablespoon increments. Mix just until all of the ingredients are incorporated. Turn the dough onto a surface and knead a few times just until it's cohesive. The dough will be undeveloped, and large chunks of butter should be visible. Divide the dough in half, gently form into neat balls, cover in plastic wrap, and press into discs. Chill thoroughly—at least 2 hours but preferably overnight.

Filling

Ingredient	Weight (g)	Volume	Baker's %
Dried cranberries	113	1 C	13
Baking apples, about 6	900	4½ C	100
Fresh ginger, peeled and grated	4	1" piece	0.4
Granulated sugar, to taste	(approximately) 134	⅔ C	15

Hydrate the cranberries in hot water for about 30 minutes, then drain thoroughly. Peel the apples and slice into thin wedges.

Assembling and baking the galette: Unwrap one piece of pastry dough and place on a lightly floured surface. Roll out to approximately 14". Combine the cranberries, apples, ginger, and sugar. Transfer the pastry to a piece of parchment and place half of the apple filling in the middle of the dough. Spread the filling to within 3" of the edge. Pull the edges of the dough up and over the filling, forming pleats. Repeat with the remaining dough and filling. Egg-wash the exposed dough. Sprinkle with a sanding of sugar if desired.

Bake at 375°F for 30 to 35 minutes.

Baking Powder Biscuits

A good biscuit is tender and flaky, and everything I do—and don't do—in making biscuits is aimed at achieving these characteristics. Do have a light touch. When mixing the ingredients together, a light touch will ensure enough gluten development so that the biscuit will hold itself together, but not so much that it cannot expand to become flaky during the quick, hot bake time. In addition, do keep the butter pieces

large and intact—this will provide the physical leavening (the expansion of the water trapped in the butter into steam) that makes biscuits flaky. Most important, don't overmix.

Yield: 9 large biscuits, each 3" square
Wood-fired or home oven temperature:
375°F (191°C). Baking powder is usually of the "double acting" type. This means it generates carbon dioxide when it comes in contact with an acid and again when the dough comes up to temperature in the heat of the oven. Baking powder biscuits need a bare minimum of 325°F (163°C) for proper leavening. If your oven is cooler than this, you'll likely get a dense biscuit with minimal flakiness. However, the second action of the baking powder means doughs or batters leavened with this ingredient can be held in the fridge or freezer and still reliably rise once they hit the heat of the oven.

Baking Powder Biscuits

Ingredient	Weight (g)	Volume	Baker's %
Bread flour	600	5 C	100
Baking powder, aluminum-free	28	2 Tbsp	4.7
Salt	12	2½ tsp	2
Granulated sugar	28	2 Tbsp + 2 tsp	4.7
Unsalted butter, cold	210	½ C + 7 Tbsp	35
Milk, cold	400	1¾ C	67
Total	1,278	—	—

Mixing: Sift together the bread flour, baking powder, salt, and sugar into a large bowl.

Cut the butter into cubes or slabs, add them to the dry ingredients, then toss lightly with your hands to coat the cubes with flour to keep them from clumping together. Flake or smear the butter into the dry mixture until most of the butter is in large, flat shards about the size of a nickel. This can be done using a pastry cutter, but we find it easier to use our hands, pressing the flour-coated butter between the thumbs and fingertips, or between the heels of our hands. Don't overdo this step! Stop when many of the butter pieces are still large and intact, almost in ribbons.

Add the milk all at once and mix by hand until barely incorporated. (There can even be a few spots of dry flour.) The kneading and folding steps that follow will continue the mix, so holding back now will help prevent an overmixed final product.

Turn the mixture onto a lightly floured work surface and gently knead six to eight times, just until the dough comes together and no more.

Roll the dough into a rectangle about 1" thick. (A cylindrical—rather than tapered—rolling pin works best here, or anytime you want to achieve a non-circular shape.) Fold the rectangle in half, turn it 90 degrees, and fold it in half again. Gently press and roll the dough into a square just shy of 9" × 9", at which point it will be about ⅝" thick. Let the dough rest, covered, for 20 minutes. Trim the outside edges of the rectangle (before cutting the nine biscuits) so all edges are freshly cut. Uncut edges will not open and rise as much. Gather the trimmed edges and press them into the bottom of the square or together to make a free-form biscuit, sometimes called a "kitty head."

Square biscuits eliminate the dough scraps created by round cutters. To cut the individual biscuits, mark a tic-tac-toe grid on the surface of the dough and use a long, sharp chef's knife to cut along the gridlines, dividing the dough into nine square biscuits. Take care to cut straight down (not a sawing motion) and wipe the blade clean after each cut.

Place the biscuits evenly spaced on a parchment-lined sheet pan and let them rest for another 15 minutes. Egg-wash only the tops of the biscuits. Egg wash that drips down a side of the biscuit can bind that side together, making the biscuit less flaky, especially if the egg wash is allowed to dry.

Bake at 375°F (191°C) for 15 to 18 minutes.

The biscuits can also be frozen immediately after they are cut. When you want to bake them, just remove from the freezer, egg-wash, and bake. There's no need to thaw the biscuit dough before baking.

PHOTO BY KATE KELLEY

Cranberry Pecan Buttermilk Scones

Pastry and all-purpose flour are blended in this formula to provide a lower protein content, which will yield a more tender scone. You can substitute any combination of dried fruit and nuts for the cranberries and pecans—just keep the weight the same. Avoid fresh or frozen fruit, which will make the dough too wet.

If the oven temperature is too high, use an inverted sheet pan to protect the bottom of the scones from getting too hard and thick.

Yield: 16 scones, 85g each
Wood-fired oven temperature window: 350°F to 375°F (177–191°C)
Home oven: Preheat the oven to 360°F (182°C).

Sift together the bread flour, pastry flour, salt, sugar, and baking powder into a large bowl. Whisk together the buttermilk and eggs.

Cranberry Pecan Buttermilk Scones

Ingredient	Weight (g)	Volume	Baker's %
Bread flour	258	2 C + 3 Tbsp	50
Pastry flour	258	2¼ C	50
Salt	5	1 tsp	1
Granulated sugar	64	⅓ C	12.5
Baking powder	28	2 Tbsp + 2 tsp	5.4
Buttermilk, cold	268	1 C + 2 Tbsp	52
Eggs	100	2 eggs	22
Unsalted butter, cold	170	¾ C	33
Dried cranberries, coarsely chopped	98	¾ C	19
Pecans, coarsely chopped	98	1 C	19
Total	1,347	—	—

Mixing: Cut or flake the butter into the dry mixture until most of the butter is in large, flat shards about the size of a nickel. You can use a pastry cutter or rub it between the palms of your hands. Incorporating the butter in one of these ways will coat the gluten strands, making a more tender scone. Make sure the butter pieces stay large and intact—this will provide physical leavening (the expansion of the water trapped in the butter into steam) that makes a flaky scone. Don't overmix!

Add the buttermilk mixture all at once and mix by hand until just incorporated—there can even be a few spots of dry flour. Add the dried cranberries and pecans; mix for 20 to 30 seconds to incorporate the fruit. Don't overmix! Turn the mixture onto a floured work surface (don't flour the bench too lightly . . . try to keep it to a minimum) and gently knead six or eight times or until the dough comes together. The fruit and nuts should be evenly distributed. Don't overknead!

Divide dough into two 680g pieces and gently shape into rounds. Let the dough rest for 10 minutes, then pat or roll the dough out to ⅝", retaining the round shape. Place on a parchment-lined sheet pan and chill for a minimum of 30 minutes.

Remove from the refrigerator and cut each round into eight equal wedges with a sharp knife. Place the cut pieces evenly spaced on a parchment-lined sheet pan, egg-wash the tops only (egg wash on the sides may inhibit the rise), and bake at 360°F (182°C) for 15 to 18 minutes.

Scones can also be frozen after they're cut into wedges. This is one of the beautiful things about baked goods that are leavened with baking powder: You can freeze them before baking, then—when the oven is right—bake them directly from the freezer. Egg-wash just before loading.

VARIATION: STEPHANIE AGANA'S ROASTED ONION AND CHEESE SCONES

For a great savory combination, replace the dried fruit and nuts with 103g (20 percent) Ember-Roasted Onions; 129g (1¼ C, 25 percent) grated cheese (Gruyère, Asiago, and white cheddar all work well—or you can try a combination of the three); and 5g (1 percent) cracked pepper. Make sure the onions are cool before you mix them with the cheese. Add the savory ingredients at the same time you would add the fruit and nuts.

Rustic Potato Pie

This is a simple food that can seem fancy. You can make the crust and filling a day in advance, which means this pie is convenient to assemble and bake for guests or yourself. In fact, the dough is easier to roll if you prepare it a day in advance and let it rest overnight in the fridge. The filling also thickens slightly and gets more flavorful as the ingredients sit overnight. Chop and add the parsley just before you fill the pies to keep it green and fresh. But don't worry if you suddenly want some of this pie and haven't made the dough and filling ahead. It can be prepped and baked a few hours later.

This can be a light meal, served with a salad in the middle of summer, or a more substantial addition to an egg dish served for brunch. It's also good cold and travels well if wrapped. One recipe tester said she became "obsessed" with this formula. Put this down as a wood-fired oven staple. The recipe was inspired by a recipe first published in the May/June 1998 issue of *Saveur* magazine.

Yield: 2 pies, each 10" diameter
Wood-fired oven temperature window: 350°F to 400°F (177–204°C). This pie *can* also be baked in an oven while there's a live fire burning; you just have to be a little more careful that it doesn't take on too much color. Position the pie near the mouth of the oven, away from the fire, so the top crust doesn't get too dark or dried out. Turn the pie as needed to prevent uneven browning, and expect the bake time to be less depending on the intensity of the heat from the fire.
Home oven: Preheat the oven to 375°F (191°C).

Dough

Ingredient	Weight (g)	Volume	Baker's %
Bread flour	284	2⅓ C	100
Salt	6	1¼ tsp	2
Olive oil	43	3 Tbsp	15
Water	142	½ C + ⅓ C	50
Total	475	—	—

Combine the flour and salt. Add the oil and water and mix until the dough comes together. Knead until smooth, about 5 minutes. Divide the dough in half and shape each piece into a ball, then flatten into a 6"-diameter disc and cover or wrap. Refrigerate for a minimum of 2 hours, but the dough will be easier to roll out if it rests overnight in the fridge.

Filling

Ingredient	Weight (g)	Volume
Yukon Gold potatoes, raw and unpeeled	680	—
1 smallish onion, diced	128	—
Parmigiano or other hard cheese, grated	30	½ C
Ricotta cheese	71	⅓ C
Unsalted butter, softened	28	2 Tbsp
Milk, whole	454	2 C
Salt, to taste	8	1½ tsp
Pepper, coarsely ground, to taste	.7	½ tsp
Egg, slightly beaten	50	1 egg
Parsley leaves, loosely packed	9	½ C

Roast or boil the potatoes and let them cool. Caramelize the onion, or use ember-roasted onions. When the potatoes are cool, grate them completely into a bowl. (If you grate them while they're still hot, they will become gummy.) Add the onion, cheeses, butter, and milk to the potatoes; add salt and pepper, adjusting to taste. Mix until smooth. Add the egg and mix until incorporated.

Assembling and baking the pies: This dough is pretty extensible (especially if rested overnight). Roll each chilled disc of dough to an 18" diameter. Use hardly any flour on the bench: The oil in the dough helps make it non-stick, and it will be easier to work on a surface with just the lightest dusting of flour. Place the dough on parchment paper or a well-floured, wooden oven peel. Chop the parsley and add to the potato filling. Deposit half the filling in the center of the rolled-out dough and spread it to within several inches of the perimeter. Fold the edges of the dough over the filling toward the center, overlapping the dough in pleats. Leave a small hole at the center to allow steam to escape. Egg-wash and bake directly on the hearth for about 30 minutes.

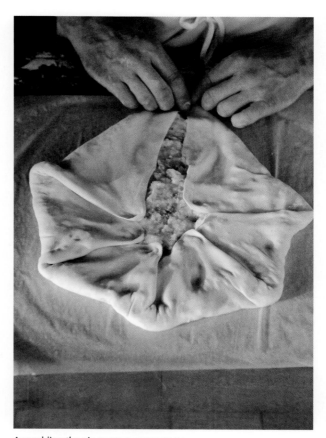

Assembling the pie PHOTO BY KATE KELLEY

Pound Cake

My first job baking handmade bread in a wood-fired oven was at a coastal restaurant named Windansea. I was the only one in the kitchen during the early morning and made enough bread for the next couple of days of dinner service. To fill the time between bread-baking steps, I started making this delicious pound cake from the venerable *Moosewood Cookbook* by Mollie Katzen. It quickly went from a dessert special to a regular menu item. When we opened One Acre Garden and Bakery, Windansea stopped being my employer and became my customer. I provided bread to them and continued to make the Moosewood pound cake, unchanged from the original recipe.

This pound cake is pretty tolerant when it comes to temperature requirements. I've baked it at 375°F (191°C) for 55 minutes and I've baked it at 325°F (163°C) for nearly 2 hours. If your oven is on the low side, slide the cake way in the back and directly on the hearth. Try not to disturb it for at least 30 minutes. If things are running a bit hot, keep the cake up front. Start the bake with the cake pan right on the hearth so you get good oven spring, but then transfer it to an inverted sheet pan so the bottom (which will end up to be the top) doesn't get too dark or dry. One other thing: This is the best pound cake ever.

Yield: 1 glorious 10" pound cake
Wood-fired oven temperature window: 350°F to 375°F (177–191°C).
Home oven: Preheat the oven to 350°F (177°C).

Grease and flour a 10" tube pan.

Sift together the bread flour, baking powder, and salt into a large bowl. Cream the butter and sugar until light and fluffy, scraping the bowl down often. Lower the speed of the mixer and add the eggs 1 at a time, letting each incorporate before you add the next.

Combine the milk and vanilla. On low speed, add the milk and flour mixtures alternately to the creamed butter and sugar, beginning and ending with

Pound Cake

Ingredient	Weight (g)	Volume	Baker's %
Bread flour	536	4⅓ C	100
Baking powder	8	1 Tbsp	1.5
Salt	4	½ tsp	0.75
Unsalted butter	454	2 C	85
Sugar	622	3 C	116
Eggs*	300	6 eggs	56
Milk	238	1 C	44
Vanilla	10	2 tsp	1.9
Glaze			
Powdered sugar	108	1 C	—
Vanilla	5	1 tsp	—
Hot water	57	¼ C	—

* The average egg weighs 50g, I've codified the amount for this recipe as 300g. However, the weight of the egg is affected by its size (of course) and its age. Use 6 eggs and you'll be fine.

flour. Take care to not overmix—have the mixture just come together.

Gently spoon the batter into the cake pan with a spatula, trying to keep it more or less level. Immediately place into a hot oven and bake for about 1 hour, until a toothpick comes out clean. (Perform the toothpick test through a crack that will form on the surface of the cake. You will get a truer reading this way than if you go through the shell of the crust.)

Remove from the oven and cool for about 10 minutes. While the cake is cooling, sift the powdered sugar into a bowl. Add the vanilla and whisk in the hot water. Keep whisking until the glaze is lump-free. Slide a knife around the perimeter of the cake and invert it onto a cooling screen or cake stand. Poke numerous holes down into the cake with a long skewer. Pour on the glaze and spread it smoothly over the top, allowing plenty of glaze to cascade over the edge and down the sides of the cake.

Try to let this one cool completely before you slice into it. This pound cake has a great shelf life. After a couple of days at room temperature, place it in the fridge.

The inverted sheet pan in the back of the oven lifts the pound cake off the hearth for the last half of the bake time, so the cake doesn't get too dark or dry.

Pain d'Epices

This is an old-fashioned gingerbread-like quick bread—the name means "spice bread." It's a holiday favorite. I've sold it, given it away as gifts, and eaten it at Christmastime for years. The main leavener is baking soda, which creates carbon dioxide when it comes into contact with the acidic honey. Unlike baking powder, which makes carbon dioxide when it becomes wet and again when it meets the heat of the oven, baking soda creates carbon dioxide only once. Make sure your oven is ready to go once you start mixing this one. Unbaked batter that sits around will lose its carbon dioxide and become heavy.

Like other dense rye breads, this bread has an impressive shelf life. It will become a bit chewier after several days, but I find it delicious toasted and served warm with butter.

This recipe was inspired by a recipe in *Saveur* magazine, issue 30.

Yield: 2 loaf pans, 1 Pullman pan, or numerous mini loaves
Prefermented flour: 0%
Wood-fired oven temperature window: 350°F (177°C) and falling
Home oven: Preheat the oven to 350°F (177°C).

Sift together the rye flour, baking soda, and spices into a large bowl and set aside. Whisk the milk and honey together over medium heat and bring to a gentle simmer. Add the orange and lemon peel and remove from the heat. Before you add the yolks, you must first temper them so they don't cook in the hot mixture. To do this, slowly drizzle a little of the hot mixture into the yolks while whisking. Now add the tempered yolks back into the liquids.

Add the liquids to the dry ingredients and mix gently just until smooth. Divide evenly between two greased loaf pans. Arrange the almonds in a decorative pattern on top of the unbaked batter.

Place the pans directly on the hearth in the 350°F (177°C) zone, and bake for 15 minutes. Then move the pans into a 325°F (163°C) zone in the oven and bake for

Pain d'Epices

Ingredient	Weight (g)	Volume	Baker's %
Whole rye flour	440	4½ C + ⅓ C	100
Baking soda	11	2 tsp	2.5
Anise seeds, ground	8	1 Tbsp	1.8
Nutmeg, ground	1.8	1 tsp	0.4
Coriander, ground	0.8	1 tsp	0.2
Cinnamon	0.8	½ tsp	0.2
Cloves, ground	0.8	½ tsp	0.2
Milk	264	1⅛ C	60
Honey	704	2 C	160
Fresh orange peel, grated on the small holes of a box grater (about 2–3 oranges)	22	¼ C	5
Fresh lemon peel, zested, grated on the small holes of a box grater	9	1-2 lemons	2.0
Egg yolks, beaten	54	3 yolks	12
Whole raw almonds, blanched	as needed	as needed	—
Total	1,516.2	—	—

approximately 25 minutes more, or until a toothpick inserted in the center comes out clean. The loaves may need to be tented with foil to prevent excessive darkening.

If you're using a home oven, bake at 350°F for 15 minutes. Reduce the temp to 325°F and bake for approximately 25 minutes more, or until a toothpick inserted in the center comes out clean. The loaves may need to be tented with foil to prevent excessive darkening.

Let the loaves cool for 10 minutes, then unmold them and cool them completely before slicing.

Taralli

Taralli are a traditional Italian baked good with the subtle flavor of anise and the crispy texture of a bread stick. These are convenient because—like scones and biscuits—they can be frozen raw and baked when the oven temperature is right.

Like bagels, taralli are placed in a container of simmering water before they're baked to gelatinize the starches, create a shiny crust, and plump up the final product through physical leavening.

A sample of taralli and the kernel of this formula came to me from a friend for whom I built an oven. Lisa's Italian grandmother sold the formula to a Connecticut bakery years ago, which is still making them to this day. It took several trials to reduce the yield from 5 pounds of flour and determine that "anise spirits" was really "anise oil." Ouzo, anisette, and anise extract don't have enough anise flavor once the taralli are baked; anise oil is concentrated essential oil. Be careful—anise oil can degrade or discolor some plastics, so measure it in glass or stainless-steel containers only.

Yield: About 30 taralli
Wood-fired oven temperature window:
350°F to 375°F (177–191°C)
Home oven: Preheat the oven to 375°F (191°C).

Grind or coarsely chop the fennel seeds.

Cream the butter and sugar in a mixer fitted with a paddle until light and fluffy. Add the eggs, water, and anise oil. Mix gently on low speed for about a minute, being sure to scrape the butter off the bottom of the bowl. It's okay if the mixture is not completely smooth.

Exchange the paddle for a dough hook, add approximately half the flour as well as the seeds, and mix on low speed until incorporated. Add the remaining flour and mix on low until incorporated.

Once all the ingredients are combined, mix on low speed for 3 minutes. You may need to stop the mixer occasionally and scrape the dough off the hook. Increase the mixer to medium and mix for another 3 minutes,

Taralli

Ingredient	Weight (g)	Volume	Baker's %
Fennel seeds	12	3 Tbsp	2
Unsalted butter	113	½ C	19
Granulated sugar	85	⅓ C + 1 Tbsp	14
Eggs	250	5 eggs	42
Water	42	3 Tbsp	7
Anise oil	2	½ tsp	0.3
Bread flour	600	5 C	100
Total	1,104	—	—

scraping the dough down off the hook as necessary. The dough is properly mixed when you can roll a small piece into a smooth rope without any lumps.

Remove the dough from the bowl, cover it, and let it rest for 15 to 30 minutes. Fill a large shallow pan with approximately 4" of water and heat until it's just shy of a boil.

Throughout the shaping process, keep the dough covered so it doesn't dry out. Divide the dough into 30g pieces. Roll each piece into a rope approximately 12" long. The pieces may not want to roll out to 12" when you first start to shape. If so, go through them systematically and roll them out as long as they will go. Then go back to the first one. The short rest time it takes to get all of them shaped will be enough to let the taralli relax. You should be able to roll them out to the full 12" on the second pass. If they are difficult to shape because they're sliding around, spritz the work surface with a mist of water. This will provide some traction for the dough, which is necessary to roll an even cylinder. Pinch the ends of the rope together and pull into an oval.

Place the shaped taralli into the hot-water bath. They will immediately sink. Loosen the taralli with a spatula if they stick to the bottom of the pan. Once they have risen, remove them with a slotted spoon and let them drain on a cooling rack while you boil more taralli.

Bake the taralli on a parchment-lined sheet pan at 375°F (191°C) for about 30 minutes.

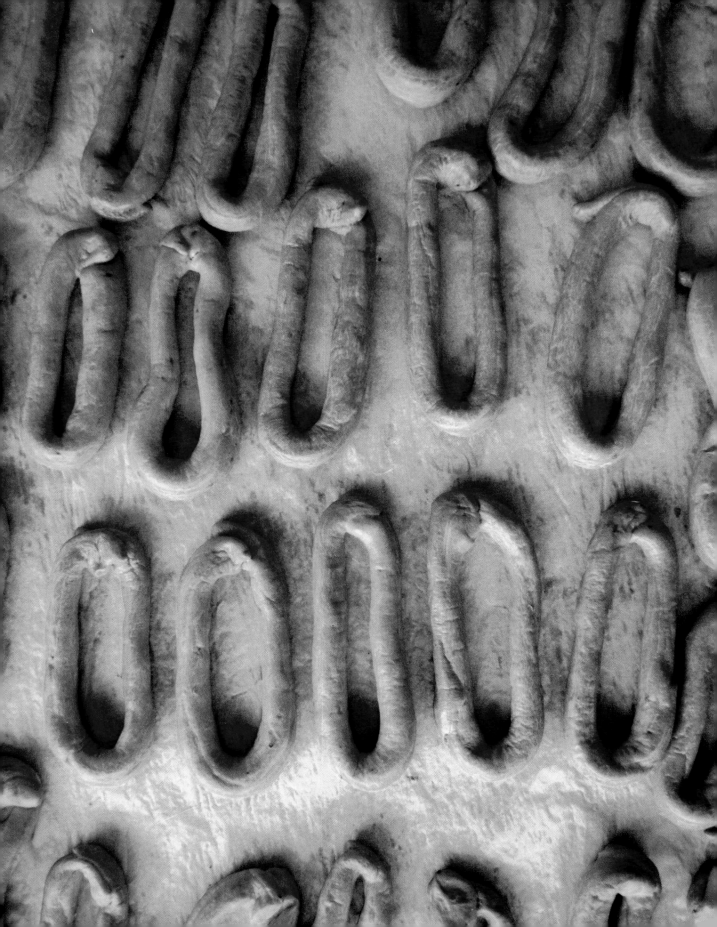

Frozen Food

The next time you make a casserole, prepare an extra, but wrap and freeze it before it's baked. Three weeks later—when you lack both ingredients and energy to make a wholesome dinner, but have a hot oven—just slip the other pan in the oven for 1 to 2 hours. Your mileage may vary, depending on the mass of your oven and the loading temperature, but a 350° F (177° C) oven should heat up a frozen casserole to a safe serving temperature in 1–2 hours.

And as far as convenience is concerned . . . I've baked box cakes, sautéed frozen pierogi, warmed up frozen burritos, and heated commercial potpies in Magdalena when the opportunity presented itself and the oven was at the right temperature. Anything you do in your home oven, you can do in your wood-fired oven. And while some purchased frozen foods do taste good, they don't present nearly the same value as if you make and freeze your own.

The taralli can also be frozen immediately after the hot-water bath. They can be baked frozen or allowed to thaw before baking.

Kugula

My family always identified itself as Polish and because we were several generations into the American experience, we retained only a few traditional Polish dishes, such as stuffed cabbage and pierogi. Still, I've always been proud and interested in my Polish heritage and I was a little disoriented when I heard through the family grapevine that we might actually be of Lithuanian descent.

In hopes of clearing up the mystery, I turned to the epic poem *Pan Tadeusz* published in 1834 by my ancestor, Adam Mickiewicz (1798-1855), famous Polish poet, political activist, playwright, and nationalist. There is an Adam Mickiewicz University in Poland and statues of Mickiewicz are in parks and squares throughout the country. I learned that Mickiewicz considered the entire *region* his home and that present day political boundaries do not accurately represent Eastern Europe during his time. What a relief to also consider myself Lithuanian without turning my back on my Polish heritage.

Adam spends considerable time in *Pan Taduesz* writing about food: descriptions of mushroom foraging, the delight of coffee, and the aromatic Polish hunter's stew

called bigos. And all of these comestibles were grown and consumed within a region he called "Lithuania." When I came across an arcane recipe for Lithuanian kugula, I had a new reason to give it a try, and realized it is perfect for a wood-fired oven. Kugula is easy to make. If you took this to a midwestern potluck, you could call it "hash-brown casserole."

In a 350°F to 375°F (177–191°C) oven, cook five pieces of bacon until crisp in a shallow 9" Pyrex baking dish, the kind that might be used for macaroni and cheese or other gratins. While the bacon cooks, peel and grate seven medium potatoes. Thoroughly rinse and drain the grated potatoes in a colander. (The rinsing step is important so the finished kugula isn't pasty.) In a separate bowl combine two beaten eggs, ⅔ cup sour cream, 2 tablespoons flour, ½ teaspoon of cracked black pepper, 1 teaspoon of salt (depends on the saltiness of the bacon), and ½ of a medium onion, grated.

When the bacon is crisp, remove the dish from the oven. Remove the bacon to cool, but leave the bacon fat in the gratin dish. Finely chop the bacon until it is almost dust. Fold the potatoes and bacon into the egg and sour cream mixture. Return the baking dish to the oven until the surface of the bacon fat starts to ripple. Take the dish back out of the oven and carefully pour the potato mixture into the hot dish. If the oven is hot enough a sizzling potato crust will immediately begin to form in the hot bacon fat. Return the kugula to the oven and bake for at least an hour or until the top gets brown and crispy.

Kugula is good hot, warm, or cold. I've read that kugula should be served with a "pitcher" of sour cream, but sometimes I just use a dollop. I also like to take scalloped tomatoes from the following recipe, puree them into a sauce, spread it on a square of kugula, top with a fried egg, and serve it all with a side salad. Oh Lithuania, my other homeland!

Scalloped Tomatoes

My parents were kitchen role models for me. They shared the tasks of cooking and each had their own specialties. Plus, their career in the air force exposed them to many different types of foods from cultures all over the world, which helped me become an adventurous eater. We would stock up on olive oil, kimchi, feta cheese, and kalamata olives when we were traveling and take it all back to 1970s mid-Michigan, where these ingredients were unavailable.

Each of my parents opened their own businesses after they retired from the air force, and although they were busy, we rarely skipped dinner. That meant a lot of late dinners, but they had the foresight to cook in advance so we could easily have a hot meal of spaghetti, stuffed cabbage, and what we called "chop suey."

These are the things comfy dreams are made of, and there is a huge variety to choose from. Mac and cheese. Shepherd's pie. Scalloped potatoes. The venerable green bean and tuna noodle casserole. You can throw lasagna in there as far as I'm concerned. I chose a simple dish my dad called Bread and Tomatoes. It involved adding a can of stewed tomatoes to some torn bread and sliced onion and baking it in a covered piece of CorningWare until the rest of dinner was ready. This was easy and hearty American fare. Once I started cooking with fire, I changed the recipe a bit.

Take the Fire-Roasted Tomatoes that are described earlier in this chapter. Or if you use canned whole tomatoes, base the following amount of ingredients on a can that weighs 794 g (a typical 28-ounce can), about 3 cups. Slice a medium onion into thin rounds and place in a coverable ovenproof dish with about 2 tablespoons of olive oil, butter, clarified butter, schmaltz, lard, or what have you. Include a teaspoon of anchovy paste and some coarsely ground pepper. Cook this preparation in a 350°F (177°C) oven until the onions start to soften.

Squeeze or chop coarsely the tomatoes and add to the onions, along with 6–7 slices of old bread, torn into pieces. I use Pain Rustique, Golden Sesame, and Miche, but whatever you have on hand is perfect. Add 2 cups of stock and a clove of minced garlic. Leave the cover off and return to the oven.

Cook until the bread absorbs some of the juice. If it gets too thick, add more stock. Once it seems well cooked, remove from the oven and top with Pain de Mie crumbs mixed with a little melted butter. Slide back into the oven.

Scalloped Tomatoes can also be poured into a casserole dish and frozen. When you need a hearty side dish, remove the pan from the freezer, top with buttered bread crumbs, and bake it again with or without flame until it's heated through and the crumbs have browned.

See chapter 13 for a Baked Bean recipe—a type of casserole (or *cassoulet* to be more exact) baked at a lower temperature for a longer time than most casseroles.

Braising

Braising is the method used for pot roast or anything you might put in a Crock-Pot, slowly tenderizing proteins while concentrating flavors all day long. To pull out the full flavors of a braised dish, sear the meat and vegetables at high temperatures, then slowly cook them in a closed vessel with seasoned stock, wine, or water. Braised dishes are incredibly satisfying and comforting and allow you to make delectable meat dishes out of inexpensive cuts of meat because the long, slow cooking process breaks down the collagen in the meat, creating a tender, tender dinner. The low cooking temperature (275–350°F/135–177°C) means part of the cooking liquid evaporates, condenses on the lid of the dish, and then drips back down, bathing the food in more and more flavor.

Follow the trick offered by Molly Stevens in her comprehensive book *All About Braising*, where she advises

Seared leeks

Seared leeks after braising in chicken stock

using a piece of parchment paper pushed down toward the surface of the food in order to reduce the headspace volume in the pot. The parchment also helps create a better seal, sealing in all the aromatic braising liquid that might leak out around the edge of the lid. Ideally, the amount of food will adequately fill the space of the baking vessel. It's important to use the correct amount of liquid—you don't want to stew the food. The idea is to bathe the food (with enough liquid to be about a quarter or a third of the way up the sides of the food in the pan) with enriched and increasingly concentrated flavors. Also, keep in mind that some foods, like celery, contribute more moisture to the cooking process than do others such as potatoes.

Braised Vegetables

You can braise meat or vegetables with the same technique. Using your wood-fired oven takes a bit of forethought, though. You want to sear the food at high temperatures before the long, slow braising period. How do you go from searing temperatures to braising temperatures? Just hold on to the braised food and wait for the oven to go into its natural cooling curve. An easy way to make some great braised meals is to sear the food the night before (at your pizza party or while you're cooking some steaks for a weekend dinner). Place the seared food directly into the braising vessel. You can even add the stock, herbs, and whatever other ingredients you want and then stash it in the fridge. The next morning, rake out the ashes, slide the prepared dish into the oven, and go have a second cup of coffee and make brunch. A couple of hours later (less if it's a vegetable braise), your lunch or dinner—and luscious leftovers for the week—will be ready and you'll have created zero dirty cooking dishes that day, save for a stirring spoon and the cooking vessel.

Don't worry if you weren't able to sear the meat in advance. You can place raw braising ingredients in the oven without the searing step. The flavor will be less complex owing to the lack of browning, of course, but you can still make a delicious braised meal.

Melba toast in Magdelena with a top-down fire
drying in advance for the next fire cycle

→→ • ←←

CHAPTER THIRTEEN

Moderate Oven, aka the Comfort Zone:
350°F to 212°F (177–100°C)

The comfort zone of the moderate oven is a part of the heat cycle I never experienced when I was baking commercially out of Magdalena, because she never got that cool. But now it's one of my favorite retained-heat cooking environments because the heat is steady, the pace is flexible, and it's the perfect environment for creating comfort foods.

Croutons

I've always been intrigued by the uses of old bread. I learned even more clever uses when I borrowed a book—Elisabeth Heinicke's *Beyond Croutons*—from Brinna Sands while I was working at King Arthur. Many of those ideas influenced my style of whole-loaf cooking and gave me uses for the half loaves that perpetually sit on the counter. But croutons are the iconic use for old bread. And like all my cooking, I try to keep these simple. No dry herbs, no extra salt and pepper. I've also gone through trials using melted butter and schmaltz as fats, but olive oil makes a lighter crouton. Any bread can be used for croutons, but I tend to make it out of Pain au Levain.

Take about half a loaf of Pain au Levain that is still moist enough to cut into ½" cubes. Toss with about 15g (0.5 ounce) of olive oil, spread on a baking sheet in a single layer, and bake in a 325°F (163°C) oven for about 15 minutes. Once cool, croutons keep in an airtight container for 2 weeks or can be frozen for 6 to 8 weeks.

Bettie Granola

Granola is a great item to make in a low-temperature oven, perhaps a day or two after a big bake day. I started developing this granola—named for our small post-office-less town, Bettie, North Carolina—to fill a vacant baking window with a salable item. This is an easy and stripped-down version of granola—just oats, almonds, honey, a little oil, and brown rice syrup, an unrefined sugar without overbearing sweetness. I prefer honey as a sweetener, but a Vegan Bettie can be made by substituting agave nectar.

Bakeries recognize granola for its extended shelf life, allowing for a sales period much longer than that for leavened bread. Wood-fired micro-bakeries can bake granola at a cool point of the temperature spectrum, in the middle of the week, and package it for sale at weekend farmer's markets.

If you would like to add dried fruit, do so after the granola is baked. The concentrated sugars in the dried fruit will burn during the baking period, even at the relatively low temperature.

Yield: About 7 cups granola
Wood-fired oven temperature window: Bettie Granola is not fussy. Bake anywhere from 250°F to 325°F (121–163°C).
Home oven: Preheat the oven to 325°F (163°C).

Bettie Granola

Ingredient	Weight (g)	Volume	Baker's %
Whole raw almonds	175	1¼ C	25
Old-fashioned rolled oats	700	6½ C	100
Brown rice syrup	210	⅔ C	30
Honey	105	⅓ C	15
Olive oil	71	⅓ C	10
Total	1,261	—	—

Coarsely chop the almonds. Combine the oats and almonds in a large bowl.

Combine the brown rice syrup, honey, and olive oil; heat gently to decrease viscosity.

Pour the liquids over the oats and almonds, and stir until well coated.

Spread onto a sheet pan or large roasting pan (the higher sides on the roasting pan help contain the granola during the occasional stirring) and bake for 30 to 40 minutes, checking every 10 minutes and stirring as necessary to promote even browning.

Bake the granola until it has taken on a rich golden caramelized color. Remove from the oven, let it cool, and check to make sure the granola is thoroughly dry. If it still feels moist, return it to the oven and bake until the moisture is gone. When the granola is thoroughly

cool and dry, store in an airtight container. This granola will keep for weeks at room temperature in an airtight container.

Melba Toast

I began making melba toast with leftover Pain de Mie, but it's so delicious that Stephanie has been known to make melba toast out of an entire loaf if she gets hold of one. Pain de Mie melba toast will be the most delicious you've ever had. To make it, cut the crust away from the loaf, then cut the loaf into ⅛" slices. Cut the square slices in half to make two rectangular pieces from each. Spread these out on a sheet pan, and dry until they're just slightly golden and thoroughly crisp. A low, receding oven works great for this—anywhere around 275°F (135°C) will produce a crisp melba in about 20 minutes. Flip them about halfway through. This is one of those dishes that can go longer at a cooler temperature and shorter if the oven is above 300°F (149°C). Just keep an eye on them and completely dry them out or they won't be crisp.

Bread Crumbs

And the crust you removed to make melba? Break it into pieces and bake in the same oven until dry. Pulverize the crusts in a blender or food processor, and store your artisan bread crumbs in the freezer. These are the bread crumbs called for in the Crab Cake and Scalloped Tomatoes recipes in chapters 11 and 12, respectively. They're perfect for tossing in some melted butter before spreading over a mac and cheese or braised celery.

Crumb-Encrusted Goat Cheese Medallions

Bread crumbs add a crust to seared goat cheese medallions. A Pain de Mie–encrusted goat cheese medallion cooked in the live fire of an oven serves nicely as a molten nugget to spread on bread or as a crown jewel on a nice salad. This recipe is included here because it is dependent on the bread crumbs dried out at a low temperature. The goat cheese medallions, however, require a hot oven. No problem . . . just save those crumbs in the freezer until the next time you fire up.

Make the salad in advance. Get a cast-iron or other heavy pan hot with about ¼" of cooking fat. Select a cylinder of goat cheese, creamy but not crumbly. Keep cold until you are ready to slice it into ½" medallions. Squeeze together with your palms if the cheese seems like it's going to fall apart. Dunk in an egg wash made of 1 egg, a bit of water, and a pinch of salt. Remove the cheese with two forks and dredge in a saucer of bread crumbs. Place in the hot pan and allow a crust to form before you flip them; use two forks when you flip so the goat cheese doesn't fall apart. Once the crust is formed on the other side, remove from the pan, drain on a piece of paper, and place on salad. These medallions also make a nice addition to a bowl of Baked Beans (below), especially if an arugula salad is served in the same shallow bowl.

Baked Beans

Baked beans are a classic—their long, slow baking cycle is perfect for the falling temperature in a cooling oven. And part of this dish's New England history indicates how convenient it is to fit into life when you don't have the time to—or simply can't—cook. The early Puritans of New England prohibited themselves from cooking on the Sabbath, so an easy way to have a hot meal was setting a bean pot in the oven on Saturday evening to cook slowly overnight. Baked beans come in many styles, but I'm drawn to the classic Boston variety with white or navy beans, salt pork, fat back or pork belly, and molasses. Traditionally, baked beans are cooked in a glazed stoneware pot that narrows at the neck and is covered with a tight-fitting lid during the 6- to 8-hour cooking period. A 2½-quart pot is just the right size for the following recipe.

Note: If the following method is too detailed for your cooking style, just put everything into a crock, place it in a 250°F (121°C) oven, and cook for about 8 hours, stirring occasionally and checking the hydration during the last 2 hours. You can follow the same process in a home oven; it works just as well.

This method is designed to start with soaked (not boiled) beans, which allows you to carry out all the steps in your oven without having to boil water on your stovetop.

Baked Beans

Ingredient	Weight (g)	Volume
Dry, white beans	454	2½ C
Fatback or pork belly, diced*	170–227	about 1½ C
Medium onion, diced	—	1 each
Molasses	85	¼ C
Bay leaves	—	3 each
Dry mustard	1	1 tsp
Pepper, coarsely ground	1	1 tsp
Water	711–948	3–4 C
Salt	9	2 tsp
Apple cider vinegar	—	2 Tbsp

* Either of these two types of meat works perfectly fine for Baked Beans, so use whichever one you can get. Pork belly has a bit more meat than fatback, and a pig has slightly more fatback than pork belly. And it's easy to guess where on the animal these two fatty cuts come from.

The day before, rinse the beans, cover with 2" of water (above the beans), and soak overnight. The next day, drain the beans and rinse again.

Build this dish by adding ingredients in stages. Many recipes have you place everything in a pot at once, but I like to have the pork, onions, and seasonings mingle before they're diluted by the beans and water. Building in stages means you bring these smaller amounts of initial ingredients up to temperature before a large addition of beans and

Getting ready to add heated water to a pot of baked beans

Beef fat

water. Heating an empty cooking vessel in advance helps bring the entire preparation up to temperature more quickly than a room-temperature vessel. This is especially true if the pot is heavy and/or the oven temperature is low (300°F/149°C). You can also warm the water for the beans in advance. A large Pyrex or other ovenproof measuring cup filled with the 3 to 4 cups of water can be warmed before it is introduced to the bean pot.

Cut the pork into ¼" to ½" chunks. Remove the heated pot from the oven. Place the pork in the pot and put it back in the oven. (I usually take the lid off during this first period and leave it in the oven to stay hot.) Find a spot around 325°F to 350°F (163–177°C) to brown the pork and partially liquefy the fat. (If the retained heat is at least 325°F or if there is a small fire or ember pile, the time to brown the meat may only be 5 or 10 minutes. Lower temperatures, or the absence of a fire, might stretch out this time to about 20 minutes.) If the oven isn't hot enough to brown the pork, don't worry. It will certainly liquefy the fat, and the long, slow cooking process will provide plenty of full-figured flavor.

Add the onion, molasses, bay leaves, mustard, and pepper to the pot and stir to combine. Place the pot back in the oven for 10 to 15 minutes or until the preparation is hot and intermingled.

Add the beans to the pot and stir to coat. Add (heated) water, enough to cover the beans by an inch.

Place the pot back in the oven. If you're on the low end of the temperature range, leave the lid off for half an hour so the radiant heat can reach the surface of the beans. At this point, an ideal temperature for your beans is in an oven (or zone) that's 250°F to 300°F (121–149°C).

From now until the beans are finished is about 6 to 8 hours. Check them a couple of times over the first few hours, mostly to stir and check the hydration. Several hours later, the beans will start to thicken as they soften and absorb water. I like to add the salt at this point; I find it is easier to properly season if enough of the beans' starches have been broken down.

After 5 hours or so, monitor the beans so they don't dry out and scorch. Adjust the salt if necessary.

Removing the lid for the last half hour gives a nice finish to the surface of the beans.

This can be served in the British way—smothered on toast. I like to serve beans together in a shallow bowl with a salad made of arugula, spinach, or greens appropriate for a wilted salad. If you skip the salad, try the beans with a light sprinkle of apple cider vinegar. A Crumb-Encrusted Goat Cheese Medallion also makes a nice addition to this simple meal.

Rendering Animal Fat

I try to bring my own rendered fat into most of my wood-fired cuisine, especially for cooking. The smoke point is higher than for most other cooking oils. And as noted in the pastry section, it also makes flaky pie crusts and biscuits.

It's important to avoid exceeding the smoke point of whichever animal fat you're using in cooking so it doesn't break down into free fatty acids and glycerol and begin to, well, smoke. At this point, off flavors will be produced and the oil surrounding your food goes from clear and pure to dark and dirty. Clarified butter begins to break down around 485°F (252°C), while regular butter starts to smoke around 275°F (135°C) and extra-virgin olive, at 375°F (191°C). Clarified butter is more pure than butter—the milk solids have been removed during the clarification process—and greater purity means a higher smoke point. Using clarified butter when you sauté at the mouth of the oven or sear a piece of fish helps ensure tastier and healthier foods from your wood-fired oven.

The resurgence of locally grown livestock and the snout-to-tail approach to using as much of an animal as possible, coupled with the wide range of temperatures in the wood-fired oven, creates some cooking possibilities that would be inconvenient in your home oven. For instance, rendering your own animal fat or infusing oils requires a steady, low heat. But who wants to have their home oven on for four or five hours? The wood-fired oven, one or two days after a pizza party, provides a perfect environment for slowly melting animal fat or infusing oils.

Pork, beef, and chicken fat are all solid at room temperature. Keep the fat cold until you're ready to use it because it will be easier to cut into small pieces, which will melt more quickly than a big chunk of fat. You can firm up the fat by sticking it in the freezer—a box grater will then help to shave it into small pieces. Put it in a heavy dish and place in a 250°F to 300°F (121–149°C) oven, leaving it uncovered so the water can evaporate. After an hour or so, check it and give it a stir. There will be some clear, liquid fat—the purest fat to be extracted.

You can draw off rendered fats at different times, which will give you fats in different grades. Each successive pour tends to be darker in color.

There will be enough pure fat at the first (and second) pour that you will be able to capture a good-sized container of rendered fat without having to strain it. For instance, a couple of pounds of chicken fat will yield 2 pints of (pretty pure) rendered chicken fat, called schmaltz, a jar of fat that will be stratified into a layer of rendering gravy, an intermediate layer of fat, and a top third that is as pure as the fat that was first poured off from the rendering vessel. With a slotted spoon, remove the large pieces of meat or skin to another container, preferably with enough space so that the meat pieces can spread out. These bits of meat are artisan pork rinds or, in the case of chicken schmaltz, Jewish gribenes, the kosher chicken equivalent to cracklings. Salt the cracklings at this point and put them in the oven to crisp a bit. Use in place of crumbled bacon.

By the second or third decantation, it's a good idea to strain the fat through a coffee filter or cheesecloth. I keep this grade separate and use it for cooking oil, or as a fat to sear vegetables like Brussels sprouts. Once rendered, pour it into wide-mouthed jars while it's still liquid.

Look to your local farmers and butchers as good sources for animal fats. Chicken fat and leaf lard may be difficult to procure in a chain market that receives most of its meat already broken down and packaged. Of the three solid animal fats described here, beef fat has the strongest barnyard smell, although it's not unpleasant. The smell of my hands after handling beef fat reminds me of my first baseball glove.

LARD

Leaf lard is the fat that surrounds the internal organs of pigs and is the highest grade of lard for rendering. The rise of the hydrogenated oil industry—and the perception that lard is unhealthful—drove lard underground during the 1980s and '90s, although in coastal North Carolina, 3-gallon buckets of hydrogenated lard are for sale in mainstream supermarkets, as are the 1-pound packages of equally processed *manteca*.

After an hour or two in a 275°F (135°C) oven, a pound of solid leaf lard melts down into plenty of liquid lard. This will be the most pure rendering. Drain it into a widemouthed container, cool, and reserve for pie and biscuit dough. Pork lard is relatively soft at room temperature, which makes it easy to scoop out of the container. If it's rendered at a higher temperature, the lard will take on more of a roasted pork flavor.

The lard left in the pot will contain bits of pork meat, or cracklings. The cracklings will become crisper as the amount of liquid lard in the rendering vessel decreases. Keep these as snacks, or use them to top salads or gratins.

Continue to melt the leftover lard, occasionally draining the liquid into your container. The yield will be less pure than the first press. I hold the later renderings as cooking fat, to be used in the sauté pan.

Lard has a smoke point around 375°F (191°C), about the same as olive oil. It does make flaky pastry crusts and biscuits. You can substitute lard for butter in the biscuit or scone recipes in this chapter, or blend it half and half with butter to split the difference between lard's flakiness and butter's taste and mouthfeel.

I've also infused lard with rosemary during the rendering process. Fresh chopped rosemary imparts a greenish cast to the lard. Be sure all the water is evaporated from the herb—otherwise the lard will become rancid more easily. I've also used dried rosemary. The color of the finished lard is more muted, but the flavor is still bright. Strain the lard to remove the rosemary leaves. I've replaced 100 percent of the butter in the biscuit recipe with rosemary lard and added 1.5 percent (of flour weight) fresh chopped rosemary. The biscuit is delicious—a bit heavier, but the flavor is lightened up by the two sources of rosemary flavor.

Different grades of decanted schmaltz

Straining gribenes out of rendered schmaltz

SUET

Suet is another name for beef fat. Lower-quality grades of it are often rendered and sold in cubes as bird food. Beef fat is also sometimes called tallow, although technically tallow can be a mixture of several different types of animal fat. As with lard, the finest grade of beef fat comes from the areas around the kidneys. Render it the same way you do pork lard. The smoke point of beef fat is around 400°F (204°C)—higher than lard, which makes beef fat ideal for frying. At room temperature, it's much harder than lard, so be sure to have it in a widemouthed jar for easier extraction. Because beef fat is such a good oil for frying, many of us still have pre-1990 memories of fast-food fries prepared in beef fat.

Deep-frying in a wood-fired oven is a method that presents the difficulties of placing the pot of oil into the hot oven and removing it, while tending to the food being fried and removing it. Working through the small, low oven door requires care so hot oil doesn't splash.

Beef Fat Fries

Making fried potatoes in your wood-fired oven is a way to make a delicious treat without splattering the top of your home oven with grease. Put several inches of rendered beef fat in a fireproof vessel and slide it into a hot oven. The fat needs to be around 350°F to 375°F (177–191°C) to properly fry. You may or may not need a live fire to achieve that temperature. Any size of raw potato can be fried—thick slices, traditional-sized fries cut on a mandoline (or even thin chips on a mandoline), and halved or whole baby potatoes. Carefully transfer them into the fat with a slotted spoon and add them slowly so the temperature of the oil doesn't drop too quickly. You can adjust the temperature of the oil

by gently moving the pot closer to the fire or the back of the oven where it's hotter. Frying time depends on the size of the potato, but it generally runs about 5 to 10 minutes. Remove the potatoes from the oil and place them on absorbent paper. The high heat of the fat will sear the exterior of the potato, creating a crispy skin that resists the absorption of oil. The interior will seem puffed, a result of the potato's rapid expansion in hot oil. If the fries seem too greasy, the fat probably wasn't hot enough. Hit them with a little salt and pepper and enjoy them hot, but be careful not to burn your fingers!

SCHMALTZ

Schmaltz is a much less widely known animal fat made from chicken, duck, or goose. It fills in nicely for cooking fat for those who don't eat pork. The globules of fat inside the body cavity are used to render schmaltz, although skin can be used to augment the bulk fat. Chicken fat is harder to come by than pork or beef fat, but may be more available during Passover. My friend Leon says that when he was a child, the granting of the gribenes was a prize treat. Schmaltz is the least hard of these three animal fats—even when cold, it can be used as a spread on bread.

You already make a type of schmaltz but may not know it. Whenever you roast a chicken, you pour off all the fat you don't need for gravy and keep it in your refrigerator. You can use this as you would rendered schmaltz, just know it will be darker and more intensely flavored.

A really nice hot meal is some boiled or roasted new potatoes tossed with a little schmaltz, chopped celery, and salt and pepper, then topped with some chopped gribenes. Make it when the potatoes are hot so the schmaltz melts. Keep the celery crisp for a nice crunch.

See Clarified Butter in chapter 14 for instructions on how to make another great cooking fat at an even lower temperature.

Figs, both whole and with popped backs, dehydrate in Magdalena

→→ • ←←

CHAPTER FOURTEEN

The Long Tail of the Temperature Curve:

UNDER 212°F (100°C)

I appreciate it when the oven temperature gets way down, as it facilitates so many traditional food preparations! At this temperature, cooking takes a long time, but products in this range enjoy a long shelf life as long as they're stored correctly.

While you might be reluctant to keep your electric or gas oven on at 140°F (60°C) for hours (or days . . .), you'll love to harvest these low, constant temperatures from your wood-fired oven. *Food Safety Alert: Be sure the oven temperature exceeds 140°F.* Don't let potentially harmful foods stay within the range of 40°F to 140°F (4–60°C) for more than 4 hours, which could promote the growth of harmful bacteria. Perishable foods must be kept either hot (above 140°F) or cold (below 40°F).

Chicken Stock

To get good stock—rich, flavorful, and gelatinous— you have to start with a really good chicken. Use the carcass of the chicken you roasted for last night's dinner to make stock in the receding oven. There are probably as many ways to make chicken stock as there

are to make red sauce. Michael Ruhlman, author of *The Elements of Cooking: Translating the Chef's Craft for Every Kitchen* and *Ratio: The Simple Codes Behind the Craft of Everyday Cooking*, among many other books and articles, makes an overnight stock. It's simple and its preparation in a 150°F (66°C) retained-heat oven provides a simmering period that makes a rich stock while keeping it at a food-safe temperature.

Pull from the carcass any pieces that could be used in a chicken salad or for a chicken sandwich. Combine the chicken carcass, enough water to cover it, some celery, a bay leaf or two, and some salt and pepper in a non-reactive pot and place this on the hearth. Ideal temperature is 200°F to 220°F (93–104°C). As long as the temperature of the stock is over 140°F (60°C) there will be no food safety issues. Simmer for as long as you like. Use the oven's retained heat to turn water into flavorful and fortified chicken stock.

It can become more even more simple. Use just the chicken carcass and water. If you roasted your chicken with onions, thyme, and lemons in the cavity, make sure to remove the lemons before you make stock so it doesn't impart a bitter flavor.

One chicken carcass will yield about 9 cups of stock.

Almond Raisin Sprouted Wheat Power Bars

Sprouted Wheat Power Bars

Sprouted Wheat Power Bars are pure goodness. They're easy to make, delicious, and incredibly nutritious. Fresh-sprouted wheat berries are ground into a coarse paste, formed and cut into bars, then baked in a very low temperature oven for a couple of hours. The conversion of starches into sugars—in combination with the dried fruit—makes the bars sweet, although they contain no refined sugar.

Yield: About 10 Power Bars
Wood-fired oven temperature window:
150–200°F (66–93°C). The slowly falling temperature of a wood-fired oven is perfect for baking sprouted grains.
Home oven: Preheat the oven to 200°F (93°C).

Sprouted Wheat Power Bars

Ingredient	Weight (g)	Volume	Baker's %
Whole raw almonds	75	¾ C	33
Dried fruit	75	1 C	33
Sprouted wheat berries	225	2 C	100
Salt	1	Healthy pinch	0.4
Total	376	—	—

Set aside roughly one-third of the almonds and dried fruit to add later in the mix. Combine the remaining ingredients and grind until smooth. I prefer a manual food mill over an electric food processor. The food mill gives a more even grind and gives you a chance to touch the dough and adjust the hydration if necessary. Three or four passes through the food mill will create a dough with a smooth consistency, although gluten strands will be visible. Add the reserved almonds and dried fruit before the last grind. If you would like a smoother power bar, grind all of the ingredients three to four times to evenly and finely grind up the whole mixture. (A food

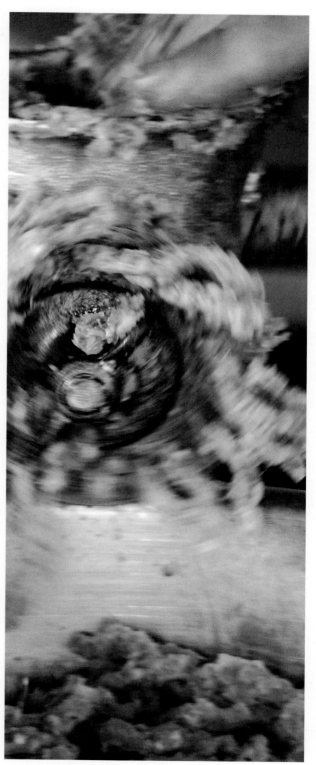

Grinding Sprouted Wheat Power Bars PHOTO BY STEPHANIE MISCOVICH

processor will not grind all the berries equally, which means a power bar with some unground berries.)

Shape into ⅜"-thick bars or a rectangle about 9" × 7½". Rolling the dough between parchment paper is a good way to get an even layer. You can also shape this dough into small loaves rather than bars. Bake at approximately 150°F to 200°F (66–93°C) for 2 hours or until firm but not dry (loaves will take longer). Flip the bars or rotate the loaves once or twice during the bake. When cooled, wrap in plastic and store in the fridge.

Other good power bar variations include pecan and dried cranberry; chocolate and dried cherry, with rolled oat coating; and fresh fruit. Keep in mind that fresh fruit will make the dough more wet. To offset the extra moisture, you can coat the bars in rolled oats or mix rolled oats into the dough.

Sprouted grain can also be used as a grain in soup or made into a delicious but fortifying salad with grated carrots, lots of parsley, olive oil, red wine vinegar, and salt and pepper. Sprouting grains is an easy and economical way to produce fresh produce, even in the middle of winter. Sprouted Wheat Power Bars also only have (literally) a pinch of salt, so they are low in sodium.

An easy way to roll Power Bars to an even thickness of about ⅜"

Cutting Cranberry Pecan Sprouted Wheat Power Bars

PHOTOS BY KATE KELLEY

How to Sprout Grains and Seeds

This process works for sprouting other types of grain to be used for this recipe. I especially like oats and spelt. Rye tastes a bit edgy when used in sprouted power bars.

Sprouting wheat means putting it into an environment that mimics the requirements of wheat seed that has just been planted and is starting to grow. Once the berry is hydrated, naturally occurring amylase enzymes begin to convert the starch stored in the endosperm into simple sugars that will fuel the first days of growth until true leaves emerge and the plant begins to photosynthesize. It's a process similar to fermentation where alpha-amylase converts starch into simple sugars used by yeast to release energy, carbon dioxide, organic acids, and alcohol. Sprouting increases the availability of many nutrients and minerals, including, but not limited to, vitamin E and vitamin C. In addition, the sprouting process is an aid to digestion. And it's exactly the process used to create the malt powder used in Pain Rustique, although malt powder used for hearth breads is usually made from barley.

Sprouting also deactivates phytic acid. Phytic acid chelates with minerals such as zinc, calcium, and iron, which means it bonds with them in a way that makes it impossible for them to be absorbed by our digestive tracts, making our food less nutritious. Sprouting is like nurturing *complete combustion*, but instead of extracting the maximum number of BTUs out of our wood fuel, it extracts as much nutrition as possible from the food we eat.

Phytic acid is also deactivated by natural leavening. (See the formula for Sprouted Wheat Flour Sourdough for more discussion about the nutritional advantages of naturally leavened breads.)

THE SPROUTING PROCESS

Be sure to clean your hands, the work area, and anything that comes into contact with the grain and sprouting equipment. Sprouting needs to be done at room temperature, and it's prudent to avoid any contamination.

Rinse any amount of grain in a colander. Place the rinsed berries in a container and cover with water.

The container can be completely closed. Or you can use a perforated lid that screws onto a mason jar and is made just for sprouting. I have a convenient piece of Tupperware that is perfect for soaking the grain and holding it once the grain has started to sprout. I've also used a colander inside a stainless bowl as a way to soak and contain grain through the sprouting process. Soak the grain for 36 hours. You can change the water after 6 to 8 hours if it starts to look dirty or sketchy, but don't feel you need to. After 36 hours, drain the berries, reserving the soaking water for rejuvelac, if desired. (There's more information about rejuvelac elsewhere in this chapter.)

Rinse the berries and allow them to sit, covered, for 24 hours, rinsing every 12 hours. A rootlet will start to emerge after about 24 hours. Cooler temperatures will slow the sprouting process. Warmer temperatures and frequent rinses will speed it up.

Sprouts are best when the rootlet is about as long as the wheat berry. Undersprouted grain won't be as sweet and may remain a little too chewy. Old sprouts get starchy, as many of the released sugars have been consumed by the young sprout in its growth into a wheat plant.

Unsprouted (green bowl), oversprouted (red bowl), and correctly sprouted (blue bowl) wheat berries

Rejuvelac

Grain beverages are satisfying, inexpensive, refreshing, and ancient. The official drink of the Eleusinian Mysteries—the annual celebration to honor Demeter, the Greek goddess of grain and agriculture, proceedings of which are now lost to the ages—was kykeon, a beverage of barley water and mint.

Rejuvelac is a light and lemony drink made from water and sprouted grain. Fermentation makes the grain beverage slightly fizzy and, of course, nutritious.

Once your wheat is sprouted, place a handful in a jar or pitcher. I like to use a clear jar so I can see how cloudy the rejuvelac gets. Fill the jar with fresh water. Cover lightly and let sit at room temperature. The beverage will ferment due to the wild yeast that settles on grain when it's still in the field or is just hanging around in your baking area.

If it's hot (above 80°F/27°C), you may want to stash the water in the fridge right away. A cooler room environment means you can leave the jar at room temperature for 6 to 8 hours to get it going. Rejuvelac can be consumed immediately or allowed to ferment for a couple of days. It remains enzymatically active until it's heated to 140°F (60°C). The lemon flavor comes from the acid production. The fizziness is carbon dioxide. If it were left to ferment, it would become alcoholic, although maybe not appealing enough for a round of rejuvelac shooters. If you aren't drawn to the flavor, you can use rejuvelac in your smoothies or in stock.

Important note: I've been sprouting for years and never had a problem with foodborne illness associated with this method. It can happen, however, especially if you don't heat the sprouts to over 140°F (60°C) before they are consumed. To sell sprouts in any form, you should determine if you need a specialized processing method variance from the FDA.

Clarified Butter

The low, slow heat of a receding wood-fired oven is a low-maintenance, high-yield way to clarify butter. Break up a pound of unsalted butter and place it in a clean, dry mason jar. Cover with a single layer of cheesecloth secured by the lid band—the permeable cheesecloth will allow water to evaporate while preventing fly ash or other debris from contaminating the butter. Place the jar in a zone of the oven that is about 200°F (93°C) for several hours. Skim the foam from the top and decant the liquid butter into a clean container. Clarified butter doesn't need to be refrigerated, but I prefer to keep it there anyway.

Pork belly on the other side of a firewall from a smoky fire

Smoked Pork Belly

The majority of the time, you'll want to concentrate on having a smoke-free fire—except when you want to use the oven as a smoker. The source where you procured your animal fats and bone marrow will likely have pork belly, and this simple technique will turn out some of the best bacon you will ever have. I learned this technique from my Johnson & Wales colleague Ray McCue, the American Culinary Federation's 2012 Rhode Island Chef of the Year.

In a large container, soak a piece of pork belly for 2 days in a solution of 1900g (½ gallon) of water, 105g (½ cup) of sugar, and 264g (1 cup) of salt. (If you're smoking more than one piece of pork belly, you may need to double the liquid.) I usually add a few bay leaves, some juniper berries, whole cloves, and a cayenne pepper. Weigh the pork belly down with a plate to keep it completely submerged. After 2 days, remove the pork from the brine, pat it dry, and let it dry-age for another 2 days. To dry-age, place the pork in the fridge on a cooling rack. The cooling rack ensures that air can circulate around the piece of meat.

The key to making good bacon is creating an oven environment that creates smoke but doesn't get so hot that the pork belly cooks and dries out. A smoky 125°F (52°C) oven for the 3 to 4 hours is ideal. The easiest way I've found to accomplish this is building a temporary firewall down the middle of the oven. (See *Use a Firewall of Bricks* in chapter 9 for more details about firewalls.)

In advance of starting the fire, soak some smoking chips or other aromatic pieces of wood. I use plenty of cedar, but also green juniper branches and fresh rosemary. Keep the fire small. You need a good, active bed of coals, but not so much heat and fuel that you build a raging fire. Place the pork belly in a lidless cast-iron pan and slide it into the oven, on the side opposite the firewall if you have an oven big enough to split into two sections.

Add some of the soaked wood to the fire and loosely replace the door. I make sure some oxygen is pulled into the oven, but try to keep the door closed as much as possible to retain the smoke inside. It takes a little fiddling, but eventually you'll arrive at the proper amount of wood to throw on the fire and the right amount of

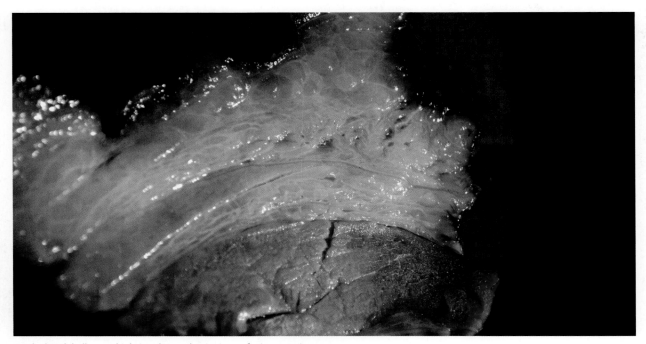

Smoked pork belly, cut thinly into bacon, beginning to fry in a cast-iron pan.

oxygen to maintain just enough combustion to create smoke. When you no longer see smoke sneak out the door, crack open the door a bit to give the fire more oxygen. Three hours later: bacon.

Chill thoroughly before cutting with a sharp knife or, better yet, a deli slicer. I try to get the pieces as thin as possible, but thicker pieces can be cut into cubes and used as lardons. Not only is using your oven in this manner fun, it also provides classic nitrate-free charcuterie.

I've smoked other cuts of pork for bacon but prefer pork belly. You won't be surprised to find out it comes from the belly region, and the fat from that area can be well streaked with meat. This meat is what you're left with when you fry your bacon until crisp. I've also smoked fatback but this cut has much less meat, which makes it more suitable for rendering, although it's not as pure (meat-free) as leaf lard. Still, when freed from the fat and fried, fatback meat yields mighty fine cracklins.

In terms of oven heat timing, you can catch the right temperature for smoking pork belly on the tail end after a bake or you can build a fire in a cold oven the day before you smoke to help warm up the firebox in advance. What you need is a low, slow, and smoky environment for 4 to 5 hours.

Beef Jerky

Throughout my childhood, I was fascinated with the preservation of meat by drying and salting. I loved the mountain man stories and the Native American techniques for preserving and tanning hides. Once I learned how to make it myself, I realized it was easy to make a flavorful jerky that wasn't too salty, wasn't overly seasoned, and still retained its meatness.

Use the economical and lean top round cut. Top round's grain makes a chewy but tender jerky. Bottom round also gives good results, albeit a bit gamier. A 680g (1 lb, 8 oz) piece of top round is a good amount for the following marinade. Firm up the meat in the freezer for about an hour. A firmer consistency makes it easier to cut thin strips about ⅛" thick. Cutting the meat on the bias against the grain makes jerky that is more tender than strips running along the grain. If you like a chewier jerky, cut with the grain.

In a container that can be covered, combine 1 bottle of beer; ¾ cup of tamari; ½ cup of Worcestershire sauce; 1 tablespoon each of black and red peppercorns, crushed in a mortar and pestle; and 10 to 12 sprigs of thyme, oregano, or marjoram—or a combination of all these—with leaves stripped and minced.

Slice the meat and submerge it in the marinade. Marinade for 6 to 8 hours in the fridge. Drain the meat from the marinade. I like to let it drip-dry in a colander for half an hour or so to let the excess marinade drain off. Arrange strips on parchment paper with about 2" between them. Place another piece of parchment on top of the raw jerky and roll with a heavy rolling pin so the pieces are about ¹⁄₁₆" to ⅛" thick. Rolling the strips like this will make them all the same thickness, which translates to a conveniently equal drying time. It also makes the jerky look more professional and, perhaps most important, it presses the crushed peppercorns and minced herbs into the jerky where they stick securely once the jerky has been dried.

Mix a new marinade for each batch of jerky. Second runs in a batch of previously used marinade suffer from a lack of salt and seasoning and are underwhelming compared with the first batch of marinated meat.

Place sheet pans in a 140°F to 180°F (60–82°C) oven and dry for about 3 to 4 hours, flipping once or twice.

Dried Fruits and Vegetables

For years I heard about using the low, slow heat of an oven for drying fruits and herbs. I realized how great it works once I dialed in the proper temperatures. The purpose of dehydrating is to remove enough water to increase a food's shelf life. You do not, however, want to cook the food. People have been drying fruits and vegetables for thousands of years, and often it was in the open with little humidity and good circulation.

Dehydrating fruits or vegetables in a wood-fired oven requires the same environment provided by an electric dehydrator: warm, dry heat

that slowly evaporates moisture. Your wood-fired oven serves the same purpose but with leftover heat instead of a fossil-fuel-driven appliance. A fan greatly aids the dehydrating process, because it helps remove water by evaporative convection, and the draft takes it out of the oven and up the flue. This is more effective than just having food dry in a still oven. The drying process will be shorter, and the food will retain more color.

Space can be an issue if you're trying to dehydrate a yield of more than a sheet pan or so. Sklips are sheet pan brackets that allow you to stack sheet pans, greatly increasing your drying space on the same footprint. You may need to flip the dehydrating food and rotate the sheet pans once or twice through the dehydrating period.

Figs are one of the fruits I dry because we have so many during the midsummer harvest. I slice them in half and turn them inside out or "pop the backs." This exposes more of the flesh and helps speed the dehydrating process.

To help retain the fruit's natural color, treat the fruit by *briefly* (about 1 minute) submerging it in a solution of 1 cup lemon juice in a quart of water. If you have a large amount of fruit to dry, treat it with ascorbic acid (which is the same as vitamin C), available in drugstores in tablet form. Finely grind the tablets; use 1 tablespoon per cup of cold water for firmer fruits like apples and 1½ teaspoons per cup of water for softer-fleshed fruit like peaches and figs. A good way to apply an even layer of the solution over the fruit is with a spray bottle.

Place the figs on a cooling rack and put the rack on top of a sheet pan. Having the fruit on the cooling racks promotes circulation and encourages evaporation.

You will increase your yield per hearth space by stacking pans with sklips.

Drying Herbs

I like to keep herbs at hand by allowing them to reseed and spread in the garden and landscape: flat parsley, thyme, rosemary, Greek oregano, arugula, and garden sage. Another useful herb, bay, is hardy here and grows into a beautiful evergreen shrub or tree. I make sure that I always have in the garden our beloved plant allies, the freely reseeding "weeds" with first-aid and tonic abilities: plantain, white yarrow, and mullein.

It's easier to dry herbs than fruit because there is less water to evaporate. Keep the temperature low, no higher than 105°F (41°C) or so—a touch lighter than the low temperature used for infusing oils. Higher temps will cook or steam the herbs instead of gently drying them. The time it takes to thoroughly dry herbs will depend on the fleshiness of the plant material. Parsley will take 4 to 6 hours at 105°F. Plantain takes 6 to 8 hours at the same temperature. Mullein's thick leaves require about 12 hours until they're dry enough to crisply crumble.

Spread the cut herbs in a single layer on a cooling rack and slide them into a low oven. This is a good time to use a fan at the mouth of the oven to help blow air over the herbs and push water vapor up the chimney. Once the herbs are dry (but not quite crisp), allow them to cool, place them in an airtight container and store in a dark place. This method yields high-quality herbs that retain bright colors and flavor. They can be used for cooking or to make infused oils (below).

Mullein (*Verbascum thapsus*) and plantain (*Plantago lanceolata*)

Oil infused with fresh rosemary by low, slow,
retained heat, the small jar also contains juniper berries

Infusing Oil

Another use of dry herbs is to infuse them into oil. Once an herb is dry, coarsely chop or grind it to expose more of the plant cells. Place the herb in a heat-resistant container (to 200°F/93°C) and add enough olive oil to cover the herb by about an inch. We like to use mason jars with enough capacity to accommodate the herb and oil and still be able to be swished about a bit during the long, slow infusion process.

We tend to use fresh herbs because that's what we have around us, but high-quality dried herbs have an advantage because the water has already been removed. Water from fresh herbs that gets trapped in the oil can cause rancidity and fermentation, and beginning with dried herbs eliminates the work required to remove the water from fresh ones. The oil can be strained after 10 days of infusing at around 100°F (38°C); a lower temperature is also acceptable, but avoid temps higher than 150°F (66°C). Be sure to squeeze the infused herb or *marc* (plant material remaining after the extraction of the soluble components) to recover as much infused oil as possible. Allow the oil to sit undisturbed for a few days. Water and organic impurities will settle to the bottom and can be removed when the oil is decanted. Two or three decantings will ensure that impurities are removed.

The long, slow, mellow tail-off heat in the window of about 100°F is ideal for infusing oils. Too high a temperature will oxidize the oils, whereas a long, slow, relatively cool infusion will protect the qualities of the oil and the herb you are using as an infusing agent. Infusing oils with rosemary, peppercorns, juniper berries, or other abundant aromatic herbs, vegetables, or seeds is an uncomplicated, worry-free wood-fired oven activity.

I make infused oils by the folkloric method taught by herbalist Rosemary Gladstar. Infused oils can be used for culinary applications and also as therapeutic ingredients in handmade medicines like plantain, calendula, and comfrey salves and lip balms.

Other Ways to Use the Wood-Fired Oven

The oven is sometimes at the perfect temperature to serve as a warm holding place for foods; of course, with this use there is the cautionary advice that the oven temperature must be above 140°F (60°C) to be safe. If the temperature is below 140°F, it's a perfect place to warm the plates when dinner is to be served outdoors on a cool evening. But there are also other ways to use a warm oven.

PORTABLE THERMAL BATTERIES

Through history people have used all kinds of objects to carry heat from the fireplace to cold winter beds, from simple bricks to long-handled metal pans that held heated stones or embers from the fire. At an oven conference Stephanie once bought a soapstone bed warmer, a common feature in northern homes but exotic in the coastal Southeast. It is a classic soapstone bedwarmer: a slab of soapstone with a wire handle . . . a simple way to absorb, transport, and then radiate heat where it's needed.

AUXILIARY HOT-WATER HEATERS

Hot-water systems don't have to be extravagant or expensive. Jeremiah Church, a mason who works with William Davenport, created a simple system of copper tubing that extends down the trough of his mobile pizza oven. The trough also serves as a fire pit while the pizza hearths extend to each side. The hot water is held in the black tank visible on the back of the trailer. It provides plenty of hot water for dish and hand washing in the middle of farmer's markets, like the one in Stowe, Vermont.

Disclaimer: Hot-water systems should be designed or checked out by a qualified plumber to avoid a dangerous accumulation of heat that could lead to an explosion of hot water.

PREHEATING WOOD FUEL

And, finally, you arrive at the beginning again. This low heat window is perfect for laying a top-down fire for the next burn, and beginning the cycle of cooking and baking again.

A soapstone bed warmer

Jeremiah Church's hot-water heater

A top-down fire structure drying before the start of the next cycle. The quantity and seasoning of this fuel is better from an efficient-combustion standpoint than the top-down burn pictured on the cover of this book.

Your hands are your most effective tools, no matter what type
of oven you build or kind of bread you bake.

General Masonry Oven Design Tips

No matter what type of oven you have or want to build, use the following recommendations to make your oven more efficient and convenient. Many of these recommendations apply specifically to barrel vault brick ovens. Some, however, such as using foam glass as an under-hearth insulator, can and should be easily incorporated into plans for any type of oven, even the simplest cob oven. A general note is that most amateur masons (myself included when I built my first oven) tend to overbuild. So build for strength, but remember that overkill is not a hallmark of good design.

Foundations

Many foundations are overbuilt, giving the impression that the oven is more formidable than it needs to be. William Rubel, author of the gorgeous book *The Magic of Fire*, has this to say about oven foundations: "Structurally, there is no point to the massive concrete bases that are almost universally specified for bread ovens. [. . .] Also, perhaps more fundamentally, building a base that is in balance with the actual structural loads is more in keeping with the spirit of returning to traditional country ways."

The foundation should also be at the right height for you. Imagine where the hearth height will be and determine if it would be convenient to work with in order to make your entire Thanksgiving dinner.

Build a Functional Facade

I'm always drawn to oven facades that facilitate bread baking and cooking. The hearth shouldn't protrude so much that it's difficult to reach into the oven. But a shelf is nice to have for resting your peels, and other small ledges are handy as permanent places to put your *lame* and other equipment—sprayer, timer, et cetera—except in the case of a larger commercial oven, where it's better to have no shelf in front of the doors so a loader can be rolled right up against it.

A functional facade might include a loading hearth or "altar" that's lower than the baking hearth. This allows easy access to load the bread into the oven without having to lift the peel up and over the altar. If you incorporate this design change, try to make the ash dump as wide as possible so the ashes have a large void to fall down without scattering over the altar.

Safety must be considered in addition to convenience. There must be sufficient clearance between combustible materials (the facade itself) and the radiating thermal mass. Insulation, of course, will help

A Le Panyol oven pedestal with nice lines and minimal bulk

The altar on Bill Freese's oven provides a convenient place for the peel when scoring loaves before loading. PHOTO COURTESY OF PETER RAY

prevent combustion and an accidental fire. Check your local codes on required clearances.

Aluminum Foil: Debunked

There's a lot of discussion among wood-fired oven enthusiasts about the aluminum foil layer Alan Scott advised placing between the firebrick firebox and additional poured cladding. Does it reduce hot spots or is it insulation? Does it serve as an expansion joint so the expansion coefficient of the firebox doesn't crack the cladding, or vice versa?

Well, it wouldn't be catastrophic if the cladding cracked, because the reinforcing mesh in the cladding prevents it from falling apart. It is disconcerting, however, to have cracks appear in the firebox. After 15 years of use, Magdalena has plenty of cracks—some that run through mortar joints and some that have

actually fractured firebricks in half. I feel these cracks have occurred mostly because of thermal cycling and the intense heat of the fire, not the firebox expanding against the cladding, especially because I did include the aluminum foil.

But why would you want an insulation layer in the middle of the mass? Any gap is going to slow the migration of heat to the outer cladding, and the goal is to have the mass heat as evenly and quickly as possible.

There are reports of foil that has been found to have disintegrated when the oven was taken apart to be repaired or removed. I have access to the front face of Magdalena's firebox (through a hole used to house the thermocouple monitor). The foil layer is still visible between the firebox and cladding and appears to be largely intact.

It's reassuring to note that the foil layer does not hurt anything or lead to problems, so you may want to go ahead and include it. You can also add a layer of foil on the very outside of the insulation, installed so the shiny side is facing the firebox. This will radiate heat back toward the firebox, slowing heat loss.

Magdalena's ash dump

Ashes, Ashes, All Fall Down

An ash dump is a slot near the mouth of the oven that penetrates all the way through the hearth slab and directs the ashes into a container under the oven. I've worked in ovens with and without ash dumps, and I'm always grateful when one is there. The absence of an ash dump means you have to use a shovel or peel to clean out the oven. Hopefully, all your fuel has completely combusted, but if it hasn't, removing it means you have to balance burning or smoking ashes and embers on a peel or shovel while you transfer them to a nearby receptacle. Cinders fall, smoke billows into your eyes, and you have a hot ash can that needs to be moved out of the area. An ash dump, however, allows you to pull all the ash forward and have it fall into a can permanently placed safely out of your work space. A simple metal trash can, with a tight-fitting lid to cut off oxygen and shut down combustion, is a good container.

Construct the ash dump so it extends completely across the entire mouth of the oven. Any ledges prevent ashes from falling into the can below. The ash dump should be outside the door so the baking chamber is sealed when the door is closed.

It's important to note that wood ash, when combined with water, makes lye. Commercial food-grade lye is sodium hydroxide, while homemade wood ash lye is potassium hydroxide. Both versions are corrosive. Skin can get burned if it comes in contact with a water solution that has a high enough concentration of potassium or sodium hydroxide. Lye solutions have traditionally been used for soap making and as a dip for pretzels before they bake. (Regarding pretzels: Although there are pretzel recipes that use baking soda instead of lye, only a lye solution will create authentic pretzel flavor. This is because the alkaline lye solution increases the efficiency of the caramelizing Maillard reaction, creating the rich brown color and the distinctive flavor.) I like to sift my ash container through fine hardware cloth, and then distribute the fine ash in the garden and around the

A safe and convenient way to remove ashes from the oven
PHOTO BY JONATHANBELLER.COM

Illumination in the oven at Rupert Rising Breads PHOTO COURTESY OF JED MAYER

base of plants that prefer a more alkaline or neutral soil. My soil is acidic, so I can spread the ash pretty much anywhere except for acid-loving plants like blueberries and azaleas.

Shine a Light

Even a small oven can be hard to see into, and installing a light in your oven as you build is not as complicated as it sounds. Jed Mayer from Rupert Rising Breads in western Vermont was worried it would create a cool spot in the oven, but family friend and masonry heater builder Peter Moore convinced him to include a simple porcelain fixture in a masonry cubby protected by heat-resistant glass and wired with high-temperature wiring. In the first nine years of its life, the bulb has had to be replaced only three times. Illumination inside the oven makes loading and checking the bread much easier. Lights shining in from the outer hearth, or bent down from a bracket outside the oven, are good options but throw more of a spotlight, instead of casting a wide warm glow over a larger expanse of hearth.

Slip Joint Hearth Slab

The suspended hearth slab design hangs from the foundation walls by rerod. This is designed to allow for expansion of the slab and to prevent heat from continually seeping into the concrete block foundation. The suspended design includes a thermal gap between the slab and the top course of cinder block. (Alan Scott also mentions that it makes moving the oven possible, although I know of only one oven that has ever been moved. People tend to move on and build another oven somewhere else; the lucky new tenant/owner inherits a nice oven.) The construction of the suspended hearth slab is tricky and labor-intensive. Holes need to be drilled into the top of the foundation to receive the ends of the rerod, and the hearth slab frame needs to be built (and, more important, removed) in a tight space. I'm not the only one who's removed a frame with a hammer and chisel.

An alternative way to pour a slab is to build a hearth slab on top of the foundation. This provides greater bearing as the entire perimeter of the slab rests on the foundation walls. Since the edge of the slab is not inside the concrete foundation, expansion will merely thrust out into space beyond the outer edge of the foundation. A slip joint of flashing along the top course of foundation block prevents a bond from forming and allows the expansion and contraction of the slab to slide across the top of the block wall. Pat Manley's hearth slab is reinforced with rerod and reinforcing mesh (concrete and cement can withstand compression but have no shear strength, so rerod is necessary to help maintain an intact hearth slab), but it's contained within the slab and is not used to suspend the slab.

Threaded rod and ratchet straps prevented the frame of this hearth slab from bulging or breaking when the concrete was poured into the frame. Slip joint flashing is visible along the top of the block walls. This is a hearth slab for a Le Panyol oven core installed at Breadhitz, Ciril and Kylee Hitz's bakery and baking school in Rehoboth, Massachusetts.

Rigid Board Insulation

The hearth slab described previously is certainly easier to install—no hearth frame to build or remove. But what about heat migrating from the hearth slab into the foundation walls? The slip joint hearth slab design turns the order of slab and insulation upside down from the suspended hearth slab design. No insulation is placed or poured under the slip joint slab. Instead, rigid insulation like foam glass or calcium silicate board is placed on top of the slab and then covered with cement backer board to avoid abrasion. The oven is then built on top of this layer. Building an oven in this order means you will avoid heating the hearth slab—the insulation will prevent heat from penetrating into the slab. You want the slab to support the oven, but why heat up thermal mass so far from the bake chamber? The hearth mass does need to be beefed up with an additional layer of firebrick to provide enough mass to bake successive batches of bread.

Foam glass is easier to install than mixing vermiculite with cement and setting it in a custom-built frame—the foam glass pieces are simply placed on the hearth slab. Foam glass is substantially more expensive than vermiculite/cement, but big bags of vermiculite are not cheap, and there are also framing materials to buy and time to spend doing it. See the image later in this appendix on page 289. The black layer under this oven built by Pat Manley at the 2010 Kneading Conference is a layer of foam glass.

Expansion Joints

The flashing between the hearth slab and foundation is not the only type of slip joint in a wood-fired oven. They're also incorporated between components of the oven itself. In fact, they may be more useful in the firebox, because the bricks undergo more expansive thermal cycling in zones that get hotter (and then substantially cooler) than the expansion and contraction experienced by the hearth slab slip joint.

Thermal cycling experienced by the materials in your oven leads to expansion and contraction. Home ovens fired for a pizza party and then cooled back to ambient temperatures before being fired up again experience more thermal cycling than commercial ovens that are refired every day (or multiple times per week), and therefore never cool back down to ambient temperature between firings. Commercial ovens tend to stay in their expanded size, while the home oven's bricks contract once it is cool. That doesn't mean commercial ovens don't need expansion joints, though.

Expansion joints are ¼" to ⅜" gaps between different planes of masonry that are filled with high-temperature insulation. (A brand called Fiberfrax is one example.) It can be purchased in rolls. The friable nature of this type of insulation means you should wear gloves and a respirator mask when handling it to avoid getting fibers on your hands or, more important, in your lungs. Also, the insulation/joint material should be set back from the edge of the brick that makes up the inner plane of the firebox. Leave a ⅜" gap that can be filled with mortar to keep the mineral wool from being exposed and shedding fibers into the firebox.

Key places to install an expansion joint are where the vaulted arch ceiling meets the back wall, anywhere a lintel is installed, and anywhere masonry is in direct contact with metal. A crack that eventually appeared in Magdalena's chimney was caused by the lack of an expansion joint at either end of a lintel. Ovens need to breathe and stretch as they heat up and cool down. Think of the flexibility of your own rib cage as you inhale and exhale.

In addition to the hearth slab, a slip joint is often incorporated where masonry meets metal, such as over a lintel.

Expansion joints can also be useful between the hearth bricks and side walls. The oven walls should bear directly on the hearth slab, instead of on the hearth bricks. This allows the hearth bricks to expand without possibly cracking the walls, but also allows you (or your heirs . . .) to replace the hearth slab if this ever becomes necessary. Hearth bricks don't have mortar between them.

An often overlooked place to achieve a thermal break is between the hearth slab and the oven core. If hearth bricks are laid directly on the hearth slab, heat

A thin metal piece of flashing provides a slip joint over the lintel. Fiber expansion joint material is also visible between bricks and precast refractory concrete that is the side of a pizza oven built by Alex Chernov at the Masonry Heater Association's annual spring conference in 2010.

Tough mama. Magdalena's hearth slab condition after 15 years of use. No worries, though; the hearth can be easily replaced.

The gap between the wall and the hearth bricks will allow the hearth to be removed easily if that's ever necessary.

will pass through the hearth bricks into the hearth slab—and it won't stop moving away from your oven until it hits a thermal break or insulation or simply runs out of energy. Alan Scott's suspended hearth slab is designed to prevent heat from seeping into the block wall foundation, turning it into a heat sink. Isolating the thermal mass of the oven can be taken one step farther by placing rigid insulation on top of the hearth slab and then building the oven core on top of that.

Locked-In Corners

This easy design modification will greatly increase structural integrity. The locked-in corners prevent the

brick that the door seats against from breaking loose due to being knocked against by the door. This happened to Magdalena after only about a year. Brick and mortar have compressive strength but little tensile strength and give way to shearing effects. The mass from several bricks behind that one would have prevented it from being dislodged.

Running Bond Walls

Tom Trout was the first Masonry Heater Association member I met, and the timing was fortuitous because I wasn't very far along in building Magdalena. I learned a lot of good masonry tips from Tom, from something as

Locked-in corner at Camp Bread 2007

simple as wearing nitrile-coated masonry gloves to the idea that the firebox walls could be built with a running bond. A running bond has staggered joints and, because it's interlocked, is much stronger than a wall made where all the mortar joints are aligned in horizontal and vertical grid lines.

Bonded Arches

Professional masons prefer to construct vaults using a bonded arch, rather than rings of arches. Bonded arches are much stronger because if one brick falls out, the rest of the arch will support itself. If one brick in a ring arch falls, then the whole structure can fail. Constructing a bonded arch means making an arch frame that covers the entire vault as opposed to a frame that only supports one of the rings at a time. Oven builder Pat Manley soaks pegboard overnight as the arch frame. Not only do the holes help the board flex into shape, but they also make handy points to help you lay bricks in a straight line.

Use Arch Bricks, if Possible

Design the width of the firebox to accommodate a series of arch bricks that make a smooth transition throughout the arch, are as close together as possible, and have thin mortar joints—not big wedge-shaped

A simpler locked-in corner for an oven with less mass than the one built at Camp Bread 2007. This photo also show the running bond wall and angle iron buttress.

A bonded arch in the oven built by Turtlerock Masonry for the King Arthur Flour Baking Education Center

A ring arch in a vaulted oven; this oven is built on a suspended hearth slab as opposed to a slab that bears entirely on the foundation walls.

These thin slices of firebrick, used as keystones, fit the space during construction but loosened after a year's worth of firing and started slipping into the firebox. PHOTO COURTESY OF GEORGE SCHUELLER

ones. This means you won't have to hold the arch bricks apart with brick chips. There are online calculators that help determine what combination of straights, #2 arch bricks, and #3 arch bricks will help you most effectively span your oven.

Straights can be used to make arches, but it's more difficult to describe a smooth arc, and the thickness of the mortar varies due to awkward spaces between straight bricks that are trying to make a smooth transition. What can happen is that the space at the top of the arch, reserved to receive the keystone, is too narrow for a full brick keystone. A slab can be cut off a firebrick to fit, but if the keystone isn't substantial enough, outward thrust isn't maximized and slack is built into the arch. A little expansion and contraction can loosen a

shim of brick acting as a keystone, allowing it to slip into the oven chamber—especially if it's positioned vertically, as keystones should be.

Vault Harness or Channel Iron Buttress

Ovens often have concrete cladding poured on top of the firebox. This adds mass and helps resist outward thrust from the arches. If you want to build a pizza or other low-mass oven and don't want the additional mass, you can resist the thrust with a channel iron buttress installed near the top of the wall.

An oven built by Pat Manley at the 2010 Kneading Conference. Pat leaves bricks sticking out of the wall as a convenient place to rest the iron before the nuts are snugged up. Clay was used as mortar for this workshop oven—it was easily dismantled after the weekend. Also, the black layer under the oven is foam glass, a rigid board insulator. Note the draft door with sliding aperture to control oxygen intake.

125 golden farm road, Bettie Beaufort NC 28516
252/504-2378

Spring and early summer 2000

ONE ACRE garden and bakery

Our traditional breads are made with stone-ground organic flours and NC Mountain spring water. Each loaf is shaped by hand and baked in Magdalena, our wood-fired brick oven.

THE BREAD LIST

We bake 4 days a week, according to this schedule:

Bread	Price	Mon.	Wed.	Fri.	Sat.
La Baguette	$2.00	✓	✓	✓	✓
petit pain .... a sandwich-sized French roll	1.00	✓	✓	✓	✓
Le Pain Rustique — Our French white dough, same as the baguette, but left in its "rustic" shape.	4.00	✓	✓	✓	
Pane Francese .. a large batard of French style ITALIAN BREAD	4.25		✓		✓
Le Pain au Levain — TRADITIONAL FRENCH SOURDOUGH leavened entirely with WILD YEAST	4.00	✓	✓	✓	
Panmarino — Rosemary Olive Oil Sourdough	4.75				✓
Pecan Sourdough — We are delighted to bring back this regional favorite.	4.75			✓	
Le Pain de Mie — a 13" loaf of delicious sandwich bread, enriched with butter and milk.	6.00	✓			
Cinnamon Spiral Bread with Golden Raisins	3.75	✓		✓	
Rye with Caraway Seeds ... a stout batard of fragrant light rye	4.25		✓		✓
100% Spelt Pita — MIDDLE EASTERN POCKET BREAD made with an ANCIENT GRAIN 4 large round pockets for	3.00	✓			
Walnut Fig Bread — English walnuts and Calimyrna figs in an Oat and spelt dough, with a crust of rolled oats.	4.50		✓		✓
Bettie Three Seed {NEW} A nutritious and flavorful bread with FLAX, SESAME, and exotic CHARNUSHKA seeds.	4.50		✓		✓
Whole Wheat Seven Grain Bread ... NOW IN A BATARD SHAPE!	4.50	✓		✓	
Rugbrød {NEW} DANISH BLACK BREAD	4.00	✓		✓	

A bread schedule from One Acre Garden and Bakery, circa 2000. Most of these breads are in this book.

Commercial Yield Formulas

Pain au Levain, 75% Hydrated

(commercial yield based on 5kg flour)

Yield: 13 loaves, 680g each
Prefermented flour: 25%

Levain

Ingredient	Weight (g)	Baker's %
Bread flour	1,250	100
Water	1,250	100
Liquid sourdough starter	250	20
Total	2,750	—

Method of preparation:
1. Combine the flour, water, and starter.
2. Mix until smooth.
3. Cover and allow to ferment for 8 hours.

Final Dough

Ingredient	Weight (g)	Baker's %
Bread flour	2,500	75
Whole wheat flour	1,250	25
Water	2,500	75
Levain	2,500	—
Salt	100	2
Total	8,750	—

Desired dough temperature: 77°F (25°C).

Method of preparation:
1. Mix the bread flour, whole wheat flour, water, and levain in a mixer until it is thoroughly incorporated. Cover and let sit for 20 to 30 minutes.
2. Add the salt and mix on first speed for 3 minutes.
3. Mix on second speed for 3 minutes.
4. Place the dough in a covered container and allow to ferment for 2½ hours, folding every 30 minutes. There will be a total of four folds.

5. Divide the dough into 680g pieces and preshape into loose balls. Cover and let rest for 20 minutes.
6. Shape into boules and place seam side up in well-floured and linen-lined proofing baskets. Let proof for about 2 hours.
7. Invert the baskets onto a peel and score each loaf.
8. Bake in a steamed 450°F (232°C) oven for about 40 minutes.

Seven Grain

(commercial yield based on 5kg flour)

Yield: 17 loaves, 680g each
Prefermented flour: 25%

Preferment

Ingredient	Weight (g)	Baker's %
Bread flour	1,250	100
Water	1,250	100
Liquid sourdough starter	150	12
Total	2,650	—

Method of preparation:
1. Scale the ingredients.
2. Combine the flour, water, and starter and mix until smooth.
3. Cover and ferment at 77°F (25°C) for 8 hours.

Soaker

Ingredient	Weight (g)	Baker's %
Grains	880	100
Water	1,000	114
Honey	290	33
Total	2,170	—

Method of preparation:
1. Scale the ingredients.
2. Combine all of the ingredients and soak overnight at 77°F (25°C).

Final Dough

Ingredient	Weight (g)	Baker's %
Water	2,150	88
Liquid sourdough starter	2,500	—
Bread flour	1,250	50
Whole wheat flour	2,500	50
Soaker	2,170	—
Instant active yeast (optional)	20	0.4
Salt	110	2.2
Honey	—	5.8
Grains	—	18
Total	10,700	—

Desired dough temperature: 76°F (24°C).

Method of preparation:
1. Combine the water, levain, flours, and soaker.
2. Hold back the yeast and salt.
3. Mix on first speed until thoroughly incorporated. (Development of the dough is unnecessary at this stage; it can still be shaggy.)
4. Autolyse for about 20 to 30 minutes

Mixing:
1. After autolysing, add the yeast (optional) and salt.
2. Mix on first speed for 3 minutes.
3. Mix on second speed for an additional 3 minutes.
4. When it's finished, the dough should be a little tacky and will resist slightly when tugged.

Primary fermentation:
1. Ferment for 2 hours, folding once after 60 minutes.

Dividing/preshape:

1. Turn the dough onto a lightly floured surface.
2. Divide into 680g pieces.
3. Preshape each piece into a loose round ball; place seam up on a lightly floured board.
4. Cover the loaves with plastic and let them rest for about 15 to 20 minutes.

Shaping:

1. Shape the loaves into boules or bâtards.
2. Place seam side up into proofing baskets or couches.
3. Allow to proof in a closed area for about 1 hour (if naturally leavened, let rise for 2 hours).

Scoring/baking:

1. Before baking, invert the loaves, seam side down.
2. Score as desired.
3. Bake in a steamed 450°F (232°C) oven for about 40 minutes. You may need to sheet pan the loaves halfway through the bake to prevent scorching the bottoms.

Golden Sesame Bread

(commercial yield based on 5kg flour)

Yield: 12 loaves, 680g each
Prefermented flour: 16%

Poolish

Ingredient	Weight (g)	Baker's %
Bread flour	820	100
Water	820	100
Instant active yeast	.8	.1
Total	1,640.8	—

Method of preparation: Combine the flour, water, and starter, and mix until smooth. Cover and allow to ferment at 75°F (24°C) for 14 to 16 hours.

Final Dough

Ingredient	Weight (g)	Baker's %
Durum flour	2,759	66
Bread flour	1,421	34
Water	2,759	66
Poolish	—	—
Instant active yeast	20	0.4
Salt	100	2
Total	7,059	—
Variation (based on half flour weight)		
Fennel seeds	15	0.3
Golden raisins	425	17

Desired dough temperature: 76°F (24°C).

Autolyse: Combine all of the ingredients except the yeast, salt, and variation add-ins. Mix until homogeneous (the dough may still be shaggy). Cover for 30 minutes.

Mixing: Add the yeast and salt. Mix on first speed for 3 minutes, then on second for 2 minutes. Scrape well throughout. The dough should be smooth and slightly tacky.

Primary fermentation: Ferment for 2 hours, with a fold after 60 minutes.

Dividing/preshaping: Divide into 680g pieces and preshape. Let the dough relax for about 20 minutes.

Shaping: Shape into bâtards. Roll in sesame seeds and place seam side up on couche.

Final proof: 1–1½ hours.

Scoring and baking: Score and bake at 450°F (232°C) for approximately 45 minutes. **Variation:** After removing approximately half of the dough weight, add fennel seeds and golden raisins on first speed until evenly distributed. Do not seed the exterior of these loaves.

Bettie Three Seed
(commercial yield based on 5kg flour)

Yield: 14 loaves, 680g each
Prefermented flour: 19%

Levain

Ingredient	Weight (g)	Baker's %
Bread flour	964	100
Water	964	100
Liquid sourdough starter	116	12
Total	2,044	—

Combine the flour, water, and starter. Mix until smooth. Cover and allow to ferment at 77°F (25°C) for 8 to 10 hours.

Soaker

Ingredient	Weight (g)	Baker's %
Flaxseeds, whole	240	56
Sesame seeds, whole	190	44
Water	430	100
Total	860	—

Combine all ingredients, cover, and soak overnight at approximately 77°F (25°C).

Final Dough

Ingredient	Weight (g)	Baker's %
Bread flour	2,040	60
Durum flour	998	20
Whole rye flour	998	20
Water	2,702	82
Flaxseeds, raw, ground	190	8.7
Sesame seeds, toasted, ground	143	6.7
Levain	1,928	—
Soaker	860	—
Salt	100	2
Instant active yeast	13.5	0.27
Total	9,972.5	—

Exterior Seed Coating

Ingredient	Weight (g)	Baker's %
Charnushka	68	12
Sesame seeds	1,359	100
Total	1,427	—

Desired dough temperature: 76°F (24°C).

Autolyse: Combine all of the ingredients except the salt and yeast. Mix until homogeneous (the dough may still be shaggy). Cover for 30 minutes.

Mixing: Add the salt and yeast. Mix on first speed for 3 minutes, then on second for 2 minutes. The dough should be smooth and slightly tacky.

Primary fermentation: Ferment for 2 hours, with a fold at 60 minutes .

Dividing/preshaping: Divide into 680g pieces and preshape. Let the dough relax for about 20 minutes.

Shaping: Shape and roll in the charnushka-sesame seed mixture.

Final proof: 1–1½ hours.

Scoring and baking: Bake at 450°F (232°C) for approximately 40 minutes.

67% Rye
(commercial yield based on 5kg flour)

꧁⚜꧂

Yield: 13 loaves, 690g each
Prefermented flour: 27%

Preferment

Ingredient	Weight (g)	Baker's %
Whole rye flour	1,330	100
Water	1,077	81
Liquid sourdough starter	80	6
Total	2,487	—

Method of preparation:
1. Combine all the ingredients.
2. Mix until all the flour is incorporated. It will have the consistency of wet cement.
3. Cover and allow to ferment at 75°F (24°C) for 12 to 15 hours.

Final Dough

Ingredient	Weight (g)	Baker's %
Whole rye flour	2,020	67
High-gluten flour	1,650	33
Instant active yeast	20	0.4
Salt	100	2
Water	2,773	77
Rye sour	2,487	—
Total	9,050	—

Desired dough temperature: 82°F (28°C).

Method of preparation:
1. Combine all ingredients in a mixer.
2. Mix on first speed for 3 minutes.
3. Mix on second speed for 3 minutes. The dough will be sticky, but gluten strands should be visible. The surface of the dough will have a slight sheen and will tug back when gently pulled.
4. Ferment in a covered bin for 45 minutes at room temperature.
5. Divide the dough into 690g units.
6. Shape into bâtards and place, seam side up, into well-floured spiral baskets.
7. Proof for 45 minutes to 1 hour. The seams will begin to rip open when ready to bake.
8. Transfer the loaves to the loaders and score across the bâtard, about 25 percent in from each end.
9. Bake in a steamed 450°F (232°C) oven for 45 minutes.

More About Baker's Percentage

The baker's percentage compares the ratio of ingredients, by weight, in a bread formula. Bread bakers find it helpful to examine the relative proportions of flour, water, salt, yeast, and other ingredients when developing or troubleshooting a formula, developing a new product, or getting some insight into the rate of fermentation. This system is also known as baker's math. Ingredient weight compared with the total weight of flour in a formula is commonly referred in the baking world as a percentage.

The baker's percentage of each ingredient is expressed as a percentage of total flour weight, and the flour percentage is *always* 100. Therefore, the total percentage of a bread formula has to be over 100 percent. **To determine the baker's percentage of any ingredient, divide the weight of that ingredient by total flour weight and multiply by 100.**

If bakers say their formula is 75 percent hydrated, they mean there are 75 units of water for every 100 units of flour. I prefer to use the metric system when using baker's percentage. US Standard Measure can be used, but all weights must be expressed in the same units.

Baker's Percentage for a Straight Dough Formula

Typical Percentages for Bread Dough Ingredients

Ingredient	Weight (g)	Baker's % Computation	Baker's %
Bread flour	1,000	1,000g ÷ 1,000g × 100 =	100
Water	690	690g ÷ 1,000g × 100 =	69
Instant active yeast	3	3g ÷ 1,000g × 100 =	0.3
Salt	20	20g ÷ 1,000g × 100 =	2

FLOUR

The baker's percentage of flour in a formula is always 100 percent. If more than one type of flour is used, add all flour weights together and divide by that quantity. Here's an example:

Two-Flour Formula

Ingredient	Weight (g)	Baker's % Computation	Baker's %
Bread flour	750	750g ÷ 1,000g × 100 =	75
Whole wheat flour	250	250g ÷ 1,000g × 100 =	25
Water	690	690g ÷ 1,000g × 100 =	69
Instant active yeast	3	3g ÷ 1,000g × 100 =	0.3
Salt	20	20g ÷ 1,000g × 100 =	2

WATER

The percentage of water in a formula is referred to as the hydration. Fermentation rate, volume, and interior crumb structure are all affected by hydration. Hearth bread formulas often strive for the highest manageable hydration.

Hydration Range in Various Types of Bread Made with White Flour

Hydration Range	Dough Consistency
65% or lower	Firm
66–70%	Soft
71% and higher	Wet and sticky

YEAST

The percentage of commercial yeast to flour varies depending on whether you're using fresh, active dry, instant active, or osmotolerant. They are manufactured differently—fresh yeast contains more water, while instant active has been dehydrated, for example—and the resulting products vary in strength per unit weight.

Type of Yeast	Typical Percentage Found in Bread Formulas
Fresh yeast	1.0%
Active dry yeast	0.4%
Instant active yeast	0.3%
Osmotolerant	0.4%

SALT

The baker's percentage of salt in hearth bread is almost always 1.8 to 2. Enriched dough formulas, or breads with a salty ingredient like olives, may have a lower salt percentage. Breads with a grain soaker may have a salt percentage slightly higher than this range.

Baker's Percentage for a Bread Formula with a Preferment or Soaker

Preferments and soakers used in a bread formula are also expressed as percentage, and the percentage of each ingredient is expressed as a percentage of total flour weight in the preferment or soaker. A formula can have a preferment that is 69 percent hydrated (for every 100 units of flour, there are 69 units of water) and still have an *overall* hydration (the percentage of all the water in the formula, including water in the preferment or soaker) of 75 percent, for example. The overall percentages are most important because they take into account all the ingredients—whether those ingredients were incorporated into the preferment(s), soaker, or final dough.

To determine overall baker's percentages add all quantities of the same ingredient, divide by the total quantity of flour in the formula (including the flour, water, et cetera in the preferment or soaker), and multiply by 100 to express as a percentage.

SAMPLE BREAD FORMULA WITH PREFERMENT:
PAIN AU LEVAIN

Levain

Ingredient	Weight (g)	Baker's %
Bread flour	227	100
Water	227	100
Liquid sourdough starter	45	20

Final Dough

Ingredient	Weight (g)	Baker's %
Bread flour	457	75
Whole wheat flour	228	25
Water	454	75
Salt	17	1.8
Levain	454	—

The baker's percentage of water—or overall hydration—is computed by adding the water in the levain and final dough and dividing by the sum of the flour in the levain and final dough:

Water in starter	227g	Bread flour in starter	227g
+ Water in final dough	+ 454g	+ Bread flour in final dough	+ 457g
		+ Whole wheat flour in final dough	+ 228g
Total water	= 681g	Total flour	= 912g

So overall hydration = 681 g ÷ 912 g × 100 = 75%.

SAMPLE BREAD FORMULA WITH SOAKER AND PREFERMENT: SEVEN GRAIN

Liquid Sourdough Starter

Ingredient	Weight (g)	Baker's %
Bread flour	250	100
Water	250	100
Liquid sourdough starter	30	12
Total	530	—

Soaker

Ingredient	Weight (g)	Baker's %
Grains	180	100
Water	206	114
Honey	60	33
Total	446	—

Final Dough

Ingredient	Weight (g)	Baker's %
Bread flour	250	50
Whole wheat flour	500	50
Water	424	88
Instant active yeast (optional)	4	0.4
Salt	22	2.2
Honey	—	6
Soaker	446	—
Grains	—	18
Levain	500	—
Total	2,146	—

The baker's percentage of water—or overall hydration—is computed by adding the water in the levain, the soaker, and final dough and dividing by the total flour in the starter and final dough:

Water in starter	250g	Bread flour in starter	250g
+ Water in soaker dough	+ 206g	+ Bread flour in final dough	+ 250g
+ Water in final dough	+ 424g	+ Whole wheat flour in final dough	+ 500g
Total water	= 880g	Total flour	= 1,000g

So overall hydration = 880g ÷ 1,000g × 100 = 88%.

APPENDIX D

Bread Production Schedule

For a printable pdf of the bread production schedule, please visit our website at www.chelseagreen.com/breadschedule.

bread production schedule

date:					
time	product 1	product 2	product 3	product 4	oven/misc.

APPENDIX E

Oven Temperature Log

For a printable pdf of the oven log, please visit our website at www.chelseagreen.com/Ovenlog.

oven log

date	time	temperature °F					what doing	comments / results
		inside door left side	mid-hearth	back wall	dome	oven air @ mid-hearth		

Starting a Liquid Sourdough Starter from Scratch

Day 1

Ingredient	Weight (g)	Baker's %
Water	96	84
Bread flour	57	50
Whole rye flour	57	50
Molasses	4	3.5
Total	214	—

Combine all of the ingredients in a stainless mixing bowl or plastic storage container. Mix until incorporated, scrape down the sides of the container, cover, and let sit in a 77°F (25°C) environment for 24 hours. This begins the fermentation process.

Day 2

Ingredient	Weight (g)	Baker's %
Water	96	84
Bread flour	57	50
Whole rye flour	57	50
Starter from preceding day	108	95
Total	318	—

Add the water and flours to the starter, mix until incorporated, scrape down the sides of the container, cover, and ferment in a 77°F (25°C) environment for 24 hours. This process of adding flour and water to the starter is called feeding the starter.

Day 3–Day 6

Ingredient	Weight (g)	Baker's %
Water	140	84
Starter from preceding day(s)	159	95
Bread flour	167	100
Total	466	—

On the third day, begin feeding the starter every 12 hours—twice a day, instead of only once a day as before. After each feeding, scrape down the sides of the container, cover, and ferment at room temperature, 77°F (25°C). Continue feeding the starter every 12 hours until day 7. By this time, your starter should be healthy and active.

Day 7

Your starter is ready to use! Increase the volume of starter as required for a particular formula using baker's percentage. You can also adjust the hydration and flour selection to accommodate a specific formula's requirements.

Choosing a Container for Your Starter

Any non-reactive, 2- to 4-quart, lidded, widemouthed container will work fine as a container for your starter. Clear containers are convenient because you can observe the general progress of your starter at a glance without opening the lid. When I want to track the growth of the starter over time, I simply mark the level with a dry-erase marker and note the time on the outside of the container.

The volume of the starter changes dramatically based on how many days it has matured and how soon it's fed after reaching maximum volume. I've started starters with this formula and purposefully created inaccuracies as a way of testing the efficiency of this approach. It has always worked, so don't worry if you have to adjust the feeding timeline.

Like all ingredients, it is best to measure starter (or a levain to be used in a final dough) by weight; volume varies greatly depending on the ripeness of a starter or levain.

APPENDIX G

Regular Maintenance:
CARE AND FEEDING OF
A LIQUID SOURDOUGH STARTER

Maintaining Your Starter at Room Temperature

Room temperature, roughly 77°F (25°C), is the preferable environment for maintaining an active starter. Feeding it water and flour can be a daily task depending on how much you bake, but it's a simple one, and you might find it less demanding than you'd think. You can always stash the starter in the fridge when daily feeding isn't convenient, but maintaining it at room temperature with daily feedings for at least a little while is a great way to become familiar with the various stages of your starter's cycle.

After you've established your starter following the formula above, feed it **once a day** as follows:

Stir the starter well and pour off all but 100g. Add 100g of water and 100g of all-purpose flour, mix until smooth, and cover. It will become ripe in about 6 to 8 hours.

Getting ready to bake: If you plan to use the starter the next day, feed it twice without pouring off any starter. There should be a minimum of 6 hours between feedings, and the last feeding should be 6 to 8 hours before you want to build a levain in order to make a batch of bread.

Maintaining Your Starter in the Fridge

When daily feeding isn't convenient, you can store your starter in the fridge and feed it once a week instead. It's also appropriate to keep your starter in the fridge if your kitchen is very warm—say, over 85°F (29°C). In a hot summer kitchen, a starter left on the counter will ferment like crazy, and you'd have to feed it very frequently to prevent it from becoming overripe.

Feed the starter **once a week** as follows:

Take the starter out of the fridge, stir well, and pour off all but 100g. Add 100g of water and 100g of all-purpose flour, mix until smooth, and cover. Allow the starter to work at room temperature for at least 2 hours before putting it back in the refrigerator.

Getting ready to bake with a starter that's been stored in the fridge with weekly feedings: Two to 3 days before you're planning to bake, you'll need to raise the activity of your starter to a more energetic level. Here's how:

Take the starter out of the fridge in the morning, feed it as usual, and let it ferment for 24 hours at room temperature. The next day, feed it twice: once in the morning, then again about 12 hours later. On the third morning, feed the starter early and allow it to ferment until it's ripe, about 6 hours. It should then be ready to use in your recipe.

Increasing the Quantity of Your Starter

To increase the quantity of your starter, simply feed the starter as usual without discarding any. You may also increase volume by increasing the amount of flour and water you add at each feeding—just remember to follow the 1:1 ratio of equal parts (by weight) flour and water.

Reviving a Dormant or Neglected Starter

When a starter has gone too long without a feeding, it will lack the usual bubbles and signs of activity, and it will have a very sharp aroma and a layer of clear, dark liquid (alcohol, a by-product of yeast that's been deprived of oxygen) on top. Although the starter appears lifeless at this point, the microflora will spring into action again as soon as they get a few good meals. Stir the liquid back into the starter, pour off all but 100g, and feed it 100g of water and 100g of all-purpose flour twice a day until it's healthy, bubbly, and active.

Sourdough starters are hearty and easily resist spoilage due to their acidic nature. The pH of a sourdough starter discourages the proliferation of harmful microorganisms, but if your starter turns ominously pink or red or shows signs of mold growth, discard it, and begin again.

Resources

The enthusiasm that started with Alan Scott all those years ago has given birth to many wood-fired oven resources. Here is a sampling of useful sources; I encourage you to check out the bibliography for a more in-depth resource listing.

Ovencrafters: Alan's business has been carried on by his daughter, Lila, and son, Nick. In addition to plans for several sizes of ovens, the site also carries thermocouples, oven doors, and books. www.ovencrafters.net

The Virtual Wood-Fired Oven

It's often challenging to find oven materials at your local brickyard—but what you will find is salespeople who aren't familiar with wood-fired oven construction. The online wood-fired oven community, on the other hand, is an informed and sharing group. Need refractory materials in your area but don't know where to go? Post an inquiry and usually you will receive some leads within 24 hours. Quite often a post goes out like this: "Anybody know where I can get high temp mortar in mid-Michigan?" Usually somebody will reply within a day: "Call Stan at Beaverton Refractories and tell him you need the same stuff he got for Albert."

Here are two public forums with plenty of information:

Yahoo Brick Oven chatgroup:
  groups.yahoo.com/group/brick-oven
Forno Bravo: www.fornobravo.com/forum

Caveat lector. Let the reader beware. Of course, any and all are allowed to post to these groups. Approach all posts with skepticism and do deeper research to make sure you're listening to somebody who doesn't just sound authoritative but is, indeed, informed.

Alsey Refractories: For over a century Alsey Refractories have refined processes to produce refractory materials, well respected by professional masons. There are other brick manufacturers, of course, but the Alsey website is included here due to its inclusion of cool photos and an informative resource page. www.alsey.com

Bee's Wrap is a reusable, breathable piece of organic cotton coated with beeswax, jojoba oil, and tree resin. Gentle warmth and pressure from your hands allows it to be molded over the top of a bowl of proofing dough or the final baked loaf. www.beeswrap.com

Bread Ovens of Quebec: The entire PDF version of this book is available at this website. Click on the chapter titles to open individual chapters. www.civilization.ca/cmc/exhibitions/tresors/barbeau/mbp0501e.shtml

Breadhitz, owned and operated by Ciril and Kylee Hitz, offers baking classes in a Le Panyol oven and earth oven building classes at a beautiful New England facility. www.breadhitz.com

Carolina Ground: Jen Lapidus, an early proponent of Alan Scott's micro-bakery idea, began this North Carolina mill to supply flour made from North Carolina grain to regional bakers. ncobfp.blogspot.com

FG Pizza & Italian is an online source for Italian-themed wood-fired oven tools, pizza supplies, books, recipes, and more, hosted at Frankie G's convivial and informative pizza oven website, www.fgpizza .com. A good source for peels and pizza tools.

Firespeaking is the website of Max and Eva Edleson, designers and builders of the barrel oven discussed in chapter 3. Max and Eva are multi-talented residential and commercial oven builders who also fabricate oven parts and accessories, including firing doors, blowpipes, and peels. www.firespeaking.com

Kiko Denzer/Hand Print Press: In addition to information about ovens, this website includes information about building and making art with earth. www.handprintpress.com

King Arthur Flour. King Arthur was the testing flour for the recipes in this book. In addition to serving the serious home baker, King Arthur provides products, support, and services to professional bakers. The Baking Education Center, located in Norwich Vermont, offers classes for all level of bakers, including wood-fired oven instruction. www.kingarthurflour.com/

Maine Grain Alliance hosts the annual **Kneading Conferences** discussed in chapter 3. www.kneading conference.com

Masonry Heater Association: A rich online resource with plenty of information about wood-fired heaters and ovens of all types, including a gallery of beautiful hand-built heaters and ovens; a library with articles, technical papers, and news; and the source for finding a mason in your area with the experience and knowledge to build you an efficient oven. www.mha-net.org

Masons on a Mission was started by Pat Manley to build efficient and healthful cookstoves for Central American families. www.masonsonamission.org

Quest for Ovens is the penultimate aggregator of online wood-fired oven resources by David S. Cargo, with all kinds of links: spbc.info/quest/links.html

Rado Hand: See Rado Hand's website for information on building masonry wood-fired ovens: www .traditionaloven.com

San Franciso Baking Institute: The baking and pastry arts school for professionals and enthusiasts and where I first learned to bake. SFBI offers a wide array of baking classes, including wood-fired oven courses in a Le Panyol. The institute also has a division that sells baking equipment and tools. www.sfbi.com

Sklip: These simple and sturdy brackets increase hearth or counter space by allowing sheet pans to be stacked in 2" or 4" increments. www.sklipco.com/

Stone Turtle Baking and Cooking School. Michael and Sandy Jubinsky's beautiful school in the Maine woods offers cooking and baking classes, the majority of which are in their wood-fired Le Panyol oven. www.stoneturtlebaking.com/

Stu Silverstein: The insightful and useful blog by earth oven builder and filmmaker Stu Silverstein: www .stusilverstein.com

The Alliance for Green Heat: The Alliance for Green Heat is a non-profit organization that promotes high-efficiency wood combustion as a low-carbon, sustainable, local and affordable heating solution. The Alliance seeks to make wood heat a cleaner and more efficient renewable energy option, particularly for those who cannot afford fossil fuel heat. www .forgreenheat.org

The Bread Bakers Guild of America has another helpful chat group, although not a public one; it is for members only. Bread bakers and oven builders are a sharing lot and will pass along fundamental information and gems of insight or new techniques. In addition to offering the chat group, The Bread Bakers Guild of America is the premier bread-baking organization in North America: www.bbga.org.

The Chimney Safety Institute of America (CSIA) is a non-profit educational organization that provides the only national certification for chimney professionals. Visit www.csia.org to find a certified chimney sweep in your area. The site also has great clear information selecting firewood, building a top-down burn and other clean burning practices.

Bibliography

Alford, Jeffrey, and Naomi Duguid. *Home Baking: The Artful Mix of Flour and Tradition Around the World*. Toronto: Random House Canada, 2003.

Alvarez, M., ed. *State of America's Forests*. Bethesda, MD: Society of American Foresters, 2007.

Assire, Jérôme. *The Book of Bread*. Translated by David Radzinowicz Howell. New York: Flammarion, 1996.

Bacon, Richard M. *The Forgotten Art of Building and Using a Brick Bake Oven: How to Date, Renovate or Use an Existing Brick Oven, or to Construct a New One; A Practical Guide*. Chambersburg, PA: Alan C. Hood, 1977.

Bittman, Mark. *How to Cook Everything: 2,000 Simple Recipes for Great Food*. 10th edition. Hoboken, NJ: John Wiley, 2008.

Boily, Lise, and Jean-François Blanchette. *The Bread Ovens of Quebec*. Ottawa: National Museums of Canada, 1979.

Bramble, Tod. "The Whole Truth About Whole Grains: Installment One." Baking Buyer (June 2011): 18-22.

———. "The Whole Truth About Whole Grains: Installment Two." *Baking Buyer* (August 2011): 18–21.

Brooks, Kimberly, and Bethan Mckernan. "Still Serving Pizza, Even During the Storm." *NY City Lens*, last modified November 1, 2013. http://nycitylens.com/?p=7748

Buehler, Emily. *Bread Science: The Chemistry and Craft of Making Bread*. Carrboro, NC: Two Blue Books, 2006.

Bushway, Stephen. *The New Woodburner's Handbook: A Guide to Safe, Healthy, and Efficient Woodburning*. North Adams, MA: Storey Publishing, 1992.

Calvel, Raymond. *The Taste of Bread: A translation of Le Goût du Pain, comment le préserver, comment le retrouver*. Ronald L. Wirtz, translator; James J. MacGuire, technical editor. Gaitherburg, MD: Aspen Publishers, 2001.

Carpenter, Anna. *The Ultimate Wood-Fired Oven Book: Design, Construction, Use*. Atglen, PA: Schiffer Publishing, Ltd, 2008.

Cayne, Bernard S., ed. *The New Lexicon Webster*. New York: Lexicon Publications, Inc., 1988.

Coleman, John T. *Here Lies Hugh Glass, A Mountain Man, A Bear, And The Rise Of The American Nation*. New York: Hill and Wang, 2012.

Colnes, Andrea, et al. *Biomass Supply and Carbon Accounting for Southeastern Forests (2012)*. Montpelier, VT: Biomass Energy Resource Center, 2012.

Cook's Illustrated Editors. *The Best Slow & Easy Recipes: A Best Recipe Classic*. Brookline, MA: America's Test Kitchen, 2008.

Crump, Nancy Carter. *Hearthside Cooking: Early American Southern Cuisine Updated for Today's Hearth & Cookstove*. 2nd edition. Chapel Hill: University of North Carolina Press, 2008.

David, Elizabeth. *English Bread and Yeast Cookery*. Newton, MA: Viking Penguin, 1977.

Denzer, Kiko, and Hannah Field. *Build Your Own Earth Oven*. 3rd edition. Blodgett, OR: Kiko Denzer, 2007.

DiMuzio, Daniel T. *Bread Baking: An Artisan's Perspective*. Hoboken, NJ: John Wiley, 2010.

Dupaigne, Bernard. *The History of Bread*. New York: Harry N. Abrams, 1999.

Dyer, Davis, and Daniel Gross. *The Generations of Corning: The Life and Times of A Global Corporation*. New York: Oxford University Press, Inc., 2001.

Edleson, Max and Eva. *Build Your Own Barrel Oven: A Guide For Making a Versatile, Efficient, And Easy to Use Wood-Fired Oven.* Blodgett, OR: Handprint Press, 2012.

Evans, Ianto, and Leslie Jackson. *Rocket Mass Heaters: Superefficient Woodstoves YOU Can Build.* Coquille, OR: Cob Cottage, 2006.

Figoni, Paula. *How Baking Works: Exploring the Fundamentals of Baking Science.* 3rd edition. Hoboken, NJ: John Wiley, 2011.

Fallon, Sally. *Nourishing Traditions: The Cookbook that Challenges Politically Correct Nutrition and the Diet Dictocrats.* Revised 2nd Edition. Washington, DC: New Trends Publishing, Inc., 1999.

Giedion, Siegfried. *Mechanization Takes Command: A Contribution to Anonymous History.* New York: W. W. Norton, 1948.

Gladstar, Rosemary. *Herbal Healing for Women: Simple Home Remedies for Women of All Ages.* New York: Simon & Schuster, 1993.

Glezer, Maggie. *Artisan Baking Across America.* New York: Artisan, 2002.

Goldenson, Suzanne, with Doris Simpson. *The Open-Hearth Cookbook: Recapturing the Flavor of Early America.* 2nd edition. Chambersburg, PA: Alan C. Hood, 2006.

Griggs, Barbara. *Green Pharmacy: The History and Evolution of Western Herbal Medicine.* Rochester, VT: Healing Arts Press, 1981.

Hamelman, Jeffrey. *Bread: A Baker's Book of Techniques and Recipes.* 2nd Edition. Hoboken, NJ: John Wiley, 2004.

Heinicke, Elisabeth. *Beyond Croutons.* Sharon, MA: Bellwether Publishing, 1996.

Hensley, Jay. "The Upside-Down Fire." *SNEWS, The Chimney Sweep News* (August 1993).

Hildegard, Saint, of Bingen. *Hildegard von Bingen's Physica: The Complete Translation of Her Classic Work on Health and Healing.* Translated by Priscilla Throop. Rochester, VT: Healing Arts Press, 1998.

Hitz, Ciril. *Baking Artisan Bread: 10 Expert Formulas For Baking Better Bread At Home.* Beverly, MA: Quarry, 2008.

Hyytiäinen, Heikki, and Albert Barden III. *Finnish Fireplaces: Heart of the Home.* Hanko, Finland: Building Book Limited, 1988.

Ingalls, Laura. *The Long Winter.* New York: Harper-Collins Publishers Inc., 1940.

Jacob, Heinrich Eduard. *Six Thousand Years of Bread: Its Holy and Unholy History.* New York: Lyons & Burford, 1944.

Jones, Holly and David. *Wood-Fired Oven Cookbook.* Leicestershire, UK: Anness Publishing, 2012.

Karlin, Mary. *Wood-Fired Cooking.* Berkeley, CA: Ten Speed Press, 2009.

Katz, Sandor. *The Art of Fermentation: An In-Depth Exploration of Essential Concepts and Processes from Around the World.* White River Junction, VT: Chelsea Green Publishing, 2012.

Katzen, Mollie. *The Moosewood Cookbook: Recipes from the Moosewood Restaurant.* Berkeley, CA: Ten Speed Press, 1977.

Kulvinskas, Viktoras. *Survival into the 21st Century: Planetary Healers Manual.* Fairfield, IA: 21st Century Publications, 1975.

Leader, Daniel, and Judith Blahnik. *Bread Alone: Bold Fresh Loaves from Your Own Hands.* New York: William Morrow, 1993.

Leonard, Thom. *The Bread Book: A Natural, Whole-Grain Seed-to-Loaf Approach to Real Bread.* Brookline, MA: East West Health Books, 1990.

Matesz, Ken. *Masonry Heaters.* White River Junction, VT: Chelsea Green Publishing, 2010.

McClane, A. J. *McClane's North American Fish Cookery.* New York: Holt, Rinehart and Winston, 1981.

McGee, Harold. *On Food and Cooking: The Science and Lore of the Kitchen.* New York: Collier Books, Macmillan Publishing, 1984.

Mugnaini, Andrea. *The Art of Wood Fired Cooking.* Layton, UT: Gibbs Smith, 2010.

Olney, Richard. *Simple French Food.* New York: Macmillan, 1974.

Ortiz, Joe. *The Village Baker: Classic Regional Breads from Europe and America.* Berkeley, CA: Ten Speed Press, 1993.

Pennick, Nigel. *The Pagan Book of Days: A Guide to the Festivals, Traditions, and Sacred Days of the Year.* Rochester, VT: Destiny Books, 1992.

Philbrick, Frank, and Stephen Philbrick. *The Backyard Lumberjack: The Ultimate Guide to Felling, Bucking, Splitting & Stacking.* North Adams, MA: Storey Publishing, 2006.

Pitchford, Paul. *Healing with Whole Foods: Oriental Traditions and Modern Nutrition.* Revised Edition. Berkeley, CA: North Atlantic Books, 1993.

Pyler, E. J. *Baking Science & Technology.* Vol. 1. Kansas City: Sosland Publishing, 1988.

Poilâne, Lionel. *Guide de l'Amateur de Pain.* Paris: Robert Laffont, 1981.

Rambali, Paul. *Boulangerie: The Craft and Culture of Baking in France.* New York: Macmillan, 1994.

Residential Wood Combustion Technology Review, EPA-600/R-98-174a. Washington, DC: EPA, 1998.

Richter, Daniel deB., Jr., et al. "Response." *Science* 324 (2009): 1390–91.

———. "Wood Energy in America." *Science* 323 (2009): 1432–33.

Robertson, Chad. *Tartine Bread.* San Francisco: Chronicle Books, 2010.

Robertson, Laurel, with Carol Lee Flinders and Bronwen Godfrey. *The Laurel's Kitchen Bread Book: A Guide to Whole-Grain Breadmaking.* New York: Random House Trade Paperbacks, 2003.

Rodgers, Judy. *The Zuni Cafe Cookbook.* New York: W. W. Norton, 2002.

Rubel, William. *The Magic of Fire: Hearth Cooking: One Hundred Recipes for the Fireplace or Campfire.* Berkeley, CA: Ten Speed Press, 2002.

Silverstein, Stuart. *Bread Earth and Fire.* Waterville, ME: Stuart Silverstein, 2011.

Spiller, Gene. *The Superpyramid Eating Program: Introducing the Revolutionary Five New Food Groups.* New York: Times Books, 1993.

Stewart, Martha. *The Martha Stewart Living Cookbook.* New York: Clarkson Potter, 2000.

Suas, Michel. *Advanced Bread and Pastry: A Professional Approach.* Clifton Park, NY: Delmar Cengage Learning, 2009.

Volz, Vivian, and Eric Stovner. "Reducing Embodied Energy in Masonry Construction. Part 1: Understanding Embodied Energy in Masonry." *Structure,* May (2010). www.structuremag.org/article.aspx?articleID=1064

Wigmore, Ann. *The Sprouting Book.* Avery, 1986.

Wing, Daniel, and Alan Scott. *The Bread Builders: Hearth Loaves and Masonry Ovens.* White River Junction, VT: Chelsea Green Publishing, 1999.

Wood Oven Recipes. Vol. 1. Trentham, Victoria, Australia: Earth Garden Books, 2009.

Wrangham, Richard. *Catching Fire: How Cooking Made Us Human.* New York: Basic Books, 2009.

Zolli, Andrew, and Ann Marie Healy. Resilience: *Why Things Bounce Back.* New York: Free Press, 2012.

Index

Note: page numbers followed by f refer to illustrations or photographs

About the Author

Richard Miscovich began baking European hearth breads in 1996 after graduating in the first class taught at the San Francisco Baking Institute. During that same trip, he visited Alan Scott and was introduced to the Scott brick oven—just as interest in artisan baking and wood-fired ovens dramatically increased. He immediately began construction of a wood-fired oven in coastal North Carolina and opened an organic micro-bakery, One Acre Garden and Bakery, specializing in organic artisan hearth breads.

Currently, Richard is assistant professor at Johnson & Wales University in Providence, Rhode Island. In addition to teaching culinary students, Richard is also a popular instructor for home bakers and brick oven hobbyists, and is a regular guest at venues around the country where he teaches artisan bread-baking techniques, wood-fired baking, cooking, and oven-building classes. In 2007, Richard organized and helped teach the first three-day wood-fired oven class track to be offered at The Bread Bakers Guild of America's biannual educational conference, Camp Bread. He served two terms on the board of The Bread Bakers Guild of America.

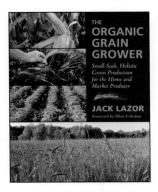

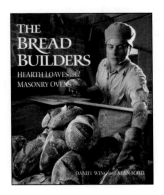
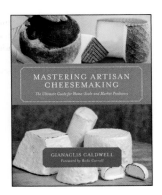

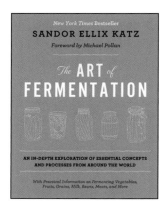
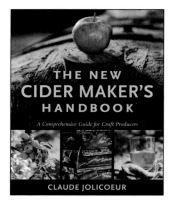
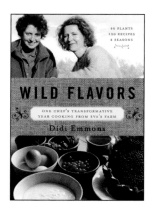